KING ARTHUR
The Making of the Legend

NICHOLAS J. HIGHAM

YALE UNIVERSITY PRESS
NEW HAVEN AND LONDON

For information about this and other Yale University Press publications, please contact:
U.S. Office: sales.press@yale.edu   yalebooks.com
Europe Office: sales@yaleup.co.uk   yalebooks.co.uk

Set in Minion Pro by IDSUK (DataConnection) Ltd
Printed in Great Britain by Clays Ltd, Elcograf S.p.A

Library of Congress Control Number: 2018953721

ISBN 978-0-300-21092-7 (hbk)
ISBN 978-0-300-25498-3 (pbk)

A catalogue record for this book is available from the British Library.

10 9 8 7 6 5 4 3 2

KING ARTHUR

Nicholas J. Higham is professor emeritus at the University of Manchester. He is the author of many distinguished works including *Ecgfrith: King of the Northumbrians, High-King of Britain* and *The Anglo-Saxon World*.

Further praise for *King Arthur*:

'A well-produced book by a serious scholar.'
David Miles, *Minerva*

'Higham's readable yet scholarly intervention is to be warmly welcomed … He roams widely, touching upon everything from ancient Greek astronomy to modern Caucasian mythography.'
Levi Roach, *Literary Review*

'The "historical" Arthur of the scholars and novelists of the last century is in fact the reflection of a particular style of nationalist storytelling; and the dismantling of this dramatic but misleading model by historians such as Higham enables us to see more clearly the racial and cultural fluidity of Britain in the century and a half after the end of direct Roman rule.'
Rowan Williams, *New Statesman*

'A very intelligent book which presents the facts and invites you to draw your own conclusions about this legendary British monarch. If King Arthur didn't exist, he should have done, and Nicholas Higham's book shows us why. A superb read: scholarly yet accessible. Highly recommended.'
Francis Pryor, author of *Britain B.C.*

'An outstanding and deeply informed overview of the various "King Arthurs" in history. Accessible and well-written, it is also a significant contribution to the debate around the historical origins of Arthur.'
Anne Lawrence-Mathers, author of *The True History of Merlin the Magician*

'It is undoubtedly the case that Professor Higham is extremely well-versed in his subject and that he has a wide-ranging and in-depth familiarity with the literature relevant to his project.'
Mark Jones, *Albion*

For Cheryl

CONTENTS

PLATES AND MAPS

Plates

Maps

ACKNOWLEDGEMENTS

This book would have been impossible to write without the prodigious amount of scholarly work undertaken by a whole legion of researchers, stretching back to the nineteenth century. It is particularly appropriate in a work dealing with King Arthur to acknowledge the sense in which I have been carried to this point on the shoulders of so many giants of scholarship working in a variety of interrelated disciplines. Arthurian studies has been an extraordinarily prolific area of endeavour over the last century and more, resulting in an exceptional quantity of published work.

Specifically, Martin Ryan very kindly read and commented on most of the chapters presented here in an early draft; as ever, I am extremely grateful to him. My thanks too go to Lindsay Allason-Jones, Frances McIntosh and Paul Bidwell for advice regarding 'Sarmatian' finds along Hadrian's Wall, to Peter Schrijver on the origin of the name Arthur, to Paul Fouracre on all matters Frankish and to Charles Insley for various fruitful discussions regarding the Irish Sea region in the early Middle Ages. Patrick Tosteven very kindly provided photographs of material in Ribchester Roman Museum (Plates 8 and 9), Paul Holder and David Langslow advised on Roman-period inscriptions and Andrew Breeze provided me with invaluable assistance regarding Celtic place-names. Ross Trench-Jellicoe set me straight on the carved stones at Maughold (Isle of Man), Rod Thomson on William of Malmesbury and Fiona Edmonds on Lancashire place-names. John Colorusso very kindly provided me with a draft of his work on the Ossetian Nart sagas prior to publication and corresponded thereon.

Anamarija Kurilić gave extraordinarily generously of her time and expertise in discussing the L. Artorius Castus inscriptions, in particular, and their
Roman Dalmatian backdrop more generally. Julie Lawton very kindly aided
me with academic French, translating passages where precise meanings
were critical. Henry Edmunds very helpfully advised me regarding recent
genetic research into the Cleveland horse breed, Barry Hobson kindly
advised me regarding the vicus at Slack Roman fort, and Duncan Sayer
both conducted me around his excavation of Roman Ribchester in 2016
and very kindly provided Plate 13. Donna Sherman gave invaluable help
and advice regarding the University of Manchester's map collection and I
am indebted to the University Library more generally for sourcing a wide
variety of monographs and other materials for my use. Bill Hanson was
instrumental in obtaining Plates 10, 11 and 12, for which my thanks go to
Visy Zsolt (Plate 10) and Andrea Vaday (11 and 12). Nenad Cambj very
kindly provided me with Plate 4 and Drazen Marsic with Plate 3. I am
grateful to John Hodgson for his help with the University of Manchester
manuscripts kept at the John Rylands Library, Deansgate, and Nigel Wilkins
for his help in accessing photographs from the collection maintained by
Historic England. Maggie Kneen drew Plate 5 with her customary skill on
the basis of a photographic record made by Roger B. Ulrich. My thanks go
to Luca Larpi for all our discussions of Arthur over the years, his advice
regarding the sword-in-the-stone story and provision of Plate 15. Many of
my students over the last few decades contributed to my thinking about
Arthur by asking questions to which I felt bound to seek answers; to all go
my thanks. I am grateful also to Heather McCallum, Marika Lysandrou,
Rachael Lonsdale and Samantha Cross at Yale University Press for commissioning this book and for all their assistance along the way, to Jacob Blandy
for his skills as copy editor and to Martin Brown for his excellent maps.

 Notwithstanding the number and scale of these many debts, all errors
are my responsibility alone.

 It is to my wife, Cheryl, though, that this book is dedicated, for she has
borne the brunt of my preoccupation with Arthur over the decades and has
found herself walking with me up hill and down dale to view sites that so
often present as just odd piles of stones. For her good humour, patience and
encouragement along the way my grateful thanks.

INTRODUCTION
Arthur, History and the Storytellers

When good King Arthur reigned with Guinevere his Queen, there lived, near the Land's End in Cornwall, a farmer who had only one son called Jack. Now Jack was brisk and ready; of such a lively wit that none nor nothing could worst him.

In those days, the Mount of St Michael in Cornwall was the fastness of a hugeous giant whose name was Cormoran.

— The opening lines of 'Jack the Giant-Killer'[1]

King Arthur today is a truth universally acknowledged, his name far better known than those of the vast majority of historical characters – a fact not lost on entrepreneurs of many different kinds, writers among them. The result has been a whole host of books and films, operas and musicals, plays, TV dramas and websites based upon his story. Arthur's name adorns country inns and the walls of community schools,[2] and promotes such heritage sites as Glastonbury Abbey (where his grave was 'discovered' in 1191) – and the live music venue, too, just up the road. He was little short of an obsession for Alfred, Lord Tennyson, poet laureate from 1850 to 1892,[3] and a keen interest of J.R.R. Tolkien.[4] Camelot, Arthur's legendary capital, was commandeered by Jackie Kennedy in 1963 in the week following her husband's assassination to serve as a metaphor for the White House during his presidency. Equally, for twenty-nine years it was the name of a children's theme park in Lancashire (it closed in 2012); today it trademarks the UK's National Lottery.

Nor is Arthur on his own in all of this; his close associates are almost as well known. The game machines used by that same National Lottery are called Arthur, Guinevere, Lancelot, Galahad and Merlin. Way back in 1879 the Ffestiniog Railway named its first steam locomotive Merddin Emrys after the Welsh version of the last of these, Rolls-Royce followed suit with its early aero engines and Merlin's name has since been used for a long-running BBC drama, an international health charity, project management software, several computer games, and various retail outlets. Guinevere was popular with artists in the Victorian and Edwardian eras,[5] and attracted film-makers in the twentieth century;[6] today her name sells bedding and antiques. Lancelot and Galahad have attracted similar attention.[7] Despite it being a fourteenth-century text in Middle English, far more editions of *Sir Gawain and the Green Knight* have been published than might have been expected were it not for its strong Arthurian connections. And the ageing Gawain is a central figure in Kazuo Ishiguro's recent masterpiece, *The Buried Giant*, the last of Arthur's knights left guarding the dragon whose breath (adapted for the purpose by Merlin, of course) causes the forgetfulness that 'darkens' the age.

Arthur's prominence is nothing new; for a millennium and more his story has been read and heard, refashioned, reinvented and retold; the process is ongoing, with new versions coming out pretty much every year, mutating from one telling to the next. And Arthur's story has long drawn in all sorts of unrelated tales – just look at the opening lines of 'Jack the Giant-Killer' quoted above,[8] or the Arthurian setting given to another tale of the same general period, 'Tom Thumb'.[9] Neither has been traced back to the Middle Ages, but in each case the connection was made soon after by authors who adopted a style of introduction that recalls the earliest Arthurian romances of the twelfth century.[10]

How we view King Arthur has long reflected how we feel about the past, and particularly the deep past – the ancient and early medieval past. Arthur has been pressed into service time and again to support any number of causes. He has represented the Romans and the British (in opposition to the Saxons), the Welsh and the Cornish (in opposition to the English), the Bretons (in opposition to the French), the Campbells (in opposition to various other Scottish clans),[11] various claims to the whole island of Britain, and the English, and ultimately the British, in opposition to continental neighbours. He has personified courage and martial prowess, an ideal of Christian leadership, chivalry, the monarchical principle, aristocratic values, conduct befitting a Victorian gentleman, romanticism, the Gothic, medievalism, barbarism, and the 'so-called *Tradition*'.[12] And Arthur and his associates have found a home too in the more mystical 'Celtic' and 'new-age' fringes of modern culture, in legends relating to the foundation of England and the authority of its early church (particularly at Glastonbury),[13] and as part of wider folk–spiritual responses to the materialism of the present day.[14]

Arthur and his friends are everywhere. Their stories, their deeds and the complex of ideas which swirl around them underpin great swathes of our literature and film. The American novelist John Steinbeck was given Malory's *Le Morte d'Arthur* as a nine-year-old and adopted it as his 'magic book', sparking a life-long love affair with storytelling in general and Arthurian literature in particular, which he sought to share by rewriting it for a twentieth-century audience.[15] Since the 1950s Susan Cooper, Rosemary Sutcliff, Kevin Crossley-Holland and Michael Morpurgo have all repackaged Arthur for children; Mary Stewart, Bernard Cornwell, Count Nikolai Tolstoy and many, many more have done the same for adult readers.[16] When the novelist Kate Atkinson has an ex-glamour-model mother tell her new nanny, 'Well, Arthur's called Arthur because his dad was into like Camelot and all that stuff', she can be sure that we will get it.[17] And when Tom Holt has the sword in the stone turn up in his hero's bedroom with the words 'Whoso draweth this sword from this stone shall be rightful king of all England' engraved upon it, we can relate immediately and smile when he adds, in smaller letters 'Please dispose of stone tidily after use'.[18] We've seen the film,[19] and many have read the book on which Disney based it.[20] We know this stuff.

Arthur in and out of history

King Arthur is, however, something of a nightmare from the historian's perspective. Despite being one of the best-known figures from the Middle Ages – even from the past more generally – there is total disagreement as to when and where he belongs. Was there a 'real' Arthur behind the legend, as so many have argued? If so, can we establish what he did, and where and when he did it? Or should we consider him less substantive than that, a figure of folklore or mythology perhaps, a remnant from pagan times? Is Arthur just a figure of legend? Was he a fiction, even, right from the start? Or should we just sit on the fence, unable to make up our minds?

Portrayals of Arthur as a real historical personage stretch back in Wales to the ninth century. Orally transmitted stories passed from the Celtic world to France and northern Italy no later than the eleventh; in England William of Malmesbury knew tales of his deeds by the 1120s. At Oxford, in the 1130s, Geoffrey of Monmouth reframed early British history, with

Arthur as his central figure. This 'historical' Arthur was translated into French by the Jerseyman cleric and poet Wace, and his story taken up thereafter both in histories and as a backdrop to romances written in the orbit of the first Angevin monarch, Henry II. Arthur's story was not, though, sufficiently well grounded in near-contemporary evidence to satisfy the greater scrutiny that began to be brought to bear on the past following the Renaissance, so lost his place in history. Even so he remained hugely popular, featuring prominently in the Victorian period, in particular, in both literature and the visual arts. Many still thought of him as 'real' in some sense, or at least wanted to, despite most historians urging caution. Then, in the 1890s, scholarly reappraisal of the main ninth-century source for Arthur's deeds encouraged scholars to think him historical once more. His stock as a figure of British history revived across the first half of the twentieth century, only to be challenged once again in the 1970s, both by historians and specialists in medieval Celtic literature.

Alongside this see-sawing debate regarding the reality of Arthur as a figure of British sub-Roman history, a few scholars have broken out of its confines to argue for very different Arthurs. The figures proposed vary in both space and time. One theory has him as a Roman army officer, associated perhaps with the Roman-period Sarmatians of the Eurasian Steppe, from whom several of his medieval stories derived; another identifies him in star-stories circulating in pre-classical Greece. Each of these lines of reasoning asserts a particular role in history for our hero, based on a unique body of source material. Arthur has yo-yoed, therefore, in and out of Britain as well as in and out of history, across the last century.

Despite the large number of books and articles dedicated to 'finding' King Arthur, the questions still remain, for there has been very little agreement. Who was he? Where did his story originate? Is there any reality lurking behind the story-book fantasies which eventually surrounded him? Should his story just be labelled legend? How should we relate Arthur to our understanding of the past?

Bookshops stock numerous volumes which claim to answer these questions, in any number of different ways. So why write another? The reason is this. Today, most specialists distance themselves from the whole issue of Arthur's reality, citing insufficient evidence to be able to judge his place in history and declaring themselves agnostic on this matter. But their silence leaves the history-reading public with insufficient guidance to the competing claims and without the specialist knowledge to judge between them effectively, for these are highly complex issues. The purpose of this book is, therefore, to set out the main arguments which are on offer, test each one against the sources on which it relies, and determine which, if any, deserve support. This will include both a range of popular 'British' solutions and the major 'foreign' alternatives that have been proposed across the last century or so. Which (if any) of these Arthurs are sufficiently supported by the evidence to stand up to scrutiny? Which arguments work and which don't? How should we resolve the historical debate surrounding King Arthur? Should we just throw our hands up in despair, admitting that we cannot know, or is there an answer to the age-old problem of the origins of the King Arthur story? That is what this book will do.

First let us just identify the main theories that we need to consider and outline how this book will be structured so as to engage with them.

The 'Dalmatian' Arthur and the Sarmatians

In 1890 it was pointed out that the Welsh name Arthur most probably derived from the uncommon Roman name Artorius. In 1925 the American linguist, Kemp Malone, directed attention to inscriptions discovered in Roman Dalmatia (modern-day Croatia) that commemorate the career of the soldier and administrator L. Artorius Castus. That this Artorius had served in Britain and had commanded 'British' troops encouraged Malone to argue that he was the legend's starting point.[21]

This thesis was left rather hanging for the next half-century or so but interest was rekindled when a new generation of scholars began to think that the mounted knights of the central Middle Ages might owe something to the heavily armoured cavalry of the late Roman army.[22] These had included men from outside the Empire, recruited *inter alia* from various Iranian-speaking peoples on the steppe. We know that Sarmatian cavalry were posted to Roman Britain, and both Alans and Sarmatians were settled in the west in the late Roman period.[23] Could similarities between stories in the Arthurian canon and tales told by classical authors about the Scythians, Sarmatians and Alans reveal debts owed by the Arthurian story cycle to tales told in Antiquity around the Black Sea?[24] If L. Artorius Castus could be linked to Sarmatians serving in the Roman army of Britain, then was it possible that the Arthurian tradition was begun by their stories becoming attached to his name?

Importantly, there is a modern witness to the tales told on the Eurasian Steppe in Antiquity. Work has long been under way to collect, translate and publish the folk literature of the Caucasus, where the Ossetians still speak a language descended from Old Iranian. This has raised the profile of a body of traditional stories known as the Nart sagas, which contain various narrative elements of great age. Across the twentieth century this corpus was scrutinised for possible connections with the Arthurian story cycle; parallels were identified and links suggested.

These lines of reasoning came together in the book *From Scythia to Camelot* by C. Scott Littleton and Linda Malcor, first published in 1994 (then in a revised edition in 2000). This argues for a link between L. Artorius Castus and Sarmatian soldiers serving in Roman Britain and highlights similarities between the Nart sagas and late medieval Arthurian literature. The resulting thesis proposes that many Arthurian legends originated on the Steppe and travelled westwards with Sarmatian soldiers who served under Artorius and then settled in Britain, to be followed later by further colonies established within the Empire. This explanation of the genesis of the Arthurian story cycle challenges the academic community to rethink the origins of King Arthur in dramatically different ways. While it has only attracted limited scholarly support, this theory has been promoted vigorously and gained a toe-hold in wider public perceptions of Arthur's backstory; it therefore requires our attention.

The 'Greek' Arthur

Stimulated in part by this suggestion of an eastern origin for the Arthurian legend, further possibilities have been put forward by the Classicist Graham Anderson, who points to figures with 'Arthur-like' names in the myths and legends of pre-classical Greece. These centre largely on stories from ancient cosmology, connected particularly with the star Arcturus (Greek Arktouros) and the constellations Ursa Major and Ursa Minor (the 'great' and 'little she-bear'). It is Anderson's view that these offer a more convincing starting point for the medieval Arthur than either the 'Dalmatian' or 'Dalmatian–Sarmatian' theories.[25] Again, his case is reinforced by parallels drawn between stories that were circulating in classical Greece and Arthurian literature of the high Middle Ages, suggesting that the Round Table, for example, derived from a tale circulating in the pre-classical world.

This theory centres, therefore, on the proposition that Arthur originated in the literature of the Greek world and passed thence into Latin and Celtic.[26] And this 'Greek' Arthur was remembered in the central Middle Ages not just in Britain but on the Continent as well, hence the rapidity with which his fame spread across Europe and even beyond. Again, this approach draws in a substantial body of new evidence that we need to consider.

The 'British' Arthurs

But such 'foreign' solutions make up only a small minority of the reactions to Arthur's lengthy exile from British history, from the seventeenth century until the nineteenth. Another was to keep him in Britain but consider him a figure of Celtic mythology. This theory enjoyed considerable support in the mid-nineteenth century,[27] then found a champion in the distinguished Celticist, Sir John Rhŷs, who argued that there were two originally separate bodies of evidence for Arthur – on the one hand, local place-names and legends, on the other the 'histories' of the central Middle Ages. These needed, in his view, separate explanations. There were two Arthurs, therefore, of whom the primary figure was mythological, to be sought in the pre-Christian Celtic world, the secondary a leader of the sub-Roman period.[28] Rhŷs's 'mythological' Arthur attracted significant scholarly support between the wars,[29] and again more recently.[30]

The mythological case rests on a body of Welsh folklore and literature written in the central Middle Ages, in which Arthur appears as a heroic figure leading a band of warriors engaged in warfare against a wide variety of opponents, both human and mythological. We find him, for example, raiding the 'other' world and bringing back magical items as booty, passing backwards and forwards between the realms of myth and man. Much of the evidence lies in Arthur's association with local place-names, two examples of which are recorded in the list of 'marvels' (*mirabilia*) which became attached to an early ninth-century Latin work written in Wales, the *Historia Brittonum* (*History of the Britons*). If a 'mythological' Arthur was already the subject of storytelling in Wales when the *Historia* was written in 829–30, then might this be the ultimate source of the 'historical' figure who first appears therein? In that case Arthur's emergence into history could be secondary to the figure of pagan mythology.

But the view that Arthur was more probably historical revived in Germany late in the nineteenth century, before being taken up by English-speaking academics keen to distance themselves from the strongly 'Germanic' emphasis of England's early history following the First World War. One such 'British' Arthur was championed by R.G. Collingwood, the leading scholar of Roman Britain of the day. Ever more 'positivist' treatments were offered by archaeologists trained within this tradition, leading to widespread acceptance of Arthur as a Dark Age figure and the entire period designated the 'Age of Arthur'. Arthur's rehabilitation peaked around 1970 with the publication of such well-known works as *Arthur's Britain* by Leslie Alcock and *The Age of Arthur* by John Morris. These provided the foundations for later writers wishing to pursue a 'positivist' approach and treat Arthur as a recoverable figure of history, producing any number of different theories regarding his origins. There is today a great mass of British candidates out there, all competing for our approval.

But the books written by both Alcock and Morris were heavily criticised, most particularly by scholars whose specialism was the Welsh texts of the central Middle Ages (on which all claims on Arthur's historicity as a British figure must ultimately rest). Many academics (but not all) have since sought to cast out Arthur once more, consigning him to the historical touchline (if not the stands). Most are of the opinion that the evidence is just not good enough to say whether or not he existed, declaring themselves agnostic on this thorny issue. There are today four competing schools of thought within the 'British' camp, therefore – those supporting a mythological Arthur, advocates of an historical figure of one kind or another, those who believe that the best we can do is be agnostic on this whole matter, and those who see Arthur as legendary or fictional. We will need to assess each of these views as we grapple with our central question: when, where and why did Arthur's story begin?

Approach and organisation

We need to take account, therefore, of many competing positions regarding Arthur – whether true or false, British or foreign – as we set about testing which, if any, are sufficiently robust to secure our vote. The focus will be less on arguments for and against a particular Arthur than assessment of the different bodies of evidence on which rival theories rest. We will begin by examining the evidence which underpins the various 'foreign' theories, starting with the 'Artorius' inscriptions from Roman Dalmatia (chapter 1), moving on to explore the potential for links between this Roman soldier and the Roman-period Sarmatians north of the Danube (chapter 2). We will then examine the Nart sagas of the Caucasus in search of material comparable to Arthur's story (chapter 3), before circling back to engage with the Arthur-like names and the tales in which they occur from Ancient Greece (chapter 4). Part II will then review the (predominantly) literary evidence on which all the 'British' theories are based, arranging these texts as far as possible chronologically. We begin where all later commentators have begun, with an examination of potential sources from the period 400–750 that have been called upon by those responsible for one thesis or another (chapter 5), then assess Arthur's role in the ninth-century *Historia Brittonum* (chapter 6) and finally turn to other works that refer to Arthur that were written later (as far as one can judge), in Latin or Old Welsh (chapter 7). At the book's close (chapter 8) we will explore how and why Arthur's stock rose, fell and rose again as a figure of British history, before finally weighing up the various different approaches to a British Arthur that are current today, offering pointers as to how best to manage the relationship between King Arthur and history in the present.

How, where and when did the legend of King Arthur begin? These are the main questions that we are seeking to address as we test all these different bodies of evidence to establish which can, and which cannot, provide us with a valid answer.

PART I

The 'Foreign' Arthurs

1

LUCIUS ARTORIUS CASTUS
A 'Dalmatian' King Arthur?

In general, the pseudo-historical Arthur (as distinguished from the
Arthur of romance) corresponds with astonishing accuracy to the
Artorius of our inscriptions.

— Kemp Malone, 'Artorius'[1]

The earliest suggestion that Arthur was 'foreign' to Britain in some
meaningful sense dates back almost a century to Kemp Malone's
proposal that the Arthurian legend began not in the British Dark
Ages but with the career of a Roman soldier named in two inscriptions
found on the Adriatic coast. This L. Artorius Castus has several advantages
as a candidate for the 'original' Arthur: he certainly existed and is on record
as doing some of his soldiering in Britain; he had command of forces that
were in some sense 'British' and he bore the Roman name from which the
Welsh 'Arthur' is very likely to have originated. All told, this makes him a
contender as the archetypal King Arthur.

The first step in assessing whether or not this individual could have
been the 'original' King Arthur is to establish as well as we can what the
inscriptions actually say – which is less simple and far less certain than one
might imagine. The second is to revisit the similarities that have been
suggested between this figure of the Roman world and King Arthur. So,
how much can we know about L. Artorius Castus and how confident can we
be of these 'facts'? What did he achieve and when? What were the events in
which he played a part? How telling are the comparisons that can be made
between this historical figure and the Arthur that we come across in the

Middle Ages? And how likely is it that his memory survived into post-Roman Britain, to re-emerge in the Arthurian legend?

Before looking in detail at the inscriptions, it will be helpful to establish when this theory first emerged, and then to track something of its later development. It was in 1873 that the longer and more informative of the two 'Artorius' inscriptions was published, bringing it to the attention of western scholars for the first time.[2] In 1890, quite independently, it was suggested on purely linguistic grounds that the Welsh name Arthur originated as the Roman name Artorius (see below, p. 30),[3] a view that gained wide acceptance.[4] When Malone developed his thesis, therefore, he was able to draw together the inscriptional evidence for L. Artorius Castus and a high probability that the name Arthur originated as Artorius. He concluded that Artorius and King Arthur were one and the same.[5]

This identification of King Arthur with a Roman soldier buried in Dalmatia found little support from British scholars between and in the immediate aftermath of the two world wars, when he was generally thought of as a 'British' figure fighting to defend his country – and civilisation more widely – against the Germans.[6] It did, though, attract some interest in post-war Yugoslavia,[7] where increasing tourism encouraged the Artorius–Arthur connection. The town of Podstrana – where the inscriptions were found – today has an Artorius Society,[8] tourist shops sell 'King Arthur' place mats and plaster replicas of the longer inscription, and a local wine is marketed as 'Artorius', its label featuring a sword embedded in the larger of the two inscribed stones (Plate 1).

Malone's thesis was eventually revived in the United States by C. Scott Littleton and his collaborators,[9] most particularly Linda Malcor. In a widely read monograph, *From Scythia to Camelot*, they argue that key elements of Arthur's story originated in the Roman period around the Black Sea and were carried from there to Britain by Sarmatians who were drafted into the Roman army in 175 CE.[10] Given that L. Artorius Castus's career included postings on the Danube frontier and in Britain, he was seen as a crucial link between Sarmatians beyond the Danube, the Roman army and stories circulating in Britain that became attached to his name.[11] It was Malcor who took responsibility for this strand of the argument, publishing two papers in 1999 alongside a revised edition of the book. She proposes that Castus immersed himself in Sarmatian culture while on the Danube frontier, that he commanded the Sarmatian warriors en route to Britain in 175 and that he then led them to multiple victories in the 'Caledonian War' fought on Roman Britain's northern frontier early in the 180s.[12] In her second paper, Malcor then proposed that the warrior Arthur whose victories were celebrated in the ninth-century *Historia Brittonum* was a distant memory of this Castus, mistakenly reassigned to the sub-Roman-period war against the Saxons.[13] Identification of the 'original' King Arthur as L. Artorius Castus is therefore an important element within the wider arguments developed by Littleton and Malcor, without which the theory that medieval stories centred on Arthur and his court originated beyond the Danube become problematic.[14] A version of this was then popularised in the film *King Arthur*, released in 2004, on which Malcor was an adviser. Obviously, we must set aside this (and every other film too) in our discussion of L. Artorius Castus.

The inscriptions

Since he is not mentioned in any other source that has so far come to light, the two inscriptions found at Podstrana, south of Split on the coast of modern-day Croatia (Map 1), provide all the information currently available regarding L. Artorius Castus. Both are from a burial context and both offer some details of his career.

It would obviously be helpful to place this information within a tight chronological framework, to give an immediate context to Castus's life. We should, though, flag up right from the start that what we do not know about him in this respect far outweighs what we do. In particular, these inscriptions provide no dates. That is not uncommon, for few burial-related inscriptions of the Roman period do, but it does introduce a degree of uncertainty that we can never entirely overcome. Stylistically the inscriptions belong to the late Principate, so the mid-second century through to the late third, with some preference for the first half of this period over the second.[15] Attempts to narrow down the date range all rely on details of the posts listed. Attention has generally focused on his role as a *dux* (military commander), since this term was rarely used of non-senatorial officers in the second and early third centuries, but it is difficult to tie down the date on that basis with any precision. The alternative is to centre on his appointment as a provincial procurator, but even then we can only establish a likelihood of this occurring in a particular time-frame. There remains, therefore, much informed guesswork regarding the dates of these inscriptions and the career that they celebrate, and risks attach to every attempt to fit L. Artorius Castus to particular historical events.

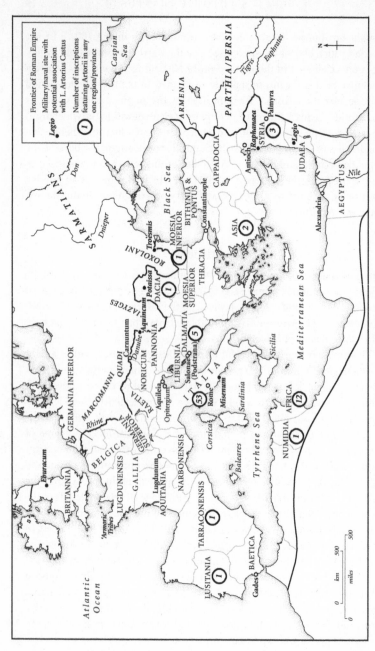

1 The Roman Empire in the second half of the second century CE: a backdrop to the career of L. Artorius Castrus.

There are two inscriptions under discussion, both damaged. We will begin with the longer and better-known one, even though there are reasons to think that this may actually have been the later of the two to be cut.

The longer inscription

Around 1840, two large inscribed slabs were used in building the cemetery wall of the church of St Martin, which stands on the coast south-east of Podstrana (ancient Pituntini), with the sea lapping the graveyard. The inscriptions were visible on the road-side face of the wall, cut onto a dense limestone quarried locally and widely used for Roman-period inscriptions at and around Salona (modern-day Solin), the capital of the province of Dalmatia.[16] Within a decade these two pieces had been recognised as parts of the same inscription.[17] The two slabs have now been removed from the wall (where they have been replaced with replicas; Plate 2), cleaned, reunited and put on display inside the church (Plate 3).[18] Bringing the two pieces together has provided an opportunity to better gauge the number of letters lost to the break,[19] facilitating reading of the text.

The larger slab was initially thought to belong to the front of a sarcophagus,[20] but has now been reinterpreted convincingly as a plaque mounted on the wall of a funerary enclosure or mausoleum.[21] It provided, therefore, an epitaph commissioned to give a fuller record than the pre-existing shorter inscription on the coffin itself,[22] of the man entombed therein.

The text was cut in capitals within a moulded inscription field and includes standard abbreviations (extended below in conventional brackets).[23] Due to damage along the break between the two surviving fragments, part of each line is lost (represented below by square brackets), with something like thirty letters missing in all.

The text reads as follows:

```
     D       M
     L•ARTORI[…]STVS7LEG
     III•GALLICAE ITE[…]G•VIFERRA
     TAEITEM7LEGIIAD[…]TEM7LEGVMA
     CITEMPPEIUSDEM[…]PRAEPOSITO
5    CLASSIS•MISENATIUM[…]AEFF•LEGVI
     VICTRICISDVCILEGG[…]MBRITANICI
     MIARVM•ADVERSVS•ARM[…]SPROCCENTE
```

NARIO•PROVINCIAE•LI[...]GLADIVI
VVSIPSESIBIETSUIS[...]IT[24]

Most of this can be reconstructed:

> D(iis)   M(anibus)
> L(ucius) Artori[us Ca]stus (centurioni) leg(ionis)
> III Gallicae ite[m (centurioni) le]g(ionis) VI Ferra-
> tae item (centurioni) leg(ionis) II Ad[iut(rici) i]tem (centurioni) leg(ionis)
> V Ma-
> c(edonicae) item p(rimi) p(ili) eiusdem [leg(ionis)], praeposito
> classis Misenatium, [pr]aeff(ecto castrorum) leg(ionis) VI
> Victricis, duci legg(ionum) [...]m Britan(n)ici-
> miarum adversus Arm[enio?]s proc(uratori) cente-
> nario provinciae Li[bur(?) iure] gladi, vi-
> vus ipse sibi et suis [posu]it.[25]

This translates:

> Lucius Artorius Castus, for the centurion of the Legion III *Gallica* and
> for the centurion of the Legion VI *Ferrata* and for the centurion of the
> Legion II *Adiutrix* and for the centurion of the Legion V *Macedonica*
> and for the *primus pilus* of the same legion, put in charge of the *Misenum*
> fleet, for the prefect [of the camp] of the Legion VI *Victrix*, for the
> commander of [?] 'British'...legions[?] against the Arm[enian]s, for the
> *procurator centenarius* of the province Li[burnia[?]] with the right to
> judge and issue death sentences, himself set [this] up while alive for
> himself and his family.

Several aspects of this reading are problematic. These issues are fundamental to the Artorius–Arthur debate, hence the need to examine each.

Firstly, there are problems regarding the cases used in the Latin.[26] On
Roman funerary inscriptions the nominative case (the subject of the verb)
was normally used of the individual whose life was being celebrated when
they themselves commissioned the work, but the dative (the indirect object
of the verb, 'to' or 'for') when the text was carved post-mortem. For an
inscription to be grammatical, the case used of the offices needed to agree
with that of the person's name. Here, the opening name is in the nominative, as is the ultimate phrase on lines 8/9 ('himself...'), but the posts are in

the dative. Until recently this was considered merely an odd lapse,[27] and the missing letters reconstructed in the nominative, allowing the offices to be read as those of the L. Artorius Castus whose name opens the inscription. But Latin was the local *lingua franca*; there are otherwise only two minor mistakes, one in a word which was probably unfamiliar to the mason (see below, pp. 20–1),[28] the other a repetition of the final letter in an abbreviation.[29] In all other respects this monument is of the high standard one would expect from production in a major workshop near the provincial capital. The designer controlled the text effectively, with letter size decreasing incrementally from top to bottom, line by line.[30] These are signs of high skill levels, incompatible with such a basic grammatical mistake.

We should probably rule out simple error, therefore. The implication would seem to be that the L. Artorius Castus in the first line was the individual commissioning the inscription, who at the close 'himself set [this] up while alive for himself and his family', but the offices listed were those of a different individual who was already dead.[31] The simplest solution is to suppose that both men were called Lucius Artorius Castus and the man commemorated was the father (or similar) of the figure commissioning this memorial – it was very common to give the father's name to the eldest son (and heir). Further inscriptions certainly suggest that the family was well established locally across the late second and third centuries,[32] so a plaque commissioned in the next generation makes good sense. On balance, therefore, the longer inscription was probably commissioned by a near descendant of the man whose career it commemorated, who bore the same name.

Additionally, there are specific words in the inscription that are problematic in some degree as regards their translation and interpretation, as follows. Then there are specific terms used in the inscription that require further comment as regards how we should interpret them.

PRAEPOSITO

Praepositus was a term generally used of an equestrian officer with logistical duties or in temporary charge of army units, for example when they were in transit or when a permanent appointment was pending. Such responsibilities could include naval units. The term was essentially a verb, meaning 'put in charge of'. I have therefore followed Tony Birley's translation here,[33] rather than treating *praepositus* as a noun requiring translation as 'commander' or similar.

[. . .]AEFF▪LEGVIVICTRICIS

The missing letters are likely to be *pr* which fit the space well, giving the abbreviated *praefecto* but with an abnormal doubling of the last consonant (FF). Assuming that the inscription pre-dates the 260s, this should be extended as *praefectus castrorum*, the third-in-charge of a legion, since this is clearly a legionary post – VI *Victrix* is specified.[34] *Castrorum* is often found on inscriptions of the mid-second century,[35] but increasingly omitted thereafter.[36] *Praef(ectus/o) leg(ionis)* followed by specification of the legion is common on second- and early third-century inscriptions.

DVCILEGG[. . .]MBRITANICIMIARVM

Duci is dative singular of *dux*, 'commander', but this term only emerged as a specific military title from the reign of Septimius Severus (193–211) onwards. Earlier it occurs occasionally as a generic used to denote military leadership in instances where lack of senatorial rank meant that *legatus* ('legate') was considered inappropriate.[37] However, from the Marcomannic Wars (*c.* 166–80) into the third century, appointment as a *dux* still generally remained the preserve of men of the senatorial class,[38] so Castus's status seems exceptional. This is an issue to which we will return.

Legg is an abbreviation for *legionum* ('of the legions') with the double consonant probably indicative of there being (at least) two.[39] There are then a small number of missing letters from a word ending with 'm'.[40] One possible reading would be [*duaru*]*m*,[41] but, having already doubled the consonant, it seems unnecessary to stipulate 'two'; additionally, the space seems insufficient. An alternative is to suppose that the lost word was [*triu*] *m*, 'three'.[42] This is not ruled out by the double consonant in *legg*, since this might require elucidation when applied to three, not two.[43] A third option is to suppose that the missing word is [*alaru*]*m*, from *ala*, literally meaning 'the wing of an army',[44] a term used for a unit of cavalry. Theodor Mommsen offered *cohort alarum*,[45] but that is far too long. Of these, *trium* best fits the space (though even this might require a ligature) and should be preferred.

All are agreed that *Britanicimiarum* is erroneous, but there is little doubt as to the core meaning, which is 'British/from Britain/pertaining to the British Isles'. *Britannicus* means 'to do with Britain'. The adjectival form *Britannicianus* occurs on inscriptions found at York and in the Netherlands.[46] *Britannicianarum* was probably therefore what was intended,[47] meaning that these legions were in some sense associated with Britain. It was commonplace in the Roman world to refer to a military unit by reference to the region in which it was originally recruited, often centuries earlier, but no legions were raised in Britain. However, units might also be distinguished by a regional name in respect of long-term service there. By the later second century recruits to Roman units stationed in Britain will increasingly have been locals, so these two categories were tending to elide.[48]

With the lost text reconstructed, therefore, as *trium*, the office can be read as a 'command of the three legions associated with Britain'. Given that the garrison of second- and third-century Britain centred on three legions, this makes good sense. L. Artorius Castus was non-senatorial so not entitled to the title of legate. Equestrian officers did not normally command legionary forces before the reign of Septimius Severus, but *dux* was occasionally used of non-senatorial officers given such responsibilities in the first and second centuries.[49]

ADVERSUS•ARM[. . .]S

Adversus means 'against'. Prior to the recent repositioning of the two slabs of the inscription, *ARM[. . .]S* was often reconstructed as *Armoricanos* – so the 'Armoricans' of north-west Gaul.[50] However, it is now clear that this would require more than the three (or so) letter-spaces available. Unless there was severe abbreviation, this seems unlikely. Furthermore, *Armoricani* do not otherwise appear on Roman-period inscriptions;[51] an adjectival form of this word occurs in Caesar's *Gallic War*, noting the 'Armoric' tribes on the Atlantic coast of Gaul,[52] but at this stage the term seems to have had only a spatial meaning.[53] That it only came to be used to define a particular people in the late Roman period makes this a doubly implausible reading of the inscription. An alternative is *Armenios* – 'the Armenians',[54] which on grounds of length must be preferred, again in all probability with a ligature.[55] This was a well-known term, used, for example by, the Roman-period geographer Strabo, and on numerous inscriptions,[56] particularly in the second and third centuries. Additionally, the earliest transcription has 'ARME'.[57] The 'E' is not now visible but if we accept this reading then *Armoricanos* is impossible. The inscription should therefore be read as referring to command over troops drawn from the three legions stationed in Britain in transit to Armenia.

PROCCE<u>NTEN</u>ARIO▪P<u>RO</u>VINCIAE▪LI[. . .]GLADI

A *procurator* was an imperial administrator. *Centenarius* refers to pay; this is the second most junior rank of procurator as measured by salary,[58] and the rank normally attained by a career soldier on this route to preferment.[59] L. Artorius Castus clearly had responsibility for a province, but the name is partially obscured. The letters LI are clearly visible,[60] followed by a vertical line with traces of a curve at the top, which suggests a 'B', 'D', 'P' or 'R'.[61] There has been a general consensus in favour of reconstructing this as Liburnia, but there are difficulties. Firstly, Liburnia is not otherwise attested as a province, though well-evidenced as a district.[62] To suppose that it was at some point detached from Dalmatia means that the province was virtually halved. While we can suggest circumstances in which this could have occurred (see below, p. 29), it must be admitted that there is no other evidence that it did. Secondly, the space is insufficient, requiring that, if this is the correct reading, it was abbreviated to four or five letters (as LIBVR, perhaps). There seems little alternative to Liburnia, however.[63] Additionally, the location of the inscriptions in Dalmatia (albeit outside Liburnia) might favour this region of the Empire as the last post held by L. Artorius Castus senior, which perhaps supports this identification.

There are difficulties, therefore, in reconstructing the text of the longer of our two inscriptions. While we can be reasonably confident of coming to an accurate reading in several areas (as for example discarding *Armoricanos* in favour of *Armenios*), there are passages where we are left balancing the probability of one reading against at least one other, with no solution which is entirely satisfactory. The weight of evidence that this text is able to bear therefore varies from one phrase to another, dependent on how confident we can be as to the reconstruction.

The shorter inscription

The shorter inscription poses fewer difficulties. This was discovered in three pieces in 1893 near the church of St Martin.[64] These were subsequently lost but one has recently been relocated in the Archaeological Museum at Split (Plate 4).[65] The slab is of fine marble from Proconnesus (the island of Marmara, Turkey), a material used for some of the finest carvings of the later Roman world.[66] As already noted, it belongs to the same general period as the longer inscription, though it is likely to have been commissioned earlier. The lettering was cut into a panel on the front of an ornate sarcophagus decorated with vertical flutes (*strigilli*). Ornamentation consists of flower heads set alongside a vine, similar to the border of the longer inscription. The text was recorded when all the fragments were available.[67] With abbreviations extended, missing letters reconstructed and gaps inserted between words, it reads:

L(ucius) Artorius
Castus p(rimus) p(ilus)
Leg(ionis) V Ma[c(edonicae)] Pr
aefec[t]vs le(gionis)
VI Victrici(s) [ex test(amento)][68]

This translates:

Lucius Artorius Castus, *primus pilus* of the legion V *Macedonica*, prefect [of the camp] of the legion VI *Victrix* by his will.

The appearance here of two of the same posts confirms that the sarcophagus which was the focus of this funeral enclosure was that of the same Lucius Artorius Castus whose career was commemorated in the longer inscription. In this instance, though, the name and the second post held are both in the nominative,[69] so it was commissioned by Castus senior in person. The significance of the two posts selected for inclusion will be discussed further below (see p. 26).

A career in time

As already established, the inscriptions belong stylistically to the later second or third centuries, with the evidence somewhat favouring the first half of this period. Use of the *tria nomina* (the three-name formula) is typical of the first and second centuries, with even an abbreviated first-name (*praenomen*) becoming rare as the third progressed. By the reign of Septimius Severus (193–211), equestrian officers were frequently distinguished by the use of complimentary language; that Castus was not termed *vir egregius* ('outstanding man'), or similar, counts against the longer inscription much postdating 200.[70] The overall layout, lettering and style of these inscriptions all favour the late second to early third centuries over the mid- to late third. The vine motif which ornaments the borders is well-evidenced across the region.[71] Flower heads likewise occur widely, though more often individually.[72] The combination of vine and flower was commonplace in the borders of funerary inscriptions regionally, for example in neighbouring Dacia.[73] The ornamental motifs on our inscriptions belong to well-established types encountered throughout the Danube provinces.[74] While the longer inscription apparently postdates the death of L. Artorius Castus, the shorter is best read as commissioned by him following his promotion to the rank of camp prefect but before the last two appointments listed on the longer.

If we are to make any headway in estimating Castus's chronology, then this can only be on the basis of the lists of posts (Appendix I). Across the last century commentators have offered a variety of dates. Malone suggested that Castus's initial service as a centurion, in Syria, will have coincided with the Judaean revolt of 132–35, so computed that his role as *dux* belongs c. 150–55.[75] However, there is no reason to think that he was in Syria at this time, for neither inscription refers to this war (or any other); Malone's solution has found no support. A more penetrating analysis was offered by Hans-Georg Pflaum,[76] who observed that the emperor Commodus destroyed many senatorial families, punishing supposed plots against him by death.[77] His praetorian prefect, Tigidius Perennis, moved against wealthy members of the senate,[78] and in Britain reportedly dismissed senators from army posts and replaced them with equestrians.[79] The *Augustan Histories* use *dux* of army commanders during his reign.[80] Pflaum therefore suggested that Castus was made a *dux* by Perennis, c. 183–84.[81] John Wilkes accepted this reasoning,[82] as have others.[83]

In 185, though, Commodus came to believe that Perennis was plotting against him and had him executed. His sons had command of the Roman army on the Danube and shared his fate.[84] In these circumstances it seems unlikely that one of Perennis's lieutenants who had only recently been appointed to an exceptional military command would have been awarded a governorship within the disgraced family's recent sphere of influence. And the *Augustan Histories* were written in the fourth century, by which time *dux* was a common term for commanders of the frontier forces of the Empire, so its use here need not be significant. The link with Perennis is not, therefore, particularly compelling.

This approach was refined somewhat by Julijan Medini,[85] who shifted the focus to Castus's appointment as a procurator, arguing that Liburnia is likeliest to have become a province during the Marcomannic Wars of c. 166–80, and suggesting that L. Artorius Castus achieved this distinction in the last year of Perennis's life, 184–85. Moving the date slightly in this way does avoid some of the objections raised above to Pflaum's dating.

However, it also shifts the removal of solders from Britain to a period when the province was a war zone.

There are difficulties, therefore, with all of these attempts to date the career of L. Artorius Castus. What we have in the inscriptions, it is worth just reminding ourselves, are lists of posts held, one just two in length, the other with nine entries. If we are to maximise our knowledge of L. Artorius Castus, the best option is to explore the posts he held in their totality. As our starting point, its greater information requires that the longer inscription serve as our guide.

The first four posts listed are all at the rank of centurion, in charge of between eighty and one hundred legionaries. In the late Principate a small minority of centurions were recruited from men of the equestrian class direct from civilian life, but far more came up from the ranks of legionaries or praetorians, or moved sideways from command of auxiliary units.[86] Given that Castus served in four different legions as a centurion before becoming *primus pilus*, his career appears to have been slow-moving in the early stages, implying perhaps that he was a man of humble background.[87] However, it is only if we assume that his career previous to appointment as a centurion was omitted from the longer inscription that we can reasonably suppose that he came from the ranks and was in origin a citizen of the third class. While that cannot be entirely ruled out, the sheer number of appointments listed and the sense of progression that they reveal is perhaps easiest read as meaning that the longer list is inclusive. On balance, therefore, he is perhaps more likely to have entered the army as a centurion direct from civilian life, so came from an equestrian background, if a somewhat modest one.

Equestrian entrants were of higher social standing and generally better educated than those from humbler backgrounds, so more suited to rubbing shoulders with officers from the senatorial elite. They had advantages, therefore, in the competition for advancement, but in any case the lot of the centurion was comparatively comfortable; their billets were spacious and even reveal signs of 'quite luxurious life styles'.[88] Many were probably accompanied by their wives – there is no good reason to think that the general prohibition on soldiers' marrying (which was in any case rescinded by Caracalla) applied to centurions.[89] Men of equestrian rank seem normally to have joined the legions in their thirties.[90] While it is often supposed that L. Artorius Castus came from Italy,[91] by the second century many such men were enlisting from the provinces, where numerous families originally from the Italian peninsula had become established.[92] Where L. Artorius Castus was born and grew up is, therefore, uncertain. That he planned his own burial near Salona while still a serving officer may imply that his family was already based in Dalmatia.[93]

Castus's first posting was to III *Gallica*, a legion normally stationed at Raphanaea (modern-day al-Rifniah), in Syria (Map 1),[94] which saw active service in the Second Jewish Revolt of 132–35, then in the campaigns of Lucius Verus and Septimius Severus against the Parthians (in 161–66 and 197–98, respectively).[95] His second commission was in VI *Ferrata*, a unit originally raised in Spain but likewise in the second and third centuries located in the east. It was in northern Arabia *c.* 119–23, then Judaea, at Legio (Lajjun) in Syria Palaestina. His third posting was to II *Adiutrix*, a legion based from 106 onwards at Aquincum (Budapest), an important crossing point on the Danube and the capital of Lower Pannonia. II *Adiutrix* participated in the campaigns of L. Verus against the Parthians in the early 160s, Severus's Parthian War in the 190s and Caracalla's eastern campaigns in 216–17.[96] From there he moved to V *Macedonica*, a legion which was stationed in the mid-second century at Troesmis (Igliţa) in Lower Moesia, facing the Sarmatians across the Danube. This unit provided troops for the Parthian wars of the 160s and was then moved to Dacia and took up quarters at Potaissa (modern-day Turda in Romania) in 167–68,[97] where it remained until the late third century.[98] This was the legion within which L. Artorius Castus was made *primus pilus*.

This was Castus's first advance up the career ladder (or at least the first that we know about). *Primus pilus* was the only promotion normally available to a centurion, attained by perhaps one in three.[99] The post was generally for only one year but attracted a salary of 100,000 sesterces.[100] It was the responsibility of the *primus pilus*, who would normally be a career soldier of long standing, to advise the legion's commanding officer, who might well be a comparative amateur in military matters. This post opened the door to equestrian rank. If Castus was not of this status already, then it will have been at this point that he achieved it. It also offered the prospect of further progression; in the later second and early third centuries this was to the office of *praefectus castrorum* ('camp prefect'), a rank exclusively available to men on this career path. L. Artorius Castus fits well within this framework, for he later served as *praefectus* in VI *Victrix*, and finally as a procurator.[101] It was the posts of *primus pilus* in V *Macedonica* and *praefectus* of VI *Victrix* that feature in the shorter inscription, on his sarcophagus; these were Castus's breakthrough appointments, therefore, that he thought warranted commemorating, and of course also brought him a substantial hike in both salary and status. Understandably enough, he was flashing the cash at this point, buying imported marble of high quality for a prestigious sarcophagus. This sequence of offices provides a terminal date for the time-frame within which his career could have occurred, for the role of the *primus pilus* changed out of all recognition during or soon after the reign of Severus Alexander (222–35); Castus's career clearly pre-dated this.

Between *primus pilus* and *praefectus*, the longer inscription has L. Artorius Castus acting as *praepositus* to the Classis Misenensis, the imperial fleet based at the western end of the Gulf of Pozzuoli, near Naples. The navy was very much the poor relation of Rome's armed services, but this was the Empire's senior fleet,[102] responsible for the security of the western seas and transportation when required of the emperor's person, family and household members. It was also the main training centre for all nine fleets and provided a strategic reserve, with a staff of praetorian status drawn largely from Thrace, Pannonia, Egypt and Syria.[103] Each fleet was normally commanded by a prefect of equestrian rank at a late stage in his military career;[104] use of *praepositus* indicates that Castus's was not a regular appointment as commanding officer. A *praepositius reliquationi classis* occurs on an inscription dated 218–35;[105] Le Bohec suggests that this officer may have been in charge of the main fleet depot and/or the reserve.[106] The term *praepositus* was certainly used of such a logistical role,[107] but with only a single mention there is little reason to think this an established post. Otherwise *praepositus* was normally used of temporary assignments, so we should probably read this as Castus serving as acting-admiral pending a permanent appointment. A *primus pilus* might be allotted such a role for a period of weeks or even months on detachment.[108] Omission of this office from the shorter inscription is consistent with this being a short-term posting while *primus pilus*, rather than a stand-alone appointment subsequent to completing that role.

L. Artorius Castus then found further advancement as camp prefect of VI *Victrix*.[109] This legion was at Xanten around 100. It may have served under Trajan on the Danube, then was moved by Hadrian in the 120s to Britain (Map 3), where it was responsible for building sections of the Hadrianic and Antonine walls. By the 160s a detachment was probably at Corbridge but its main base lay at York and would remain there for most of the remainder of the Roman period. In the early 180s, VI *Victrix* was almost certainly involved in war in the north.[110] In the early 190s it was part of the army of Clodius Albinus that was defeated at Lugdunum (Lyon) by Septimius Severus; it returned to Britain around 195, after which it was engaged in fighting beyond Hadrian's Wall and was for a time stationed at Carpow on the Tay.[111]

The job of *praefectus camporum* was created by Augustus (emperor 27 BCE–14 CE), and reserved for ex-centurions by Claudius (41–54 CE). Until the 260s, when the prefect became the legion's commanding officer, this officer was third-in-charge of the legion beneath the legate and senior tribune. As such he had responsibilities which have been compared with those of the modern quartermaster:[112] he assisted the legion's commander in planning and operations; oversaw army discipline; supervised the centurions; managed communications within the legion; sited camps on the march, oversaw the supply of pack animals, firewood and straw, and controlled pay and rations. The role was largely office-based and normally held for around three years.[113] At this stage in his career, L. Artorius Castus was probably in his early fifties.[114]

His eighth posting, as *dux*, is more problematic, only in part because of difficulties in reconstructing the text. Firstly, as Pflaum recognised,[115] until the 190s (and to an extent later still) overall command of any force including legionaries was normally reserved to members of the senatorial class. Since there is no suggestion that Castus ever achieved that status, his tenure is difficult to reconcile with a date prior to the civil wars won by Septimius Severus. Thereafter the senatorial monopoly on high military rank gradually weakened,[116] until Gallienus (260–68) finally replaced senatorial with equestrian officers across the board. The office of *dux* does occur earlier,[117] but was standardised as an equestrian office with command over frontier forces only in the late third century.[118]

However, the wording of the office to which L. Artorius Castus was appointed is unique, which counts against it being either a field command in the context of the civil wars of the 190s or an established post of the third century. Rather it should probably be understood as another ad hoc appointment of a temporary nature. Although such were uncommon, they are recorded from the first century through into the third quarter of the second and were occasionally held by equestrians.[119] C. Velius Rufus, for example, rose from *primus pilus* to become *dux* in command of an army in Africa, eventually serving as a procurator,[120] and Sextus Flavius Quietus was a *primus pilus* who led an army in Mauretania.[121] On balance, therefore, we should probably view Castus's as an exceptional command of men from the legions in Britain while in transit to the east. There were numerous conflicts with the Parthians and, later, the Sassanid Empire, in which Armenia figured heavily.[122] Being already in Britain and with previous experience of Syria, Castus may well have seemed an obvious choice.

Finally, L. Artorius Castus served as *procurator centenarius* of the province of Liburnia(?). Castus brought to the role a CV which included service on the eastern and northern frontiers, a short-term command of the premier imperial fleet, a posting in an essentially logistical capacity at York and command of detachments in transit to the eastern front, which must have travelled in part, at least, by sea. When might such skills have been particularly needed on the Adriatic? As Julijan Medini recognised, the likeliest time was in the late 160s to early 170s, during the emergency of the Marcomannic Wars. Ad hoc reorganisation of war-affected provinces was a strategy repeatedly used by Marcus Aurelius as he sought to match effective leadership to the forces available. The three Dacian provinces were placed under a single command in 166, divided again *c.* 169 then reunited and combined with neighbouring Moesia Superior *c.* 170.[123] We should concur with the most recent reassessment of the career of L. Artorius Castus, by Željko Miletić, therefore, who suggests that Dalmatia was split in two around this same time, with Castus appointed Liburnia's first (and probably only) procurator.[124]

In 170 an imperial expedition on the Danube frontier suffered severe reverses, triggering a retaliatory invasion of northern Italy, the sack of Opitergium (Oderzo on the Venetian Plain) and a siege of Aquileia. Salona was hurriedly fortified and walls were built elsewhere in the region.[125] The Liburnian city of Tarsatica (modern-day Rijeka in Croatia) lies a mere 37 miles from Aquileia. Urban defences will have been a priority there and elsewhere and Liburnia was a region best suited to the movement of men and equipment by sea.[126] It was probably a separate province for only a brief period,[127] placed under the command of an old soldier with the necessary experience and whose own estate was conveniently close by, at a moment of national emergency.[128]

If his role as procurator be pulled back near to 170 (Miletić suggests the envelop of 167–74), then Castus's service as *dux* best fits the war triggered in 161 by a Parthian invasion of Armenia. The Roman response involved the movement of key personnel to the east, including that of M. Statius Priscus, governor of Britain, to Cappadocia.[129] Alongside, soldiers from other frontiers (including legions I *Minervia* from Bonn and II *Adiutrix* from Aquincum) were transferred. It seems quite likely that it was in these circumstances that the experienced career soldier, Castus, who was at this point serving at York, was ordered to lead a force drawn from Priscus's 'British' legions to the east.

This chronology would place Castus in Syria in the late 140s or early 150s, at Aquincum in the early to mid-150s and in Lower Moesia in the mid- to late 150s, before a period of service at York straddling 160. Each of these theatres was comparatively peaceful at these dates, as far as we know. But this comfortable career track was then energised in 161 by the outbreak of war in the east and the need to redeploy troops there. Following his role as *dux* in charge of a force drawn from Britain, Castus may well have retired to his estate just south of Salona, where he already seems to have made provision for his burial. But his emperor called on his services one more time, to defend Liburnia in the emergency occasioned by a Marcomannic invasion, *c.* 170.

Close examination of these two inscriptions has therefore allowed us to explore the life of L. Artorius Castus to the extent that we are able. What has become clear, though, is that the chronology is less than certain. The likeliest solution is to place his service as *dux* during the Parthian War of 161–66 and as procurator in Liburnia *c.* 170. But that is merely the best-fit scenario; we can come to no firm conclusions on the basis of the evidence available (Appendix I). The longer inscription was probably commissioned posthumously by a descendant who may well have had no first-hand experience of government or army service so this may be a somewhat informal record of his ancestor's career. It would be unsurprising therefore if its language was not always quite standard (and the Latin of Roman inscriptions can be inconsistent even at the best of times), hence our inability to be clear just what is meant by certain posts. Castus had a very successful career but he did not achieve the ultimate accolade of promotion to the senate, nor the string of lucrative procuratorships that might have gone along with that. Even so, *primus pilus*, camp prefect and a single procuratorship were well-paid and highly respected positions which will have given Castus considerable status in his provincial retirement.[130] He will certainly have been a man of influence in and around Salona and we should read both inscriptions in that context. Use of imported marble for the sarcophagus suggests an individual flaunting new-found wealth. The longer inscription suggests a family interested in keeping his memory alive but at more modest expense.

L. Artorius Castus and King Arthur

We know less than we would like, therefore, about L. Artorius Castus. The fact remains, though, that the medieval Welsh name, Arthur, is very likely to derive from the Roman Artorius, with the long 'o' transmuting into 'u', the 't' thickening to 'th' and the ending discarded.[131] The case is unproblematic phonologically, although that does not entirely rule out other possibilities.[132]

As Malone pointed out, Artorius was not a common name in the Roman world,[133] despite being that of a *gens* ('tribe', in the sense of 'extended family'), and no trace of it has otherwise been discovered in Roman Britain. He went on to argue that we could not assume that the name was even in use there, though that does of course remain perfectly possible (indeed, likely). But this leaves L. Artorius Castus as the only figure known to us who both bore the Roman version of the name and is recorded as having been in Britain at some point. Although we now have more examples of the name, that situation has not changed significantly. The Epigraphik-Datenbank Clauss/Slab offers eighty inscriptions from the whole Empire (Italy included) that refer to Artorii (Map 1). Excepting only the longer of the two from Podstrana, none has any connection with Britain. Fifty-three were found in Italy, with Africa (twelve) having the most of any of the provinces, followed by Dalmatia with five. The remainder are scattered widely in the south and east of the Empire; none have so far been found in either Britain or Gaul.[134] Of course, surviving inscriptions only reference a tiny proportion of Roman army officers,[135] so there may well have been other Artorii connected with Britain, but in the current state of knowledge there are no other candidates from the Roman world.

Malone built on this by drawing parallels between the careers of L. Artorius Castus and King Arthur: not only do the names equate but he considered it significant that both defended Britain against barbarians and both led 'British' armies to conquests in Gaul. There is only one 'British' Artorius, Malone suggested, and only one Arthur, so it is no great stretch to suppose that they were the same man: 'as matters stand, the only historical character with whom Arthur can with any plausibility be connected is the second-century L. Artorius Castus'.[136]

What of this case today? Clearly, Malone's comments regarding the name still stand. On that basis alone there is a *prima facia* case for seeing L. Artorius Castus as a possible starting point for the legend. That does not, though, mean that he was.

First of all, there are difficulties as regards Roman naming practices. L. Artorius Castus has three names in the style characteristic of the early Empire. First comes the abbreviated *praenomen* – the personal name given soon after birth. There was a very limited range of *praenomines* in use and Lucius was so common as to be of little value outside the immediate family in distinguishing this individual from others (there were, for example, over one hundred consuls with this *praenomen* between 298 and 1 BCE). Then comes the *nomen gentilicium*, the name of the family, but in the extended sense rather than the nuclear, signifying the clan or tribe to which he belonged. One reason why Artorius was uncommon is the lack of an emperor with this family name. All who bore it, therefore, are likely to have descended from the original extended family or their freedmen. Lastly comes the *cognomen*. From the late Republic onwards it was increasingly the *cognomen* rather than the *praenomen* which was used as the principal name by which an individual would normally be identified – think Gaius Julius Caesar.[137] L. Artorius Castus would have generally been known as Castus,[138] therefore, not Lucius nor Artorius; any successes associated with him will have attached to this name, not Artorius.

Naming practices, though, were changing across the later Roman period. The *praenomen* fell out of use universally. In Britain individuals were recorded either with two names,[139] or more commonly just one.[140] The phonetically adapted single name, Arthur, better fits the period which witnessed abandonment of the *tria nomina*, not the late Principate. Again, this militates against any connection between Arthur and the second-century L. Artorius Castus.

We must also revisit those facets that Malone considered common to L. Artorius Castus and King Arthur. To what extent is it reasonable to argue that they both defended Britain against barbarians? Clearly, the Arthur that we meet in the *Historia Brittonum* does fit that description, for he fought against the incoming Saxons (see below, p. 185).[141] But for Castus all we have is his service as prefect of the legion stationed at York. Malone interpreted this as corresponding to a regimental colonel,[142] but unless Castus belongs later than 260 this is to go far too high up the ranks of modern equivalents. Earlier, the camp prefect was primarily an administrator and only third-in-charge of the legion, as we have seen. Whether or not VI *Victrix* saw active service while he was attached is unknowable but even if it did it seems unlikely that the legion's backroom staff would have engaged in much actual fighting; Castus will only have held command in an emergency. It seems highly unlikely, therefore, that his role as *praefectus* at York could have originated the legend of King Arthur.

In fact, there are few wars in northern Britain which could have relevance to Castus's career. Hostilities seem to have broken out in the mid-150s and perhaps also in the 160s, though the matter is very obscure.[143] A war did occur in the early 180s but we have only one near-contemporary description and that is of poor quality, since this section of Dio Cassius's *Roman Histories* survives only in an abridgement made by an eleventh-century Byzantine monk. The relevant passage concentrates on the general,

Ulpius Marcellus, with little regarding the actual war: 'For when the tribes in that island crossed the wall separating them from the legions of the Romans, and cut down a general with his soldiers, Commodus became alarmed and sent Ulpius Marcellus against them ... Such a man was Marcellus and he ruthlessly put down the barbarians in Britain'.[144]

Who the senior figure was who was killed is unclear. Peter Salway suggested that he was a legionary legate, in which case he was most likely the commander of VI *Victrix*. There are though no signs that a legionary fortress was attacked or substantial casualties inflicted,[145] so this would need to have occurred while inspecting the northern garrisons or directing operations beyond the Hadrianic barrier. But given the use of the same word, 'general' (στρατηγός), for both the stricken leader and Ulpius Marcellus, it seems likelier that this referred to the previous governor,[146] probably in similar circumstances. Ulpius Marcellus had already served in Britain in the late 170s. The loss of his successor was made up by his return. It was Ulpius Marcellus who was responsible for Rome's success in the subsequent war.[147] That Castus was even in Britain at this time is no more than speculation (the reconstruction of his career offered above places him at York two decades earlier). That he somehow took the credit for the victory is to contradict all the evidence available to us and should be dismissed as special pleading.

Nor is the second point that Malone made any more convincing, that both L. Artorius Castus and King Arthur led British armies to victory in Gaul.[148] Malone was formulating his theory when the longer inscription was understood to read *Armoricanos*; with the two pieces repositioned, that interpretation is no longer viable. Therefore an expedition led by Castus to Gaul does not fit even the little we do know. That the 'Armoricans' play a significant role in Arthurian storytelling is not in doubt, but they are Arthur's close allies, not his enemies. There is no mention of the Armenians, though Geoffrey imagined that the Romans had brought in Parthians, Medes, Libyans, Egyptians, Babylonians, Bithynians, Phrygians and Syrians, among others, to fight against Arthur.[149] But all that is immaterial if we accept *Armenios* on the longer inscription. And Arthur was not credited with waging continental wars until the appearance of two works of the central Middle Ages, the Breton *Legend of Saint Goeznovius* (see below, pp. 242-3), and Geoffrey of Monmouth's pseudo-historical *History of the Kings of Britain* (below, pp. 250-1), neither of which can be accepted as a reliable source for a much earlier period. The second of Malone's parallels between the careers of L. Artorius Castus and King Arthur is therefore no more convincing than the first.

Linda Malcor is responsible for easily the most elaborate interpretation of Castus's life currently on offer and it is to this that we should now turn. 'There is,' she writes, 'precisely one military action known to have been led by a *dux* in the late second century ... to Armorica in 185, which is documented by Herodian ... the officer had to be Lucius Artorius Castus'.[150]

This is highly problematic. Herodian did not use the term *dux*; he wrote in Greek not Latin and he made no mention of an expedition from Britain to Armorica. This passage focuses on an army deserter called Maternus, who turned to a career of brigandage, initially in Italy, then Gaul and Spain. It was the governors of the affected provinces, not the commander of Britain's legions, who were ordered to act against him.[151]

The cities that he attacked are not named, but given that Maternus was active on both sides of the Pyrenees we should probably look to the south – the provinces of Aquitania and Narbonensis – as the area of Gaul most affected, not the northern Atlantic coasts, where there were in any case very few cities. And of course, fresh readings of the longer inscription have virtually eliminated the possibility that Castus led detachments from the 'British' legions against 'Armoric' opponents. Clearly, there is not one scrap of evidence linking Castus and Maternus.

Malcor used a scheme of internal dating to reconstruct Castus's career, on the basis of 'tours of duty' averaging four years each. He served, she supposes, six tours, of which five are detailed in the longer inscription. His service as a centurion in III *Gallica*, VI *Ferrata*, II *Adiutrix* and V *Macedonica* make up the first four, with his elevation to *primus pilus* the last. It is as a centurion in II *Adiutrix* that she begins to argue for a connection between Castus and the Sarmatians on the Danube frontier: Castus, she writes, 'would have had to entertain any visiting diplomats, and in Aquincum the diplomats came from – among other tribes – the Iazyges ... Castus would have become familiar with the Sarmatian culture, language and fighting techniques'.[152]

But all this is pure speculation. Aquincum does lie on the Roman frontier with the Iazyges in the Carpathian Basin and, if the subsequent posting was to Troesmis, this similarly bordered Sarmatian territory. However, if this transfer postdated 167–68, as Malcor suggests, then the legion would have been at Potaissa in Dacia,[153] where Sarmatians would have been thin on the ground. While centurions did occasionally serve as ambassadors and travel out beyond the frontiers,[154] there is little sign that they were normally expected to have much to do with envoys arriving on Roman territory.

Other than their styles of warfare, just how much junior officers needed to know about neighbouring tribes is unclear. Relations with the Iazyges were normally peaceful across this period, with the exception of wars in 117–18 and 169–75. There were two broad language groups facing Rome on their northern frontier. The dominant peoples confronting Marcus Aurelius initially were the Marcomanni and Quadi, both Germanic-speaking. The Iazyges on the other hand were Sarmatians who spoke Old Iranian. Castus was one of fifty-eight centurions serving in II *Adiutrix* if it was up to strength. The inscriptional evidence for the presence of specialist translators on the Danube frontier makes it unlikely that any of the legion's centurions were expected to learn the language of either of the groups beyond the Danube, let alone him in particular (see below, p. 49).

Malcor then asserts that he 'was assigned a post that is not detailed in the surviving portion of the main inscription.'[155] She supposes in a footnote that the abbreviation PRAEF should be reconstructed in the central damaged area of the text in line 4, as if his office of *praefectus* was the normal next stage of the *cursus honorum* of a member of the *equites*. This reading is impossible. Castus was not following the standard equestrian military career path (the *tria militiae*) of cohort prefect, legionary tribune and prefect in charge of a cavalry *ala*, but the parallel track starting with the centurionate. Her assertion that Castus was then responsible as *praefectus* for the transfer of 5,500 Iazyges from the Danube frontier to Britain merely piles speculation upon speculation.

'In 181,' Malcor then claims, 'Lucuis Artorius Castus was sent back to Britain – and into legend.'[156] This is stirring stuff but does not bear up to close examination. The longer inscription has [PR]AEFFLEGVI•VICTRICIS at this point, which translates unproblematically as 'prefect of legion VI *Victrix*'. This was as camp prefect. Malcor, however, rejects this and insists that Castus served as *praefectus* of the auxiliary force stationed at Bremetennacum (Ribchester, central Lancashire). Certainly, there were Sarmatian cavalry at Ribchester in the third century, to whom we will return (see below, pp. 58–65), but there is not a shred of evidence that Castus was ever their commander. Rather, *praefectus castrorum* was the standard promotion from *primus pilus*; Castus served in this capacity at York. On balance, he is most likely to have been stationed in Britain *c.* 160, significantly earlier than the Sarmatian troops posted there in 175.

Malcor's second article builds upon 'what we know about the life of Lucius Artorius Castus's (i.e. her first piece),[157] and brings to it for the purpose of comparison events linked to or attributes of Arthur derived from texts that

she terms 'primary',[158] stretching from the *Historia Brittonum* in the early
ninth century to such insular writers as Gerald of Wales and Laȝamon in the
decades around 1200.[159] She concludes that: 'The parallels between Castus
and Arthur are striking not only in their number but also in the variety of
levels on which they occur ... Castus [is] a powerful candidate for the title of
the historical Arthur.'[160] Her parallels include them both being warriors: active
'in Britain at some time in the past'; 'associated with Roman legions', either as
an ally or enemy; identified as 'the historical leader of a group of armoured
horsemen who fought using swords, lances and shields'; commanding 'troops
from a fortress which is variously identified'; using similar standards (the
Pendragon); fighting to defend 'civilised' parts of Britain against 'barbarian'
invaders, who are sometimes identified as the Saxons, though 'most texts
quickly shift to Picts and Scots and Irish'; who consolidated Britain following
infighting after the death of the previous ruler; who were both entitled *dux*;
and who had some connection with a Roman Lucius.

But these comparisons cannot stand if the career of L. Artorius Castus
was significantly different to the one which Malcor imagines; in reality most
are in any case of very little or no weight. Numerous figures with the same or
similar names were active in Britain without our needing to identify them as
the same individual. Association with Roman legions, either for or against,
again applies to numerous leaders; Castus was self-evidently a Roman soldier
but no one has ever suggested that King Arthur fought alongside Rome's
armies and he was only depicted as opposing them in works written in and
after the twelfth century. There is no reason on the basis of the inscriptions
to associate L. Artorius Castus with cavalry, however armed; centurions
normally commanded legionaries (i.e. heavy infantry), with only occasional
secondment to take charge of auxiliary units, only a minority of which were
mounted, and there is no evidence that Castus held such a post. Equally the
medieval Arthur was portrayed as a commander of cavalry only after the rise
of the knight post-1000, when such became virtually obligatory.

We have no idea what banner L. Artorius Castus fought beneath, but it
was presumably the emblem of his legion of the day. There is no evidence
for Arthur's standard which is remotely contemporary. The inscriptions
make no reference to Saxons, Picts, Scots or Irish, and the earliest 'Arthurian'
texts have only Saxons (as per the *Historia Brittonum*) or leave Arthur's
enemies unnamed (as per the *Annales Cambriae*). There is not a scrap of
evidence that L. Artorius Castus consolidated Britain following infighting
associated with the death of a previous ruler, and it is only late versions of
the Arthurian legend which offer a comparable scenario for King Arthur,

following Uther's death. With rejection of the Armoricans as opponents of L. Artorius Castus, comparison between his and King Arthur's supposed expeditions to Gaul necessarily falls. Certainly, Castus had the *praenomen* Lucius, but there is no meaningful connection between his name and that of the emperor who demanded tribute of King Arthur in Geoffrey's account.[161] Firstly, Lucius was an extraordinarily common name. Secondly, one was the *praenomen* of a candidate for the archetypal Arthur while the other is that of his most senior opponent. Thirdly, Geoffrey's emperor was named Lucius Hiberius (though Hiberius was in some manuscripts replaced by Tiberius, the emperor from 14 to 37 CE), but no such name is likely in the classical period.[162] Fairly obviously, this emperor was one of Geoffrey's numerous inventions, as was his letter to Arthur, with its reference to its author as 'procurator of the republic' – hardly an apt title for a real Roman emperor in a piece of high diplomacy. This is language designed to seem convincing to a twelfth-century audience with no knowledge of Roman protocols. It would have been unthinkable in the late Principate.

At the core of Malcor's analysis, though, is an attempt to read Arthur's battle-list in the ninth-century *Historia Brittonum* as commemorating a war fought by L. Artorius Castus against northern invaders in the early 180s.[163] She is not the only scholar who today considers the list historical,[164] though all others have accepted a post-Roman chronology for these events. Could the *Historia* contain a memory of warfare between the Roman army in Britain and its northern enemies, which was later reimagined as a conflict between Britons and Saxons? It is certainly possible to argue for a northern bias in the battles, to the extent that they can be located at all, but the overwhelming sense is our inability to locate most of them with any real confidence. In practice, many of the identifications proposed by Malcor find absolutely no support in place-name studies and have been rejected by every other scholar who has examined this thorny problem (Appendix II). If her identifications cannot stand then nor does her attempt to depict Arthur's warfare as against Rome's Caledonian enemies.

What is left to us? There are just two connections between L. Artorius Castus and Britain that we can make. The earlier is his office as camp prefect of VI *Victrix* at York. In rather general terms, we can be reasonably sure what sort of responsibilities went with this post, which are very unlikely to have offered a platform for heroic leadership in battle.

The second connection of Castus with things British is more problematic and there is no generally agreed solution to the difficulties posed by the inscription. This is his last military role, as *dux*. If his career lay in the second century, then he was one of only a very small number of individuals of equestrian rank to have been recorded in association with this term. But if the people against whom he led his forces were the Armenians, this posting has nothing to do with a campaign launched into Gaul. Recent readings of the longer inscription effectively negates any attempt to associate L. Artorius Castus with Geoffrey of Monmouth's King Arthur. This appointment seems likeliest in the early to mid-160s, when Britain's governor was transferred to the east, but this can only be considered a best guesstimate; the chronology remains a matter of probability, not certainty.

The 'Dalmatian connection'

When the evidence is examined closely, none of the attempts so far made to identify the historical L. Artorius Castus as the 'original' King Arthur seem convincing. Although the name Arthur is very likely to have derived from Roman Artorius, there is no good reason to connect the medieval legends with the L. Artorius Castus known to us from inscriptions found in Dalmatia. Beyond entirely general points which are shared too widely to have much significance, none of the similarities so far claimed between the careers of Castus and the later Arthur have any substance. And the name Arthur is more likely to derive from naming practices in late or post-Roman Britain than from those of the late Principate, when L. Artorius Castus would almost certainly have been remembered as Castus, not Artorius.

Our approach in this chapter has been to scrutinise the two inscriptions found at Podstrana as closely as possible, much aided by the recent cleaning and repositioning of the larger one. While there remain some problems of interpretation, we now have a much better understanding of this text than previously. This is a time for re-evaluation but also for recognition of the limitations of what we can know. There are difficulties in reconstructing damaged sections of each line of the longer inscription, several of which cannot be resolved with any real certainty. In particular, we should problematise the claim that Castus was appointed *dux* at the close of his military career, for this was a very rare advancement for an equestrian officer before the mid-third century. His appointment as procurator perhaps best fits events around 170, so we should arguably seek to reconstruct the chronology of his career back from that point, but the results cannot be considered better than probable.

L. Artorius Castus was a Roman soldier who enjoyed a distinguished career, bringing him wealth enough to establish his family at the heart of

Dalmatia, where he was eventually buried and commemorated. But beyond the name, which he presumably shared with various other members of his *gens*, there is no good reason to think him the archetype on whom King Arthur was later based. His connection with Britain was slight, amounting to a stay of unknown length in a backroom post at York, then a poorly understood command as *dux* of soldiers drawn from the legions stationed in Britain on their way to the east. With that record it seems extraordinarily unlikely that any Briton of the post-Roman period will have even heard of him, prior that is to publication of the Dalmatian inscriptions in the late nineteenth century, which was what brought him to Malone's attention.

The onus must be on those putting forward theories to come up with persuasive arguments, not their opponents to disprove them. On close examination, the case for connecting the historical L. Artorius Castus and the medieval legend of King Arthur is entirely unconvincing. We should therefore dismiss the proposal. That L. Artorius Castus was not the 'original' King Arthur is, therefore, something of which for the moment we can be reasonably confident. It is time for Arthurian scholars to release their interest in Castus back to the Classicists to whom he more properly belongs. King Arthur was not buried at Podstrana: for now that is fact.

2

THE 'SARMATIAN CONNECTION'

> A troop of 5,500 Sarmatian heavy cavalry, or *cataphractarii* ... posted
> to ... Britain in AD 175 ... who belonged to a tribe known as Iazyges ...
> introduced what later became the core of the Arthurian legends.
> — C. Scott Littleton and Ann C. Thomas, 'The Sarmatian Connection:
>   New Light on the Origin of the Arthurian and Holy Grail Legends'[1]

A reader opening this book for the first time here might well ask,
'Why should a study of the origins of King Arthur be interested in
barbarian society during the Roman period north of the Danube?'
The answer, because Scott Littleton and his collaborators proposed that
several of the more important Arthurian stories circulating in the Middle
Ages originated there, and it was incomers from this region who introduced
these tales to Britain during the Roman period (as the quote above).[2] To
date, early medievalists have given this thesis little consideration: in my
own earlier study of King Arthur I noted the idea but only alongside many
attempts to locate Arthur in various different regions of Britain; I did not
assess it.[3] Caitlin Green (writing as Thomas Green) considered the
Sarmatian thesis 'imaginative and intriguing', but felt the chronological
problems to be so great that any connection between Arthurian storytelling
and the Sarmatians can only belong to the later Middle Ages so have no
bearing on the origins of King Arthur.[4] Guy Halsall has more recently
dismissed the notion, beginning with '*King Arthur was a Sarmatian*' as a
heading, followed immediately by 'No he wasn't', and concluding 'whatever
the historical Arthur was, we can I think be sure that he wasn't Sarmatian'.[5]

That is, though, to somewhat misrepresent the thesis: Littleton and his collaborators did not so much argue that King Arthur was himself a Sarmatian as that elements within the medieval Arthurian stories originated on the Eurasian Steppe, were transmitted to Britain by Sarmatians in 175 and there became attached to the name of the Roman officer L. Artorius Castus. Despite words of caution,[6] Littleton's thesis has circulated widely and attracted considerable interest. The 'Sarmatian connection' was central to the storyline of Jerry Bruckheimer's film *King Arthur* in 2004 (see above, p. 15); in that same year Graham Anderson remarked that 'there is a great deal of promise, if some missed opportunities and unguarded enthusiasm, in the Littleton–Malcor view'.[7] Likewise, the archaeologist of the Near East, Warwick Ball, has written that 'Recent studies have suggested that such Sarmatian cavalry units within the late Roman army might have been one of the sources of the Arthurian legends ... Bremetennacum, modern Ribchester ... became ... a Sarmatian settlement'.[8]

The 'Sarmatian connection' has gained a degree of traction, therefore, so requires testing. In chapter 1 we assessed the claims that King Arthur originated as the 'Dalmatian' L. Artorius Castus and found them unconvincing. We must now explore relations between Rome and the Sarmatians and assess whether or not Sarmatian warriors recruited into Rome's armies are likely to have transmitted stories from around the Black Sea to Britain. For the Littleton–Malcor thesis of a Sarmatian origin for Arthurian legend to be viable, such stories need to have passed from Old Iranian into Latin and Brittonic, been taken up by both the clerical and vernacular traditions in post-Roman Britain then been adopted into literature written predominantly in French from *c.* 1150 onwards. The very complexity of this proposal and the long time scale require that we examine each strand of the thesis with due care. I reserve discussion of parallels between Arthurian literature and oral storytelling in the Caucasus for the next chapter.

Sarmatia and the Sarmatians

The Sarmatians inhabited the Steppe of Eurasia (across the south-east of central Europe and south-western Asia) during the classical period (Map 2). We can recognise over a dozen of their tribes by name, but not all were necessarily considered 'Sarmatian' by contemporaries at all times and some were probably subsections of others,[9] for names went in and out of use. Overall, the term is best viewed as somewhat fluid, encompassing a family of peoples some of whom might at any one time be distinguished by other names. They were never gathered within a single political structure and it seems unlikely that the Sarmatians formed a single community in the genetic sense; rather they were formed from what had earlier been several different peoples, who achieved a degree of cultural homogeneity through processes of contact, assimilation and conquest. From the very beginning, therefore, we should acknowledge that the use of 'Sarmatians' as a term requires a degree of elasticity in our thinking.

Historically the Sarmatians are known in the west primarily through the geographies, ethnographies, histories and memorials on stone produced by their neighbours, in Greek or Latin, for they have left us no texts; indeed, there is little to suggest that they used writing. Various configurations of names, peoples and tribal geographies are provided by ancient writers, suggesting a degree of confusion regarding their internal arrangements and/ or changes across time. They spoke Old Iranian, though which branch – or indeed branches – of that language is debated. Classical authors noted that they had numerous dialects, and it is far from certain that they were all mutually comprehensible. Sarmatian personal names occur on inscriptions around the Black Sea and scribbles on pottery from Greece provide snatches of Scythian (likewise a form of Old Iranian).[10] Beyond these, though, and their tribal or group names, the ancient language is almost entirely lost. A modern descendant from this language group is Iron,[11] spoken by the Ossetians in the Caucasus, but this probably comes from the language spoken by the Alans, who remained east of the Sarmatians until the fourth century and only settled modern-day Georgia in the late Roman period.

Today scholars also study these peoples via their material remains. In the early modern era finds looted from rich graves in the Ukraine and southern Russia attracted wealthy collectors, including several Russian tsars who amassed a vast collection at St Petersburg.[12] Over the last half-century technically rigorous excavations have been shedding important new light on these societies and their culture across southern regions of the Russian Federation, Ukraine, Moldova, Bulgaria, Romania, Slovakia and Hungary, as, for example, the burial ground at Filippouka (Orenberg, Russia), where a grave rich in metal artefacts was excavated.[13]

Turning to the classical authors, from the fifth century BCE onwards western writers made various references to the Sauromatae or Sarmatae.[14] The Greek historian Herodotus (c. 484–25 BCE) offered an origins story, suggesting that they descended from a union between Amazon women and Scythian men, who agreed to live separate from, but as neighbours to, the Scythians.[15] This legend probably derives from an awareness of the

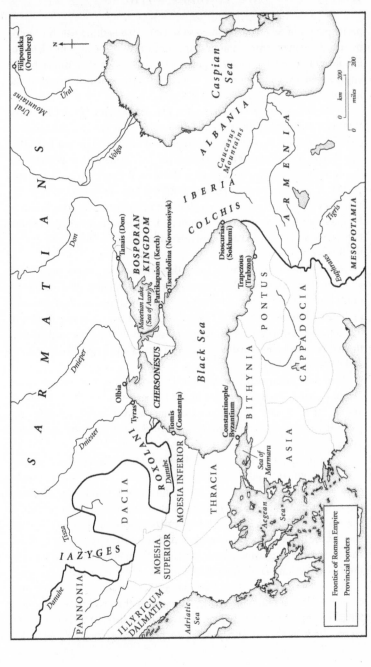

2 The 'Sarmatian connection': areas of Sarmatian settlement during the Roman period around the Black Sea and adjacent regions of the Roman Empire.

participation of Sarmatian women in warfare – something which is noted by several ancient writers and perhaps confirmed by the high incidence of female graves with military equipment.[16] Indeed, it was probably the engagement of some Sarmatian women in warfare which triggered the legend of the Amazons in the first place.[17]

In the fifth century BCE Herodotus placed the Sauromatae east of the Scythians, beyond the River Tanais (the modern-day Don), with a territory stretching fifteen days' journey northwards from the Maeetian Lake (the Sea of Azov).[18] Ancient authors considered the Sarmatians responsible for the destruction of 'Greater Scythia' in the second century BCE.[19] From this period onwards Sarmatian groups took over new territories around the Black Sea. This process is far from clear-cut in the surviving texts, however, for many authors found it difficult, and perhaps unnecessary, to distinguish between Scythians and Sarmatians, often presenting the latter as a subset of the former.[20]

Around the time of Christ, Sarmatian tribes were present west, north and east of the Black Sea. The Roman poet, Ovid, spent the last nine years of his life in exile at Tomis (modern-day Constanța) on the Black Sea coast of Moesia Inferior, where they posed a major threat: 'Greater hordes of Sarmatae and Getae go and come upon their horses along the road. Among them there is not one who does not carry a quiver and bow, and darts yellow with viper's gall.'[21]

They were ever-ready to strike. Raids launched in winter over the frozen Danube were a particular concern; the barbarians were 'strong in steeds and in far-flung arrows', their attacks were sudden and destructive, and when these occurred only flight to the walled city offered the prospect of safety.[22]

The geographer Strabo, a contemporary of Ovid, likewise noted 'wagon-dwelling Scythians and Sarmatians' on both sides of the River Danube (though he thought them mostly on the further side), and stretching from there right round the Black Sea to the Caucasus. In his day, the Sarmatian tribe called the Iazyges held the lands north of Tyras (on the north-western coast of the Black Sea).[23] He noted their diet as consisting of honey, milk and cheese, but 'nothing living',[24] and thought of them and their neighbours to the east as predominantly nomadic, though some he described as farmers.[25]

Ancient writers viewed such nomads as the very antithesis of their own, city-centred communities, yet they recognised the existence of nomadic kingships as proto-states with internal structures.[26] In reality, many Scythians do seem to have farmed. Their origins story featured a plough, a yoke, an axe and a cup, all in gold, representing an agricultural at least as much as a pastoral lifestyle.[27] But it seems fair to assume that the Sarmatians placed a high value on their livestock, and many sectors of society practised trans-humance, at least. For long periods their seasonal migrations were prob-ably confined to specific territories,[28] with ox-drawn wagons supplying distant herders with shelter and water. Repeated use of the same seasonal pastures is implicit in Herodotus's depiction of a Scythian kingdom divided into administrative districts, each with a governor. The occupation of comparatively 'fixed' territories likewise seems the best explanation of their traditions of pottery manufacture,[29] which will have required regular access to clay and fuel. Repeated visits to specific sites is also implicit in the best-known archaeological evidence attributed to the Sarmatians – burial mounds, termed 'kurgans', which were erected over timber chambers (or occasionally stone), set into the natural ground surface and containing elite burials sometimes accompanied by a wealth of artefacts.[30] The variety, quantity and at times quality of finds discovered in such tombs implies a comparatively stratified society, led by mounted warriors and their imme-diate kin.[31] Herodotus referred to 'Royal Sarmatians',[32] Roman texts mention Sarmatian kings, and the larger mounds and richer burials are best consid-ered princely graves.[33]

Although the second-century CE Greek writer Pausanias asserted that the Sauromatae had no dealings with foreigners,[34] their tombs yield imports from China, India, Afghanistan, Uzbekistan, Armenia, Mesopotamia, the Bosporan Kingdom, the Greek world and the Roman Empire.[35] Some objects could have come from raiding but most probably reflect access to such trading sites as Partikapaion (Kerch, the capital of the Bosporan Kingdom), Tomis, Olbia and Dioscurias (Sokhumi, Georgia). Some finds, including fine-quality silver and bronze table-ware sets, may have been diplomatic gifts from the Bosporan Kingdom; others came from Italy and Dalmatia, reflecting exchange or official contact with the Roman Empire.[36]

Sarmatian material culture was not merely eclectic. Their artisans were responsible for pottery vessels of various kinds, glass beads, high-quality brooches, metalwork in an ornate and imaginative animal-style, horse trap-pings, armour and weapons. Alongside, though, the richer graves do suggest a link between status and exotic imports, particularly as regards pottery and metal vessels. One illustration of this is the appearance of what are termed 'tamga' signs – small non-alphabetic marks and symbols which occur predominantly on metalwork around the Bosporan Kingdom, but spread outwards from there onto the Steppe. Their purpose is disputed,[37] but they were long lasting, with a history traceable well into the Middle Ages.[38]

Today some archaeologists are critical of the long-held view that cultures identified archaeologically in the Volga, Don and Ural Steppe should necessarily be termed 'Sarmatian',[39] pointing instead to the plurality of communities in the region during the classical period, with Greek cities on the coast interacting with Thracians, Dacians, Celts, Getae, Basileians and Urgi,[40] as well.[41] As the archaeological community has long recognised, pots and other artefacts are not necessarily diagnostic of particular peoples, nor in themselves a safe indicator of population replacement; changes in material culture do not always mean fresh waves of incomers.[42] It is, therefore, helpful to widen out the research agenda in seeking to understand cultural shifts in the region.[43] Clearly, there were many other factors feeding into the variability of material culture, including changing patterns of trade, diplomatic contacts, social structures and warfare, and there was a plurality of ethnic groups, with the divisions between many less than clear-cut and sometimes highly negotiable.

That said, migration was important over a very long period. The distribution of Indo-European languages, from the British Isles, Germany and Spain in the west to northern India in the east, speaks to processes of both contact and migration from the fifth millennium BCE onwards that arguably began on the Steppe and quickened following domestication of the horse.[44] In the classical period, movement was predominantly from east to west,[45] triggered to an extent at least by conflict between China and its nomadic neighbours to the north-west, the Hsiung-nu (though whether or not they should be equated with the Huns is debated[46]). Despite Roman emperors attempting to fend off their nomadic neighbours, the Steppe peoples pushed ever further south-westwards. From the first century CE, an expanding Roman Empire was confronting these new neighbours on its north-eastern borders. Coastal settlements were vulnerable to pressure from nomadic peoples in the interior, but Roman thinking seems to have been to stabilise relations, discourage marauding and provide a degree of protection to settled communities around the Black Sea.

It was late in the first century BCE and early in the first century CE that Sarmatian groups pushed west of the Black Sea. Several factors were involved. Rainfall on the Steppe is low and unreliable, generally today between 200 and 500 millimetres (8 to 20 inches) per year. The availability of fodder for flocks and herds in any particular area therefore fluctuated. Conditions are thought to have been particularly arid between c. 150 and

250 CE,[47] encouraging greater competition and further mobility. It is widely supposed that the Iazyges migrated into the middle Danube valley in part at least due to pressure from another Sarmatian group, the Roxolani, who took their place west of the Black Sea.[48] Tensions between rival groups seem to have played a part in the alliances that they made, both with the Roman Empire and its enemies. Sarmatians fought on both sides in Rome's wars, or one group was in conflict with Rome but another unaffected.[49] Alongside internal tensions, other nomadic peoples moving westwards across the Steppe created a domino effect that pushed the more westerly groups towards Roman territory. The Huns, in particular, swept other groups ahead of them, eventually forcing the Alans, too, westwards from around the Caspian Sea. The Germanic Vandals and Goths were also moving southwards into the Eurasian Steppe, applying further pressure on communities caught between them and the Roman Empire.

The Iazyges, Marcus Aurelius and Sarmatian cavalry

Sometime around the Augustan period (27 BCE–14 CE), the most westerly Sarmatian group, the Iazyges, began to relocate to the Carpathian Basin, settling on the Great Hungarian Plain between the middle Danube and the River Tisza in modern-day Hungary and Slovakia. In the third quarter of the first century, Pliny noted:

> The higher parts of the Danube and the Hungarian Forest as far as the winter quarters of Pannonia at Carnuntum and the plains and level country of the German frontiers there are occupied by the Sarmatian Iazyges who have driven out the Dacians.[50]

This region had been inhabited by Germans, Celts and Dacians. These the Sarmatians apparently subdued; certainly some remained, forming a polyglot mosaic of different ethnicities, lifestyles and economic systems.[51] Strong Germanic traditions continued in the hilly areas north of Budapest, where excavation of Roman-period sites generally yields a mix of Roman, Germanic and Sarmatian material.[52] The Germanic Quadi seem to have expanded eastwards at the expense of the Iazyges following their arrival, apparently without conflict between them. Such a process suggests long-term collaboration between these peoples, who we know to have been allies in the later second century. Finds indicative of 'Celtic' traditions of manufacture were still being deposited in the late second century CE in the north of the Carpathian Basin, suggesting a degree of interchange between pre-existing communities and Sarmatian incomers.

Sarmatian penetration of the region seems to have occurred over several generations. Archaeology confirms settlement initially in the north, in the foothills and mountain valleys, then spilling onto the Great Hungarian Plain between the Danube and the Tisza. There followed a gradual withdrawal from the far north, a shift southwards and, following Trajan's conquest of Dacia early in the second century, a push east of the Tisza. The migration seems to have been largely over by around 120, with the tribal hierarchy successfully transplanted to the new region. The entire Carpathian Basin (centred on the Tisza and its tributaries) came under Iazygan control.[53]

Relations between Romans and Sarmatians seem to have been generally co-operative during the settlement period. Indeed, the Romans may have welcomed the arrival of the Iazyges so as to weaken the Dacians. However, other Sarmatian groups were less amenable to Roman ambitions or respectful of her territory. Josephus wrote of a Sarmatian raid across the Danube into Moesia in the reign of Vespasian (69–79), killing a consular legate.[54] Hadrian was later credited with keeping the Sarmatians in check on the Danube during Trajan's reign, but raiders struck at Moesia once more following his accession.[55] These (and the Sarmatians featured on Trajan's Column) were probably Roxolani from the lower Danube, allies of the Dacians against Rome (on whom see pp. 51–2).

Trajan's conquest of Dacia (see Map 1) did much to stabilise the Danube frontier: the danger posed by the free Dacians was largely eradicated; the new Roman territory divided frontier tribes to east and west and a better watch could now be kept on their activities.[56] Roman Dacia separated the Iazyges from their kin around the Black Sea and meant that they were surrounded by Roman territory other than to the north. In general, relations seem to have remained peaceful, with the Romans establishing routeways between Pannonia and Dacia across Sarmatian territory.[57] Roman goods appear in the Carpathian Basin from around 100 CE, with finds centred on the more important river crossings. Occasional Roman inscriptions and Roman-style buildings occur, which suggest either high levels of Romanisation or the intrusion of military and diplomatic posts.[58] There is a wide spread of Roman material of the second and early third centuries, its distribution particularly concentrated opposite Aquincum, the capital of Pannonia Inferior, and from there running eastwards across the Tisza valley.[59] Rome sought to keep control of the Danube corridor on both sides of the river,[60] as well as the main route-ways. On the whole, therefore, the Iazyges should be viewed as little short of a client community, tied to the Roman interest through diplomacy, gifts and trade,[61] though they could at times be turbulent bedfellows.

In the second century there was only a single Roman legion garrisoning this section of the Danube, at Aquincum. The governor had the task of managing relations with both the Sarmatians and sections, at least, of the Quadi. It is there that we find evidence for diplomatic exchanges with tribes beyond the river, with both 'interpreter of the Sarmatians' and 'interpreter of the Germans' occurring on inscriptions.[62] The absence of legions further south gives the impression of a generally peaceful frontier. Over forty military sites were strung out along the 500-mile border of Pannonia Inferior, garrisoned by only around thirty auxiliary units, implying that many forts were only thinly or discontinuously occupied. At the southern end, a double-strength cavalry unit was the largest force facing the Sarmatians.

Relations between the Empire and its northern neighbours deteriorated in the reign of Marcus Aurelius (161–80). There were several causes. War erupted in the east early in the 160s necessitating the removal of troops to counter the Parthians,[63] weakening the garrisons of the Danube frontier in the process. The expense of this war resulted in a drop in the currency's precious metal content of around 10 per cent across the reign.[64] Any subsidies the Empire had been providing to barbarian rulers beyond the Danube are likely to have been reduced in value, therefore, or even discontinued. Another factor lay in pressures exerted by tribes further north; the Goths were moving southwards, pushing the Vandals into the Carpathian Basin. By the late 160s the Marcomanni, Quadi and Iazyges were all seeking Rome's protection, either via resettlement below the Danube or incorporation of their lands within the Empire.[65] That Marcus Aurelius twice resolved to push the frontier northwards reflects these political realities. Inclusion of the nearer tribes would have much reduced the border's length and provided fresh resources of manpower for Rome's armies, but his intentions were frustrated first by revolt in the east and ultimately his own death.

Under these pressures, the Marcomannic War erupted in 166–67, with the German tribes raiding in force across the Danube into Pannonia, and the Iazyges attacking Pannonia and Dacia. The Dacian garrison was reinforced, including the legion V *Macedonica* being relocated at Potaissa on its return from the east. The co-emperors Marcus Aurelius and Verus arrived on the Danube in 168 but plague was raging and Verus's death (probably early in 169) led the imperial household to return to Rome. In

170 a barbarian invasion of northern Italy and the Danube provinces trapped the surviving emperor in Aquileia.

This campaign resulted in a damaging outflow of loot and captives but Marcus Aurelius reacted with determination. Roman forces defeated the Marcomanni in 171 and destroyed their fighting strength. The emperor then shifted his base to Carnuntum (in Lower Austria) for the period 171–73 and decisively defeated the Quadi. In 174 he moved to Sirmium, the main town in the south of Pannonia Inferior, and across the following two campaigning seasons defeated the Iazyges on the Hungarian Plain.

It was a rebellion launched by Avidius Cassius in the east that forced Marcus Aurelius to conclude this campaign in 175. Dio tells us that the emperor did this with reluctance, having been so angered by the Iazyges that he wished to annihilate them. Their king, Zanticus, came to terms but this treaty was more onerous than those concluded with the Marcomanni and Quadi: the Sarmatians were required to recognise a wide *cordon sanitaire* along the Danube, keep off islands in the river, refrain from using their own boats thereon and banned from assembling together for any purpose. They also had to return their captives – Dio put the number at 100,000.[66]

On these terms Zanticus was allowed to renew his people's alliance with the Empire, 'and at once he supplied as their contribution to the alliance eight thousand horsemen, of whom he [the emperor] sent five thousand and five hundred to Britain.'[67] Just what sort of soldiers were they? The Sarmatians were consummate riders, on that all are agreed; they fought as cavalry. Their equipment changed, though, across the period and across their different groupings, depending on developments in warfare and various social factors. Those who claim a connection between the Sarmatians of the second century and Arthur's knights in the literature of the high Middle Ages (as the quotation at the start of this chapter) have long argued that the Iazyges who surrendered to Marcus Aurelius were heavily armoured cavalry of the kind represented by the Greek term *cataphractoi*. To what extent is this likely?

We need to backtrack a little if we are to address this issue effectively. Domestication of the horse occurred comparatively early on the Eurasian Steppe, probably in the fifth millennium BCE, initially as a food animal. By the end of the third millennium, horses were being worked in harness, chariot warfare had developed and was taken up by city states and empires in Asia Minor.[68] Thereafter, in the early Iron Age, riders replaced charioteers. Mounted Scythians and Cimmerians were raiding their neighbours from the eighth century BCE onwards,[69] and several early kingdoms in the Middle East – including the Assyrians and Medes – included cavalry in their armies. Archery was the favoured weapon of these warriors but light cavalry was generally ineffective when faced by determined ranks of heavily armoured infantry, such as Greek hoplites from the fifth century onwards, later the Roman legions. This led to a shift of tactics and adoption of heavy cavalry by several peoples. Equipped with lances or sabres these warriors could be used as shock troops to attack opposing armies head on and attempt to sweep them from the field.

The Persian Empire certainly deployed such units, though most of their cavalry were always light raiders. So too did Alexander of Macedonia, who personally commanded an elite company of heavy horse in the campaigns which destroyed that empire in the later fourth century BCE. Alexander's quite extraordinary success can only have encouraged neighbouring peoples to adopt similar tactics, including the Massagetae, an Iranian-speaking people whose territory lay near the Aral Sea (modern-day Kazakhstan and Uzbekistan).[70] The Massagetae were successful in creating an extensive hegemony in Central Asia; when that eventually disintegrated, one group re-emerged as the Alans,[71] who eventually migrated westwards and came to the notice of Roman authors.

Whether heavily armoured cavalry reached the Black Sea region initially by migration of this more easterly branch of the Iranian-speaking community or via emulation is unclear, but the latter seems the more likely, with body armour increasingly adopted by tribal elites across the late centuries BCE. The nature of this armour seems to have been very variable. Pausanias remarked on a breastplate that he attributed to the Sarmatians which he had seen in the sanctuary of Asclepius at Athens. The Sarmatians, he reported, had no iron but used bone to tip their weapons, and they split horses' hooves to make hard scales which they then pierced and sewed together onto linen to manufacture armour which was the equal to the metal used by their contemporaries in the Roman world.[72]

There is no reason to doubt that this trophy derived ultimately from Sarmatia. However, Pausanias's remarks must be read with caution, since excavations clearly reveal that the Sarmatians excelled in working various metals. Even so, Tacitus likewise referred to armour made of 'hard hide'.[73] Writing in the late fourth century, the Roman historian Ammianus Marcellinus similarly pointed to horn as the material from which the Sarmatians fashioned armour,[74] though there is of course a danger that later authors were merely repeating the testimony of their predecessors.

By far the most revealing depiction of Sarmatians in the second century CE comes in a scene on Trajan's Column, completed in 113. This was erected to glorify the emperor's conquest of Dacia. Scene 37 shows Roman cavalry, on the left, pursuing Sarmatians fleeing right, leaving a casualty on the ground as they speed off. Both the Sarmatians and their mounts are covered with armour visually reminiscent of snake-scales. This image warrants our close attention (Plate 5), created as it was little more than sixty years before the warriors who surrendered to Marcus Aurelius were despatched to Britain. The Sarmatians wear conical helmets, fastened with a chin-strap over near-shoulder-length hair, and what look very like padded onesies, covered all over with scales and girded at the waist by a narrow belt or cord. Reins are much in evidence but in no instance is there a saddle or any of the associated straps, in comparison with the very visible chest-straps of the Roman mounts. Rather, these warriors are depicted riding bare-back. Few of the men have any weapon: there is no attempt to represent any type of spear; one has a short sword-sheath, but no sword; another is shooting with a bow over his horse's croup. The Sarmatian horses look spirited but comparatively small, with the riders' feet close to the ground.

The lack of any kind of spear or sabre, the absence of saddles, the failure to depict garments realistically and the comparatively small horses all suggest that we should be very cautious about interpreting these horsemen as heavy cavalry. The small size of the horses is borne out by excavations, which generally reveal animals of between 12 and 14 hands. While these mounts were famously fast and enduring, there must have been a limit to the weight they could carry.[75] In detail, the armour is unrealistic: in particular, scales on the inside legs of horses seem highly improbable. The designer had probably never seen a Sarmatian so was relying on somewhat imprecise descriptions. This tableau on Trajan's Column should be read, therefore, less as a detailed representation of Sarmatian warriors than as a cartoon.

It is also important to remember that this scene did not depict the Iazyges but a different group, most likely drawn from the Roxolani, fighting alongside the Dacians. It was Sulimirski's view that the Iazyges did not share in the general Sarmatian adoption of heavy cavalry tactics which he dated to the second century BCE, with the development of iron-headed lances and long swords. In any case he suggested that these tactics were in retreat by the second century CE, when the so-called 'Hunnic' bow, able to pierce body armour, became available.[76]

Even those Sarmatian groups that adopted the heavy-cavalry tactic did so only in part. While richer and higher-status sections of society invested in body armour for themselves and their mounts, others will have had less defensive equipment and will still have focused predominantly on archery, as Ovid witnessed (see above, p. 44). Even Sarmatian communities that had adopted heavy cavalry would in practice field a mixed force, with a core of armoured horsemen accompanied by light cavalry. Tacitus's depiction of the Roxolani implies a close relationship between elite status and armour:

> when they attack the foe on horseback, hardly any line can resist them. On this occasion, however, the day was wet and the snow melting. They could not use their lances or the long swords which they wield with both hands, for their horses fell and they were weighed down by their coats of mail. This armour is the defence of their princes and all the nobility; it is made of scales of iron or hard hide and, though impenetrable to blows, nevertheless it makes it difficult for the wearer to get up when over-thrown.[77]

Strabo remarked that both the Scythians and Sarmatians castrated their horses to make them easier to manage, and that they rode small, exceedingly swift animals.[78] He seems to have been describing not heavy cavalry so much as lightly armed raiders, and Ovid, as we have seen, saw them as mounted archers. We can be reasonably confident, therefore, that the Sarmatian troops despatched to Britain in 175 CE were better suited to raiding than full-scale warfare and pitched battles. Dio used the neutral term *hippeas* (ἱππέας), 'horsemen', of them. Few (if any) are likely to have been cataphracts, as Littleton and his collaborators supposed.

The Sarmatians in Britain

We have nothing more than Dio's word for it that 5,500 Sarmatians were despatched to Britain in 175. This section of his work has come down to us only via an abridged version (see above, p. 32), and concerns regarding the reliability of the text can only introduce doubts regarding the content. That said, the main problems are likely to be of omission, not invention. We can draw some confidence from the fact that the numbers are expressed in words rather than numerically, reducing the likelihood of error. Dio was a contemporary of these events and well placed to know about such matters, being a public servant for much of his life, a member of an influential senatorial family and for a time the governor of Pannonia. On balance, therefore, we should accept his statement, albeit with a degree of caution.

Why did Marcus Aurelius send much of this levy to Britain? The Antonine Wall was abandoned early in the 160s, perhaps in part due to troop withdrawals triggered by war in the east. This led to the recommissioning of Hadrian's Wall and some of the forts in its hinterland. With renewed garrisoning of the Pennines, there seems little likelihood of the type of unrest of which there are signs in the 150s. If the province was not on a war footing in the early 170s, this leaves two possibilities, which are not mutually exclusive: one, Britain was somewhere from where these warriors could not return to their homeland without permission (making them virtual hostages);[79] two, he was restoring to the governor some of the military strength which had been drawn away over the previous decade and a half and these were the troops that were to hand at a moment when regular troops were once again having to be despatched to the east.

The Romans had a long history of recruiting cavalry from their allies; in the early period 'native' irregulars generally served under their own leaders near to home, disbanding once the war was over. Caesar, for example, recruited horsemen from allied tribes to assist his conquest of Gaul, led by members of the tribal elites.[80] But events in 175 were very different, with the cavalry surrendered unconditionally to Rome and for use as the emperor thought fit, as part of a treaty to conclude the recent war.[81] This was not a temporary arrangement, therefore, and there was no prospect of their returning home. Rather, these Iazyges were to be absorbed into the Roman military at the lowest level, as *dediticii* (literally, 'the surrendered'). This was not an elite force; quite the opposite.[82]

Even so, if we accept Dio's numbers these irregulars comprised around 10 per cent of the normal strength of the Roman army in Britain. Given the size of this contingent and our ability to recognise archaeologically quite small, 'foreign' groups within the Roman garrison,[83] we might expect to be able to identify some at least of the sites where they were based. In practice, though, these Sarmatians have proved surprisingly difficult to locate, despite the excavation of so many Roman forts over the last century and more. Sulimirski stated with confidence that they 'were stationed on the northern border in units of 500',[84] noting their presence at Morbium and modern-day Chesters, Ribchester and Chester (Map 3).[85] However, it is no more than guesswork quite how, and in most cases where, they were deployed. Without far more evidence than we currently have at our disposal it is premature even to theorise regarding the size of the units into which these Sarmatians were divided. The scarcity of distinctive finds can only imply that they arrived with very few possessions and without their families.

3 Roman Britain: Rome's north-west frontier on the edge of the known world.

Strangely, the best evidence that we have today for the Sarmatians' legacy may come from the bloodline of their mounts: Cleveland Bay horses (originating in and named after the Cleveland region of North Yorkshire) have been shown genetically to be closely related to the horses of modern-day Ossetia.[86] It seems reasonable to suppose that this link derives from horses that Marcus Aurelius's Sarmatians brought with them. Perhaps those responsible for the supply of mounts to the Roman army bred from this stock in preference to others, thereby establishing the bloodline locally. Unfortunately, though, we know very little about such processes. Late Roman writers commented on horses from such regions as Parthia and North Africa,[87] but not on stock from Sarmatia. It is difficult, therefore, to be sure how this genetic profiling relates to the Roman-period Sarmatians. If we focus just on the region where the Cleveland Bay breed originated, there was certainly a need for mounts in the Roman forts at Binchester, South Shields and Lanchester, but none of these have displayed archaeological evidence of a Sarmatian presence.

Setting this genetic link to one side, we can only re-examine the evidence on which Sulimirski based his identifications. First Morbium, which is in a rather different category to the remainder, deriving as it does exclusively from a textual reference. This is listed as one of the commands under the *dux Britanniarum* (the commander of the northern army) in the *Notitia Dignitatum*. The entry reads:[88] '*Praefectus equitum catafractarium, Morbio* [Prefect of the cataphract horsemen at Morbium].' There are two difficulties here. Firstly, Morbium is not securely located.[89] This section of the *Notitia* begins with the sixth legion, then lists three cavalry units south of the Wall under the command of the *dux*. None is identified with full confidence – Dalmatian horsemen were stationed at Praesidium, probably at York;[90] another troop was at Danum, which may be Doncaster.[91] Morbium could have been any cavalry fort in Britannia Inferior not on the Wall and not otherwise mentioned. Piercebridge is a possibility, particularly given the fifth-century horse fittings found on the site.[92] There may be some corruption in the name, since no Celtic root has so far been identified.[93] Secondly, Sulimirski seems to have assumed that any reference to cataphracts could safely be read as meaning Sarmatians, but that reasoning is far from secure. There are eight units of *equites* referred to in these terms in the *Notitia*. In three instances the people from whom they were originally raised is specified – the Albigenses were German,[94] the Ambianenses and Biturigenses Gaulish.[95] None are explicitly Sarmatian. In addition there is an *ala* of cataphracts listed under the command of the *dux* of Egypt,[96] but again they are not said to be Sarmatians. In fact, there are only two explicitly Sarmatian army units listed in the *Notitia*, that at Ribchester (for which see below, pp. 58–65) and another in Egypt.[97] Given that this is distinguished as the seventh such regiment, there had presumably been at least a further six at some point, but these go unmentioned. And neither of those listed was termed cataphracts.

The Roman army had begun using heavy cavalry by the reign of Hadrian,[98] and this arm of the military was expanded in the third and fourth centuries CE, when the military commentator Vegetius wrote approvingly of their capabilities.[99] Some units were recruited beyond the frontier but these were not exclusively Sarmatian;[100] most were probably raised within the Empire. Virtually the only archaeological evidence so far recovered for Roman horse-armour comes from Dura-Europos, on the eastern edge of Syria, where bardings for horses and a *graffitus* depicting an armoured cavalryman astride a mount wearing a barding have been uncovered.[101] The site was destroyed in 256–57, providing a clear end-date for these finds. Given use of cataphracts by the Persians who were responsible for the site's destruction, it comes as no surprise that evidence for Roman heavy cavalry should surface here, but there is nothing 'Sarmatian' about this frontier post.

With this in mind, the cataphracts at Morbium could have come from any number of different communities and were probably in any case local recruits by the late fourth century, when the *Notitia* lists relating to Britain are likely to have been written. On several grounds, therefore, we must reject this entry as evidence of Sarmatians in the army of late Roman Britain.

If we turn instead to the artefactual evidence, it must be said that it is very thin indeed. A horse's eye-shield and five beads which may be of Sarmatian origin were found at the fort of Chesters on Hadrian's Wall (Plate 6),[102] but although this began as a cavalry fort, it eventually housed infantry units from Dalmatia and the Rhineland. Flat, hexagonal or prism-shaped beads similar to one of those from Chesters have come from Richborough and Verulamium, which may or may not be Sarmatian.[103] Additionally there is a possible Sarmatian bone artefact from Great Chesters,[104] but this was an infantry fort. These finds occur in such small numbers that they could have arrived via any number of mechanisms – for example with troops who had served on the Danube, so we cannot assume the presence of soldiers from this particular ethnic group. More convincing is the funerary relief carving found at Chester,[105] of a mounted warrior wearing a conical helmet of the type which we saw on Trajan's Column, with a tubular standard held overhead in the left hand (Plate 7). The cloak or jacket billows behind; the lower right arm is damaged but a sword sheath is visible behind the right thigh; scholars have claimed to be able to see armour on the figure (but not his mount),[106] but this is now hard to confirm. This seems to depict a *draco-narius*, carrying a 'dragon-banner' of the type which originated in Sarmatia. The dragon standard was widely adopted by the Roman army,[107] but the 'ethnic' dress may imply burial of an actual Sarmatian. He was, though, being commemorated in very 'Roman' terms,[108] and at a military centre with a garrison of heavy infantry.

It is only at the Roman fort of Bremetennacum, on the north bank of the River Ribble at Ribchester,[109] that there is substantive evidence of a Sarmatian cavalry unit in Britain (Map 3). This comes almost exclusively from inscriptions, for to date artefactual evidence indicative of the Sarmatian presence is limited to a single possible 'tamga' sign in lead (Plate 8).[110] Otherwise finds include armour in copper alloy from third-century levels, but of a fineness that would arguably have made it militarily non-functional; harness fittings are predominantly from deposits earlier than the late second century, so derive from the previous garrison.[111] The material evidence for a Sarmatian presence here has on occasion been much exaggerated.[112]

Bremetennacum was a standard cavalry fort, initially built in the first century CE, rebuilt in stone in the second century and occupied at least up to the late fourth,[113] though falling into a dilapidated condition that could indicate abandonment around 200.[114] The original garrison troops were Spanish cavalry, the *ala Asturum*, and the fine-quality parade helmet found here will have been worn by a member of that unit.

The seminal study of Ribchester's Sarmatian garrison is that of Sir Ian Richmond, published in 1945.[115] It was he who first recognised the advantages of reading and analysing the two longest inscriptions in tandem for the light each might shed on the other. These are a plaque commemorating the restoration of a temple,[116] and an inscribed shaft which formed the base of a Jupiter-column-like monument.[117] Both present significant difficulties of interpretation.

First the plaque: this will originally have been fixed to the wall of a temple located outside the fort to mark its rebuilding, but was eventually reused as a flagstone within the fort. While the left-hand and lower margins of the inscription survive, the right-hand margin was dressed for reuse, and only three small fragments remain from the upper margins. The surviving inscription is around 120 centimetres wide by 64 centimetres high. The lettering is of a high standard, using 'elegant monumental capitals'.[118]

The inscription is partially reconstructed, as follows:

    [P]RO
    [SA]L(VTE) IM[P(ERATORIS) CAES(ARIS) AL]EX[ANDRI
    AUG(VSTI) N(OSTRI) ET
    IUL(IAE) MAMAEAE MA]T[R]IS D(OMINI) N(OSTRI) ET
    CASTR(ORVM) SV[B CVRA]
    VAL(ERI) CRESCENTIS FVLVIANI LEG(ATI) EIVS PR[O
    PR(AETORE)]
5   T(ITVS) FLORID(IVS) NATALIS LE(GIONIS) C(ENTVRIO)
    PRAEP(OSITVS) N(VMERI) ET REGI[ONIS]
    TEMPLVM A SOLO EX RESPONSV [DEI RE-]
    STITVIT ET DEDICAVIT D[E SVO]

Collingwood's translation reads:

To [name of god] for the welfare of our Emperor Caesar Alexander
Augustus and of Julia Mamaea the mother of our Lord [the emperor]
and of the army, under the charge of Valerius Crescens Fulvianus, his
propraetorian governor, Titus Floridius Natalis, legionary centurion and
commander of the contingent and of the region, restored from ground-
level and dedicated this temple from his own resources according to the
reply of the god ...[119]

Second, the monument base, which has suffered badly from weathering,
apparently as a result of its standing outside for a long period in Antiquity.
The surviving stone measures c. 61 centimetres across, is 130 centimetres
in height and 51 centimetres deep. On the right-hand face Apollo is
represented with lute and quiver; the rear has two female figures, one
passing a box (or similar) to the other. Richmond interpreted these as a
junior figure representing the local *regio* ('administrative region') receiving
a remission of taxation from the senior figure representative of Britannia
Inferior (the more northerly of the two third-century Roman provinces
of Britain).[120]

The text is in standard Roman capitals, laid out within a moulded
frame (Plate 9), with abbreviations and ligatures to control line length.[121]
This is an inscription of sixteen lines but neither Collingwood nor
Richmond felt able to read beyond the eleventh. Their reconstruction is as
follows:

DEO SAN(CTO)
[A]POLLINI MAPONO
[PR]O SALUTE D(OMINI) N(OSTRI)
[ET] N(UMERI) EQ(UITUM) SAR-
5   [M(ATARUM)] BREMETENN(ACENSIUM)
[G]ORDIANI
[A]EL(IÚS) ANTONI-
NUS C(ENTURIO) LEG(IONIS) VI
VIC(TRICIS) DOMO
10   MELITENIS
PRAEP(OSITUS) N(UMERI) ET R(EGIONIS)

This translates:

> To the holy god Apollo Maponus for the welfare of our Lord [the emperor]
> and of Gordian's own unit of Sarmatian cavalry of Bremetennacum
> Aelius Antoninus, centurion of the Legion VI *Victrix*, from Melitene,
> commander of the contingent and the region ...

Richmond was interested in these inscriptions as evidence for the Sarmatian
troops stationed at Ribchester. On the basis of Dio's remark, he assumed that
this unit arrived *c.* 175 and consisted of Iazyges from the Carpathian Basin.
Since they originated outside the Empire, he reasoned that they could not
return home when they retired so arrangements were made for them locally.
He noted that the Ravenna Cosmographer referred to Roman Ribchester as
Bremmetenaci Veteranorum[122] – 'Bremetennacum of the Veterans'. It is
generally agreed that the *Ravenna Cosmography*, a compilation made *c.* 700
CE, was based on road maps of the Roman period that still existed at
Ravenna.[123] Richmond supposed that the veterans alluded to in this place-
name were the Sarmatians of the inscription, who he reasoned retired onto
land officially set aside for them. The commanding officer's authority over
the *regio*, the 'region', which Richmond read on the temple inscription, then
logically grew out of the responsibility for settling Sarmatian veterans, which
began around 200 CE, as the recruits of 175 CE completed twenty-five years
of service. He supposed that this occurred predominantly in the Fylde,
which he considered 'good champaign country [which] only requires
drainage to develop its potentially fertile soil',[124] and pointed to a Roman
road running from Ribchester via Kirkham towards the mouth of the Wyre
that could have connected Ribchester with veterans settled thereabouts. At

Ribchester he saw the considerable investment in religious facilities as evidence of deliberate Romanisation, with the military authorities at York providing not just centurions from the legion to act as the unit's commanding officers but also the designers and masons responsible for these high-quality inscriptions.[125]

Richmond's analysis was scholarly, surefooted and confident; understandably it has exerted considerable influence on later scholarship. Elements of it are uncontroversial: certainly, there can be no doubt regarding the presence of a 'Sarmatian' unit at Ribchester in the third and fourth centuries. A tombstone which probably came from the vicinity was set up by Julius Maximus for his son, wife and mother-in-law and names the garrison as *ala Sar[matarum]*;[126] another inscribed fragment of a tombstone found in 1604, since lost, references the same unit.[127] The late presence of this same force is confirmed by an entry in the *Notitia Dignitatum*, which reads:[128] *Cuneus Sarmatarum, Bremetenraco* ('wedge of the Sarmatians, Ribchester'). *Cuneus* occurs widely in the *Notitia*, in thirty-four entries in the east and fourteen in the west.[129] Of the latter, one was attached to the main field army and the remainder – this one apart – were on the Danube. Except at Ribchester, *cuneus* always occurs in combination with *equitum*, indicating a cavalry unit, so it can reasonably be inferred here. Most entries using this formula include an additional term. A few offer an adjectival form of an emperor's name, indicating the reign in which the unit was raised; rather more name the people from whom they were originally recruited (most commonly Dalmatians) or specify the particular nature of the unit (as for example 'shields-men', 'armoured men'). Other than the omission of *equitum*, the entry at Ribchester conforms to this formula. This is the sole mention in the *Notitia* of Sarmatians in a *cuneus*.

But while it is established that Ribchester was garrisoned across much of the third and fourth centuries by a unit originally comprising Sarmatians, there are issues regarding other aspects of Richmond's analysis. We need to revisit his reading of the main two inscriptions, his assumption that this unit was made up originally of Iazyges entering Britain in 175, and finally his understanding of the 'region' over which the commanders at Ribchester had authority, how that related to the 'veterans' of the *Ravenna Cosmography*, and the reliability of this place-name.

Firstly, the text of the 'Apollo' monument. A new reading by Geza Alfoldy has allowed Ben Edwards to offer the entirety of this text.[130] The difficulties of deciphering a badly eroded inscription obviously detract from the reliability of lines 12 to 16,[131] but there are differences even in the first eleven lines. Edwards has the following:[132]

```
        DEO SAN(CTO)
        [A]POLLINI MAPONO
        [PR]O SALVTE D(OMINI) N(OSTRI)
        [ET] N(VMERI) EQ(VITVM) SAR-
5       [M(ATARVM)] BREMETANN(ACENSIVM)
        [G]ORDIANI
        IVL(IVS) ANTONI-
        NVS C(ENTVRIO) LEG(IONIS) VI
        VIC(TRICIS) DOMO
10      MELITENIS
        [P]RAEP(OSITVS) ET PRAEF(ECTVS)
        V(OTVM) S(OLVIT) L(AETVS) M(ERITO)
        [DE]DIC(ATVM) PR(IDIE) KAL(ENDAS) SEP (TEMBRES)
        IMP(ERATORI) D(OMINO) N(OSTRO) GORDI
15      [ANO A]VG(VSTO) II ET PON-
        PEIA[NO] CO(N)S(VLIBVS)
```

In translation, Edwards offered:

> To the holy god Apollo Maponus for the welfare of our Lord [the emperor] and of Gordian's unit of Sarmatian cavalry of Bremetennacum, Julius Antoninus, centurion of the Victorious Sixth Legion, from Miletene [Melitene], commander and prefect, willingly, freely and deservedly fulfils his vow. Dedicated on the first day of the Kalends of September in the year when Gordian Augustus was consul for the second time together with Pompeianus.

While a minor change in the name of the dedicatee matters little, it is important to note that this new reading makes no reference to a *regio*. Richmond's assumption that the text alluded to authority over Sarmatian veterans as well as the garrison troops is therefore far from secure, placing in doubt the connection that he made between the 'veterans' of the *Ravenna Cosmography* and a local 'region' over which the commander had authority.

We then need to reconsider the chronological framework. The emperor whose welfare Antoninus was seeking to promote is unnamed, but, given the reference to Gordian, he cannot have reigned earlier than 238. Which Gordian? Gordian I and Gordian II reigned jointly for a mere twenty-two days in 238; the reference is more likely therefore to have been to Gordian III, who was on the throne from 238 to 244.[133] If we accept Alfoldy's reconstruction in detail, then the date of composition narrows down to 241.[134] If not, then a slightly broader envelope is possible; all we can say for certain is that the inscription cannot pre-date 238.

Richmond overlooked the fact that the cavalry regiment actually bears Gordian's name, which implies that it was raised in his reign. If so – and this is by far the most plausible reading – then this unit had nothing to do with the Iazyges despatched to Britain in 175;[135] rather, it had only just arrived here when this monument was erected, most probably by its first commander, a centurion seconded from the York legion. There is, of course, no good reason to think that 175 was the only year in which Sarmatians entered the Roman army or were sent to Britain but the more the surviving evidence points to later groups the less we know regarding those despatched by Marcus Aurelius.

This reading of the evidence finds some additional support. While we can be confident that an *ala* of Spanish horse provided the early garrison at Ribchester, it is not clear precisely when it departed.[136] There is a hint that Ribchester housed German horsemen for a time at the start of the third century.[137] That possibility does nothing for Richmond's assumption that there was a Sarmatian outfit at Ribchester continuously from *c.* 175 onwards. Of course, more than one unit could have been stationed here on a temporary basis during the build-up to the Severan campaign in Scotland, but these are legitimate concerns. Additionally, the fort may even have been disused for a time late in the second or at the start of the third century, in which case there was perhaps a gap between the departure of the *ala Asturum* and the arrival of the Sarmatian *numerus*.

Finally, we need to reconsider the evidence for a veteran settlement. The sole reference to veterans at Ribchester comes from the *Ravenna Cosmography* (see above, p. 60). This is its only mention of 'veterans' in any Romano-British place-name, despite there being known veteran settlements like Colchester.[138] There are nine other names from south of the Wall with two elements, with the second a genitive plural, but these are all civilian settlements which include the names of the tribes in which they lay.[139] Ribchester is the only fort, and the only place with a common noun as the second element.

Given its exceptional nature we should perhaps be rather suspicious of Ribchester's name in the *Cosmography*. Veteranorum was not appended to this fort-name in the late-Roman *Notitia Dignitatum*, yet the scribe responsible for that list presumably used the nomenclature then in official parlance. But the Cosmographer is hardly likely to have known a name coined later than the *Notitia*, given how little revision to maps of Roman Britain was likely to have been attempted at Ravenna post-410. One possibility is that Veteranorum does not refer to Ribchester at all, but is a separate name on the ageing map he was attempting to decipher that he mistakenly attached to Bremmetenacum;[140] names beginning 'Ve-' are comparatively common in Roman Britain,[141] as are names ending in '-um' in the *Cosmography*. And there are quite a few otherwise unrecorded names in northern Britain listed in this text, most of which must refer to quite minor places. Therefore the assumption that there was a veteran settlement at Ribchester may rest on nothing more than the Cosmographer's misunderstanding or misreading of his source. In light of these uncertainties, Richmond's reliance on the *Ravenna Cosmography* for evidence of a colony of Sarmatian veterans established in the early third century should be considered highly suspect.

If we then turn to the archaeological evidence for veterans, there is a worrying lack of support for Richmond's thesis. As he was aware, such settlements in the early Empire were normally either *coloniae* – so comparatively urban in character, or quite haphazard, with the ex-soldiers living pretty much wherever they could purchase properties. In fact, soldiers were long barred from acquiring land in the province in which they were stationed. Only in the fourth century do we come across settlements of barbarian irregulars focused on a city and taking over parts (at least) of its territory (or its land tax). While Ribchester had a settlement outside the fort (a *vicus*) which was in some sense fortified, its occupation peaked in the second century and it was virtually abandoned in the later Roman period.[142] Surviving inscriptions indicate the presence of no fewer than eight temples, but the evidence is again mostly early.[143] We currently know of only a single extramural complex in use in the late third and fourth centuries – the military baths. This was no *colonia*, therefore, even on a small scale, with soldiers settled in a nucleated settlement and allotted land in the neighbourhood.

Richmond argued instead for land having been made available in the Fylde, north-west of Ribchester, but there is not a scrap of evidence for 'Sarmatian' communities there. No characteristically 'Sarmatian' burial mounds have so been discovered either here or anywhere else in Roman Britain, despite their prominence in Hungary, for example, throughout the Roman period (Plate 10), nor settlements. Indeed, there is very little evidence of Roman-period rural settlements in this region of any kind.[144] Richmond seems to have been unaware that much of the Fylde was raised bog, hardly conducive to the horse-breeding which he supposed would have engaged these communities.[145] This was never what Richmond termed 'good champaign country'. While place-name evidence suggests some sparse occupation in the early medieval period, drainage barely began before the later Middle Ages and made only limited progress before the eighteenth century;[146] only the last two centuries have seen this area converted to large-scale arable. There seems very little likelihood that the Romans established veterans here in any systematic sense; this was mostly intractable mossland.

We can be confident, therefore, that there was a unit of cavalry initially recruited from Sarmatians garrisoning Ribchester from the mid-third century through the fourth. Beyond that, the whole matter is far less clear-cut than Richmond supposed. Firstly, there are hints at least of another cavalry regiment here between the initial Spanish troops and the arrival of the Sarmatians. Secondly, the addition of Gordian's name to that of the Sarmatian *numerus* implies that this was a force raised no earlier than 238. Thirdly, the evidence for a veteran settlement is little, late and unconvincing. Fourthly, there is no reason to think that warriors serving in Sarmatian *numeri* would have been granted land on completion of their service.[147] Fifthly, the archaeological evidence coming from Ribchester is as 'Roman' as that from any other fort site; excepting only one lead 'tamga' there is nothing indicative of Sarmatian material culture. It was entirely normal for military units recruited from beyond the frontier to be Romanised during the second and third centuries, and this process was much assisted by local recruitment, which was the norm by *c*. 200. By 300, the Sarmatian presence at Ribchester will have amounted to little more than a name attached to the garrison, as was the case in any number of similar units stationed on the Roman frontiers. That the bath house is the only external structure known to have been in use across the later Roman period underlines the sense in which this 'Sarmatian' unit adopted standard 'Roman' behaviours.

The fate of the Iazyges sent to Britain in 175 is unknown; there is no evidence that they were officially 'retired' in Britain. They were troops of the very lowest status with few if any rights, no pay scale and no established period of service. It is a mistake to imagine that in the first generation they enjoyed status akin to auxiliary units of cavalry in the Roman garrison of Britain, for whom retirement was a right. Perhaps they never retired at all.

Sarmatians and the later Empire

The peace imposed on the Iazyges in 175 did not hold for long, but warfare during the reign of Commodus settled the frontier region. Extensive reconstruction occurred in both Dacia and the Pannonian provinces, and the region seems to have been prosperous and comparatively peaceful across the Severan period (193–235 CE).[148] This left the Iazyges hemmed in, by Vandals to the north but otherwise by Roman territory. There may be signs of fresh Sarmatian incomers, with the possibility that members of the Roxolani were arriving in the late second century, then Alans still later.[149] This may have been the main period of Sarmatian colonisation of territory east of the River Tisza, establishing settlements even across the low-lying lands fringing Dacia.[150] There is growing evidence of both burials and settlements in other areas, around Miskok, for example, the settlement and cemetery excavated at Kiskundorozsma, dating from the late second to the mid-third centuries, the cemetery at Madaras from the later second to the mid-fifth;[151] excavations at Tiszaföldvár have likewise produced characteristically Sarmatian artefacts as late as the mid-fifth century (Plates 11, 12). There was a significant Roman contribution to Sarmatian material culture in the region, with coins appearing in around 10 per cent of graves, many of which lie inside ring-ditches or under barrows. Clearly, this frontier community was not entirely nomadic, with plentiful evidence of sunken-floored houses and workshops, kilns and smokehouses, associated with both livestock husbandry and cereal cultivation. Given the constraints imposed on them during this period by their Roman neighbours, it seems likely that they were among the more settled of the Sarmatian peoples, though such evidence could relate in part at least to their clients.

The growing weakness of the Roman state from the 230s onwards, with successive barbarian invasions, devaluations of the coinage and civil wars, led in the 270s to the emperor Aurelian withdrawing from Dacia back to the Danube. This left the Carpathian Basin exposed to the east; fresh Gothic settlement dominated events, building pressure on the Iazyges. Whereas they had been contained by Roman territory on three sides, now it was the Germanic peoples who were their neighbours to the east as well as the north. These pressures seem to have come to a head during the reign of Constantine the Great. Bank and ditch systems were constructed on the northern and eastern borders of Iazygan territory. These, the so-called *Limes Sarmatiae*, are massive works: one section, the Csörsz-ditch ('Devil's Ditch'), is today in places still 3 metres deep.[152] Finds of Roman material may imply a degree of imperial involvement in their construction. The Iazyges are likely, therefore, to have been closely tied to the Empire for much of the fourth century, and there is every reason to think that the Roman cultural impact remained significant.[153] The tribal name ceased to be used in classical texts, however, with a reversion to 'Sarmatians'.

Even so, tensions between Rome and its neighbours occasionally resurfaced. In 320 Constantine defeated the Sarmatians and Goths; his son, Constantine II, allied with the Sarmatians when he campaigned against the Goths in 332. Two years later, large numbers of Sarmatians fled their own lands to escape a revolt by their subject peoples, with 300,000 reportedly settling in Thrace, Scythia, Macedonia and Italy, 'of different ages and both sexes'.[154] Ammianus Marcellinus noted that Sarmatian and Quadi warriors, 'whose habits are better suited to brigandage than to open warfare', struck at the Pannonian provinces and Upper Moesia but were defeated and brought to terms by Constantius in 358.[155] They attacked Pannonia again in 365 and were defeated in 374.[156] Valentinian died at Aquincum in 375 while campaigning against the Quadi, the Sarmatians having already surrendered.

The arrival of the Huns on the Eurasian Steppe in the 370s led the Goths in turn to seek resettlement in the Empire; the Sarmatians and Alans were no less affected. Some fled westwards, others were slaughtered or swept up into the Hunnic confederacy. Some of those pushing west sought refuge inside the Empire – groups entered Italy and Gaul. Others joined their Germanic neighbours and invaded across the Rhine c. 405,[157] then divided once more when inside the Empire. Some gained Roman employment; we hear, for example, of King Goar following imperial instructions to punish the Armoricans, probably early in the second third of the fifth century.[158] Others were among the barbarians pillaging Spain, where they were defeated savagely by the Goths in the second decade of the fifth century. The survivors divided again; some joined the Vandal migration into North Africa, while others settled in Galicia (north-western Spain) with the Asding Vandals and Suevi.

There were Alans in the army put together by the Roman general Aëtius in Gaul to confront the Huns, and the sixth-century Roman historian Jordanes considered that they were 'infesting' Gaul,[159] engaged in brigandage there. Neither the Sarmatians nor the Alans had ever been politically unified and their migrations resulted in further fragmentation, with disparate groups either destroyed or gradually absorbed by others.[160] By the sixth century, notice of Sarmatians and Alans draws to a close among writers in the west. In the east, Alans continue to attract some attention, primarily as allies of the Persians, occupying Colchis (Map 2).[161] For those settling in the west, the ending of an even semi-nomadic lifestyle and the comparatively localised nature of their colonies necessarily encouraged acculturation. By the end of the sixth century, at latest, we can be reasonably sure that surviving groups had been assimilated into the predominantly Germanic elites taking over in Gaul, Italy, North Africa and Spain.[162]

In Britain, only Ribchester preserves any trace of a Sarmatian presence to the later fourth and into the fifth centuries, and here it almost certainly meant very little beyond the name. The latest coins discovered belong to the reigns of Gratian (died 383) and Valentinian (died 392) but some were very worn by the time they were deposited. The final phases of occupation are now revealing industrial activity, including glass manufacture.[163] Recent re-examination of fort sites across northern Roman Britain has encouraged the view that many were occupied into the later fifth and on occasion even the sixth centuries.[164] The current campaign of archaeology at Ribchester, led by Duncan Sayer, is demonstrating that the same was true here (Plate 13). The presence of a medieval church built on the fort site might even hint at continuity,[165] but this is neither aligned on the Roman buildings nor strictly east–west. Given that it is largely constructed of recycled Roman masonry, the location was probably selected to take advantage of the ample supply of squared stones. The dedication to St Wilfrid cannot pre-date his death in 710 (though it could, of course, have replaced a pre-existing British dedication).

King Arthur and the Sarmatians

The proposition which we have been testing in this chapter is that Sarmatians recruited into the Roman army of Britain in 175 might have transmitted stories from north of the Danube to Britain, where they eventually re-emerged within the Arthurian tradition. We have explored this so-called 'Sarmatian connection', assessing to what extent there was a specifically Sarmatian presence in the army of late Roman Britain which could have provided a conduit for such stories and motifs travelling from one frontier of the Roman Empire to another.

Clearly, there were Sarmatians serving in the Roman army in Britain, alongside men from numerous other peoples from the frontier regions and beyond. But there is nothing to suggest that they long remained a distinctive element capable of injecting much of themselves into local culture. Despite Dio's account of Marcus Aurelius having despatched 5,500 Sarmatians to Britain, it is extraordinarily difficult to locate them. Beyond the Danube, the Sarmatians have left us substantial evidence of their material culture from the second century through to the fifth; there is virtually nothing from Britain. Only at Ribchester is there convincing evidence for a

Sarmatian unit, but this seems to have consisted of men recruited *c.* 238, not in 175. That these came from outside the Empire is implied by use of the term *numerus*,[166] but the same garrison was also referred to as an *ala*, implying eventual incorporation into the mainstream of the Roman cavalry.[167] For a time this regiment was officered by centurions on detachment from York. That perhaps reflects awareness of the need for careful oversight until these 'foreign' troops settled in. Ribchester seems to have been a place where a special effort was made to promulgate Roman attitudes and practices. These Sarmatians were therefore under pressure to become 'Roman'; there is every reason to believe that they did so. Even so, Ribchester's entry in the *Notitia Dignitatum* does flag up this garrison as different. While all the other entries listed under the command of the *dux Britanniarum* use the formula *praepositus* or *praefectus* of unit X, here it is the unit, not its commander, that is described. It may be significant that no other British garrisons are treated in the same way.

We do not know how large the unit was at Ribchester but it is unlikely to have exceeded five hundred men, and was perhaps smaller.[168] There is no archaeological evidence that this garrison maintained a distinctively 'Sarmatian' material culture across the later Roman period: they were probably no more 'Sarmatian' by, say, 300, than the first garrison there had been 'Asturian' by *c.* 180. Local recruiting predominated. On examination, the evidence on which Richmond's argument for a distinctively 'Sarmatian' veteran settlement seems unconvincing.

Culture and language

This brings us to the problem of the languages spoken. When Gordian's cavalry first took up residence, it seems reasonable to suppose that they spoke Old Iranian, but their gradual absorption into the army of Britain, its command structures, its religious practices and its supply system, required that these men learn Latin. As a spoken language, Old Iranian is likely to have been abandoned comparatively early, most probably after the first generation. While there is a slight possibility that some stories passed from Iranian into Latin, it is a commonplace that the loss of lifestyle and language results in the abandonment of stories and legends too.[169] There is nothing to suggest a community that continued to think itself Sarmatian, as opposed to Roman or Romano-British, even at Ribchester. In reality, virtually all the evidence for a Sarmatian presence comes in typically 'Roman' forms, as inscriptions associated with Roman-style monuments or burials.

There are issues here regarding linguistic status. In the Roman period, cultural influence was predominantly (though not exclusively) top-down, from the dominant community to the subservient. Although words from other languages did enter Latin, far more marked was the disappearance of local vernaculars across the Western Roman Empire and widespread adoption of the imperial language. Alongside, Roman deities, classical literature, stories and mythologies, architecture, literacy and education all disseminated top-down through provincial society. While there were regions – Britain included – where these processes were far from complete by 400, there can be no doubt of the potency of Roman culture and its close identification with regional power structures. In such circumstances, it is very difficult to imagine the presence of Sarmatian warriors in Britain with the cultural status necessary for their stories to cross the language barrier and be taken up within a broader community.

A comparative approach may assist us here. By the fourth century, there was far greater potential for 'foreign' cultures to transplant successfully into the Roman Empire than there had been in the late second or third. The majority of barbarians then serving in the Roman army were Germans of one sort or another, but there were also numerous others.[170] Some of these groups were very large, the Goths and Franks in particular, and by the end of the century many were serving under their own leaders with virtually no Roman command structure. The larger groups entered the Empire with their families and were granted rights of settlement. Retention of their own elites and the arrival of entire communities, as opposed to just bands of warriors, are factors likely to have encouraged cultural resilience.

The Sarmatians were among the peoples who entered the Empire in some numbers. Some of their settlements were still on the imperial radar around 400, when the *Notitia* records the officers responsible for barbarians established in Italy and Gaul. All seventeen 'barbarian' commands in Italy were Sarmatian.[171] In Gaul, six Sarmatian settlements are detailed, including at Poitiers and Paris (not all are certainly identified). Some of these were probably comparatively large, providing far greater opportunities to retain elements of their own cultural identity across the following generations than had the Sarmatians despatched to Britain in 175, or a single unit raised *c.* 238. There is, though, very little sign that any of the barbarian groups settling inside the late Western Empire achieved this in the medium term, or even that they sought to do so. Despite their undoubted political and military successes, the Goths made little lasting impact on western European culture; other than in the frontier region, the Franks abandoned their own language and religion in favour of those of the Roman provincials. The Vandals, Suebi and Burgundians are known to us from writers using Latin and Greek but left very little of their own cultural identities behind them.

Even more does this apply to the Sarmatians and Alans. There is no trace of the Iranian language or Sarmatian material culture in fifth-century Italy. In Gaul, material evidence of Alano-Sarmatian influence is limited to a handful of graves of the late fourth and early fifth centuries,[172] and a small body of name evidence. This last has two strands: one centres on the popularity of Alan as a personal name in Brittany in the central and later Middle Ages; the other the use of *alain* (or similar) in French place-names.[173] But there is no certainty that either derives from the Alans as a people. *Alan* occurs in Welsh and Breton both as a common noun and as a name (Alun in Welsh); the personal names evidenced in France arguably derived from Breton. The suggestion that Lancelot originated as 'Alanus-à-Lot', so derives from the Alans,[174] should be set aside as implausible. The name dates from no earlier than the late twelfth century, when the French poet Chrétien de Troyes came up with it for a knight who demeaned himself by riding in a cart.[175] The 'alain' place-name element may come from a Roman personal name, such as Aelianus;[176] its use with French suffixes (as Alincourt, Allainville, Alamont), not Breton, implies a name-forming element exclusive to proto-French. These were clearly formed in the Romance vernacular, so should be considered 'French' place-names; they are unlikely to have had anything to do with the Alans.

The *Notitia* provides evidence of Sarmatian settlement in Italy and Gaul but no record of similar groups in Britain. There has never, to my knowledge, been any claim that Iranian influenced place- or personal names in Lancashire,[177] or anywhere else in Britain for that matter, and there is no artefactual evidence of the sort being excavated in modern-day Hungary. Sarmatian units that had been posted to the Roman army in Britain in 175 had apparently been transferred out, died off or become thoroughly Roman by 410. They are most unlikely either to have retained their linguistic and cultural identity or to have passed on their own stories to local communities. And there were greater linguistic complications in Britain than elsewhere, with Latin having spread less uniformly than on the Continent. Brittonic was still widely spoken in 400, particularly in the west and north (where any Sarmatian units are likely to have been stationed) but even to an extent in the lowland zone.[178] While Latin will have been the *lingua franca* at third-century Ribchester, local farmers are likely to have spoken Brittonic first and Latin, haltingly, only when dealing with the authorities. In the fifth century, Latin began its long slide to oblivion as a spoken language in Britain, under pressure from Old English in the eastern lowlands and from Brittonic, later Old Welsh, in the west and north. Even if Sarmatian story-telling somehow managed to jump the gap between Iranian and Latin, it needed to achieve yet another leap to escape oblivion. Given the parallels, such seems extraordinarily unlikely.

Sarmatian cavalry and medieval knights

Much has been made by those who favour the 'Sarmatian connection' of similarities between modes of warfare practised by the Sarmatians in the classical period and the knights of western Europe in the central Middle Ages, and also of the standards used by Sarmatians on the one hand, and King Arthur on the other. To take the second matter first, we do not, of course, know anything about the types of standard used in early medieval Britain, or even whether or not such existed. Connections between the medieval literary King Arthur and the red dragon are likely to have been encouraged by the prophetic story central to the *Historia Brittonum*, which has a 'red worm' (arguably with the sense of 'serpent' or 'dragon') symbol-ising the Britons (or Welsh) and a white one the Saxons (or English).[179] This passage had nothing directly to do with Arthur, but its appearance in the same text only a few pages earlier than his deeds may well have encouraged the connection to be made by later Arthurian storytellers. Geoffrey of Monmouth depicted a dragon as a portent of the successes awaiting Uther and then Arthur.[180] That the standard of a serpent serving as a primitive type of windsock derived ultimately from the Sarmatians is well established. This was, though, adopted both by the Parthians and the Romans, so should be seen as a near-universal accompaniment to any army of the later Empire. Vegetius referred to *draconarii* with standards of this type attached even to infantry cohorts,[181] but it was probably adopted initially by the Roman cavalry.[182] Across the central Middle Ages the *Epitoma* of Vegetius was widely read, so it is hardly surprising that storytellers and manuscript illu-minators adopted this image to illustrate Arthur's battles. That it is referred to quite matter-of-factly by the German poet Wolfram von Eschenbach in *Parzival*, flying above the pavilion of a maiden,[183] shows how common-place the device was *c.* 1200. This neither implies nor requires any direct borrowing by medieval writers from Sarmatian culture;[184] the likeliest source was Roman literature.

Of course, there were similarities between Sarmatian cavalry and medieval knights: both are known to have worn protective armour of one kind or another, used long spears or lances and fought from horseback on the field of battle. In the late Roman period, such similarities were probably closest with the Alans, who had only recently arrived within the Empire. While the Sarmatians gradually disappear from histories written in the late Roman period, the Alans remained a significant presence. Jordanes, for example, stereotyped them at the battle of Nedao (in 454) 'drawing up a battle-line of heavy-armed [men]'.[185] Such allusions are rarely by eye-witnesses and are not always accurate,[186] but they distinguished major groups of barbarian peoples from one another in Roman eyes, in particular the horsemen of the Steppe from the infantry of the Rhineland.

But such similarities do not require, or even imply, that the medieval knight was directly descended from the Alans, as some have argued.[187] There were many different types of Roman cavalry. Some did resemble medieval knights,[188] but these were not all Sarmatians or Alans. And there seems to have been a near-complete absence of cavalry in western Europe across the later centuries of the first millennium CE.[189] In addition, it should be noted that there are significant differences in the equipment used. We do not hear of Frankish knights wearing armour made from sheets of metal, hide, horn or hoof; rather chain mail was standard. Sarmatian cavalry are represented using a long spear or sword two-handed, tactics entirely alien to the horsemen fighting the battle of Hastings, for example, or the First Crusade. And Sarmatians are frequently linked with other styles of warfare entirely, particularly archery, which barely appears in the repertoire of the knight in the central Middle Ages. When writing in honour of Stilicho in the late fourth century, Claudian referred to 'the on-rushing Alan, the fierceness of the nomad Hun, the scimitar of the Geloni, the Getae's bow, the Sarmatian's club'.[190] Such word-pictures were quite variable and do very little to establish the image of Sarmatians as the 'original' medieval knights. And the knight of the central Middle Ages was inseparable from the castle, while the Sarmatians were at least semi-nomadic. These may seem technical differences but they do nothing to sustain the view that Sarmatians and medieval knights were in any sense connected. Rather, such dissimilarities underline the obvious problems posed by the lengthy gap between the disappearance of Sarmatian and Alan cavalry in the late Roman period and the emergence of the knight in medieval Francia. It was only with the Avars, against whom the Franks fought c. 800, that we begin to find evidence for the metal stirrup; the knights of the Middle Ages relied heavily on this development in their use of a couched lance in the charge.

The sword in the stone

Lastly, we need to review the parallels which have been claimed between the Arthurian sword-in-the-stone motif and religious rites practised by the Scythians and Alans in Antiquity.[191] In the fourth century Ammianus Marcellinus remarked that the Alans' 'savage custom is to stick a naked sword in the earth and worship it as the god of war, the presiding deity of the regions over which they range'.[192] Marcellinus was a well-educated Greek (though he wrote in Latin) and may well have been drawing here on the much fuller description of this rite by Herodotus in the context of the Scythians; their sanctuary consisted of a platform built on bundles of sticks, with an ancient iron sword to represent the god. At an annual festival, animals were sacrificed and prisoners of war despatched: some had wine poured over their heads and their throats cut, with the collected blood poured over the sword; then the right arms of these unfortunates were cut off, hurled in the air and left where they fell; finally the remainder of the captives were slaughtered.[193]

There are parallels with Herodotus's description of the Scythian practice of oath-taking,[194] which again involves a sword and the mingling of blood and wine. However, the Arthurian sword-in-the-stone episode has very little in common with either passage. While among the Scythians and Alans the sword represents the god of war and his propitiation through blood sacrifice, in Arthurian literature his ability to withdraw the sword distinguishes the one true claimant to the throne as determined by Christ. This has closer parallels with the origin story of the Scythians, in which only the youngest son was able to collect up the four golden objects which fell to earth from the heavens, his elder brothers having found them too hot to touch. The youngest, therefore, became king and possession of these sacred objects legitimised his descendants.[195] Similarly the sword in the stone provides a means of determining God's choice for the succession, so engaging the divine in issues of royal succession (see below, p. 100). In the Middle Ages this should be understood as a secular type of miracle – something which had an obvious appeal to a writer of romance. There is no need to suppose that it owed anything whatsoever to the Scythians.

Such tests are rare in folklore.[196] The sword-in-the-stone motif entered Arthurian literature comparatively late and in French – it is absent from the works of Geoffrey of Monmouth, Wace and Laʒamon (and everything earlier). It appears first in *Merlin*, a work that was long attributed to the late twelfth-century French writer Robert de Boron but is now thought to have been written by a continuator *c.* 1200.[197] There are parallels in, for example, the *Life of Saint Edward*, written in the early 1160s in the context of his canonisation, and (more distantly) in the career of Siegfried,[198] but there is no better evidence that the author of *Merlin* was aware of these than that he drew on ancient Scythian practices. There seem to have been king-making rituals involving stones in the Celtic world, such as the rock footprint perhaps used for this purpose at Dunadd, Argyll (Plate 14); it is possible that some trace of such ideas could have filtered into Celtic stories circulating in twelfth-century France, but not a scrap of evidence that it had (and this is hardly a close parallel).

A likelier source for this motif can be found in the cult of St Galgano, an Italian knight who died at Montesiepi near Siena in 1181 and who was the first candidate for sanctity to go through a new, formal process of canonisation prescribed by the Vatican, beginning in 1185. His sword, lodged in a rock, was an important feature of his story; San Galgo Abbey was established there early in the thirteenth century.[199] This was a site being developed by the Cistercian order of monks, who were much in favour at Rome at this date; the strength of Cistercian networking can have only increased the likelihood of this tale reaching *Merlin*'s author. This late twelfth-century cult, publicised at Rome and Siena (Plate 15), provides a far likelier route for this motif to have entered Arthurian storytelling than the possibility that it had somehow descended from Scythian, Sarmatian or Alan practices a thousand years earlier.

Arthur and the Sarmatians

At the end of the day, the 'Sarmatian connection' is a theory capable of stimulating all sorts of thoughts, and it takes us on an interesting journey. But when the evidence on which this theory rests is subjected to close inspection, the complex web of suppositions that it requires fails pretty well every test. Rather, we can be as certain as the nature of the evidence permits that elements of the Arthurian stories were not carried to the west by Iazygan warriors posted to Britain by Marcus Aurelius in 175. There is no evidence linking L. Artorius Castus with these Sarmatians, nor with the group who were established post-238 at Ribchester, by which point he was almost certainly long dead.[200] That this was the only unit in Britain to be still recognised as Sarmatian at the close of the fourth century implies that the much larger group of incomers in 175 experienced very different treatment from the Roman authorities; they left hardly anything behind, excepting perhaps the bloodline of their horses. What happened to these warriors we do not know but whatever it was it seems to have wiped out any traces of their Sarmatian identity.

The Ribchester garrison had a different history which should be viewed separately. Unlike the large influx of Sarmatians two generations earlier, these incomers seem a special case in that their group identity was long remembered. Yet even here there is no evidence that Sarmatian culture had an impact on local communities, among which forms of Britishness, and eventually Englishness, prevailed. And there is not a shred of evidence that, as Malcor postulated, L. Artorius Castus led this troop in twelve glorious victories against the Caledonians which would later be remembered as if a sub-Roman general's battles against the Saxons.[201] We must dismiss the 'Sarmatian connection' from our histories, therefore, and look elsewhere for the origin of medieval stories about Arthur.

KING ARTHUR AND THE NARTS

... many of the medieval legends of King Arthur and the Knights of the Round Table are remarkably similar to the Nart sagas of the Ossetes ... [who] are directly descended from the ancient Alano-Sarmatians.
— C. Scott Littleton, 'The Holy Grail, the Cauldron of Annwn, and the Nartyamongas'[1]

In 1969, a French scholar, Joël Grisward, noted close similarities between the death of King Arthur in stories told from the thirteenth century onwards and that of the Nart hero, Batraz, in stories from the Caucasus, east of the Black Sea. He supposed that they must be connected in some way and suggested that tales may have been shared between the early Celts and the ancestors of the Iranian-speaking Ossetians – the Alans.[2] Grisward's discovery attracted the interest of folklorists and anthropologists, among them Georges Dumézil, the doyen of Nart scholarship, and Helmut Nickel.[3] Scott Littleton had recently read Grisward's essay when he was alerted to Dio's report of the emperor Marcus Aurelius having sent large numbers of Sarmatians to Britain. This was his 'lightbulb' moment, so to speak, that led him to formulate the 'Sarmatian connection'. These Steppe warriors, Littleton proposed, brought their own traditional stories to Roman Britain; elements of these stories eventually resurfaced in Arthurian tales in the Middle Ages but alongside they continued to circulate in their Caucasian homeland. It is now time, therefore, to turn our attention to the Nart sagas, to ascertain what they are, how old they may be, and how closely they resemble Arthurian legend. Might there be links between the Arthurian canon and storytelling beyond the Roman frontier on the Danube? Could Arthur and his knights derive in some meaningful sense from Nart heroes?

We will begin by exploring who the Narts were, what these stories consist of, who told them and how ancient they may be. We will then move on to reconsider those parallels between the Nart sagas and Arthurian literature that have been cited as evidence of a connection, exploring possible links between them.

The Nart sagas

The Nart sagas consist of a body of interrelated oral tales, told or sung in and around the Caucasus Mountains between the Black and Caspian Seas, in what are today disputed border regions where the Russian Federation meets Georgia (Map 2).[4] Like Greek mythology, these are stories set in a remote past, in what seems always to have been understood as a different, preceding age. Collectively they make up a substantial corpus which has a degree of integrity as regards narrative shape, characterisation and style. The sagas are set in a cultural and societal landscape which is broadly similar from one language to another. The Narts of the sagas are a mythological people who are defined by kinship, beyond all else – largely by membership of a mere handful of families;[5] their group identity is reinforced by shared language, behaviours, traditions and beliefs. There is a strong sense of their being separate from and superior to other groups – most obviously the giants (with whom they alone initially seem to have shared the world) but also the 'little people',[6] and eventually various other human communities. The giants, in particular, are generally considered enemies, though that does not entirely rule out social interaction and even mutual assistance.[7] Stories are almost all told from a Nart viewpoint; the audience is expected to empathise with the hero of the tale and the Narts collectively.

Although some Narts live at a distance, the leading figures have homes within three close-set settlements. Each 'village' is dominated by a single family; feasts take place in a large house and the Narts hold open-air meetings. State apparatus, aristocracy or kingly figures are almost entirely absent.[8] Rather, Nart society is oligarchical, overseen by the senior men from the leading families. The Narts live off the land through a mix of pastoralism, agriculture, hunting and raiding. The sagas reveal a 'Nart-world', with recurring features and behaviours and an established value system. Most stories centre on expeditions to hunt, raid or seek women, but there are also numerous references to dances, feasts, meetings of the elders and various domestic scenes.

At their core, the Nart sagas centre on the deeds of a small number of interrelated hero-figures, mostly but not entirely male, whose life stories they tell as a succession of adventures. These heroes are all from the Akhshartaggata family, whose members are renowned warriors. The family descends from Warkhag, 'one of the eldest of the Narts',[9] who has twin sons, Akhshar and Akhshartag (whose name came to denote the family).[10] While guarding the 'apple tree of the Narts',[11] Akhshartag shoots and wounds the dove that stole the magic apple, pursues it to the shore and then into the depths of the sea. There he enters the realm of Donbettir, lord of the oceans, finds, heals and marries the beautiful girl who had transformed herself into the dove, but on returning to the shore with his bride Akhshartag kills his twin out of over-hasty and needless jealousy, then himself from remorse. His widow, Zerashsha,[12] travels to his village to give birth to the twins Urizhmag and Khamis, and eventually marries her father-in-law Warkhag. After her death, Washtirji, guardian spirit of warriors, inseminates her corpse in the tomb, resulting in the birth of a posthumous daughter, Shatana.[13] On reaching maturity, the beautiful Shatana supplants Urizhmag's wife, Eda, and herself marries her half-brother, but their offspring are ill-fated.[14] Khamis's only son is Batraz, who avenges his father's death at the hands of the Narts and in so doing brings the sagas to an end.

Shatana is by far the most important female figure, repeatedly characterised as highly desirable, the wonder-working and omniscient mother-figure of her own family (and on occasion of the entire Nart community), providing counsel on a wide variety of difficult matters. Her name means 'mother of a hundred',[15] and she should arguably be considered as in origin a divinity. She is, though, particularly the confidant and adviser of Urizhmag and others of the Akhshartaggata, seeking to keep them safe and aiding them even against other Nart kindreds.

Given the 'mother-goddess' role of Shatana, close interactions between individual Narts and guardian spirits or deities, and the way in which some Narts pass backwards and forwards between heaven and earth, it is tempting to think of the Narts as having originated as pagan gods or demigods who were euhemerised in the Middle Ages.[16] In reality there was no ancient people called Narts, so in that sense they exist only within these stories. There is a great variety of characters, including both heroes and villains, much like Norse mythology. As in other ancient literatures, the Nart sagas provide a world in which there is close contact and interaction between deities and humans – for parallels think of the *Ramayana*, the works of Homer, and Virgil's *Aeneid*. Leading figures may have non-human blood, as well as human; deities take an active role in their affairs; magic, fore-knowledge and prophecy are all present. In an important sense, therefore, the Narts are mythological, and we need to be aware of the numerous parallels between the Nart sagas, Norse mythology and the tales told of Greek gods and heroes.[17] But they also show human characteristics: the Narts pray, but are not prayed to, and they frequently rely on divine aid and support. Many tire easily, they suffer from hunger and physical pain, they age and die, or can be killed, and they fear death and the world of the dead. The Narts occupy some sort of halfway house, therefore, between mankind and the gods.

Although tales about the Narts are told among communities that speak several different languages, they originated in Old Iranian, which is ancestral to Iron,[18] the language of the modern-day Ossetians, a group who are genetically closer to the Iranians than to other Caucasians.[19] Not only is the term 'Nart' Iranian, but so too are the names of many of the core characters, particularly in the earlier generations.[20] Many archaic linguistic features which are absent from modern Iron are retained in the tales, confirming their antiquity.[21] That specific themes and motifs which feature in the stories find parallels in tales told in Antiquity about the Scythians, and to a lesser extent the Alans,[22] confirms that the tales retain a core of very early material. The notion of burial beneath a mound is commonplace, reminiscent of the elaborate kurgans constructed in the classical period (as Plate 10).

It is, therefore, generally accepted both that there is an ancient north Iranian kernel to this material irrespective of the language of delivery today,[23] and that the tradition exhibits considerable conservatism. There is, for example, no sign of the Zoroastrianism which was the state religion in Iran up to the seventh century CE, and only comparatively superficial traces of Christianity and Islam. At their core, these stories recall a thought-world that was pre-monotheistic, with a pantheon of deities. Take, for example, the gift-giving by the gods to the infant Shoshlan which occurs in the home of Shafa, spirit protector of the domestic hearth and his foster-parent: Washtirji offers his sword; Afshati a share of his wild beasts; Falvara protection of his herds against the wolves; Wasilla donates wheat, Kurdalagon ploughshares, Galagon the wind for winnowing and Donbettir the water to drive mills.[24] This compares with the story that Herodotus recorded of the Scythians, explaining how the gods provided the means by which their people might live.[25] While there has been some Christianisation of gods' names,[26] their roles and responsibilities seem ancient enough.

There is also a strong folkloric and magical element, with, for example, one-eyed or multi-headed giants, shape-shifters,[27] speaking animals, and Narts able to converse with them.[28] Some individuals have foreknowledge of events or the ability to perceive things at a distance, and magical felt whips can transform people into animals. Such folkloric motifs and the deep-rooted pagan elements clearly stem from the pre-Christian era. Sir Harold Bailey suggested that the tales came into being no later than 500–700 CE;[29] others have generally avoided offering specific date ranges but have tended to assume that certain elements date back further still, to the first millennium BCE. Some stories are demonstrably old. There are, for example, close parallels to the Greek myth of Prometheus (first referenced by Hesiod, c. 700 BCE), who is pinned on a mountain and his liver eaten by an eagle for providing mankind with fire.[30] In Homer's *Odyssey*, Odysseus is imprisoned with his followers in a cave by the cyclops Polyphemus. They escape by blinding the monster with a fire-hardened tree-trunk and then hiding beneath his sheep to slip through the exit.[31] This likewise dates to the close of the eighth century BCE; the same tale appears in the Nart sagas, with Urizhmag as the hero.[32] Given its early date it is of course tempting to assume that the Homeric version was borrowed into the Nart sagas, but this story is so widespread that there is no particularly good reason to assume that it originated in either Greek or northern Iranian. Rather, this is a folkloric tale which circulated very widely in the pre-classical period;[33] its origins could be earlier still. These examples stand alone in that they are identified in an early written form, but it may be no more than an accident of survival that other stories cannot be shown to be as ancient. Whether or not, this confirms that at its core the sagas have elements which are both very early and have exhibited a remarkable degree of stability over a long period of oral dissemination.

That said, individual stories frequently appear in different versions, implying local reinterpretation of what were once common traditions. Differences can be substantial. For example, what seem to be the same stories feature different heroes. So, Sasruquo, Shoshlan and Batraz are all tempered by the smith-god; though there are differences in detail, and the latter's story is by far the most elaborate, these seem essentially the same tale.[34] Numerous individual motifs recur across different stories, suggesting that they come from a common stock. Even family relationships are inconstant. Shatana's origins differ markedly from one tradition to another and, in the Abaza Nart corpus, Batraz (here Bataraz) plays the role of Urizhmag

in the tale of Shatana's marriage (here Satayana) as told in
the Ossetian version,[35] and the young Sasruquo stands in for the Ossetian
Batraz.[36] There is a degree of fluidity, therefore, to the corpus, with individual tales dropping or picking up scenes or motifs from the general
memory bank available to their tellers and mutating over time.[37]

There are further difficulties in addition. Much of what survived of
these stories only a couple of hundred years ago is now lost, for the oral
cultures which preserved them were seriously impacted by Russian colonisation. Ever since the eighteenth century, efforts have been made to recover,
record and codify these tales, but this has been only partially successful.[38]

We can only focus on what survives. A major problem is how to distinguish early material from later. If we start from the present and work back,
there is a broadly identifiable late medieval–modern horizon in the stories,
characterised by written letters,[39] cannon, gunpowder, cartridges,[40] firearms,
and words referencing lordship that derive from neighbouring languages.[41]
But beyond this 'late' material there are far greater difficulties. John Colarusso
suggests that the earliest stratum is to be found in mere snatches of story,
and particularly in individual motifs which are incidental to the main thrust
of the narrative, retained as inconsequential relics of earlier versions within
an otherwise oft-revised tale.[42] The principal value of this approach is in
identifying elements which might have been circulating in the Proto-Indo-
European period, but such rarely comprise entire stories. Between these two
extremes of the comparatively late versus the very early, it is hard to weigh
up the internal chronology.

Perhaps the best approach is to assume that the corpus is today characterised both by the high degree of conservatism already identified and yet
also by successive revisions, with some late composition. The tension
between these two extremes is tangible. For example, derivation from the
Scythian, Sarmatian and Alan horsemen of Antiquity requires that the
sagas initially featured communities of graziers on the open Steppe, on
occasion living in wagons (see above, pp. 44–5). The Narts, however, inhabit
permanent villages of stone houses which are multi-roomed, equipped
with hearths and feature high towers and cellars (Plate 16). This is the
settlement pattern of the hill-country they were inhabiting in the Middle
Ages and later, not the Steppe.[43] While there are occasional references to
ox-drawn wagons as a means of transport,[44] these are very much the exception.[45] Ox-carts are otherwise two-wheeled farm transport;[46] Nart heroes
ride out on horseback from, and return to, the permanently occupied
villages where their women, children and old folk remain throughout.

These are not migratory communities, therefore; although they do make forays onto the Steppe, and occasionally into deserts beyond, the Narts of the stories do not normally inhabit the open plains.

Mountains and forests are important elements of the landscapes reflected in these tales, with wooded ravines, dense thickets, woodland glades and caves all abundant. Clearly, whatever their original form, the sagas have been refashioned to accommodate life in a mountainous region. Yet the sea, or perhaps several seas, and great rivers also appear, including by name the Don, Volga and Dnieper (Map 2), reflecting the legacy of an ancestral territory which transcends the Caucasus mountains and their immediate hinterland. The mental geography of the sagas therefore does still embrace the Steppe to the north, and the seas to west and east, but only as adjuncts to the Narts' normal lives among the mountains. Unfortunately, several places or districts which are named are now unlocated, but the inference must be that there was a landscape evoked in earlier versions which was both known, or at least knowable, to the audience and more extensive than the Caucasus. We are dealing with a performance literature which is rooted in an age when the horizons of the storytellers were significantly broader than they later became, but shrank to conform to the narrower world in which they found themselves. Such changes are systemic.

Across much of the canon, therefore, the chronology is complex and difficult to unravel. There are, though, certain horizons which can aid us. One is the arrival of Christianity among the Alans in what is now Georgia (medieval Alania). While the coastal region and parts of the Caucasus were Christianised early, conversion of the interior was still ongoing during the patriarchate of Nicholas I Mystikos (901–7, 912–15). His letters to Peter, archbishop of Alania, refer particularly to the problems of bringing marriage practices into line with Christian norms.[47] We find such non-Christian arrangements in the sagas, for example in Warkhag's marriage to his widowed daughter-in-law,[48] and Shatana's to her half-brother.

To the extent that it occurred at all, therefore, Christianisation is unlikely to have begun impacting the Nart sagas much before the close of the first millennium CE. This process was never more than superficial, as in the replacement of the names of deities with Christian characters, as Washtirji (St George), 'the spirit protector of warriors and travellers' who was a 'benefactor to the Narts since ancient times',[49] and the god Wasilla/Elia (the prophet Elijah).[50] However, the divine is often referred to in the sagas in the singular, suggestive of the Christian or Islamic God, giving us prayers to 'God of gods, my God',[51] 'all highest',[52] the 'will of God',[53] 'God's blessing',[54] 'the Lord God',[55] and the 'hands of God'.[56] Several stories could owe something to biblical miracles, as for example the heap of wheat that never reduces in size,[57] which perhaps parallels the New Testament story of the feeding of the five thousand,[58] and babies carried by the river to a new home of high status,[59] reminiscent, at least, of Moses.[60] Christian ideas may have had some impact, therefore, but Christian rites, priests and churches are notable by their absence. Rather, when such female characters as Shatana and Karmagon seek divine aid, they bake honey-cakes and pray over them,[61] then carry them to a place of special significance to themselves,[62] or one set aside for ritual – such as the 'mountain where sacrifices were made'.[63] This implies that pre-Christian traditions long retained a degree of familiarity, at least, among the stories' audiences.

There is additionally some Mongolian influence, including personal names and titles. Such is likeliest to have occurred in the thirteenth and early fourteenth centuries, when the Alans were subordinate to the Golden Horde. Islam was discouraged by the Mongols but gradually became the dominant religion across much of the Caucasus thereafter with the rise of Turkish power. This too has left its mark, though only rather superficially. Personal names also offer us some chronological indicators. Shoshlan is an important figure in the sagas; the name was in use in the region in the late twelfth to early thirteenth centuries CE. The name Shatana is otherwise known from the writings of the fifth-century Armenian, Movsēs Xorenac'i.[64] Such at least offer some notion of the periods in which names encountered in the sagas were current.

The Nart sagas do therefore contain early material, but no individual story should be described in its totality as ancient. Rather, our assumption should be that none are; we find elements drawn from many different periods contained in most if not all the tales, which are difficult to disentangle.

The story of Batraz

We must now explore the parallels that have been suggested between the medieval Arthurian story cycle and the Nart sagas. By far the most impressive comes in a story of the sword-in-the-water type,[65] which we find in one version of the death of the Nart hero Batraz, and as a preliminary to Arthur's departure for Avalon that first appears in French literature early in the thirteenth century. Firstly, some background.

Batraz is a prominent character in the Nart sagas, with a major role in some twenty-six of the eighty-nine sagas collected from among the

Ossetians,[66] and a minor part in others.[67] He also occurs in tales circulating among the Circassians and Abazas in the western Caucasus.[68] In the Ossetian tales his life story opens with his father Khamis out hunting, meeting and marrying Bisenon, a diminutive maiden of the Donbettir. A beautiful woman by night but a frog by day,[69] she eventually leaves Khamis to return to her own people, leaving him the parting gift of their son, who is then born from an abscess on his father's back. Batraz is made of steel so at birth has to enter the sea to cool down, causing it to boil and resulting in clouds and torrential rain. He grows up on the sea bed among his maternal kin the Donbettir, but is lured out by the sight of his paternal uncle Urizhmag having his head and beard shaved on the shore.[70] As a small child in Khamis's house, he triumphs in archery contests against other Nart youths (particularly the Borata boys).[71] While still a youth he displays prodigious strength by killing 'the giant with the mottled beard' who has stopped the Narts pasturing their livestock.[72] He has himself hardened in the forge of the heavenly smith, Kurdalagon, and again has to cool off in the sea, causing it to boil and resulting in downpours.[73]

In saga 57, Batraz intervenes to stop the Boratas killing his uncle Urizhmag, leaving many of them dead, then he and Shirdon recover a young Nart, Burazag, from Black Dollars, an enemy of the Narts whose arms they wrench off before flinging him into the sea.[74] Then when the spirit Tykhyfyrt Mukara takes a tribute of Nart girls, Batraz rescues them.[75] When Alaf, the son of giant Afsharon, wounds Nart youths who were dancing the Shimd ring-dance, Batraz pays him back in kind then intervenes to rescue his father and uncle when Afsharon seeks to avenge himself on them.[76] In a parallel story, Batraz rescues his father, his uncle and Shoshlan when they are captured by giants. He avenges the death of the Nart Uraz at the hands of the giant Akshualy, following advice offered by a maiden whom the giant had stolen.[77] In a very different type of story, in saga 64 Batraz is sold by his kin into service at a time of famine – this tale has parallels with the biblical Joseph, so may be comparatively late; he proves a model worker but when he kills a giant who is oppressing the village he feels insufficiently respected so returns home driving his owner's herds before him. In saga 65, Batraz kills the prince of Khizh for stealing Shoshlan's wife and restores her to her husband, then saga 66 provides a version of the story of the magic Nart drinking vessel, Wasamonga (see below, pp. 111–13), with Batraz boasting of his achievements but the cup rising at his instruction to the lips of his father, Khamis, rather than to his own.[78]

Saga 67 tells the long and complex story of Batraz' marriage to the beauty Akola, who requires that he first rescue the Nart Uon, enslaved by the seven-headed giant Kanzargash, whom he slays. When his bride is insulted by Zvar, the spirit of fertility, Batraz beats the spirit and pursues it from the house of one deity after another.[79] At a meeting of the Nart elders, Khamis claims three valuable pieces of fine cloth on behalf of Batraz, on the grounds of his great wisdom, valour and nobility, his restraint and honesty, and his respect for women. Shirdon proposes a sequence of tests which Batraz undertakes, culminating in his seeking out and carrying off God's daughter from His palace, following a terrible trek across Steppe, desert and ocean.[80]

We move then to the terrible finale. Burafarnig of the Boratas plots with Shirdon and Chief Shainag against Khamis, whom Shainag kills in single combat. Following Shatana's advice (which he forces her to give him[81]) Batraz kills Chief Shainag with his own sword, then Burafarnig and his seven sons. He overcomes but spares Shoshlan to recover his father's horses. But Batraz believes the Narts to be collectively guilty of his father's death and he sets them a succession of tasks which they cannot achieve. Eventually he has himself bound to a giant arrow and fired against the Warp fortress to attack the spirits that Shirdon claims had instigated his father's killing. The spirits complain to God, who demonstrates His power to Batraz. But the hero slays three of the seven sons of Washtirji (St George), the protector of warriors, and three of the seven sons of Elia (Elijah), god of thunder, when they ride against him. Finally, trapped on the Steppe under the artificially concentrated rays of the sun, Batraz kills seven of the remaining eight of these spirits but finally dies when his body overheats and he cannot find the water necessary to cool himself. His body gives off poisonous vapours until it is taken to the 'Shofya vault', which it resists entering until God sheds three tears over the body.[82]

This synopsis provides no more than the bare outline of his life and it conveys little of the richness and complexity of these stories, but I hope that it offers a framework for discussion. There are several different themes discernible in the tale overall.

Firstly, this is a story of bitter rivalry between two prominent families, the Akhshartaggata and the Boratas, leading to the premeditated killing of Batraz's father. The resulting blood feud ultimately ruins both families and the Narts as a people. In that sense it is a tragic tale told to warn of the dangers that may arise when traditional customs are taken to their ultimate conclusion.

Secondly, Batraz clearly relates to the weather. The torrential rain caused by his need to plunge into water to cool off implies that he originated as a god of storms, thunder and lightning. In that sense he is equivalent to Zeus,

Jupiter, Indra, Thunor, Thor or Taranis,[83] though without the 'head-god' role which characterised several of these. Batraz stands somewhat aside from the main tradition of the Nart sagas and his status is ambiguous. Although he is generally portrayed as a Nart – a member of the Akhshartaggata family, nephew to Urizhmag, son to Khamis and foster-son of Shatana – he repeatedly transcends that role, spending time 'in the heavens' or on the sea bed, from where he responds to the pleas of his kin, returning to succour or avenge them. The manner in which he comes down from on high to aid the Narts supports the view that he began as a deity, and has only been somewhat imperfectly euhemerised.[84] While there is good reason to suppose that all the Narts originated in the world of mythology, the transition to human status in Batraz's case seems less complete than many of his peers.

Thirdly, this is a story about metallurgy, and in particular the use of quenching as a means of hardening steel. This was a technique known in both China and the Roman Empire by the end of the first millennium BCE. The Latin for steel is *chalybs*, derived via Greek from the name of a people famous for making steel in early Pontus (Map 2). Steel-forging therefore seems to have reached the Greek and Roman worlds from the Black Sea region. The hardening of the body of Batraz, along with other Nart heroes,[85] reveals a keen interest in the technique, reflecting the importance of high-grade steel to the Steppe peoples in Antiquity. Batraz's need to immerse himself in water is a recurring theme. He cools himself in the sea in sagas 51, 56 and 59, on a mountain glacier in saga 60, and is finally overcome by the concentrated heat of the sun out on the Steppe, far from cooling water, in saga 72. This follows, of course, from the processes by which he is formed and then tempered, with repeated heating and cooling. The contrast with normal flesh and blood is spelled out in saga 60, when the giant Alaf reacts to the injuries done him by Batraz by in turn seeking to be hardened in Kurdalagon's furnace, only to be consumed in the fire. Batraz bears comparison with Homer's Achilles, who likewise has a divine mother, a magical birth and a body that was near-indestructible.

Finally, Batraz's story reflects societal and religious changes confronting storytellers and their audiences across the Middle Ages and later. Batraz is the epitome of traditional values: he is 'the best man among all the Narts';[86] the strongest and bravest warrior, the most honest speaker, ever respectful of his elders, a committed protector of women and of his kin, and the champion of his people.[87] It is to Batraz therefore that the task falls to uphold the Nart tradition against encroaching monotheistic religions and alien political structures.[88] The fictional world responds to the same issues as were confronting the 'real' world. His wife Akola's disagreement with Zvar, spirit of fertility, arguably relates to the shifting patterns of thought inherent within a conversion situation and the loss of faith in traditional remedies. We find Batraz at odds too with the Christian God; he battles the sons of Washtirji and Elia, and peace is only achieved by depositing his body in a vault within Hagia Sophia at Byzantium, the mother-church of eastern European Christianity. His story therefore epitomises Christianity's triumph over paganism. Equally, Batraz champions the Narts against encroaching lordship and the state, as we saw above (p. 86). These struggles reveal Batraz as the champion of 'free' Nart society, heroically, but ultimately vainly, contesting new forms of religion, lordship, governmental diktats, taxation and the castle-building of the feudal world. With Batraz dead, the Narts dwindle away: the heroic age is over; there can be no new sagas.

How ancient is the tale of Batraz? Clearly, some of the folkloric elements are likely to be very early. For example, the rescue of Uon from the giant Kanzargash has numerous folkloric motifs which we find elsewhere, including the means of capture of the old man's horse, the horse's role as an adviser, passage between two 'head-butting' mountains, a multi-headed giant, an enemy who has to be despatched with his own sword, a lake with rejuvenating properties and travel on a magic carpet. That what is basically the same story has been recorded among the Abazas, though the man rescued is different,[89] suggests an early tradition from which these two versions have evolved independently. There is no reason to suppose that this was originally part of Batraz's story at all.[90]

The Abaza corpus offers two different versions of the marriage of Khamis and his death.[91] In the first, Khamis meets a hunter of the 'little Spe people' and marries his daughter, Isp, promising her that he will never call her a 'little wretch'.[92] Isp becomes pregnant with 'Pataraz' (Batraz), but when she is slow to prepare food for her husband when he is going raiding he makes the mistake of calling her this. She therefore departs before he returns home. Khamis thereafter lives alone but his seduction of the women of neighbouring families (he is a serial womaniser throughout the canon) leads to a conspiracy against him and his enemies shoot him dead. In saga 31, Batraz is cast out as a child when his foster mother realises that only this may save her people, but he returns as if from the dead to avenge his father, using guile as much as his own prowess to overthrow the Narts. The blood price he demands is impossible for the elders to pay, bringing ruin upon his people. As Colarusso notes, Batraz is here the converse of Christ, returning from death to bring not salvation but destruction.[93]

The other version of the death of Khamis recorded among the Abazas has him out hunting and meeting with a huntsman of the Marakwa, traditional enemies of the Narts.[94] Again he marries the huntsman's daughter, and gives his word not to call her 'short'. Again he breaks his word when kept waiting. This time, though, his companions on his journey are Marakwas who are plotting to kill him. They encounter a giant whom Khamis slays after a long struggle but he is exhausted and his sword blunted so the Marakwas take the opportunity to murder him. His widow returns home once she has given birth to Batraz, who is raised in secret by an old couple but quickly reveals what a heroic figure he is destined to become. The saga then switches to the story of his marriage to the daughter of Wazarmis and the subsequent rescue of his father-in-law from the clutches of a terrible giant (as above).

Looking across the entire corpus, these tales display sufficient similarities to be sure of common roots. Their differences, though, speak to successive reformulations and diverging oral traditions. Potentially early motifs are scattered throughout many of the tales and some may be very ancient indeed. For example, shaving as a key to the rite of passage from youth to adult status is found in the Welsh story *Culhwch and Olwen*,[95] and among the Germanic Chatti as told by Tacitus, *c.* 100 CE.[96] Likewise, the notion of a beard as a trophy is evidenced in both Scythian and Celtic traditions.[97] Such may even derive from a distant Indo-European past. Shatana's approach to God at 'holy hill' suggests pagan practices,[98] as too, perhaps, does Batraz's wrenching off the arms of his defeated opponent, for which Herodotus provides parallels in the context of sacrifice to the Scythian wargod.[99] Khamis's threat to kill and stuff his horse, when that beast (very sensibly) urges him to avoid the ambush set by Chief Shainag, recalls the burial rites accorded Scythia's kings.[100]

But there are also indications that important elements of these stories are late. The name Batraz is not Iranian; it has been thought Mongolian but is more probably Circassian,[101] entering the Ossetian storytelling tradition from their western neighbours only once Alan communities had settled in the Caucasus. While elements of Batraz's life story may well be early, therefore, these tales coalesced around him no earlier than the late Roman period. Stories that centre on Batraz contain more allusions to Christianity than all the rest of the sagas combined, uniquely featuring the One God as an active character. It seems reasonable to suppose that this material entered the corpus when the oral tradition was interacting with Christianity. References to styles of lordship alien to Nart society are likewise concentrated in Batraz's

story, again implying that the narrative entered its current form comparatively late. And there is a concentration of very recent motifs, including the
use by his bride of a horse-drawn carriage mounted on springs.[102]

What we have, therefore, is a story with multiple chronological horizons.
While some motifs probably date back to Antiquity, an unusual number of
elements within Batraz's story are more recent and show signs of having
been composed in response to challenges to the traditional values enshrined
in the Nart sagas, in or after the central Middle Ages. To a greater extent
even than many other sections of the sagas, therefore, these tales have
evolved within the shifting cultural context to which storytellers and their
audiences found themselves needing to respond across the Middle Ages
and beyond.

Batraz, Arthur and the sword in the water

To this point, there have been no close parallels drawn between the Nart
sagas and the Arthurian legends. There is, though, another account of Batraz's
death, which was translated into Russian in the nineteenth century and
published in French by Dumézil in 1930,[103] a version of which is included by
Colarusso and Salbiev in their new volume.[104] A passage at the close of this
narrative bears close similarities with the death of Arthur as that is described
in the late medieval tradition, best known from Sir Thomas Malory's *Le
Morte d'Arthur*.[105]

The story goes as follows. Batraz wreaks vengeance on the Narts for his
father's murder, forcing them to prepare the forge in which he then tempers
himself. He continues to harass them, cutting some down with his sword;
others are devoured by his horse. He then has them fire him as a human
cannonball at the Warp fortress, where he subdues the resident lord. As an
apostate, Batraz incurs the wrath of God, who afflicts him – and through
him the Narts more generally – with disease. Tiring of his struggles, Batraz
agrees that he is ready to die, but only after his sword Dzus-quera has been
thrown into the sea. What follows is a translation of Dumézil's version
(Batraz is speaking at the opening of the quote):

'... it must be added that I cannot die until my sword has been thrown
into the sea.' The Narts succumbed to despair, for how were they to throw
the sword of Batraz into the sea? They decided to deceive the hero, to
persuade him that his sword had indeed been thrown into the sea and it
was now time for him to die. They approached him accordingly in his

sickness and swore that his fate was fulfilled. 'What marvels did you witness when my sword fell into the sea?' he asked them. 'Not any', the Narts responded, with concern. 'Then my sword has not been thrown into the sea, otherwise you would have seen wonders.' The Narts at last resigned themselves: they deployed all their power, harnessing many thousands of draught-beasts; in the end they were successful in dragging the sword of Batraz to the shore and threw it into the sea. Immediately the waves and storm rose, the sea boiled and then turned the colour of blood. The Narts were astonished and elated. They hurried to inform Batraz what they had seen; convinced, he breathed his last.[106]

It is this passage that attracted Grisward's attention. As Littleton and Malcor put it, 'one need not be a specialist in the Arthurian romances to see the striking parallels [with] ... the death of Arthur.'[107] *Le Morte d'Arthur* provides by far the best-known version of the latter:

'Therefore,' seyde kynge Arthur unto sir Bedwere, 'take thou here Excaliber, my good swerde, and go wyth hit to yondir watirs syde; and whan thou commyste there, I charge the throw my swerde in that water, and com agayne and telle me what thou syeste there.' 'My lorde,' seyde sir Bedwere, 'youre commaundement shall be done, and lyghtly brynge you word agayne.' So sir Bedwere departed. And by the way he behylde that noble swerde, and the pomell and the hauffte was all precious stonys.

So rich was it that Bedivere was unwilling to throw Arthur's sword away so hid it instead; but his report of what had occurred did not convince the king, who sent him back. Again though he failed to carry out his task. It was only at the third time of asking that:

... he bounde the gyrdyll aboute the hyltis, and threw the swerde as farre into the watir as he myght. And there cam an arme and an honde above the watir, and toke hit and cleyght hit, and shoke hit thryse and braun-dysshed, and than vanysshed ... with the swerde into the watir. So sir Bedyvere cam agayne to the kynge and tolde hym what he saw.[108]

Arthur was convinced at last so able to leave by ship for Avalon, where his wounds would receive the care that they required.

As Littleton and Malcor remark, 'the need to throw Excalibur into the lake, the attempts on the part of the grieving Bedivere to deceive the dying king, and even the magical events that occurred ... recall the central elements of the Ossetic story.'[109] These are indeed similarities which invite exploration.

We should, though, note that this is one of only very few motifs within the two stories which bears close comparison and even here there are differences: Batraz's sword is too large and heavy to be thrown away, Arthur's too rich; the Narts fail once, Bedivere twice; the strange things that have to be reported are dissimilar. Arthur and Batraz are otherwise very different: one is a king, the other a gigantic hero; one is Christian, the other apparently an apostate; they are dying for very different reasons and their relationships with those accompanying them are very different. It is only, therefore, the need to dispose of their swords in water preliminary to their respective deaths (or potential afterlife, in Arthur's case) and their companions' attempts to deceive which bear close comparison.

In addition, we should recognise that there is a logic internal to both stories, such that neither is obviously out of place within its own tradition. The tale of Batraz places such a strong emphasis on this hero's composition of hardened steel, his frequent quenching and cooling in water and his upbringing on the ocean bed that to find both water and steel featuring in his death-scene seems consistent with much else within this story. Indeed, Dumézil considered that Batraz was mystically joined to his sword.[110] What better way to effect his death than to return it to the ocean, where the same boiling resulted that Batraz had himself repeatedly caused, followed by the sea washing away the blood of the Narts whom he had slaughtered? Viewed through a Christian lens this might even represent forgiveness of Batraz, equivalent to the baptism and absolution necessary prior to the Christian entombment that, in one version, he received.

And repeated lies followed by eventual acquiescence is a motif which occurs elsewhere in the Nart sagas, as for example in the false claims made to messengers that he was ill by Urizhmag before he attended a meeting of the Narts at which he (correctly) anticipated an attempt on his life.[111] In the situation of Batraz's death the initial dishonesty raises dramatic tension regarding what marvels would occur and injects an element of doubt as to whether or not Batraz would finally die and so bring peace to his people. This is a story consistent with what else we know concerning the narrative tradition, therefore, but one which is also suggestive of comparatively late, Christian influences.

The tale in which Batraz's sword has to be disposed of in the sea is just one of several versions of his death. There are enough elements in common with the wider story of Batraz among the Ossetians to recognise that it is part of the common stock, but it bears the hallmarks of late composition.[112] The motif of something too heavy for yokes of oxen to move occurs in relation to Batraz's own body in another variant of the tale,[113] which must likewise postdate contact with Christian missionaries. A cannon, gunpowder and shot in this version replace the giant arrow to which Batraz is attached in another, suggesting post-medieval modification, at the very least.[114] And other stories are compressed or excluded; gone are all the traditional elements (there is no magic, no giant, nor other Nart heroes); gone too is the moral justification for Batraz's quarrel with the Narts responsible for his father's death. Rather his career of destruction is unexplained, he is neither heroic nor impelled by justifiable motives. There is an assumption that he has been Christian in the past but has lapsed. The audience is expected to have monotheistic sympathies; uniquely, Batraz is here not an empathetic character but the proper target of divine anger; the story favours his victims.

The sword-in-the-water motif occurs, therefore, only in what seems the most 'modern' version of Batraz's end, and the least sympathetic portrayal of Nart tradition reaching us from any part of the corpus. While we cannot entirely dismiss the possibility that this is a *bona fide* element stemming from an ancient oral tradition, its survival exclusively in an apparently late version of the death of a figure whose name is not Iranian and whose story betrays exceptional influence from both Christianisation and feudalism must militate against this. Its modern-seeming characteristics make it virtually impossible for us to consider this Ossetian sword-in-the-water tale the source of a story of Excalibur's disposal in water already circulating in the first half of the thirteenth century. Certainly, this tale cannot have been introduced to Roman Britain in anything remotely resembling its current form and thence imported to the Arthurian tradition from Celtic storytelling.[115]

Turning to the west, there is a long tradition of potential relevance to Excalibur's committal to the sea or lake. In Britain, weapons were being deposited in 'watery' locations in prehistory: think of the late Bronze Age Tattershall hoard from close to the River Witham, the late Bronze Age or early Iron Age hoard found at Llyn Fawr in southern Wales, or the late Bronze Age finds from Broadward.[116] During the Roman period the connection between water and deposition continued – as, for example, at the temple of Sulis Minerva at Bath and the cult of Coventina at Carrawburgh, though weapons are absent. Weapon-deposition then resumed in the post-Roman era, with seventy or so riverine finds of the Viking Age so far recovered.[117]

On the Continent, too, weapon-deposition in wet locations has a long history. The practice features in Orosius's description of a Roman defeat by

the Cimbri in 105 BCE at Arausio in southern France,[118] and is well known
archaeologically in Germany and Scandinavia across the Roman Iron Age
and Age of Migration.[119] It seems likely that cross-fertilisation during the
Viking Age reinforced – perhaps even reintroduced – the practice in Britain
late in the first millennium CE. Similar ideas were still circulating in
the later Middle Ages, though by then no longer involving weapons. There
are large numbers of sacred springs in both Britain and France, many of
which attracted ritual deposition; notions of propitiation or wish-fulfilment
earned by throwing a coin into a fountain or spring remain with us still
today across western Europe.

And there were already parallels within Arthurian literature for the
repetitive behaviours of Arthur and his knight and the latter's failure to fulfil
his lord's command. Chrétien de Troyes's *Story of the Grail* has Perceval lost
in contemplation of drops of blood in the snow which recall his beloved's
face. The king's squires think him asleep in the saddle; three times Arthur
commands a knight to go out onto the heath and bring him back with them.
The first and second messengers fail (each is overcome by Perceval), and
only the third, Gawain, succeeds.[120] While there is no deceit here, there are
obvious parallels. Or we might invoke the contest of Gawain and Bertilak de
Hautdesert (later revealed to be the Green Knight), in which the latter
proposes and the former accepts a proposal that three days running they
should each give the other their winnings. While Bertilak each day goes
hunting and gives his kill to his guest, Gawain finds himself having to fend
off the amorous advances of his host's wife and fails to surrender the magic
girdle that she gives him on the third day. The Green Knight then three
times brings the axe down on his opponent's neck, on the third occasion
cutting but not severing it. While the degree of deceit is less than in Arthur's
'death' scene, the thrice-repeated exchange is again reminiscent.[121]

We can, of course, look to early Celtic literature for the use of threefold
divisions within a story,[122] but behind such motifs in the medieval period
also lie biblical exemplars, and particularly the Trinity and the thrice-
repeated denial of Christ by St Peter,[123] as his master had foretold.[124] The
New Testament is very likely to have influenced a story cycle composed by
medieval authors working under the long shadow of Christian learning.

Arthur's approach to Avalon

Malory's account is best viewed as a late stage within successive reimaginings
of Arthur's death or departure from the world of the living, which stretch

across the central and later Middle Ages. The starting point is a brief entry in the mid-tenth-century *Annales Cambriae*: 'The battle of Camlann, in which Arthur and Medraut fell, and there was a mortality in Britain and Ireland' (see below, pp. 223–5).[125] While Arthur had already featured in an earlier entry (*c*. 516) in this text, this is the earliest mention of both Camlann and Medraut (later Mordred). What supposedly occurred is unclear: the annalist established neither whether or not Arthur and Mordred were enemies,[126] nor who won the battle. Geoffrey of Monmouth interpreted this in a typically imaginative fashion, making Mordred Arthur's nephew and his appointee as regent while he fought on the Continent; Mordred thereby becomes the 'foul traitor' who rebels against Arthur in his absence, forcibly marries his wife and seizes the throne.[127] Geoffrey placed the final battle on the River 'Camblan' – the Camel in Cornwall (this region features prominently in Geoffrey's work[128]), with both armies virtually annihilated in an epic struggle:

> The illustrious king Arthur too was mortally wounded; he was taken away to the island of Avallon to have his wounds tended and, in the year of our lord 542, handed over Britain's crown to his relative Constantine, son of Cador, duke of Cornwall.[129]

For Geoffrey this brings to an end the grandiose achievements of Arthur's reign which form the climax of his work. That the illustrious king was brought down by treachery was perhaps influenced by the dynastic infighting at both the beginning and end of the reign of Henry I (1100–35). Henry died without a legitimate son surviving him, having pressured the Norman establishment into recognising his daughter, Mathilda, as his successor. She was, though, the countess of Anjou, traditionally Normandy's enemy, when Henry died. His barons gave their support instead to his nephew Stephen of Blois (1135–54). Geoffrey is generally considered to have been finishing his great pseudo-history in the late 1130s (at latest in 1139[130]). From *c*. 1138 Stephen was actively opposed by a faction favouring Mathilda led by Henry's illegitimate son Robert of Gloucester, to whom Geoffrey dedicated his *History of the Kings of Britain* (*Historia Regum Britanniae*).[131]

This is our earliest encounter with Avalon (Geoffrey offers 'Avallon'). What Geoffrey meant is best explored via his later work, the Latin verse *Life of Merlin* (*Vita Merlini*):

> The island of apples [*insula pomorum*] which men call 'the Fortunate Isle' [*fortunata*] gets its name from the fact that it produces all things of

itself; the fields there have no need of the ploughs of farmers and all cultivation is lacking except what nature provides. Of its own accord it produces grain and grapes, and apple trees grow in its woods from the close-clipped grass.[132]

Geoffrey then remarked that this was where Arthur went after Camlann,[133] placing the identification beyond doubt. Avalon stems ultimately from the Elysian Fields or Isles of the Blessed of early Greek literature, a paradise on earth to which heroes might retire at the close of their active careers.[134] He was also familiar with Christian, otherworld paradises attainable within this world in such well-known works as the Irish *Voyage of Saint Brendan* (*Navigatio Sancti Brendani*).[135] It is unclear how much the *Navigatio* owes to the classical legend, for its main influences are clearly Christian.[136] Even so, there seems at least a distant echo of the ancient tradition in the grapes, apples and loaves provided by God on islands called 'Delightful Island',[137] and the 'Isle of Anchorites',[138] where communities of monks never age or grow feeble, there are no extremes of temperature, no illness and a perpetual harvest provides foodstuffs without the need for labour.[139]

By the Roman period the 'Isles of the Blessed' were thought to lie out in the Atlantic (indeed, all the Atlantic islands, Britain and Ireland included, were presented as somewhat otherworldly).[140] In the mid-first century Pliny the Elder placed them off Cape Finisterre (Spain), terming them 'the six islands of the gods, which some people have named the Fortunate Isles [*Fortunata appellavere*]'.[141] Plutarch considered that: 'They offered a benign climate and without labour yielded: pleasant fruits to their happy inhabitants ... A firm belief has made its way, even to the barbarians, that here are the Elysian Fields and the abode of the blessed of which Homer sang'.[142] This occurs in Plutarch's *Life of Sertorius* (died 72 BCE),[143] who was closely associated with Spain, so his 'barbarians' should be identified as western Celts. To the extent that their knowledge of the 'Isles of the Blessed' derived from classical texts, Pliny's widely circulating *Natural History* was perhaps the main source.

Geoffrey's *History of the Kings of Britain* provides the earliest link between Arthur and Avalon.[144] However, Plutarch's remark suggests that the underlying motif had passed into the Celtic world,[145] and the name Geoffrey adopted indicates that his source was Celtic at least as much as classical, for 'Avalon' derives from the word ancestral to Old Welsh *aball*, meaning 'fruit tree' or 'apple tree' (there were cognate terms in Old Irish, Old Cornish, Breton and the Gaulish language – from which comes Avallon in Burgundy).

The Celtic name apparently reflects the fruitfulness of the classical 'Isles of the Blessed', its adoption perhaps encouraged by Pliny's use of the verb *appellavere* (see above).[146] That Aballava was the name of the Hadrianic fort of Burgh-by-Sands demonstrates that the Brittonic term was in use as a place-name element in Roman Britain,[147] though that is likely to have been entirely independent of the myth.

The centrality of an apple tree to the Garden of Eden and the story of the 'Fall' cannot have escaped the notice of those perpetuating this motif in the central Middle Ages and probably gave it renewed vigour, with the prospect of passage to the garden of creation and/or a worldly paradise preparatory to heaven. That Arthur was there not to experience death but for his wounds to be healed finds parallels in an island described by the early Roman geographer Pomponius Mela off Brittany, where nine priestesses supposedly performed feats of healing.[148] It is consistent with Arthur's positioning as a secular type of the Christ-figure who might come again, reinterpreting for a Christian milieu what began as a notion of the idyllic resting place fit for the greatest pre-classical heroes.[149]

Avalon probably stems, therefore, from a Christianised, Romano-Celtic version of the myth of the 'Isles of the Blessed'. Whether or not Geoffrey of Monmouth was responsible for linking this with Arthur is not clear but it is entirely possible. The name originated either in Brittonic (in or before the Roman period) or Old Welsh, so was not Geoffrey's invention; he was familiar both with the Welsh name and what it meant, rendering it in Latin as 'island of apples' in his final work. His description is reminiscent of Pliny, and even Strabo's *Geography*.[150]

It is Geoffrey who first connected Arthur's sword with Avalon, for he tells us that:

> Arthur ... buckled on *Caliburnus*, an excellent blade forged on the isle of Avallon, and graced his hand with his spear, called *Ron*.[151]

Ron is perhaps an abbreviation of *Rhongomyniad*, the name of Arthur's spear in *Culhwch and Olwen*, simplified for a non-Welsh-speaking audience. *Caliburnus* is a rendering of the word ancestral to Welsh *Caledwlch* and Breton *Kaledvoulc'h*, which in turn derived from classical Latin *chalybs*, meaning steel (and medieval Latin *calibs* may well have influenced Geoffrey here).[152]

Geoffrey may of course have found Arthur's sword to have been forged in Avalon in an earlier tale, but this is something of a departure from depictions of the 'Isles of the Blessed' in classical texts, which never mention weapons, let alone their manufacture. But one of the islands in the *Voyage of Saint Brendan* is inhabited by smiths, which may have provided the necessary inspiration.[153]

The connection between the manufacture of Arthur's sword and Avalon was retained by Wace, in his Norman-French-verse rendering of Geoffrey's work, the *Roman de Brut*, completed in 1155. He likewise at the close depicted the king, having received 'a mortal wound to his body', 'carried to Avalon, for the treatment of his wounds'. Here we have rather more than Geoffrey had offered on the possibility of Arthur's return. Wace looked back to Geoffrey's *Merlin* as his authority:

> Arthur, if the chronicle is true, received a mortal wound to his body. He had himself carried to Avalon, for the treatment of his wounds. He is still there, awaited by the Britons, as they say and believe, and will return and may live again. Master Wace, who made this book, will say no more of his end than the prophet Merlin did. Merlin said of Arthur rightly, that his death would be doubtful. The prophet spoke truly: ever since, people have always doubted it and always will, I think, doubt whether he is dead or alive. It is true that he had himself borne away to Avalon, five hundred and forty-two years after the Incarnation.[154]

A generation later the poet Marie de France introduced Avalon into her *lais* (lay), 'Lanval', to provide a suitably heroic ending for her hero and his beloved. The same images persist: 'He went with her to Avalon / So we're told by the Bretons [or Britons] / To an isle of much beauty'.[155] 'Lanval' is the earliest 'Arthurian' *lais* in French (generally dated *c.* 1170–90); that it is centred on Carlisle implies an Anglo-Norman patron – though presumably born in France, Marie is generally thought to have written in England.[156] 'Lanval' may of course owe something to Celtic oral tradition, as Marie claimed, but its topography seems entirely dependent on Wace.[157]

The poet Laʒamon, writing (probably) during the reign of King John (1199–1216),[158] provided an English version of Wace's *Brut* which he described as 'the noble origins of the English'.[159] He was particularly taken with the Arthurian section, which he extended in several passages, but given that both Geoffrey and Wace had depicted Avalon as an island, a boat was already implicit in their accounts; Laʒamon made this explicit, added further mystique and invested in the expectation of Arthur's return:

And I will go to Avalon, to the loveliest of all women, to Argante the queen, fairest of fairy women, and she shall make well all my wounds; make me all whole with healing draughts. And afterwards I will come again to my kingdom, and dwell with the Britons with mickle joy.

With these words there came moving in from the sea a short boat...'[160]

Arthur and the sword in the water

The story of Arthur's passing was gradually being elaborated, therefore, in works composed in and up to the early thirteenth century, albeit with little in the way of a break in the tradition. The sword-in-the-water scene is the final addition and by far the most dramatic. It appears first in *The Death of King Arthur* (*Le Mort Le Roi Artu*),[161] one of the linked prose romances in French known variously as the *Vulgate* or *Lancelot-Grail Cycle*, written *c.* 1215–35. Malory found the story here and in the *Stanzaic Morte Arthur*,[162] an anonymous, fourteenth-century English poem which was itself based on the earlier French work. Once again, Arthur would be carried from the sea shore by a ship crewed by women, but a new scene was inserted as preparation for his departure, centred on the disposal of Excalibur and the unwillingness of Girflet, the last of Arthur's knights, to obey the king and throw it into the water (Malory later substituted the better-known Bedivere).

Why was such a radical alteration made to a story that had to this point only diverged slowly from that told by Geoffrey and Wace? To a degree, this is explicable by reference to the shift from the 'historical' (or more correctly 'pseudo-historical') style of the *Brut* to the romance form that Chrétien originated, that presented Arthur and his court in new and far more imaginative ways. But such changes also reflected the interests and concerns of the intended audience.

What we see emerging is an alteration to the ways in which royal authority is perceived and to the passage of kingship from one generation to the next, engaging the divine as a guarantor of both the succession and good kingship. Geoffrey and Wace had both depicted Arthur inheriting the kingdom quite matter-of-factly on the death of his father, with the unquestioned support of the political elite. Here is Wace: 'The bishops sent word to each other and the barons assembled; they summoned Arthur, Uther's son, and crowned him at Silchester.'[163] Arthur then in turn divested himself of the kingship by nominating his young kinsman, Constantine, before departing for Avalon. This assumes the sovereign's right to determine the succession – particularly in the stress of war – so represents kingship as very much a personal matter. But in the decades centred on 1200, Richard's near continuous absence from England and his excessive taxation were followed by John's usurpation of the throne, his tyrannous rule and the loss of France. The result was a steep rise in the tensions between the crown and the baronage, leading to moves designed to limit the monarch's freedom of action (as *Magna Carta* and attempts to impose collective decision-making on Henry III).[164] These concerns found their way into Arthurian literature.[165]

It was a French work of *c.* 1200, *Merlin*, that first introduced the famous sword-in-the-stone scene as the means by which the young Arthur obtained the crown (see above, pp. 74–5). To this point, Arthur's sword had been merely a weapon, alongside various others in his armoury,[166] but this reimagining of Arthur's acceptance as king required that the sword be understood as something more. Before the main porch of the church 'a great square block of stone and an anvil appeared, and in the anvil was fixed a sword'.[167] On it is written that 'whoever should draw the sword from the stone would be king by the choice of Jesus Christ'. The sword symbolises 'a king and leader to uphold Holy Church and to guard and save the people.'[168] Many try to extract it but only Arthur succeeds. By this token he is Christ's candidate; repetition eventually gains him the acceptance of the assembled nobility.[169] That Arthur is the son of the previous king is known to the audience but this becomes clear to characters within the story only once he has been crowned;[170] the archbishop presides over this pivotal scene.[171]

The author of *Merlin* therefore injected divine oversight and notions of consent into what had to this point been a process of inheritance,[172] which highlighted the good kingship expected from the successful claimant. Necessarily, this had implications for how Arthur should ultimately surrender the kingdom. Given that it was his drawing-out of the sword that marked his succession, the sword's disposal should now symbolise the laying-down of his kingship, allowing him to 'retire', as it were, to Avalon, and ultimately to death (for the *Mort Artu* describes his tomb[173]). In *The Death of King Arthur*, therefore, Arthur no longer nominates a close kinsman as his successor; attention switches instead to Excalibur, 'a fine rich sword, [almost] the best in the world' as the symbol of his kingship. Arthur wishes to hand it on to Lancelot, 'the noblest man in the world and the finest knight', who is the real hero of this work,[174] and the only figure worthy to succeed to Arthur. But Lancelot is unavailable. Arthur decides, therefore, that the sword should be cast into a lake, and he commands his sole surviving companion to carry this out. But Girflet considers it too rich to discard. First he asks for it for himself but Arthur denies him on the grounds that 'it would not be put to good use' (i.e. he is unworthy), then Girflet agrees to do the king's wishes and carries the sword away to the lake but: 'he began to look at it and it seemed to him so good and so beautiful'. He hides Excalibur, therefore, and throws in his own sword instead. But when he cannot account for what occurs next, Arthur angrily sends him back. This time he throws in the scabbard and hides the sword. Only on the third occasion does Girflet finally obey the king, throw in Excalibur, and witness 'a hand come out of the lake, which revealed itself up to the elbow', that 'seized the sword by the hilt and brandished it in the air three or four times.' Once this has been reported back, Arthur can depart. He dismisses Girflet, who only witnesses the king's departure by ship from a distance, as he shelters under a tree from the (much-deserved) rain.

The literary device of a royal command obeyed only belatedly provides space for exploration of the symbolic nature of the action and raises dramatic tension by causing delay which might prove fatal to the stricken king. We have already noted parallels in Chrétien's *Story of the Grail*,[175] which has Arthur twice ordering knights to bring Perceval into camp to no avail, before this was achieved by Gawain.[176] Again, there is the New Testament parallel of St Peter's denial of Christ. But repetition was also a feature of *Merlin's* sword-in-the-stone scene, with Arthur extracting it five times in all before the barons agree to accept him.[177] The story of Excalibur's disposal compliments and is driven by the miraculous story of Arthur's accession, therefore, the two scenes serving to bookend the reign. Lancelot's absence lends pathos; the implication is that he would have made a fitting successor to Arthur as wielder of Excalibur and protector of the kingdom, despite being unrelated. It would be his ending with which the author finally closed this work.[178] But retention of Avalon as Arthur's destination, so of the shoreline as the setting for his last scene – combined with still-current notions regarding the disposal of metal objects in rivers (see above, p. 94) – are likely to have triggered this 'watery' end for his sword.

The thirteenth-century Arthurian romances had moved a long way from the genealogically structured pseudo-histories of Geoffrey and Wace, therefore, to engage with the thought-world of an audience drawn predominantly from non-royal sections of the elite. They accommodate this group's views on the need to temper royal authority, ensure its transmission to a worthy successor and secure good lordship.[179] This shift in the story of Arthur's ending reveals a writer sensitive to changes elsewhere in the tradition, as well as his audience's interests. Such plot development is fully explicable without reference to 'foreign' material, whether current or in a remote past.

The deaths of Batraz and Arthur: parallels and possible origins

It seems entirely possible, therefore, that sword-in-the-water scenes developed independently in the Caucasus and the west. If this is not acceptable (and the evidence is not conclusive), then there are three mechanisms that could in theory link these two narratives. We can rule out the first of these (see p. 93), for the relative chronology means that this comparatively late version of a Nart saga cannot have entered the Celtic world as part of a wider transfer of stories from the Caucasus to Britain in the Roman period (as Littleton and his collaborators supposed). Influences running in the opposite direction are possible, with thirteenth-century Arthurian literature contributing the sword-in-the-water motif to the Nart sagas. Alternatively, both could derive from a common ancestor, in which case the two stories bear witness to a very long-distant parent.[180]

The longevity of ritual deposition of weapons in wet places might support this third option, the so-called 'genetic model' of story-transmission. But that requires that the basic elements of the sword-in-the-water story were already present in storytelling before the third millennium BCE, when the eastern branch of Indo-European (later to split into Greek, Armenian and Aryan) separated from the western (including Italic and Celtic).[181] Certainly, there are motifs common to the Nart sagas and Celtic mythology sufficient to harbour this possibility, such as the unnaturally rapid growth of babies to adulthood,[182] the interest in giants,[183] and use of threefold numbering. Against this, however, must be set the absence of this motif from every witness earlier than the thirteenth-century *Mort Artu*, in the west, and a version of Batraz's death which is not evidenced before the nineteenth century. While this could have resulted from the loss of earlier manifestations of this scene, emergence of this story in both Arthurian literature and the Ossetian tales comparatively late in each tradition is easier reconciled with independent generation or a late borrowing from west to east.

That Arthurian literature fed into the Nart sagas is a possibility. An oft-quoted passage from a commentary by the so-called 'pseudo-Alanus de Insulis' remarks on how widespread knowledge of Arthur had become:

> What place is there within the bounds of the empire of Christendom to which the winged praise of Arthur the Briton has not extended? Who is there, I ask, who does not speak of Arthur the Briton, since he is but little less known to the peoples of Asia than to the Britons, as we are informed by our palmers who return from countries of the east? The eastern peoples speak of him as do the western, though separated by the breadth of the whole world. Egypt speaks of him and the Bosphorus is not silent. Rome, queen of cities, sings his deeds, and his wars are not unknown to her former rival Carthage. Antioch, Armenia and Palestine celebrate his feats.[184]

This author took it for granted that Arthur was in origin British,[185] but recognised that his fame had spread far and wide. While the author is unlikely to have had much knowledge of the Bosporus, Egypt or Carthage,[186] the audience for French romances at this date included westerners resident in the eastern Mediterranean. Parts of Syria and Judaea were under Frankish control from 1099,[187] facilitating the passage of clerics, soldiers and many others to and fro; German and French armies under royal leadership were at Jerusalem in the late 1140s, then numerous senior figures with their followers through to the early 1170s. Antioch and Palestine were very much part of the Frankish world, with ruling elites who are likely to have been eager for the latest stories.[188] Jerusalem fell to Saladin in 1187 but Acre was retaken by the Third Crusade in 1191 and served as the capital of a smaller Christian kingdom for a further century. Byzantium (earlier Constantinople) was then taken by Crusaders in the spring of 1204. Although Greek rule of the bulk of the Empire continued, the ancient capital and its European hinterland were only reconquered in 1261; Antioch held out until 1268. There were significant connections between these eastern Frankish territories and the homelands of French romance, for Baldwin I, ruler of the crusader state of Byzantium, was married to Marie of Champagne, the daughter of Chrétien's sometime patron, Marie of France. Western writers had good reason to take an interest in the east, therefore, and there were various often rather clumsy efforts to include the eastern Mediterranean in Arthur's story.[189]

Byzantium commanded the southern entry to the Black Sea and was a focus of mercantile activity. French literature is likely to have been prized there across the early to mid-thirteenth century. There were therefore several decades during which the Arthurian sword-in-the-water story could have been carried along trade routes linking Byzantium to the further shores of the Black Sea. There is no actual evidence that the story travelled from west to east but that seems far likelier than the reverse.

In the last resort, there is no clear solution to the problems thrown up by similarities between the high medieval Arthurian story of the sword-in-the-water and the tale of the disposal of Batraz's sword. Coincidence remains a possibility, given that we are speaking of so few motifs among so many. In that case, what look like very similar notions emerged independently in two very different traditions. So too is parallel development from a single, ancient origin, though the late appearance of both stories rather militates against this. Finally, a borrowing from Arthurian storytelling into the Nart sagas seems possible, and this is perhaps the likeliest explanation. In contrast, the notion that it travelled westwards in the Roman period is entirely at odds with the available evidence. While we can be certain that this motif was present in French texts in the first third of the thirteenth century, it need not have entered the Nart sagas until centuries later and cannot possibly have featured in Sarmatian stories circulating in the second century CE.

The second main area in which parallels between Arthurian traditions and the Nart sagas have been drawn is in the portrayal of various drinking or cooking vessels. Littleton and his collaborators argued that both the grail and various other vessels that appear in Celtic stories stemmed from a magical cup or bowl in the Nart sagas, the Wasamonga.[190] We will now examine these fictional vessels, their nature and possible origins, so as to ascertain whether or not they could have derived from early storytelling on the Eurasian Steppe. Is there a meaningful relationship between the western tales and either Scythian stories recorded in Antiquity or the Nart sagas of the Caucasus? It is to these issues that we must now turn.

The Holy Grail

The Holy Grail is one of the best-known components of the Arthurian legend as that developed across the later Middle Ages but its origins are much debated. Some have argued that it developed from Celtic folk tales,[191] while others focus more on its religious meaning and see it primarily as a Christian symbol.[192] It has been prominent in the more 'mystical' portrayals of the Arthurian story, centred particularly on Glastonbury.[193]

The grail first appears in medieval literature in the unfinished poetic romance *The Story of the Grail* (*Le Conte del Graal*), generally considered Chrétien de Troyes's final work, composed *c.* 1190. But despite its presence in the title,[194] the grail appears only fleetingly in this work. Chrétien's interest lay predominantly elsewhere, for this is largely a meditation on the wisdom that a knight needed in making good judgements and how such is best inculcated. While the hero, Perceval, was born to knighthood and was both courageous and naturally skilled in war, a childhood spent in seclusion had not prepared him for the life to which his paternity and aptitude propelled him. The poem opens with the stock motif of a naïve youth mistaking knights for angels; finding that they are human he then bombards their leader with questions. While he belatedly receives advice from his mother his attempts to apply it are misconceived (even comical), and some of it he rejects. Later he is mentored by Gornemant of Gohort, but his urging to be reticent then discourages him from questioning the grail-keeper – which is where his difficulties multiply.[195] Perceval's problems are, therefore, largely a consequence of the mismatch between his heroic character and the inadequacy of his preparation for knighthood.

It is not until line 3208 of the poem that we actually encounter the grail. Perceval arrives at a castle where the maimed Fisher King invests him with a magnificent sword. He then witnesses a procession headed by a squire bearing a white lance from the tip of which blood trickles, followed by two more young men carrying golden candelabras, and a beautiful girl, noble-looking and richly attired, bearing a grail in her two hands. After her follows another maiden carrying a silver carving platter, but Chrétien focuses attention back to the grail, remarking that it is of pure gold with precious stones inset. Perceval and his host wash their hands, a fabulous table of ivory and ebony is brought in and they eat a delicious meal as the grail is once more carried across the room in front of them. Nothing is said, despite Perceval feeling that he should ask as to the meaning of both lance and grail. In the morning he leaves the castle without meeting a soul but comes across a maiden (his own cousin), who on hearing of his experiences laments his failure to pose questions regarding what he has seen. Her rebuke is reiterated on his return to Arthur's court by an extraordinarily ugly maiden (the 'Loathly Damsel') who rails against him for not enquiring concerning the individual whom the grail was intended to serve, asserting that great ill has resulted. Perceval therefore commits himself to return and ask regarding both grail and lance. But the tale switches at this point to the adventures of Sir Gawain,[196] who rides off on a different quest which then becomes the poem's focus.[197]

When Chrétien eventually turns his attention back to Perceval,[198] he utilises his confession to a hermit on Easter Friday as a means of explaining the mystery of the grail. The hermit is speaking:

> The man served from it [the grail] is my brother. Your mother was his sister and mine; and the rich Fisher King, I believe, is the son of the king who is served from the grail. And do not imagine that he is served pike or lamprey or salmon. A single host that is brought to him in that grail sustains and brings comfort to that holy man – such is the holiness of the grail! And he is so holy that his life is sustained by nothing more than the host that comes in the grail. He has lived for twelve years like this, without ever leaving the room which you saw the grail enter.

The term used is 'graal', meaning a salver or shallow bowl in which food was conveyed from the kitchen to the table in an aristocratic household.[199] Where did this 'graal' originate? Certainly, Chrétien did make use of orally transmitted traditions; many have followed the great Arthurian scholar Roger Loomis in postulating that he was drawing here on 'some ancient myth of food-producing vessels, perhaps but not necessarily of Celtic origin'.[200] There are several of these in Welsh literature, as, for example, the unfillable food-bag featured in *Pwyll, Prince of Dyfed*, and the capacious hamper which appears at the close of *Lludd and Llefelys*,[201] and further examples in Irish stories. However, the Welsh romance which is closest to Chrétien's, *Peredur Son of Efrawg*, has at this point 'two maidens coming in, a great salver between them, and a man's head on the salver, and blood in profusion around the head'.[202] While this version connects with Welsh mythology in the person of Bran, *Peredur* is later than Chrétien's work, derivative of it and to an extent oppositional as well.[203] And Chrétien's grail is the very antithesis of these Celtic cornucopias, for it contains only a single Mass wafer. It is not until the German poet Wolfram von Eschenbach rethought the nature of the grail that it became an inexhaustible source of fast food.[204]

Overall, therefore, the appeal to folkloric antecedents need offer little more than what we might term 'mood music' to contemporary understandings of the grail. Chrétien's parade seems to mix two images, one of food and drink being carried into the great hall for a feast, the second a procession of clergy and their supporters bearing the Eucharist. Sources of light born aloft will have been a common element of both, along with vessels of various kinds, some of which would frequently have been valuable. The host reflects the ecclesiastical scene but it is the integration of these two scenarios which lend it mystique; its power derives ultimately from the symbol of Christ's body, making the grail a 'vessel of grace'.[205]

The American scholar Joseph Goering has recently provided new insights to the origins of a maiden bearing a grail, drawing attention to a group of frescoes painted in the late eleventh and early to mid-twelfth centuries in the valleys of the Pyrenees.[206] Particularly significant, he suggests, is the wall painting which decorated the church of St Clement at Taüll, completed in 1123, which includes the Virgin Mary holding a bowl (others have a cup or chalice), emitting flames.

Goering teased out the means by which such scenes in churches in the upland march of Catalonia might have influenced French writers further north.[207] The service rendered by Count Rotrou II of the Perche (on the borders of Normandy) to his cousin the king of Aragon may be relevant; his son, Rotrou III, moved in the same circles as Chrétien. Marie de France (1145–98), the daughter of Eleanor of Aquitaine and Louis VII, was wife to Henry I, count of Champagne (1164–81) and one of Chrétien's patrons.[208] Eleanor is credited with having introduced the southern French Troubadour tradition to northern France.[209] Either connection could potentially have supplied Chrétien with accounts of wall paintings in churches in the mountain valleys bordering Aquitaine. While the precise nature of the link remains elusive, that Chrétien's grail was influenced by a recent tradition of church wall paintings featuring the Virgin Mary has much to commend it.

Although Chrétien offers no interpretation of the lance carried at the head of this procession, he may well have intended this as an allusion to the spear by which Christ's side was pierced on the cross.[210] This was an important relic regarding which there were competing claims,[211] including one retrieved from Antioch in 1098. Indeed, as the object heading the procession this should perhaps be considered the more prominent and religiously significant article in this first telling, but we may also be able to pick up other contemporary resonances. Chrétien at least began this work for Philip I, count of Flanders, whom he lauded in the introduction (it may have been interrupted by news of Philip's death in 1191). Philip's career, his familial connections and the highly cosmopolitan culture of his court may all have influenced the tale, particularly the count's participation in two crusades and his kinship with Baldwin IV, the 'leper king' of Jerusalem (1174–85).[212]

The grail here is generic, rather than specific, without the definite article from which it later becomes inseparable. The dish is part of a tableau, with the lance, the grail, the light it sheds,[213] the host which it bears, the hand-washing, the meal and the sacral number of years during which the Fisher King's father has been kept alive all contributing symbolic meaning.

Robert de Boron, writing closer to 1200, took up the story of the grail in his prose *Joseph*,[214] but shed Chrétien's mysterious procession and Arthurian connections to focus on the vessel itself and its guardians. In the New Testament, Joseph of Arimathea is credited with asking for and obtaining the body of Christ, winding it in linen, adding spices then laying it in a tomb. This follows the blood and water coming from the wound caused by the spear with which soldiers had pierced Christ's side.[215] The *Gospel of Nicodemus* elaborates what happened thereafter to various characters, Joseph of Arimathea included. This was probably written in the early fourth century; it descended in numerous recensions in both Greek and Latin, retaining significant popularity across the Middle Ages.[216] The attraction of such works lay largely in their focus on the crucifixion scene and it was in that context that the character of Joseph was fleshed out.[217] Robert built on this tradition, reinterpreting Chrétien's grail as both the cup of the Last Supper and the vessel in which Christ's blood was captured in the cruci-fixion story, which he envisaged as preserved thereafter at His command by Joseph. Of course, a cup or chalice had already appeared on several of the Pyrenean wall paintings;[218] it is possible that this late twelfth-century author in north-east France was aware of the mutability of the image in that setting, shifting from a shallow bowl containing the sacramental body of Christ to a cup containing His blood. Robert's was a highly imaginative 'history' of this sacred object, which sought to construct links between the west in the present and the crucifixion, Joseph and early Christian Palestine. The anonymous continuator responsible for *Perceval* developed further connec-tions between Chrétien's tableau and Christ's death on the cross, endowing the scene with new spiritual meanings:

> this is the lance with which Longinus struck Christ on the cross. And this vessel, called the Grail, holds the blood that Joseph gathered as it flowed from His wounds to the earth. We call it the Grail because it delights the hearts of all worthy men and all those who can stay in its presence – it will not tolerate the presence of the sinful.[219]

This explanation of the name is obviously fanciful, but from this point the grail assumes new symbolic meaning and takes centre stage. That 'it will not tolerate the presence of the sinful' reflects, of course, the barring of those who are unshriven from receiving Communion.[220] The Mass is central to this story.

However imprecise, the geography of Chrétien's narrative is predominantly insular in intent, though his familiarity with English places far outweighed that of any other part of Britain.[221] Robert's continuators seem to have recognised this.[222] With Chrétien's 'graal' bearing a single host reinterpreted as the cup of the Last Supper and the receptacle for the capture of Christ's blood from the Crucifixion, they 'chronicled' this relic's passage to Britain. Chrétien's 'graal' occurred within an Arthurian romance; connections were now forged between the apocryphal gospels and a newly elaborated grail, making them part of the same story; in *Merlin* and then *Perceval*, these strands were linked back to Arthur, following his story to its culmination in the war with Mordred, the king's fatal wounding and his retirement to Avalon. This 'British' connection proved attractive, with swift accommodation of both Joseph and the Holy Grail within insular histories. The opportunity was seized at Glastonbury, particularly, to lay claim to all of Joseph (as Britain's earliest missionary), Arthur and Avalon.[223]

Reworking Chrétien's cryptic tale offered a feast of opportunities, therefore, leading eventually to an extensive and well-trodden story cycle linked to Arthur (if sometimes rather loosely). Robert's contemporary Wolfram von Eschenbach was responsible for perhaps the most ambitious version, though his interpretation of the grail as a precious stone with magical powers attracted few imitators among the wider *literati*.[224] Even so, Wolfram's debt to Chrétien is obvious, with new material appearing predominantly where he was adding episodes to the pre-existing story or elaborating its sparer scenes.[225] Subsequently, the *Vulgate Cycle* replaces Perceval with Galahad (introduced as the illegitimate son of Lancelot) as the grail knight, whose virginity enables him to succeed in a quest denied to his adulterous father and the far-from-perfect Perceval. This staunchly moral tale proved extraordinarily popular, becoming an important element of Arthurian storytelling across the later Middle Ages.

For our purposes there is no need to follow the grail any further forward in time, for later developments of the great pseudo-relic which Chrétien and then Robert de Boron bequeathed their audiences were driven not by new material emerging from the past but by the evolving needs of its authors and their audiences to fit these stories to their own world. The origin of the grail story is clearly Christian, belongs to the late twelfth and early thirteenth centuries, and owes very little to influences external to western Christianity.

The cauldron of Annwn

The 'cauldron of Annwn' occurs in an anonymous Welsh poem, *Preiddeu Annwn*, which is preserved in the *Book of Taliesin*, written early in the fourteenth century.[226] Composition is not closely dated but probably lies within the period 850–1250; its form perhaps favours the first half of that period.[227] The poem is in the first person; given its inclusion in this collection, it seems safe to assume that the authorial voice was intended to be that of the legendary sixth-century poet Taliesin.[228] In reality Taliesin's authorship can safely be discounted; this persona had been adopted by a poet serving one of the Welsh princes.[229] The author was a skilled poet, composing to a high technical standard in late Old Welsh. He seems to have assumed his audience would be aware of the traditional body of Welsh mythology and legend, some of which is now lost.[230] This rather obscures the meaning of a work which was in any case written in a highly allusive style, with relatively little narrative. What story there is centres on an expedition launched by Arthur to 'Annwn' – the 'Otherworld'. As in *Y Gododdin* (see below, pp. 166–9), the author identifies himself as one of only a small number of survivors (here seven), who make it back. The poem consists of just sixty lines, arranged in eight verses of unequal length.

The 'cauldron of Annwn' occurs in lines 13 to 17:

It was concerning the cauldron that my first utterance was spoken:
It was kindled by the breath of nine maidens.
The cauldron of the Chieftain of Annwn; what is its faculty?
Dark [ornament] and pearls around its rim
It will not boil the food of a coward; it has not been [so] destined.[231]

As Marged Haycock notes, the reference to 'nine maidens' perhaps alludes to the same source story as was used by Geoffrey of Monmouth for his description of Avalon (in his *Merlin*), which was he says staffed by nine maidens; Taliesin was Merlin's putative informer therein.[232] This probably originated in the same island off the French coast that we have already referred to (above, p. 97),[233] and perhaps implies a degree of confusion between Annwn and Avalon resulting from their phonetic similarity. Whether or not, a cauldron was a cooking vessel of a kind well known across the Old World. That specific powers might be invested in such vessels is evidenced elsewhere in Welsh literature. Take for example the vessel featuring in *Branwen Daughter of Llŷr*, as a gift given by Bendigeifran to the Irish king Matholwch which served as a 'cauldron of rebirth' by which to restore warriors to life (though not to speech).[234] Such examples perhaps point to some earlier Celtic story featuring a magic cauldron which was sufficiently mutable to allow insertion in varying forms into different tales.[235]

Cauldrons are widely present in British prehistory, with two periods of manufacture particularly well evidenced, the late Bronze Age to early Iron Age (1200–600 BCE) and then the late pre-Roman Iron Age (200 BCE–100 CE). Like weapons (see above, pp. 93–4), many were deposited in 'watery' locations, apparently as votive offerings. Their costly manufacture and central role in elite social settings, for the preparation of food and perhaps also of alcoholic drink, rendered them particularly suitable as gifts to the gods. Such include the magnificent 'Battersea Cauldron', dated c. 800–700 BCE, which was recovered from the River Thames (Plate 18), and the enormous example from Llyn Fawr which dates to c. 750–600 BCE.[236] Cauldrons were among the vessels occurring in seemingly ritual deposits in Britain beyond the frontier during the Roman period,[237] and they were used in high-status households in the post-Roman period.[238] Metal cooking vessels have a long history thereafter right across Europe. Wolfram von Eschenbach has Kay, Arthur's steward, refer to himself and a German counterpart as men to whom 'the cauldron is subject',[239] implying that his southern German audience c. 1200 was familiar with their use. It is not therefore surprising that cauldrons feature in medieval storytelling; indeed, it would be strange if they did not.

The Wasamonga

The last of our three fictional vessels, the Wasamonga,[240] plays an important role in the Nart sagas:

> The Narts had many treasures, but highest among them they valued their drinking bowl Wasamonga. That bowl had this precious property: if someone among those feasting spoke the truth about his feats, his valour and his honour, the bowl lifted itself up to his lips, but if someone boasted falsely, then all was in vain. The bowl would sit unmoving.[241]

This was, therefore, a magical drinking bowl able to distinguish true claims from false ones. This attribute is not confined to drinking vessels in the sagas, for it is also ascribed to a cauldron,[242] and to wine barrels, which burst or overflow in confirmation of the truth.[243] Clearly, the motif of a vessel containing liquid that was capable of filtering out untruth is well-established within this oral tradition. This was presumably a response to the difficulty of assessing the validity of boasts made by warriors regarding deeds to which there were no witnesses;[244] thus the Wasamonga distinguishes false claims from true ones within an elite culture in which social status depends largely on individual achievement. In so doing, it reflects a common difficulty experienced in the lives of those listening to these stories.

This connection between a drinking vessel and the achievements of a warrior is of considerable antiquity. As already noted, Herodotus said of the Scythians that: 'Once a year the provincial governor mixes a bowl of wine and all the Scythians who have killed an enemy that year drink from it. Anyone who has not, does not partake but sits to one side in disgrace.'[245] The warrior who could claim to have killed two enemies receives two glasses of wine, and so on. Here the cup is not of itself expected to judge the warrior's claim, but many of the same ideas are present; only those with true claims had the right to the esteem derived from drinking from the bowl.

Comparable drinking and feasting tropes were recorded of various ancient peoples. The work compiled by the Greek ethnologist (and all-round polymath) Posidonius in the first century BCE only survives in fragments, but feasts feature prominently. Among others he commented on the Celts:

> When many of them sup together, they all sit in a circle, and the bravest sits in the middle, like the leader of a chorus, because he is superior to the rest either in his military skill, in birth or in riches; and the man who gives the entertainment sits next to him, and then on each side the rest of the guests sit in regular order according as each is eminent or distinguished in anything.[246]

He went on to add that the hindquarters of a pig might be placed on the table to be claimed by the bravest man present, with single combat deciding the issue should more than one come forward.[247] Like the Scythians, therefore, the Celts were credited with mechanisms for establishing status in a social setting. Perhaps strategies of this kind began in deep prehistory, in which case the story told by Herodotus of the Scythians might be related, however distantly, to that offered by Posidonius regarding the Celts. Whether or not, such conventions were clearly present in both communities long before 175 CE, the point at which Littleton and his collaborators argue that Sarmatian storytelling first entered Britain.

We can only conclude, therefore, that such fictional Celtic vessels as the cauldron of Annwn are reflective of a long-established tradition of manufacture and use of metal containers in western Europe. These parallel the similarly long-established traditions of the steppes which resulted in the Wasamonga of the Nart sagas. Clearly, there are parallels between these traditions but no more than should be expected, given the similarities between the proximate societies underlying these literary traditions. There seems no good reason, though, to suppose that either tradition was indebted in significant ways to the other. Rather, each tradition seems complete in and of itself.

The grail tradition should be considered separate. This has no deep roots in prehistory but emerged out of the Christian interest in relics, and particularly those primary relics with the potential to link back to the person of Christ. The grail story was initiated no earlier than the late twelfth century, when a 'graal' was the term used for a shallow dish containing the Mass wafer. This image was then reimagined in the context of the story of Joseph of Arimathea, with the shallow dish metamorphosing into both Christ's cup from the Last Supper and the receptacle in which His blood was collected during the crucifixion scene. The chronology is such that we can safely put aside the arguments made by Littleton and his collaborators in favour of Alans having brought the kernel of this story from the steppes to France in the fifth century. There is no connection, therefore, between the grail and the Wasamonga of the Nart sagas, and little enough with the range of magical vessels that occur in various Celtic tales.

King Arthur and the Narts

The Nart sagas deserve recognition as one of the richest seams of oral storytelling still recoverable from any part of the world, a northern Iranian tradition worthy of celebration alongside those of Ancient Greece, India and Scandinavia. But much like the Finnish oral tradition,[248] which is in some respects comparable, the Iranian corpus was only transcribed very recently. Any attempt to assign the composition of individual stories to a particular period is problematic. While some aspects are consistent with formulation in or even before late Antiquity, others reveal later influences. Oral recitation over long periods has provided a somewhat fluid mechanism, therefore, for the perpetuation of 'original' material. As circumstances have changed, so have these stories: mountains have replaced the Steppe, forests and vales the grasslands; fixed settlements have trumped life in the wagon, which was a standard of classical writers;[249] pagan practices have been watered down in the face of the Bible and the Quran, and the traditional society depicted in the sagas was eventually tempered by the arrival of feudalism and state-formation.

It is against that backdrop that we must read the multiple versions of the death of Batraz, only one of which includes a sword-in-the-water motif comparable to that appearing in Arthurian literature. The non-Iranian name of this hero implies that his part in the sagas derives from a later time than other family members. Batraz's role in contesting Christianity suggests an origin for this story in the central Middle Ages, or at least its revisualisation at that stage. His prominence as an opponent of various forms of government and lordship similarly implies late development, as does the concentration of modern features in these tales. While the story of the disposal of Batraz's sword had taken hold on the Black Sea coast before 1900, it need not be many centuries older; certainly, it cannot date back millennia, at least in anything close to the form in which we have it. Aspects of the story parallel other of the Nart sagas, suggesting a narrator calling upon long-established motifs but shaping them to his own purpose. That this story uniquely shows a Nart hero in an unsympathetic light is easiest reconciled with its composition only once the audience for the sagas had lost some of their respect for the traditional social mores which otherwise characterise the canon. This is likely, therefore, to be the last of the several versions of Batraz's death now available, and a late addition to the sagas as a whole.

That the sword-in-the-water motif which first appears in the Arthurian story cycle in French early in the thirteenth century owed anything to the Nart sagas is therefore extraordinarily unlikely. We can trace the story of Arthur's death across the central Middle Ages. Geoffrey of Monmouth elaborated the brief entry in the *Annales Cambriae* by establishing Mordred and Arthur as close kin but in adversarial roles, then despatched the king at the close to Avalon, having nominated his successor. Two generations later Robert de Boron's continuator reworked Arthur's ascent to the throne in *Merlin*, introducing the sword-in-the-stone scene. Christ's support now trumped the fact, only revealed later, that Arthur was son to the previous king, so the true heir by descent; his sword symbolises his kingship. Downgrading the hereditary principle at the start of the reign rendered it less necessary to its ending. In the *Mort Artu* Arthur therefore no longer names his heir. Disposal of his sword in a fashion as mysterious as its acquisition becomes the principal act required before Arthur departs to healing or death. That the sword hilt has the form of a cross and water is the medium of baptism can only have added Christian resonances to the story, which amounts to a secular type of miracle. We can find parallels for some aspects of this sword-in-the-water story in both the Bible and Chrétien's poetry, but we should recognise that this was primarily the imaginative achievement of an anonymous thirteenth-century writer who we should allow was thinking through his response to changes recently introduced to the narrative by the author of *Merlin*.

When we turn to look at other parallels which have been marshalled in support of the 'Sarmatian connection', parallel development seems the likeliest explanation. There is no reason to doubt that the grail (eventually the Holy Grail) originated in a thoroughly Christian milieu. The cauldron of Annwn arguably stems from a tradition of metal cooking vessels stretching far back into British prehistory and is unconnected. The cultural roots of the Wasamonga of the Nart sagas seem at least as ancient, but there is no good reason to suppose any causal link between the drinking vessels of the Scythians and Sarmatians and cauldrons used in Antiquity and thereafter in high-status households in the west. The pursuit of such parallels has the advantage of encouraging exploration of each of these traditions but it tells us nothing about the origins of King Arthur.

Debates regarding the potential connectedness of such phenomena have a very long history. When Plutarch set about writing brief biographies of Roman worthies he thought it necessary to confront the assumptions of his own day that similarities between life stories necessarily carried historical meaning:

> It is perhaps not to be wondered at, since fortune is ever changing her course and time is infinite, that the same incidents should occur many times, spontaneously. For, if the multitude of elements is unlimited, fortune has in the abundance of her material an ample provider of coincidences; and if, on the other hand, there is a limited number of elements from which events are interwoven, the same things must happen many times, being brought to pass by the same agencies. Now, there are some who delight to collect, from reading and hearsay, such accidental happenings as look like works of calculation and forethought.[250]

Plutarch's point is the more apt when the life stories are fictional, as here. We cannot be absolutely certain in such matters, but it is most unlikely that Arthurian literature written in the late twelfth and early thirteenth centuries owed anything at all to storytelling among speakers of northern Iranian, late versions of which have come down to us in the Nart sagas.

4

KING ARTHUR AND THE GREEKS

> ... we must all accept that this figure [Arthur] simply cannot have begun life in the British Dark Ages if he is older than Hesiod (*c.* 700 BC) in some form.'
>
> — Graham Anderson, *The Earliest Arthurian Texts*[1]

I t was long assumed that, whoever King Arthur might actually have been he was in some sense British. Across the twentieth century, though, arguments in favour of L. Artorius Castus, then development of the full-blown 'Sarmatian connection', encouraged scholars to widen out the search. What if King Arthur's roots lay outside Britain, somewhere further east within Eurasia, and the raw materials of his story came to the Celtic west only via processes of cultural osmosis?[2] The last 'foreign' theory that we need to explore stands apart from the closely linked Dalmatian, Sarmatian and Nart hypotheses discussed so far; this is the proposal that King Arthur's story began in pre-classical Greece.

This 'Greek connection' is the brainchild of the classicist Graham Anderson, who set out his argument initially in his book *King Arthur in Antiquity*, published in 2004, then refined it and provided the literary evidence in a follow-up volume, *The Earliest Arthurian Texts*.[3] It must be said at the very beginning that the 'Greek Arthur' has one notable advantage over other 'foreign' theories of Arthur's origin. Although it is widely accepted that the names of characters can often be substituted as stories and snatches of narrative pass between languages,[4] the total lack of correlation of Arthurian, Sarmatian and Nart personal names can only detract from attempts to weave connections between them. In contrast, there are characters in several early Greek tales whose names are very like the Old Welsh Arthur; this is even more the case if we take account of forms of the name recorded on the Continent from the eleventh century onwards (to include Artusus, Artusius, Artuxius, Artus and Artur).[5]

Additionally, Anderson points out that the name Arthur 'does not so far as we yet know produce meaning related to its legendary character in any language but Greek.'[6] It can though be derived very satisfactorily from a combination of two words, *arktos* (Ἀρκτος), meaning 'bear', and *ouros* (οὖρος), 'guardian', 'watcher' or 'ward'.[7] 'The Greek form is Arktouros [Ἀρκτουρος], loaned into Latin as Arcturus, and subject to a very predictable consonantal reduction as Arturus.'[8] An equally predictable loss of the word ending then leaves us with Artur, resulting in Old Welsh Arthur.[9]

This throws down a significant challenge to the long-running near-consensus that Arthur's name in the early Welsh sources (in both Latin and Old Welsh[10]) derived from the Roman family name Artorius.[11] In addition, Anderson reminds us that no root for Artorius has so far been identified in Latin, opening the door to the possibility that here too the name came from the Greek. That, though, is to press this line of reasoning rather further than it can reasonably go. Agreed, the stem of the name Artorius should probably be sought in one of the languages with which Latin came into contact during the Roman conquest of Italy in the third century BCE. Greek was, of course, one of those languages, but the long '-ou-' of Arktouros is unlikely to have metamorphosed into the short '-o-' of Artorius;[12] that the Roman name stemmed from Greek seems improbable, therefore. Malone suggested that this was a loan from Etruscan.[13] A likelier derivation, though, is from Gaulish; names based on Celtic *Arto- ('bear') were common in the Roman west (and in medieval Wales and Ireland).[14] There was a substantial Gaulish community in Ancient Italy, parts of which are likely to have been incorporated in the Roman state as that expanded – this family name was first recorded late in the third century BCE, so at the right time for this to have occurred. It seems likely, therefore, that the family name derived from a leading Celtic family in one of the Italian regions colonised from Gaul that succeeded in transforming itself into a Roman one. Such would help explain the comparative infrequency of its occurrence in the Roman period.

But the possibility that the Welsh name Arthur derived independently from Arktouros requires that we explore the option of a Greek origin of the Arthurian tradition. Anderson also suggests parallels between stories featuring various Greek Arthurs and the Arthurian story cycle of the Middle

Ages, arguing for example that Arthur was first connected with a table in pre-classical Greece – with potential relevance to the origins of the Round Table. If confirmed, such parallels might support the case for a Greek derivation.

We need, therefore, to investigate this 'Greek Arthur'. There are numerous questions that we can pose. What roles do these names play in early Greek literature? Are there possible connections with the early British Arthur? Did stories featuring one of these Greek 'Arthurs' spread to the west, where they could have provided a launch pad for the later figure of pseudo-history and romance? The means of transmission of such tales must be uppermost in our minds: how widely was Greek spoken in Roman Britain? To what extent did Greek mythology spread westwards, either in Greek or in Latin, and how well could any such transmission have survived the cultural shifts occurring across late Antiquity? Finally, we must examine the parallels which have been put forward, and weigh up whether or not the British Arthur really could owe a long-overlooked debt to Greek mythology.

The Arktouros tradition

The case for a Greek Arthur is complex and multi-layered, but at its core lie stories relating to the night sky. Like many others, Greek stargazers divided the heavens into constellations – largely a matter of joining up the stars into pictures of people, animals or things.[15] Though they seem to have given names to only a few of the thousand or so stars that they observed,[16] those that they did included the more visible examples. One of these, the brightest star in the northern hemisphere, they named Arktouros (Ἀρκτουρος), Latin Arcturus, the 'Bear-Ward'. The bear in question was the constellation that we call Ursa Major, following the Latin, the 'Great She-Bear'. Arktouros lay within or adjacent to a constellation known variously as Arktophylax (the 'Bear-Watcher', 'Bear-Guardian'), or Boötes (the 'Ox-Driver').

These names were already in use by c. 700 BCE, as attested in Homer's *Odyssey*:

> [Odysseus] sat and guided his raft skilfully with the steering-oar, nor did sleep fall upon his eyelids, as he watched the Pleiads, and late-setting Boötes and the Bear which men also call the Wagon which ever circles where it is and watches Orion, and alone has no part in the baths of Ocean.[17]

Likewise, the *Iliad* has Hephaistos crafting a shield for Achilles:

He pictured on it earth, heaven, and sea, unwearied sun, moon waxing, all the stars that heaven carries for garland: Pleiades, Hyades, Orion in his might, the Great Bear, too, that some have called the Wagon, pivoting there, attentive to Orion, and unbathed in the Ocean stream.[18]

An association between bears and these northern constellations is common to several Indo-European languages, suggesting that the connection pre-existed their separate emergence. Indeed, Ursa Major is arguably 'the most solidly reconstructed' Indo-European constellation (though admittedly competition is not stiff).[19] But the link between the northern night sky and the bear is not unique to the Indo-European languages, occurring also in Basque, Hebrew, languages spoken by various Siberian peoples and pre-European peoples in the New World.[20] The distribution of stars in neither constellation actually much resembles a bear; nor did it in Antiquity. Coincidence therefore seems unlikely, implying that a link between the bear and the northern night sky may even pre-date flooding of the Bering land bridge.[21] An association between bears and the far north would have made good sense in the Palaeolithic, given their prominence in northern regions. It seems reasonable, therefore, to see this as a very early tradition indeed,[22] already widespread when Indo-European came into existence, thereafter discernible in several of the successor Indo-European languages.[23]

But by c. 700 BCE this representation of the heavens was being contested. The Greeks acquired new ways of interpreting the stars from Babylonian astronomers,[24] who identified the seven principal stars of Ursa Major as 'the Wagon'. Homer was familiar with both traditions. This injection of eastern star-lore led to the overlaying of parts of the pre-existing Greek astronomical system, with Boötes – the 'Ox-Driver' – alongside the Wagon (or Wain, later the Plough or Big Dipper). This more 'agricultural' representation of the heavens spread across the ancient world; in Latin *septentriones* – literally 'seven yokes of oxen' – was used of the north generally but applied specifically to the Great and Little She-Bears. What Babylonian astronomy offered was an update to interpretations of the night sky better attuned to farming, with annual shifts in the heavens now used to calendar the agricultural year. We are here witnessing the cosmic resonances of the shift from hunting/gathering to farming and the domestication of animals, so the Neolithic Revolution.

Written around the same time as Homer,[25] Hesiod's *Works and Days* marked the beginning of spring by the rise of Arktouros and its departure from the night sky in autumn prompted the grape harvest.[26] Successive authors followed his lead, culminating in the first century CE in Virgil's *Georgics* and Columella's *Res rustica*. Even writers less focused on farming took notice of the northern hemisphere's brightest star; in his *Natural History*, for example, Pliny paid particular attention to Arcturus.[27]

The work of such astronomers as Eudoxus in the fourth century BCE helped standardise the constellations. Alongside, Greek writers showed considerable ingenuity in melding astronomy with mythology. This tradition is exemplified by a work known as *Catasterisms*, erroneously attributed to the scholar Eratosthenes, head of the Alexandrian library from 245 BCE onwards. The original is largely lost, but it is known to us via an abbreviated version of the first century CE. Arktos (the Bear) and Arktophylax were among the figures attracting attention. It is these stories which we need to explore as a possible starting point for King Arthur.

Our witnesses are a mix of Greek and Roman writers spread across several centuries. Hyginus, a Latin writer of the first century CE,[28] provides a good starting point, offering the Greek story to his Latin-speaking audience:

Therefore, as we said above, we shall begin with the Great She-Bear. Hesiod says that she is named Callisto, the daughter of Lycaon who ruled in Arcadia, and she was drawn by love of hunting to attach herself to Diana; and because of their mutual interest she was very dear to her. Afterwards however, when she had been raped by Jove, she was afraid to reveal the truth to Diana, though she was unable to conceal it for long; for with her belly now swollen, while she was washing her body, tired out by her exertions in the river and already close to her time, Diana realised that she had not preserved her virginity. The goddess exacted no small penalty for so great a suspicion. For she took away the appearance of a young girl and changed it to that of a bear, called *arktos* in Greek, in that form she gave birth to Arcas.

... And when she was wandering as a wild beast in the wood, she was captured by some Aetolians and brought to Lycaon in Arcadia with her son for a reward; there she is said to have thrown herself into the temple of Jove Lycaeus, unaware of the prohibition of entering it. Therefore, when the Arcadians pursued them and sought to kill them, Jupiter remembered his misdeed, placed Callisto with her son among the stars and called her the Bear, her son he named Arctophylax, concerning whom we will speak later.[29]

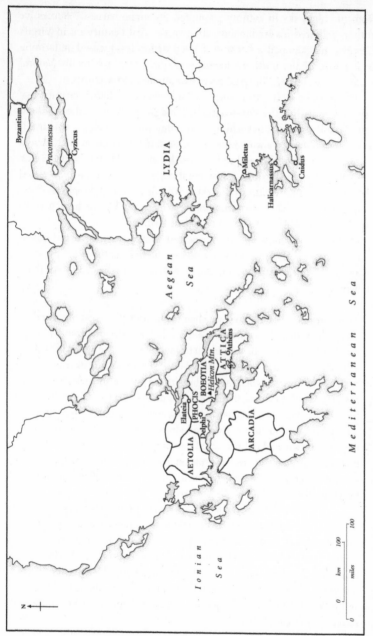

4 Ancient Greece: a backdrop to the 'Greek Arthur' hypothesis.

We find almost as many versions of this story as we have surviving texts, but this provides as good an outline as any. Callisto becomes the constellation Ursa Major and her son Arcas the neighbouring star-group Arctophylax (the 'Bear-Guardian'). Hyginus developed this tale further, adding a macabre story of Arcas's murder by his grandfather King Lycaon:

> Arctophylax. Concerning this it is said that it is Arcas by name, the son of Callisto and Jove, whom it is said Lycaon, when Jupiter came to be entertained in his house, cut up and served him with other meat in a banquet ... But the limbs of the boy, collected and reunited as one, he [Jove] gave to ... one of the Aetolians to raise; as a young man, when he was hunting in the woods, he saw his mother without recognising her, changed as she was into the form of a bear. Thinking to kill her he pursued her into the temple of Lycaeon Jove, to enter which brought the death penalty ... Jupiter took pity on them and placed them up among the stars, as we said before; he too from this is seen following the Bear and attending the Bear he is called Arctophylax.[30]

This reads as a doublet of the story of Tantalus, who reputedly cooked and served up his son Pelops to the gods – a tale which was widely repeated in classical works, including by Hyginus.[31] Given its centrality to the Tantalus legend, the story's origin is more likely to lie there than with Arcas, but the reference back to Hesiod may mean that borrowing was already ancient.

Pausanias provides another Arcas story, this time as the eponymous king of Arcadia (Map 4):

> After the death of Nyktimos, Arcas the son of Callisto came to power. And he introduced domestic crops, under the teaching of Triptolemos, and he taught how to make bread and weave clothes and other things; wool-working he learned from Adristas. From his kingship onwards the land was called Arcadia instead of Pelasgia and its people Arcadians instead of Pelasgians. And he lived, they used to say, with a woman who was no ordinary mortal but a Dryad ...[32]

Icarius was the subject of another set of stories, this time linked specifically with the star Arcturus. Here is Hyginus again:

> When Father Liber [Bacchus, or Dionysus] came to mankind that he might show them the sweetness and pleasant taste of his fruits, he

enjoyed the liberal hospitality of Icarius and Erigone. He gave them a
skin full of wine and ordered that they should propagate [it] in other
lands. Icarius loaded a cart with his daughter Erigone and dog Maera
and came to the shepherds in the land of Attica and showed [them] how
sweet it was. The shepherds drank immoderately, so fell down drunk;
thinking that Icarius had given them bad medicine they killed him with
cudgels. However, the howling dog Maera showed Erigone where her
father lay unburied; when she arrived, she committed suicide by hanging
herself on a tree. Angry because of this Dionysus afflicted the same
penalty on the daughters of the Athenians. They sought an explanation
from Apollo, who replied that the cause was their ignoring the deaths of
Icarius and Erigone. In response they punished the shepherds, insti-
tuted a festival day for Erigone to commemorate the plague of hanging,
and [decreed] that they should pour a libation to Icarius and Erigone of
the first fruits of the vine. By the will of the gods they were placed among
the stars; Erigone [is] the sign of the Virgin, who we call Justice, Icarius
is called Arcturus among the stars, the dog Maera is Canicula.[33]

The Arcas story told by Pausanias provides a culture-hero for part of the
Greek Peloponnese, through whom the name of the people is explained.
That this was an addition to pre-existing foundation legends seems likely
given the 'invention' of houses and founding of cities before his time in this
same account. His value here centres on the name-shift from Pelasgians
to Arcadians. Arcas was developed therefore as an eponym for Arcadia,
attracting tales which had probably earlier centred on different figures.

These are among the fuller stories that have come down to us. Brief
references are much more common, posing problems of interpretation to
their audiences. Aratus's astronomical poem, written in the first half of the
third century BCE, is a key source: 'Behind Helice there comes, like a man
driving, Arktophylax, whom men call Boötes, because he is seen to be just
touching the Wagon-Bear. All of him is very conspicuous; below his belt
circles Arktouros itself, a star distinct from the rest.'[34]

On the one hand, Aratus was treating the Bear (i.e. Ursa Major) as a
discrete constellation, but in the same work he was having to grapple with
the confusions resulting from the two naming systems, one based on the
Bear and Bear-Ward the other on the Wagon or yokes of oxen and the
Ox-Driver. His attempt at reconciliation merely adds to the difficulties,
entangling these originally separate traditions. A commentary on Aratus
increases the confusion,[35] by seeking to explain the resemblance of

Arctophylax to a driver: 'because he is carrying a *kalaurops* in his right hand, as if holding onto the cart, called the bear, as Boötes, who is driving the oxen from it carries a *kalaurops*, which is a club.'[36]

Cicero looked to Aratus as a source. In his *On the Nature of the Gods* (*De Natura Deorum*), written in 45 BCE and structured as a debate between exponents of rival philosophical traditions, he focused on the two bears which never set, circling round the pole:

> One of these two the Greeks call Cynosure [the 'Dog's Tail'; Ursa Minor], the other Helice [the 'Helix'; Ursa Major] is named, and the latter's extremely bright stars, visible to us all night long, our countrymen the Septentriones [Seven Yokes of Oxen] call and the little Cynosure [Ursa Minor] consists of an equal number of stars similarly grouped, and revolve round the same pole.'

Phoenician sailors, he remarked, use the Cynosure as an aid to navigation:[37]

> After the Septentriones comes Arctophylax [the 'Bear-ward'], commonly called Boötes, because he drives the Bear yoked to a pole … for with this Boötes beneath his bosom fixed appears a glittering star, Arcturus, famous name, and below his feet moves the Virgin bright, holding her ear of corn resplendent.[38]

Arktos, Arctophylax and Arcturus are still present, therefore, but heavily overlain by the later, 'agricultural' tradition.

Like Cicero, Latin poets of the early Principate knew their Greek mythology. In his *Fasti*, a lengthy poem left unfinished when he was banished to the Black Sea in 8 CE, Ovid made several references to the star legends. The second book, centred on the month of February, reveals his familiarity with the Callisto story, her ancestry, rape by Jupiter, transformation into a bear and subsequent birth of a child who then unknowingly attempted to spear her, then: 'They both were caught up into the mansions on high. As constellations they sparkle beside each other. First comes what we call the Bear, Arctophylax seems to follow at her back.'[39] In book six, centred on June, he briefly returned to the legend: 'On the third morn after the Nones it is said that Phoebe chases away [the grandson of] Lycaon, and the Bear has none behind her to fear.'[40]

Ovid clearly expected his audience to know the myth of Callisto and her son, for the Arcas tale could not be reconstructed from this work alone.

Likewise, Virgil (died 19 BCE) was aware of the story. He referred at different points in his *Georgics* to both Arctos (the Bear) and Arcturus,[41] but these are mere allusions. Though Virgil named Lycaon he did not include Callisto, Jupiter, Zeus or Diana, so left responsibility for their familiarity with the tale with his audience. The *Aeneid* is even less instructive. Here is the scene at the close of book I, with Aeneas and his men feasting as Dido's guests at Carthage:

> And Iopas of the long hair took his lyre bound with gold, and his music rang. The great master, Atlas, had been his teacher; he sang now of the wandering moon and the labouring sun; of the origin of men and of beasts, of rain, of fire, of Arcturus and the Hyads which foretell the rain, and of the two Bears.[42]

Implicit, once again, is knowledge of the origin stories of Arcturus and Ursa Major, but we are offered no detail and any member of the audience who did not already share this knowledge was none the wiser. Virtually the same line recurs later in a scene which recalls navigational lore.[43] The *Aeneid*'s allusive treatment has important consequences for the tradition, since this was the most widely read, pagan-period Latin work throughout the late Roman and sub-Roman periods.

Aratus's *Phaenomena* was revised early in the first century CE in a Latin text ascribed to Germanicus Caesar.[44] This alludes to the Callisto tale,[45] but also offers an entirely different origin for the bears: 'The Bears of Crete, called Arctoe, or in Latin, Ursae, guard it [the North Pole] on the right hand and on the left. They are also called Ploughs, and the shape of a plough is the closest to the real shape formed by their stars.'[46] These bears were the nursemaids of Jupiter, who shielded him in infancy from the wrath of his father Cronos. Again, we have the plough as an alternative. The author eventually turns to Arctophylax, whom he conflates with Icarius:

> An old man, threatening his animals with a walking-stick [*baculum*], follows, he is either Arctophylax or Icar[i]us, slain because of his services to Bacchus and rewarded for the loss of his life with a place among the stars ... only one of his stars has its own name. Men call it Arcturus.[47]

Unsurprisingly, when the author returns to this constellation it is as Boötes, the 'Ox-Driver'.[48] The two traditions were by now hopelessly confused.

As members of the Roman intelligentsia, Virgil, Ovid and Germanicus were conversant with Greek mythology, but it was their characteristically allusive references that became the predominant *entrée* to this material across the western provinces, not works in Greek. Romano-Celtic society is not therefore likely to have had detailed access to the Arktos stories. Nor was even Latin culture particularly accessible in the western provinces beyond a classically educated minority; most provincials were excluded, hearing only the tales that their family and friends told, into which Greek myth percolated only fitfully. It was a homogenised Graeco-Roman culture that prevailed in the west, even in elite circles.

We should also note that astrology came to overshadow and then displace astronomy in the Roman world. Augustus (emperor 27 BCE–14 CE), and particularly Tiberius (14–37 CE), led the way in seeking a better understanding of terrestrial events via heavenly portents (it was Tiberius who is thought to have appointed the first astrologer to the imperial court). Astronomy had pretty much lost its way by the end of the second century and was little more than astrology's fall-guy across the remainder of the classical period.[49] By the fourth century it was effectively dead, along with many of the star-stories which it had earlier popularised. The trend was increasingly towards a more encyclopaedic approach to learning, recirculating and commenting on pre-existing works within a Neoplatonic thought-system based on belief, not observation. The eclecticism of writers such as Pliny played well in this milieu; his work was copied many times and remained in circulation in the early medieval west. But the astronomical content of his *Natural History* is slight and its attention to the northern bears even less; Pliny consistently used Septentriones for the Great and Little Bears, and discarded Arctophylax in favour of Boötes.[50] Apart from the star Arcturus,[51] bears were absent from his night sky.

More specialised works attracted only small audiences, were copied infrequently and were eventually lost to view, in the west particularly. Pausanias is a good example. His *Description of Greece*, thought to date to the reign of Marcus Aurelius (161–80 CE), provides a guide to the traditions local to one city-territory after another. But it was overly cumbersome to serve as a practical guide on tour – there are almost nine hundred pages in the Teubner edition, suggesting a text that would have been very difficult to consult (it will originally have been in the form of a scroll). Few seem to have made much use of it and it survived in only a single manuscript, probably lodged in one of the great libraries of the east. Pausanias's preference for ancient over newer religions (including the Imperial cult) marked him as a conservative,[52] and he was writing just as philhellenism was waning among even the Roman elite. Christian Habicht considers his work to have always been obscure, low on contemporary impact and something of a failure.[53] Others scholars are less pessimistic, but his detailing of pagan myths necessarily rendered the *Description* unattractive to the Christians who were increasingly dominant by *c.* 400 CE.[54] The Arcas tradition was popular locally in the Hellenistic period, when the Arcadians erected a monument at Delphi that celebrated his story,[55] but there is no reason to think that this interest survived to the later Empire, nor that it spread far outside Greece.

To engage with the intellectual interests of the Roman aristocracy in the late fourth century we must turn instead to such authors as Macrobius. His name is Greek and he was familiar with both Latin and Greek literature, but perhaps more comfortable with the former. His longest work, now surviving only in part, the *Saturnalia*, is a dialogue between participants in the festival of that name that uses extracts from earlier material and is highly antiquarian in tone. The first book reveals an interest in the calendar; it includes some mythology, but Arcturus, Lycaon, Icarius and Arcas are all absent. Books III to VI explore the *Aeneid* from various perspectives.[56] Though Bacchus receives honourable mention,[57] Callisto and Arcas do not.

Macrobius' surviving works also include a *Commentary on the Dream of Scipio*. The original *Dream* was written by Cicero in the 50s BCE as part of his *De Republica*, but it circulated independently, surviving largely because it became attached to the *Commentary*. Astronomy is under discussion at the beginning, but the focus is on Neoplatonic interpretations of the Universe, the sun and eclipses.[58] Book IV likewise covers the Platonic spheres and the planets, and book V the music of the spheres. Given the range of mythology on display, the absence of all of Arcturus, Arcas, Lycaon, Icarius, Ursa Major and Callisto is noticeable. The style is once more antiquarian, with frequent references to Homer and Virgil, from whom he probably lifted his reference to the Pleiades, Hyades, Orion, the Septentriones and the Dragon.[59]

It is a similarly much-reduced understanding of classical Greek astronomy that we find in another Latin work compiled in late Antiquity, *On the Marriage of Philology and Mercury* (*De Nuptiis Philologiae et Mercurii*), written by Martianus Capella early in the fifth century. Again, there are no bears other than the star Arcturus, though that had now been substituted for Arctophylax as one of two names of the constellation:

From one direction, Herdsman Boötes, brilliant in the northern light, is wont to watch Septentriones ... The northern constellations are found

in the region of the zodiac towards the Septentriones ... The northern
sector is occupied by the two Septentriones; by Draco, which winds
about and glides between them; by Arcturus, also known as Boötes ...[60]

The sense of 'watching' is perhaps a leftover from the ancient Greek tales
but there is nothing more which is even reminiscent of the early myths.
Capella's interest in the stars was primarily astrological. His work would be
highly influential in introducing the sevenfold structure of knowledge that
was adopted in the monastic schools of the early Middle Ages. By this date
Ptolemy's work was unknown in the west and interest in astronomy had
dissipated. That pagan star-stories were suspect to Christian thinkers
further discouraged the circulation of tales which sought to explain the
heavens without recourse to Genesis.

Bishop Isidore's *Etymologies*, written in southern Spain early in the
seventh century, reflect the state of knowledge two hundred years later in
what had arguably been the most Romanised region of Atlantic Europe:

> The first of the signs is Arktos, which, fixed on the pole, rotates with its
> seven stars revolving around it. Its name is Greek, and in Latin it is
> called Ursa. Because it turns like a wagon, we call it the Septentriones.
> For *triones*, strictly speaking, are ploughing oxen ... Their proximity to
> the pole causes them not to set, because they are on the pole. Arctophylax
> is so named because it follows Arktos, that is the Great Bear. People have
> also called this constellation Boötes, because it is attached to the Wagon.
> It is a very noticeable sign with its many stars, one of which is Arcturus.
> Arcturus is a star located in the sign of Boötes beyond the tail of the
> Great Bear. For this reason it is called Arcturus, as if it were the Greek
> 'tail of the bear', because it is located next to the heart of Boötes.[61]

Bishop Isidore was conscious of the basic naming conventions of the Greek
and Roman constellations, therefore, but confusion resulting from the
overlaying of terminologies had by this point led to the rise of new understandings of what the names meant and how they had arisen. The Greek
stories known to earlier Latin authors do not register here.

Turning to early medieval Britain, Greek was taught at the Canterbury
School while Archbishop Theodore was in post (669–90), and a few of his
graduates seem to have attained a degree of fluency.[62] This was a new beginning, however, and short-lived, for there is no evidence that knowledge of
the language lasted in England beyond the next generation. Bede noted that

Theodore taught astronomy and ecclesiastical computus,[63] but this will have been primarily for religious purposes, specifically the Christian calendar. Unfortunately, there are no astronomical texts surviving that we can associate with Theodore, so we cannot be sure precisely what was on the syllabus.[64]

Bede knew the works of Pliny, Virgil, Macrobius and Isidore, but the astronomical content of his *On the Nature of Things* (*De Natura Rerum*), written *c.* 703, is slight indeed:

> ... some stars are stimulated spontaneously at fixed times, like the rising of the Haedi, and of Arcturus which ascends on 13 September with a tempestuous hailstorm, and like stormy Orion, and Canicula (Sirius), which, giving off excessive heat, rises on 18 July.[65]

Bede was dependent on Latin sources for the little he knew. This is virtually the totality of his entry under the heading 'Stars';[66] the astronomy inculcated among his students was minimal and lacks all of the mythology regarding star-names that was circulating even a half-millennium earlier. Max Laistner was unconvinced that Bede had access to much more than book two of Pliny's *Natural History*, and suggested that he was prone to quote classical authors at second hand, via late Roman grammarians and Isodore's *Etymologies*. In Bede's later works 'quotations from pagan literature other than Virgil are exceedingly rare.' His knowledge of Josephus's *Antiquities* was probably via a Latin translation, and his historical perspective rested on the works of Latin writers, including Orosius, Jerome, Rufinus, Eutropius, Cassiodorus, Prosper, Marcellinus, Isidore, Gregory of Tours, Vegetius and Gildas.[67] While this list underlines the quality of the manuscripts collected at Wearmouth–Jarrow, it is clear that Bede accessed few if any Greek texts and there is no certainty that he could read even elementary Greek.

A renewed interest in astronomy and astrology characterised the court of Charlemagne (768–814) but this renaissance relied heavily on works assembled by the Northumbrian scholar Alcuin; Bede had pride of place, alongside Pliny, Macrobius and Capella.[68] Greek stories explaining the names Arktos, Arctophylax and Arcturus were absent. His attention to meteorological phenomena, the night sky, earthquakes, eclipses and comets has led the anonymous biographer of Louis the Pious, Charlemagne's son and successor, to be dubbed 'the Astronomer',[69] but his interests are better described as astrology. He was for example consulted by the emperor regarding what such a 'dire and sad portent' as Halley's Comet might threaten, apparently suggesting recourse to prayer, masses and alms-giving.

Were the Celtic regions better served with classical astronomy than Anglo-Saxon England and Carolingian Francia? Our answer must surely be 'no'. Levels of literacy were low in Atlantic Britain in the early Middle Ages, writing was reserved primarily for matters of authority, be those secular or ecclesiastical, and the supply of 'foreign' manuscripts was very limited indeed.[70] There is no evidence to suggest that there was an appetite for Greek texts in early medieval Wales, nor that any survived there. Nor are Latin astronomical works likely to have been available, beyond allusions to the stars in the *Aeneid* and the material that Isidore included in his *Etymologies* (see above, p. 129); while both these were known in Wales, neither offer anything on the 'Greek Arthur'.

It seems safe to conclude, therefore, that the 'Greek Arthur' was unknown in western Britain in the early Middle Ages, when the 'British Arthur' first begins to emerge. There is another possibility, though, that we need to consider, that Greek astronomical knowledge and the star-stories which accompanied it had been absorbed into their own culture by the western Celts at an earlier date, in which case they could have been present in some different, more 'local-looking' guise.

Greek influences in pre-Roman Britain

We must now go back in time to explore the nature of interactions between the Greeks and the inhabitants of the British Isles before the Roman Conquest of 43 CE. Certainly, the Atlantic provinces of the Empire were receptive to some elements, at least, of Greek mythology. For example, the concept of the 'Isles of the Blessed', as first encountered in the works of Homer (see above, p. 96), was taken up in Atlantic Europe in the Roman period, later re-emerging in the central Middle Ages (see above, p. 97). The Greeks certainly played a part in the naming of the British Isles: Latin Britannia derives ultimately from Celtic but via Greek Prettania; Albion reached Latin from Greek (also meaning 'Britain'), as did Thule (perhaps Iceland; the derivation is obscure); Latin Hibernia (Ireland) derives from Greek Iouernia (though again this probably came originally from Celtic).

Greek communities in the western Mediterranean in the first millennium BCE were conscious of Britain's importance for its tin mining. A small number of early Greek artefacts have been discovered in Britain, such as the early Bronze Age Rillaton Gold Cup.[71] A scatter of Greek coins from southern Britain,[72] and occasionally even beyond, probably reflects the presence of Greek traders who had travelled overland from the Mediterranean then crossed the Channel. As British leaders began to mint their own coins in the late pre-Roman Iron Age, they initially looked for inspiration to Gaulish issues, on which representations of animals were common, with horses, eagles and boars predominating.[73] Bears are rare, though: of just four examples identified, one is accompanied by a trainer,[74] so is obviously not the bear of the northern cosmos.

A major change occurred in British coining following Caesar's conquest of Gaul. From *c*. 20 BCE, insular rulers commissioned coins with new levels of realism in their design. Roman coinage was obviously a major influence, particularly following the opening of a mint at Lugdunum (Lyon) to pay the Rhine army.[75] The coiners were probably incomers, since these coins were 'wholly classical in style and often fully classical in content'.[76] The inscriptions were in Latin, but coiners adopted various motifs from Greek coins, including Heracles (Hercules) and Apollo, a krater or vessel, the vine-leaf, grain-ear, a star's rays, the centaur and the sphinx. Some of these images potentially have astronomical meaning.[77] While most of the Greek originals were of the late third century BCE through to the early first century CE, a minority date to *c*. 400 BCE, suggesting that a wide variety of Greek coins were available as exemplars.[78]

There is also the possibility of Greek ships reaching Britain's coast directly from the Mediterranean. Around 400 CE, the Latin writer Avienus, from Etruria, wrote a short work, the *Ora Maritima*, describing the sea voyage to Britain from the Mediterranean. This contains material written in the pre-Roman period by a Massilian (from Massilia, modern-day Marseille), who had taken ship as far as Gades (Cadiz) and there gathered information about the Atlantic coastline up to Brittany, Ireland and Britain.[79] This early traveller may have been Pytheas, whose work (now lost) was referred to by both Strabo and Pliny.[80] Pytheas had, Strabo tells us, travelled all over Britain and assessed its coastline at 40,000 stadia.[81] However, without further written or archaeological evidence, there is little opportunity to assess the cultural impact of such Greek visitors before the Roman period, and every reason to think it comparatively slight. Unlike southern Gaul, where Celtic inscriptions were cut using Greek letters, there is no evidence that the Greek language, its alphabet or its mythology took root in pre-Roman Britain.

Roman Britain and Greek culture

The Roman Conquest, beginning in 43 CE, opened the door much wider to continental influences. Roman culture at this date was heavily infused with Greek but, even so, there seems little chance that Greek star-stories had much impact. To explore this remote possibility, we need to examine the evidence for a Greek cultural presence in this, Rome's most northwesterly province, so as to assess the likelihood that the Arktos/Arktouros myths might have become embedded here.

First of all, we need to establish the extent to which the Greek language was used or understood. Latin and Greek were the main languages of the Empire, but by far the biggest linguistic impact on Britain came from its large garrison. This consisted predominantly of soldiers from the Western Roman Empire: the legions came from Latin-speaking provinces (the most easterly being legion XX *Valeria Victrix* from Illyricum via Lower Germany) and were in any case recruited exclusively from Roman citizens, so speakers of Latin. The auxiliary units were mostly from Celtic or German regions, with some twenty-six drawn from Gaul or Gallia Belgica, eighteen from Germany and around twelve from Spain.[82] Others are recorded from Latin-speaking Pannonia (six), Dalmatia (four) and Raetia (two). Only a small minority came from regions that were Greek-speaking – including six from Thrace, one from Syria – but even regiments based in the east in the first and second centuries CE normally spoke Latin, as did all army officers. We can be quite sure, therefore, that the *lingua franca* of the Roman army in Britain was Latin, not Greek.

While many governors and the better educated of their staff will have been bilingual, Latin was always the language of government and administration. Numerous merchants traded goods into the province, but very largely aiming at the army, government officials and the emergent tribal aristocracy, so these too used principally Latin. A burial inscription erected outside the frontier fort at modern-day South Shields on Hadrian's Wall commemorates the British wife of Barathes, a Syrian merchant in both Latin and Palmyrine;[83] Barathes is almost certain to have understood Greek, but that was neither his native language nor one normally heard at this army post. His wife's first language will have been Brittonic but it seems likely that they conversed in Latin. As British families began to adopt Roman names, they selected predominantly from the Latin repertoire, less often Greek, but with numerous Celtic names Latinised and remaining in use throughout the Roman period.[84]

Setting aside depictions of the chi-rho as a Christian symbol, there is very little use of Greek lettering on stone beyond the two altars found at Chester, both commissioned by Greek-named doctors (Plate 19).[85] As R.G. Collingwood and R.P. Wright remarked, such specialists are likely to have been attached either to the legion or to the household of its commanding officer. Otherwise there is a bilingual altar (with Latin on the front and Greek on the back) from Lanchester, again with medical connections.[86] Greek inscriptions are even rarer on mosaics in the north-western provinces.[87] Just one of the dozen or so with any lettering so far uncovered in Britain offers anything in Greek: the single word *HELEKON* (ʹΕΛΗΚΩΝ) occurs at Aldborough (Yorkshire), denoting the mountain of that name in Boeotia (mainland Greece) with which the muses were associated (Map 4).[88] Of the graffiti recovered from Roman Britain, almost all are in Latin.

Occasionally Greek lettering occurs on portable items found in Britain: the names of six gods have been identified,[89] among a total of sixty-three Greek inscriptions and a further ten in the Greek language but transliterated into Roman letters. But of around five thousand personal names recorded in *Roman Inscriptions of Britain*, volume 2, only twenty-one are in Greek characters. Greek lettering occurs predominantly on objects of high value and is absent from the far more numerous objects of base metal, such as bronze brooches made locally. Greek was therefore an occasional feature of imports intended for elite consumption, in most instances added already before their importation. Given the thousands of such inscriptions in Latin, the incidence is very low indeed.

Well over two hundred curse tablets have been recovered from the sacred springs at the Romano-British temples of Bath and West Hill, Uley near Stroud (Map 3).[90] Excepting some which either offer no text at all or seem the work of illiterates, all but three or four are in Latin. The exceptions are thought to be Celtic;[91] none are in Greek. Tablets seem to have been written mostly by members of the urban middle and lower classes and more prosperous sections of the peasantry, many of whom had Celtic names. Not only could these petitioners speak Latin but most could write it as well. The archaeological distribution of styluses similarly implies that, in the Lowlands at least, literacy was comparatively widespread.[92] Efforts were made on some curse tablets to disguise their messages, for example by folding the lead sheets or using ciphers; one from Uley has a Latin text written in Greek letters.[93] Knowledge of the Greek alphabet had clearly percolated down to this middle-ranking individual, but while his effort to obscure the text reveals his own knowledge it has the further implication that few shared it. This curse tablet therefore marks the very edge of Greek literacy.

Of course, men with some knowledge of Greek were probably common enough in the villa-rich Cotswolds. Comparison with Gaul suggests that by the second century schools will have been teaching grammar and rhetoric to young men from the better-off families at the tribal capitals, with some Greek featuring on the curriculum. A secretarial post in an elite household may well have required competence in the Empire's alternate language. This will have been particularly true of a Christian household in the second and third centuries, when the Gospels were exclusively in Greek, but by the later fourth century western Christianity was becoming Latin-based, the preserve of a monolingual civilian elite.[94] The persistence of Brittonic, though, rendered the linguistic situation more complex in Britain than across much of the nearer Continent. Abandonment of Latin as a spoken language early in the Middle Ages long encouraged the view that it had made comparatively little progress in Roman Britain outside the towns and the country houses of the aristocracy.[95] This now looks overly pessimistic, but Celtic was certainly more widely spoken in Britain than in the more Romanised parts of Gaul or Spain.[96] We should probably conclude that Latin was widespread in late Roman Britain, particularly in the Lowland Zone, and literacy along with it, but Celtic was still heard everywhere and was for many their first language – particularly in the north and west. In contrast, Greek remained very much a learned language, acquired only by a minority of the small number wealthy enough to attend the schools, and then generally only at a basic level.

The absence of Greek is evidenced by insular works from the period when Roman government was ending. St Patrick's *Life* and *Letter*, written probably in the mid-fifth century, reveal extensive knowledge of the Latin Bible but no acquaintance with texts in Greek.[97] One might put that down to the interruption of his education in his teens, but the British, Christian scholar Gildas, writing a couple of generations later, similarly reveals no awareness of Greek literature, despite his apparently being a native Latin-speaker who had been classically educated.[98] Bilingual witticisms imply that Gildas and his immediate audience understood Celtic,[99] and there is even a single word of Old English,[100] but there is no sign that he knew Greek, despite his much-vaunted erudition.

Patrick and Gildas are likely to have been members of those same land-holding families who in the fourth century had ornamented the reception rooms of their houses with mosaics and wall paintings. Here images which originated in Greek mythology are common, including Apollo, Orpheus, Bacchus, Medusa, the Naiads, Actaeon and Oceanus. Individual panels within a single mosaic contain scenes which seem randomly selected (perhaps from a style book), with little in the way of a coherent story. Quotations incorporated into either mosaics or wall paintings are mostly from Virgil's *Aeneid*.

Dolphins, dogs, deer and lions were commonly represented, with other members of the cat family and elephants also appearing. The seasons were popular, perhaps reflecting the importance of time in the Neoplatonic world-view. These, again, often feature animals; House VII in Insula XI at Caerwent, for example, represents the seasons by a boar or lion, a hunting dog, a lion, and a paired hare and hound.[101] While mosaics do sometimes include animals with which the villa-owners would have been familiar, most are exotic beasts such as leopards, lions, tigers and elephants.[102] Bears are very rare and no character in the stories associated with the Greek Arktos/Arktouros has so far been identified.

Perhaps the mosaic most relevant to this discussion is the fourth-century floor of room XII of the villa at Brading on the Isle of Wight.[103] A visitor entered via a frieze featuring Tritons and Nereids to a rectangular floor centred on the head of Medusa in a roundel, with the four winds in triangular panels to the sides and four two-figure scenes from mythology on the diagonals, depicting Lycurgus and Ambrosia, Ceres and Triptolemus, Attis and the nymph Sagaritis, and a badly damaged scene of an amorous pursuit. This connects with the second main block via a threshold panel featuring a male figure, seated and pointing with a rod towards a globe, with a sun-dial on a column behind and a bowl with a leafy twig beside him on the ground. This is widely thought to depict an astronomer (in the sense of an astrologer: Plate 20).[104] Lines around the globe dividing it in four perhaps invoke the seasons; the sundial represents time. This figure is therefore marking relationships between the passage of time, the globe and the seasons.

This panel then leads on to the larger of the two areas, laid out in a nine-panel grid. Of the four main rectangular panels only one survives near-complete, representing Perseus and Andromeda seated, with the hero holding aloft the head of Medusa. Busts of the four seasons occupy the corners. Other panels may feature Cadmus and perhaps Hercules, constellations in the polar region,[105] but extensive damage makes it impossible to be sure. But despite the apparent interest shown here in the northern night sky, the seasons, and the figure of the astronomer linking these mosaics, there is no attempt to represent Ursa Major or Minor, Arctophylax, Boötes or Arcturus. Nor have they been identified anywhere else in Romano-British art. What the Brading mosaic room XII offers us, therefore, is some insight to the contents of the style books available to a patron with interests in the heavens as they were understood in elite society in the fourth century. The choices made are illuminating, but only in the negative sense; we cannot show the 'Greek Arthur' to have been of interest to either mosaicists or their patrons.

Mosaics were not laid much if at all after 400. The fifth century witnessed not just the collapse of this form of artistic endeavour but also of the whole of the late pagan high culture which so many of its scenes reflected. While Christianity took on a great deal from this thought-world, there would be no more insular representations of the stars or their stories, Greek or otherwise, in Britain for many centuries.

The name Arcturus

Perhaps the best test of the 'Greek Arthur' hypothesis remaining to us is to focus on the name itself. Firstly, we need to assess the extent to which Greek and Roman star-names are likely to have been adopted in Britain as personal names. Although the Greeks named comparatively few stars, the brightest ten were among these, plus a further four of particular significance for calendrical purposes.[106] James Evans lists these stars: Arcturus; Sirius; Procyon (Antecanis); Antares; Canopus; Aix (Capella); Lyra (Vega); Aëtos; Stachys (Spica); Basiliskos (Regulus); The Pleiades; Protrygeter (Vindemiatrix); Eriphoi (Haedi); Onoi.[107] Searches of relevant databases reveal that collectively these are rare as personal names in the west. Most, including Arcturus, simply do not occur.[108] Arctus is recorded once in Pannonia, Arcus four times in Spain, Artus three times in Gallia Belgica, and Artius in Wales, but these are all likely to be Romanised Celtic names of peregrine type stemming from 'Art-', not from Arcturus. Otherwise, Basiliscus occurs once, in Italy, Canopus once in Gallia Narbonensis, Aeto- several times in Gallia Belgica and Dalmatia (though other origins for this name are likely), and Sirius once in Dalmatia. Capella, Spica and Regulus are all encountered but these are common nouns in Latin (meaning 'goat', 'ear of wheat', and 'petty-king' respectively) so as names need have no connection with astronomy, particularly as a cognomen. Of these, only Regulus has been identified in Britain, on the northern frontier.[109]

The *Onomasticon Provinciarum Europae Latinarum* is based on inscriptions on stone, so biased in favour of wealthier social groups, but the fact remains that it is a very large database. To check its value to our investigation, a search for Orpheus/Orfeus reveals two instances of the name in Italy and one in Gallia Narbonensis. In contrast, Arcturus does not occur. Nor do any of these names appear on surviving curse tablets, nor on the thousands of portable objects found in Britain which bear personal names. Were the name Arcturus in widespread use in the Western Empire, we might expect to register at least one example. An absence of evidence is of course not proof of absence, but it does seem unlikely that there was much use of Arcturus in particular, and Greek star-names in general, in personal nomenclature in the western provinces. Given the top-down nature of Romanisation, this conclusion probably holds good too for lower levels of society that are unrepresented by the inscriptional evidence, where Celtic personal names are likelier to have always predominated.

If not in Britain, and the Western Empire more generally, where did Arktouros/Arcturus occur as a personal name? Neither Ἀρκτουρος nor related forms have been recorded on mainland Greece, the Aegean islands, Cyprus, Cyrenaica, Sicily or Magna Graecia (Italy westwards), occurring only in Asia: Arcteus (Ἀρκτεύς) has been identified in Lydia, Arctoria (Ἀρκτωρία) at Cyzicus in Mysia (Anatolia), and Arcas (Ἀρκάς) at Halicarnassus and Miletus (Map 4).[110] Again, this does not support the view that Arcturus was a personal name likely to have become established in Roman Britain.

That does not mean that Greek personal names were entirely absent. That some were in use is confirmed by the Greek-originating name of the British heresiarch Pelagius, and the Elafius mentioned by Constantius of Auxerre.[111] These, though, were names that occur elsewhere in the Western Empire. Pelagius is evidenced twice in Italy, three times in Spain and four in Gallia Narbonensis, while Elafius/Elaphus has been recorded in single instances in Gallia Narbonensis, Gallia Lugdunensis and two of the Spanish provinces. They had, therefore, 'gone native'.

Anderson objects to Artorius as the source of Arthur on linguistic grounds: 'It should be stressed that any form ending in –ius (such as Artorius) is an adjectival form indicating connection with or descent from Arthur.'[112] This in his view counted against it having been the origin of Old Welsh Arthur. But is this a valid criticism? There are several points that we should consider. Firstly, unlike Arcturus, the family name Artorius is well evidenced, during the Republic as well as the Empire. While the inscriptional references belong to the first to third centuries CE, Artorii were recorded in the context of the Second Punic War (218–201 BCE) and the civil wars which led to the supremacy of Octavian.[113] Around 100 CE,

Juvenal wrote disapprovingly of an Artorius in his *Satire 3*, implying that he was a social-climbing 'outsider' (i.e. not from the city of Rome).[114] The name was, therefore, already present in the west before the full impact of Hellenism on Roman society in the second century BCE; it continued at least into the third century CE (to include the presumed descendants of L. Artorius Castus in Dalmatia). This provides a far more solid foundation for the migration of a Roman name into Britain than we can muster in support of Arcturus.

Secondly, it is a fact that Roman family names ending in –ius were very common. This is particularly true under the Republic. For example, the first forty consuls, from 298 BCE onwards, all had family names exhibiting this adjectival form. Such names are not as all-pervasive in the late Empire but they are still numerous. Of the last ten emperors in the west (covering the period 425–76), nine had some element of their name ending –ius. In the third century, newly enfranchised citizens generally adopted as their family name the adjectival form of the name of the emperor or consul of the day, causing a wide spread of names ending in –ius. And to look closer to Britain, the Roman commander in Gaul to whom Gildas reported that the Britons sent a plea for aid was Flavius Aëtius (died 454), whom Gildas termed Agitius,[115] and the later general with whom he is sometimes confused was Aegidius (died *c.* 464). The leader who Gildas credited with fighting off the Saxons was Ambrosius Aurelianus,[116] and one of the tyrants who he addressed in the present was Aurelius Caninus.[117] Celtic names ending '–orix' seem often to have been Latinised as '–orius',[118] and other local names were formed in the same way.[119] This style of name-formation outlasted the Western Empire; when, *c.* 800, an Irish cleric was constructing a Roman-style name from Old Irish *iasc*, 'fish', he opted for Iasconius.[120] Artorius fits comfortably, therefore, into everything we know about personal naming in the British Isles in and after the Roman period. Arcturus, in contrast, does not. Clearly, the adjectival form of the name is no bar to Artorius having been the origin of Arthur in Old Welsh.

Excalibur and the Round Table

An important component of Anderson's thesis lies in the similarities that he detected between Greek stories and tales within the Arthurian canon. There is neither time nor space here to examine all the suggested parallels so I propose to focus on two of the more prominent. Could Arthur's sword Excalibur or his Round Table have originated in Ancient Greece?

First let us focus on Excalibur. This is a rendering into French of Geoffrey of Monmouth's Latin *Caliburnus*, which descends, whether directly or indirectly, from the word ancestral to Welsh *Caledwlch* and Breton *Kaledvoulc'h*,[121] and medieval Latin *calibs*. All descend from classical Latin *chalybs*, meaning 'steel', and ultimately from Greek (see above, p. 87).

As already noted, a Greek commentary on the *Phaenomena* of Aratus offers: 'because he [Arktophylax] is carrying a *kalaurops* [or '*kalabrops*'] in his right hand, as if holding onto the cart, called the bear, as Boötes, who is driving the oxen from it carries a *kalaurops*, which is a club.'[122] This commentator was hopelessly confused by the two originally separate naming systems – bear versus cart, and Arktophylax versus Boötes – which Aratus had attempted to reconcile. The result is complete nonsense. But what attracted Anderson's attention was the variation in the spelling of *kalaurops*, leading him to point to the similarity of *kalabrops* and Geoffrey of Monmouth's *Caliburnus*.[123] But *kalaurops* is a common noun, not a name, and this is an agrarian term (it was a shepherd's staff used in herding cattle) not a soldier's weapon. Additionally, the variant spelling *kalabrops* is present in only one branch of the manuscript tradition.

For this to have influenced Geoffrey's Caliburnus, then both the *Phaenomena* and this variation of the commentary need to have jumped the language barrier into Latin and Old Welsh and circulated in Britain, but there is no evidence for this occurring. The *Phaenomena* circulated widely in the early Empire but seems to have lost out thereafter; the Latin version ascribed to Germanicus fared no better, and in any case offers an entirely different interpretation of the cosmic bears. Neither Aratus nor 'Germanicus' refer to a *kalaurops*; this occurs only in a commentary which is not known to have been translated into Latin. There seems very little likelihood of it circulating anywhere in the later Roman west, let alone in Britain. The *Almagest*, by Ptolemy, written in the second century CE, similarly refers to something carried by Boötes but uses the term *ropalon*, 'a club'. Ptolemy's was by far the best-known work of ancient astronomy in the later Middle Ages, but was only translated into Latin from Arabic some two generations after Geoffrey wrote the *History of the Kings of Britain*, so had no influence on the name of Arthur's sword.

To summarise, we can be reasonably certain that none of the *Almagest*, the *Phaenomena* or the *Commentary* were available in Britain in the 1130s. Nor did they leave any discernible footprint within western European literature prior to the *Almagest's* translation *c.* 1200. Without a viable route of transmission, arguments in favour of the migration of a specific word from an obscure Greek commentary via Brittonic and Old Welsh to Geoffrey's Latin pseudo-history are unconvincing. As already noted (see above, p. 87), classical Latin *chalybs* was a loanword from Greek *Chalups* (Χάλυψ), in origin a people of ancient Pontus.[124] Out of respect for their fame as steel-makers, the Greeks formed the word *chalubdikon* (χαλυβδικόν: 'steel', literally 'cast-by-Chalybes'). The root-word was borrowed into both Latin and the Celtic languages, and eventually gives us both Caliburnus and Excalibur. There is no reason to think that there was any connection with *kalaurops*, the meaning of which is very different. This argument is one that rests on nothing more than the 'sounds-a-bit-like' principle, which surfaces repeatedly in Arthurian studies.

Turning now to Arthur's legendary Round Table, Anderson has brought together several texts which refer to the foundation of the city of Trapezous (Τραπεζους: see Map 2). A surviving fragment of *Catasterisms* reads:

Concerning Boötes, also known as Arktophylax: It is said that it is Arcas, son of Callisto and Zeus; he lived around the temple of Lycaion Zeus. When Zeus raped Callisto, Lycaon pretended not to know and entertained Zeus, according to Hesiod, and having cut up the child he laid it on the table. Zeus overturned it and gave its name to the city Trapezous, and he blasted Lycaon's house with a thunderbolt, outraged at the man's cruelty. Lycaon he turned into a beast and made him a wolf. And Arcas he put together again, and he was brought up by a goatherd.[125]

This was probably the source, whether directly or indirectly, of the story told by Hyginus (see above, p. 123). The word used here for 'table' is *trapeza* (τράπεζα); clearly this was the root of the city-name; τρᾰπεζεύς means 'at/ of a table'. Trapezous, modern-day Trabzon, was founded by Milesian colonists in the eighth century BCE. The 'table' element in the name is likely to reflect the use of tables, for example in trading. That the citizens were conscious of the root of the name is evidenced by their coins, some of which bore the image of a table, but it was surely the city's name's coincidental inclusion of 'zeus' that suggested the false etymology that we find in the *Catasterisms*. The connection is purely phonetic and has absolutely nothing to do with Arcas.

Is it reasonable to see some connection between this story and the Arthurian Round Table? Several factors suggest not. Firstly, the origin of the word *trapeza* is *tetra-peza* (τετρά-πεζα), meaning 'four-legged'.[126] Though not proscriptive, this suggests a rectangular table, rather than one which was necessarily round: the table on the coins certainly seems rectangular. It is only the roundness of Arthur's table which is distinctive, so shape matters in this instance. If the table that Zeus overturned in the story was not specifically round there seems little reason to make the connection.

Secondly, the Arthurian Round Table does not appear before the *Roman de Brut*, written by Wace in Norman French and completed in 1155.[127] This work was based closely on Geoffrey's *History of the Kings of Britain*,[128] with some passages omitted (particularly the prophesies of Merlin) and others expanded. Here we have an example of the latter. There was a logic to the changes made. Geoffrey had remarked that, following Arthur's settlement of Scotland and rout of the Irish, the king

> began to increase his household by inviting all the most doughty men from far-off kingdoms and conducted his court with such courtesy that he was envied by distant nations. All the noblest were stirred to count themselves as worthless unless they were dressed and armed in the manner of Arthur's knights.[129]

Wace elaborated this to further raise Arthur's prestige:

> He [Arthur] never heard of a knight who was considered in any way worthy of praise who would not belong to his household, if only he could recruit him, and if such a one wanted reward for his service he would never deprive him of it.[130]

Awareness of the likely consequences of the resulting surfeit of knightly egos at Arthur's court led Wace to proceed:

> On account of his noble barons – each of whom felt he was superior, each considered himself the best, and no one could say who was the worst – Arthur had the Round Table built, about which the Britons tell many a tale. There sat the vassals, all equal, all leaders; they were placed equally round the table and equally served. None of them could boast he sat higher than his peer; each was seated between two others, none at the end of the table.[131]

In reality it seems very unlikely that Wace took this from a British source,[132] for he seems not to have used any texts that could fall under this description, Geoffrey's excepted. The idea could have come from a round table thought to be that of the Last Supper reputedly seen by Crusaders in the Holy Land,[133] or from one left in Charlemagne's will, as told in Einhard's *Life of Charlemagne*,[134] though that was of silver so presumably very small, but there is no actual evidence that either of these influenced Wace. This development of the story was clearly his own and no source is really necessary; indeed, his table was conceptual rather than material and would remain so for much of the next century.[135] Wace reputedly dedicated his *Brut* to Queen Eleanor and we know that Henry II later commissioned his work on Norman history, so there is nothing improbable in his interest in how a court as splendid and well populated as Arthur's might best function. He therefore toned down Arthur's ferocity, elaborated Guinevere's beauty, expanded Geoffrey's brief account of the time of peaceful court life which preceded war with Rome,[136] and gave thought to such matters as precedence and competition among Arthur's military retainers. It was these issues that the Round Table was intended to address.

Wace's introduction of the Round Table to Arthurian literature was a practical solution to an imagined problem, therefore, which there is every likelihood he came up with himself. There is certainly no reason to suppose that it derived from an ancient tradition which he came across in either Celtic or Latin literature. There is far too little correspondence between the Greek and French narratives to suggest a causal connection and no plausible route of transmission by which the much earlier example might have reached the Latin, Celtic and Romance west. Wace's elaboration of Geoffrey's story is easiest explained as his own, with or without some stimulus from references to round tables in an earlier medieval context. Without much more compelling evidence, we should discount the suggestion that the Arthurian Round Table has any connection with the ancient city-name, Trapezous. This is coincidence.

Arthur and the Greeks: in conclusion

The main strength of the theory of a 'Greek Arthur' lies in the presence in early literature of a set of interconnecting names very similar to Arthur. One of these, Arktouros, passed into Latin as Arcturus and is still used today for the brightest star in the northern night sky. Linguistically, Arcturus could be the source of Old Welsh Arthur. There is a case, therefore, for arguing for a connection between the medieval King Arthur and stories told in the classical period about Arktouros, Arktos, Arcas and various other hero-figures of Greek legend and mythology. Anderson has very usefully set out and commented upon the numerous texts which we need to take into account. While there are too many to discuss here in detail, we have looked at several of the more important.

Given the depth of time, it is particularly the transmission of these stories that must come under scrutiny; for the Arthurian trail to extend back to pre-classical Greece, we need to be able to demonstrate that an ongoing tradition is at least a reasonable possibility. In practice, though, that seems extraordinarily unlikely. While Greek mythology was well known to the philhellene elite of the early Roman Principate, knowledge of it dissipated thereafter, particularly in the west. In late Roman literature, references to the 'Greek Arthur' are limited to the Latin star-name Arcturus. Astronomy was superseded by astrology and pagan mythology was already giving way to Christian thinking about the nature of the heavens as the Roman period drew to a close. The literary output of the period c. 350–800 CE offers no hint of any traditions relevant to the 'Greek Arthur'.

Exposure to Greek culture was very limited in the north-west provinces of the Empire, and in Britain in particular. The Greek language was little used, Greek lettering is rare and Greek names few. While a largely Greek-inspired classical mythology featured on the mosaics with which the elite decorated their villas, particularly in the fourth century, it is the *Aeneid* which features in any attempt to link mosaics and literature, from which potentially Arthurian material is absent. Neither Patrick nor Gildas display any knowledge of the Greek language, Greek literature, or the 'Greek Arthur' tradition, even in translation. A sample of the more detailed claims likewise does little to support the 'Greek Arthur' thesis. The similarity of Greek *kalaurops* and Geoffrey's name for Arthur's sword, Caliburnus, is almost certainly coincidental and there is no causal link discernible between the Greek city-name, Trapezous, and the Arthurian Round Table that we first encounter in Wace's mid-twelfth-century *Brut*.

History can rarely demonstrate a negative, but theories are worth retaining only when they can be argued through effectively. That there were figures in Greek mythology whose names were sufficiently Arthur-like to have given rise to the Old Welsh name Arthur is now established. Without far more convincing evidence of an ongoing tradition, though, the claim that the medieval Arthur could have begun with the 'Greek Arthur' can be no more than speculation. The Greek personal name is unknown west of Roman Asia, leaving the star-name Arcturus as the sole survivor of this ancient 'Arthur' tradition, lodged in Isidore and the Bible.[137] By the central Middle Ages this name carried none of the stories that had clustered around it a millennium earlier. We can safely conclude that the medieval King Arthur owed nothing beyond his occasional confusion with the Latinised star-name Arcturus to pre-classical Greek mythology.

PART II

The 'British' Arthur

5

A DARK AGE KING ARTHUR

...no historian is entitled to draw cheques in his own favour on evidence that he does not possess, however lively his hopes that it may hereafter be discovered. He must argue from the evidence he has, or stop arguing.

— R.G. Collingwood, *An Autobiography*[1]

Throughout the Middle Ages, early post-Roman Britain was where Arthur's story was believed to have begun. It is to this period that we will now turn. This is a very congested space, though, with more theories regarding who he may have been than it is possible to even consider here. This chapter will seek to focus on the earliest 'British' Arthurs to have been proposed in recent years. First we will consider the view that Arthur began not as a figure of history but as a Celtic god or demi-god of the pre-Roman or Roman periods. Secondly we will examine the textual evidence for Arthur being identified as the fifth-century, British ruler, Riothamus. Finally, we will turn to several works in either Latin or Old Welsh written in Britain between *c.* 500 and *c.* 800 to see what, if anything, they can tell us regarding Arthur.

The mythological Arthur

An option which has recently gained renewed support is to view Arthur as a figure primarily of mythology – as Lord Macaulay, Sir John Rhŷs and others advocated in the nineteenth century. Certainly there is much about the early Arthurian tradition that might fit a god or supernatural hero. Several Welsh tales depict his arbitrary behaviour, his lustfulness and tendency to violence,[2] his ease of travel to other worlds and his encounters with giants and mythical beasts. This Arthur seems to belong in a world of 'magical realism',[3] set apart from the abodes of man.[4] He is even sometimes a giant himself.[5] His attachment to obscure landscape features seems compatible with other uses of the supernatural in Cornish and Welsh folklore.[6] As Anton van Hamel noted, Arthur emerges from the Welsh literature of the central and later Middle Ages as a figure comparable to the Irish Fionn – leading a band of heroes in the wilderness, fighting off invaders (both human and supernatural), raiding into the underworld (from which great treasures might be recovered) and protecting society at large.[7] There can be no doubt of Fionn's mythological origins: his name means 'fair one'; he was depicted as an archetypal hero battling an otherworldly opponent, and his name occurs in Roman-period place-names on the Continent (including Vindobona, modern-day Vienna). By the tenth century he had been thoroughly euhemerised.[8] Parallels between Fionn and the Welsh folkloric Arthur make the latter's mythic origin well worth exploring.

We encounter difficulties, though, when we try to establish Arthur as a god. In her survey of the religions of Celtic Britain, Annie Ross discussed the possibility of a bear cult and concluded, 'this evidence is impressive ... in later times, the divine qualities envisaged as being possessed by the bear would become transferred to find expression as heroic epithets in a heroic milieu'.[9] Certainly, the bear was used metaphorically for a warrior in early Welsh poetry,[10] but this theory is plausible only if Arthur is interpreted as a euhemerised form of the bear, thereby treating his story as evidence for the earlier divinity. There is an unwelcome circularity to this argument which calls the whole approach into question. In reality, evidence for a bear cult is far stronger on the Continent than in Britain: a Roman-period bronze of the goddess Artio offering fruit to a bear was found at Muri near Bern in Switzerland; inscriptions invoking her were discovered near Bollendorf (Rhineland-Palatinate),[11] and Mercury Artaios occurs in Roman Gaul.[12] Various river-names share the same first element as this 'god' name,[13] though it is unclear when these were formed and they need not signify a cult as late as the Roman period. In Britain, the only inscriptions of even marginal relevance are two naming Artius, a centurion, from near the auxiliary Roman fort of Bremia (at Llanddewi Brefi, Ceredigion: Map 3),[14] but the site was only occupied c. 75–130 CE and his rank denotes a continental at this date.[15] Jet amulets ornamented with bear images have been found at York, Malton and Bootle, but whether or not these have any religious significance is unclear. Otherwise bear amulets are occasional finds in child burials, perhaps representing a female protective force equivalent to the astronomical figure.

To get around this, an 'Arthur-deity' honoured only by the lower classes has been suggested, whose followers lacked the wherewithal to commission inscriptions;[16] alternatively a 'protector/guardian of the bear' type of demigod equivalent to the Greek myth has been proposed, who has somehow escaped art-historical and archaeological notice.[17] But this is just clutching at straws; theories for which there is no evidential support whatsoever can be no more than speculation; unless and until relevant evidence surfaces, there is no justification for making an Arthur-deity our starting point.

And even if there were such a cult, any connection with our Arthur would be highly speculative, at best. Welsh *arth-gŵr* (Old Welsh **arto-*wiros*), 'bear-man', is likely to result in the medieval name Arthwr. Without exception we encounter 'Arthur' in early texts,[18] a name that more naturally derives from Roman 'Artorius' (see above, p. 30). There has been concern that medieval texts refer to Arthur, Arturus, Arcturus, Artur (and similar), but never Artorius,[19] but that should not surprise us. A series of sound changes occurred, most simply expressed in the succession Artorius > Arthur > Artur > Arturus/Arturius, as the name passed from Latin to Brittonic and Old Welsh, then centuries later back to Latin and then French, at each stage adapting phonetically. Some medieval writers were of course also aware of the star-name Arcturus (see above, pp. 144–5), and on occasion substituted this for Arturus, but that should be seen as convergence, without significance for the name's origin. Since 'Artorius' was left behind comparatively early in this succession of sound-changes, it was no longer an option; it neither reappeared nor was ever likely to.

The final obstacle to viewing Arthur as a deity is the fact that, unsurprisingly, Celtic gods uniformly bore Celtic names.[20] If Arthur's name is in origin Roman (even if the root of the Roman name might be Celtic), then that effectively excludes him from their ranks. Nor was Artorius an imported 'foreign' deity (of which Roman Britain of course had large numbers), for this name identifies a god nowhere in the Empire. Given that, on linguistic grounds, the Greek Arktouros could equally well have given birth to the Welsh name, this must be considered too, but there is no evidence of an Arktouros/Arcturus cult in the Roman west (see above, p. 137), nor of its use as a personal name there, so that too is a dead end. The lack of evidence is such that we must dismiss the possibility that Arthur originated as a god or demi-god of the pre-Roman or Roman periods.[21]

Riothamus

We must turn next to a figure of late fifth-century Gaul known as Riothamus. Geoffrey Ashe has long argued that King Arthur should be identified with this figure, who led a British army against the Goths.[22] Riothamus is historical, though we know little enough about him beyond his defeat c. 470.[23] But Geoffrey of Monmouth later depicts Arthur as a British leader who campaigned on the Continent. Could his Arthur have somehow stemmed from memories of this war fought by a British king against German enemies deep inside Dark Age France? That the name Riothamus derives from Brittonic *rig- ('king') in a superlative form, so means something like 'most-kingly-one', has encouraged Ashe to suppose that this was less a name than a title. If Arthur was the 'most-kingly one', then the puzzle is solved: Arthur was a fifth-century British king who led his army across the Channel to fight against the Goths but whose deeds were recorded under his title, not his name.[24]

There are two sources for Riothamus. The earlier is a letter addressed to him written by Sidonius Apollinaris, who became bishop of Clermont c. 470. The letter complains that the anonymous bearer's slaves had fled to join Riothamus's army. But it was Sidonius, not the messenger, who wrote (presumably at his request). The familiar style of this letter, addressing 'my friend Riothamus',[25] suggests that these two men had previously been in contact and had perhaps even met.[26] Such seems very unlikely were Riothamus normally in Britain, where Sidonius otherwise seems not to have had any connections.[27] It seems far more likely that Riothamus was a ruler of the Britons in Armorica (modern-day Brittany), so a member of the continental elite with whom Sidonius was extremely well connected. This would certainly justify the anonymous letter-bearer's otherwise bizarre request that Sidonius should write a letter for him to deliver.

The Roman author Jordanes also tells us something about Riothamus in his mid-sixth-century abridgement of a now-lost history written by the well-connected Roman aristocrat Cassiodorus, some two decades earlier:

> Now Eurich, king of the Visigoths, perceived the frequent change of Roman Emperors and strove to hold Gaul by his own might. The Emperor Anthemius heard of it and asked the Britons for aid. Their king Riothamus came with twelve thousand men into the tribal territory of the Bituriges by way of Ocean, and was received as he disembarked from his ships. Eurich, king of the Visigoths, came against them with an innumerable

army, and after a long fight he routed Riothamus, king of the Britons, before the Romans could join with him. So when he had lost a great part of his army, he fled with all the men he could gather together, and came to the Burgundians, a neighbouring tribe then allied to the Romans.[28]

In 468 Anthemius (emperor 467–72) attempted to recover Africa from the Vandals, but his campaign ended in an expensive defeat;[29] the effort to restore imperial authority in Gaul the following year fared no better.[30] Although Riothamus answered the emperor's call, neither the Burgundians nor sufficient Roman forces mobilised in support. The alliance seems a hasty and somewhat ramshackle affair, put together by an emperor who had few resources to add to the mix and who was hamstrung by infighting within his own regime.[31] In such circumstances it seems most unlikely that he was calling in help from across the Channel. That Riothamus transported his men by ship via 'Ocean' suggests that they embarked in western Brittany and travelled down the coast before entering the Loire. Ashe's thesis requires that Riothamus was a ruler in Britain. The unlikelier this seems, the less plausible his argument becomes.

Nor is there a shred of evidence that 'Riothamus' was anything but a personal name. 'Kingly' names were widely used in the Celtic world;[32] there is nothing exceptional about Riothamus as a name of the period. And he is actually referred to by Jordanes as king Riothamus (*rex Riotimus*). Should we see this as a double title, then, 'king-very-kingly', used of someone of an entirely different name? Obviously not. Jordanes meant what he said, this was a kingly figure named Riothamus. Ashe's identification of King Arthur with this fifth-century British leader is without merit and should be set aside.

Ashe's is not the only attempt to claim Arthur for France, for there has been interest also in the possibility that Avallon, a town on the River Yonne in Burgundy, might be that Avalon to which Arthur supposedly travelled having been mortally wounded.[33] That, though, rests on the possibility that the earliest reference to Avalon in Arthur's story, as told by Geoffrey of Monmouth in the twelfth century, has something meaningful to tell us about his hero as an historical figure. Such seems utterly implausible. As already noted, the Celtic word for apple is likely to have been a common name element in Gaul, Spain and the British Isles (see above, pp. 96–7),[34] so we should not be surprised to come across names of this derivation in any region where Celtic place-names have come down to the present in any number. We have seen that the classical legend of the 'Fortunate Isles' became embedded in the Celtic world under this name (see above, p. 96), but there is no reason whatsoever to link any particular example of the name with this ancient story – and this candidate is thoroughly landlocked.

Nor do the tales celebrated at the cultural centre at Rennes which is dedicated to Arthurian literature and legend (the Centre de l'Imaginaire Arthurien) have anything to contribute to a search for his origins, centred as they are on stories which cannot be pushed back much beyond the twelfth century, many of which were only collected much later.[35]

Arthur and Gildas's *De Excidio Britanniae*

There are significant numbers of British texts written in the sub-Roman period but the vast majority are brief inscriptions on stone. These reveal something of the linguistic, religious and commemorative culture in parts of western and northern Britain but none name Arthur,[36] so they are only somewhat distantly relevant to our topic. Extended texts of the period are limited to the works of Patrick and Gildas,[37] but Patrick's belong very much to the mission to Ireland, mention neither Saxon incomers nor Arthur and seem remote from our quest. Only Gildas offers anything approaching a near-contemporary account of the sub-Roman period and the British wars against Saxon incomers. Despite the fact that he does not actually name Arthur, down the centuries committed Arthurians have repeatedly sought to interpret Gildas's work as evidence of a glorious period of British success – an 'Age of Arthur' – between the British victory at Badon and the time of writing. We must start, therefore, with Gildas (as has virtually every commentator at least from the eighth century onwards), to assess whether or not these claims stack up.

We have some letter fragments and a brief 'Penitential' (a text of monastic discipline), but *De Excidio Britanniae* (*The Ruin of Britain*) is Gildas's only complete surviving work. It consists of 110 short chapters totalling about 22,000 words. Gildas termed it a 'history of lamentation',[38] but his conception of 'history' was very different to ours. Later writers have often regarded it as a sermon,[39] in the form of an open letter written for the purpose of moral exhortation. It is heavily influenced by the Bible – indeed, it consists very largely of biblical passages which he held up as a mirror to contemporaries to reveal the causes of their difficulties and recommend remedies.[40] Although it has become conventional to divide the *De Excidio* into sections – one of which (and by far the most often read) is 'The History of Britain' (chapters 2–26) – such subheadings and divisions are not original to the text and are in some respects unhelpful. Gildas's purpose is best understood by reading the entire work, however unappetising this extended indictment of his own people may seem to a modern audience. He was urging his fellow citizens to abandon their sins, be obedient to God in all things and thereby regain His protection: 'In this letter I shall deplore rather than denounce; my style may be worthless, but my intentions are kindly. What I have to deplore with mournful complaint is a general loss of good, a heaping up of bad.'[41]

Gildas's 'historical' introduction is offered not out of any desire to write history *per se* but as a means of building an inescapable relationship between the Britons' obedience to the Lord, His treatment of them and their well-being (including their success in withstanding invaders).[42] This strategy makes Gildas's work difficult to use as an historical source, but the problems do not rest there. It is unclear who Gildas was,[43] and where he was based, if anywhere,[44] so to what part of Britain his comments particularly apply. There have been attempts to locate him in the north or North Midlands, perhaps in or around Chester,[45] but recent readings of the *De Excidio* have preferred somewhere south of the Thames, perhaps around Dorset, Devon or Wiltshire.[46] This is, though, only a matter of inference, incapable of bearing much weight.

The chronology is also debatable. Gildas's death in *c.* 570 was entered into what is generally considered a near-contemporary chronicle written at Iona.[47] His correspondence with *Vennianus* – probably the St Uinniau (Finnian) of Moville (on Strangford Lough: Map 5) who taught St Columba[48] – was mentioned in a letter written by Columbanus in the 590s,[49] which may also refer directly to the *De Excidio Britanniae*.[50] Gildas offered no dates but some of the events described can be assigned years by reference to external evidence. The latest securely dated incident is Magnus Maximus's bid for the Empire in 383–88,[51] but this is too early to provide a secure platform for dating the fifth century. The British appeal to 'Agitius thrice consul' offers a less secure but significantly later anchorage-point, but only if Gildas was actually quoting from a *bona fide* text. That he had already lamented that he had no insular writings casts some doubt on that assumption.[52] Aëtius was thrice consular in the years 446–54 but was the senior military figure in Gaul already by 430.

Any estimate of Gildas's internal chronology also needs to take account of the fact that there are significant errors of fact in his ordering of events. These are concentrated early on.[53] While such mistakes have generally been ascribed to ignorance, it has also been suggested that Gildas was influenced by Stephen's address to the Sanhedrin in the New Testament.[54] Just as Stephen adopted a cavalier approach to relative chronology,[55] so too may Gildas have disregarded the actual sequence of events in favour of an order that better suited his rhetorical purpose. In that case exploration of the internal chronology has little value prior to his grandparents' era.

It has recently been suggested that Gildas's reference to 'a very dense cloud and black night of their sin' which so looms 'over the whole island' could mean that he was writing in the aftermath of the environmental disaster that has recently been identified in *c.* 536–37 through dendro-chronology.[56] It does seem reasonable to think that Gildas would have interpreted such a phenomenon as a sign of divine displeasure and he might have been stirred thereby to circulate concerns which he had been cogitating for the last ten years, as he says.[57] But while this perhaps has some merit, it is far from conclusive,[58] for Gildas couched it in moral, not experiential, terms; the darkness and blindness of sinful man are metaphors that he used repeatedly, as in the preceding passage.[59]

Then there is the riddle of Gildas's cultural context. While his bilingual punning on personal names implies that he and his intended audience understood the Brittonic language, Michael Lapidge has argued convincingly that Gildas had the benefit of the type of Roman education that signalled an intended career in legal or civil administration.[60] His literary style invites comparison with the Romano-Gaulish writers, Sidonius and Salvian, in the second half of the fifth century,[61] and reference to *rectores* (literally 'governors') and *speculators* ('scouts') might imply some sort of Roman-style government still in being at the time of writing.[62] We do not know how long Roman governance or the traditional style of Roman education continued in Britain but it would surprise most commentators to think either was still functioning by *c.* 500 CE. That his contemporary, Maglocunus (Maelgwn, king of Gwynedd), had apparently received a similar education reinforces the point.[63] These observations might encourage the view that Gildas was educated within the fifth century, not the sixth. Additionally, there are external reasons to think the Saxon power-grab in Britain significantly earlier than it has traditionally been placed. The *Gallic Chronicle of 452* notes in an entry for 441 that: 'The British provinces have been handed over across a wide area through various catastrophes and events to the rule of the Saxons.'[64]

How precisely this fits with Gildas's account is unclear but fit it must if both are to be accepted as in some sense historical; the *Gallic Chronicle* is arguably the nearest thing we have to a contemporary witness, however distant its author was geographically.[65] And archaeology provides us with evidence of Germanic-style settlements and burials in southern and eastern Britain at least from the 420s onwards – which again needs to be factored into Gildas's narrative. The material record fits comfortably alongside a Saxon takeover of parts of southern Britain in the decades running up to c. 441. Such considerations tend to pull the De Excidio earlier.

Close dating of the De Excidio Britanniae is, therefore, problematic. The best that we can do is to say that it was written sometime between c. 500 and the mid-sixth century. A death date of c. 570 is consistent with authorship in the second quarter of the sixth century, as is often surmised,[66] but there remain reasons to think it might be earlier.[67]

Since we can have little confidence in either Gildas's sequence of events or his chronology, his is a far from reliable guide to the period prior to the epoch of his own grandparents. The De Excidio does not, therefore, offer us a very transparent commentary on the fifth century,[68] despite it being the go-to text from which later writers found themselves having to extract the story. That is its main significance here, for as we have already made plain Gildas did not actually name Arthur. This is often excused by reference to the fact that he mentioned few individuals.[69] Between his remarks concerning Magnus Maximus (in 13, 1) and the present, there are at most three: 'Agitius' (the Roman general Aëtius: 20, 1) and Ambrosius Aurelianus (25, 3) are comparatively uncontroversial, though the latter is not mentioned in any other near-contemporary source. More problematic is the anonymous 'proud tyrant' (superbus tyrannus: 23, 1), in modern editions.[70] Bede named this figure Vurtigernus (Vortigern),[71] the manuscript of the De Excidio Britanniae in Cambridge University Library has this same name, and the spelling is reconcilable with a fifth- or sixth-century date.[72] There is some merit therefore in Kenneth Jackson's view that Gildas may originally have included the personal name.[73]

'Agitius' was neither British nor an insular figure, and Ambrosius Aurelianus is treated as in some sense 'Roman' by Gildas, albeit he was active in Britain. Only Vortigern, whose name does not certainly even appear, is fully representative of the British 'homeland' (patria). In line with the author's overall prejudices, it is Vortigern alone of these three who is condemned (he is labelled 'blind' and 'stupid' and compared to Pharaoh who opposed the Israelite Exodus). Had a militarily successful Arthur appeared, therefore, Gildas might have presented him too as in some sense Roman, rather than British.

Attempts to locate Arthur in the De Excidio generally start from the assumption that he was responsible for the only British victory against the

Saxons that Gildas names, the 'siege of the Badonic mountain' (*obsessio Badonici montis*),[74] since this was the final battle allotted to Arthur in the ninth-century *Historia Brittonum*.[75] This is, though, rather to put the cart before the horse, for the *Historia* cannot be considered a reliable guide to the *De Excidio* (see below, pp. 212–15), so should not be allowed to influence our interpretation of this passage in the earlier work. That the *Historia* gave responsibility for Badon to a figure who Gildas does not mention has historical value only if we can be reasonably confident that its author was drawing on some other near-contemporary source which provided this information. However, he almost certainly was not. If we reject the *Historia* as an aid, then Arthur remains absent.

Division of the *De Excidio Britanniae* into chapters and paragraphs in modern editions has rather separated Badon from the one leader against the Saxons whom Gildas does both credit with victory and name – Ambrosius Aurelianus. However, this structure is absent from the earliest surviving manuscript, written *c.* 1000.[76] Although this was damaged in the fire that swept through Sir Robert Cotton's library in 1731, the relevant page remains legible.[77] The passage in which mount Badon occurs translates as follows:

> Their leader was Ambrosius Aurelianus, a gentleman who, perhaps alone of the Romans, had survived the shock of this notable storm [i.e. the Saxon rebellion]: certainly his parents, who had worn the purple, were slain in it. His descendants in our day have become greatly inferior to their grandfather's excellence. Under him our people regained their strength, and challenged the victors [the Saxons] to battle. The Lord assented, and the battle went their way. From that time now the citizens [Britons], now the enemy [Saxons], were victorious as in that people [the Britons] the Lord could make trial, as He is wont to do, of His latter-day Israel to see whether it loves Him or not. This lasted right up until the year of the siege of the Badonic mountain and almost the most recent slaughter of the convicts [Saxons], and certainly not the least. That was the year of my birth; as I know, one month of the forty-fourth year since then has already passed.[78]

Both Oliver Padel and Michael Wood point out that this passage is consistent with the victory at Badon having been achieved by Ambrosius Aurelianus, leaving no obvious role for another leader.[79] The point is well made, but Gildas credits Ambrosius Aurelianus with having led the Britons to victory in open conflict (the word he uses is *proelium*). Badon in contrast was a siege; there seems little need for the principal British general to have been present here, particularly if the Britons were the defenders. Given Gildas's lurid portrayal of 'all the major towns' being sacked by the Saxons,[80] several sieges may have occurred simultaneously and no leader could be in every place that was threatened. Successful resistance might easily be construed as a significant victory, particularly in that locality. It is not a question, therefore, of Ambrosius Aurelianus or Arthur commanding at Badon, for there are numerous other possibilities. But that Arthur is absent from Gildas's account must place in doubt each and every reconstruction of his deeds that relies upon his playing a leading role in this 'war of the Saxon federates'.[81]

We should also note that most modern interpretations of this passage are highly problematic. A consensus has arisen that Badon was the culminating British victory over the Saxons that determined the outcome of the war, as in the following quotations:

> The great battle of Mount Badon in the year of Gildas' own birth, which was a resounding victory over the Saxons, so much so that the land had peace ever since up to the time of writing ...
>
> Badon was the 'final victory of the fatherland' ... The British ... stood alone in Europe, the only remaining corner of the western Roman world where a native power withstood the all-conquering Germans.
>
> At Mount Badon Arthur fought and won a decisive battle that stopped the Saxon incursions for forty-four years, said Saint Gildas ...
>
> The last of these battles, which clearly was intended as Badon Hill, mentioned by Gildas, had the effect of entirely conquering the Saxons ...
>
> The evidence points to him [Arthur] being a highly effective commander who dealt the Anglo-Saxons a major shock at the Battle of Badon in perhaps 509 AD.[82]

But this is not what Gildas says, nor even what he implies.[83] He is our only near-contemporary witness, so his account carries enormous weight. We must be very mindful of the theory of history running through this work, that the experiences of the Britons were governed not by historical processes of the type that we might seek to apply but solely by the shifting nature of their relationship as a latter-day people of Israel with their God. Setbacks stem from British disobedience and the divine punishment that followed, achievements from God rewarding His loving people.

The 'war of the Saxon federates' has its roots in the events referred to in chapter 23, in which Gildas condemns the hiring of Saxons by the British council and 'proud tyrant' as an act of 'desperate and crass stupidity'. The original contingent was reinforced by new arrivals, uninvited and more numerous than the first. 'In just punishment for the guilt [*scelera*]' of the Britons, these Saxons then rebelled (as agents of God, by implication), devastated 'the whole surface of the island' and sacked all the cities.[84] Some Britons were killed, others enslaved; some crossed to 'lands beyond the sea' (almost certainly Armorica); others held out. But once the Saxons had withdrawn 'home',[85] so, by implication, divine chastisement was at an end, 'God gave strength to these survivors'; led by Ambrosius Aurelianus, they 'challenged the victors to battle. The Lord assented, and the battle went their way'.[86]

There followed a period of warfare characterised by both victories and defeats, as – in Gildas's version – God weighed His people in the balance 'to see whether it loves him or not'. This 'mixed' phase of the war came to an end in the year in which the siege of mount Badon occurred. Badon was 'almost the most recent slaughter' inflicted on the Saxons,[87] so there was at least one more British victory thereafter; clearly, Badon did not end the war.

Gildas may have been alluding to this same siege in his contents list (chapter 2) when he referred to *postrema patriae victoria, quae temporibus nostris dei nutu donata est.* Winterbottom's translation reads: 'the final victory of our country that has been granted to our times by the will of God'.[88] This is, though, unnecessarily ambiguous; a better rendering is 'the last victory of our country that has been granted in our times by the will of God' – the meaning of which is subtly different (though still not entirely accurate if we take note of the 'almost' of chapter 26).

How important a victory was Badon? Obviously, it was sufficiently memorable for Gildas to have considered it an effective means of recalling the year for his audience. To that extent, it was notable. However, the nature of his text required that Gildas was writing for a very small audience that shared his Christian values and was both sufficiently well educated and biblically literate to appreciate it. The interest taken in his 'Penitential' in those under a monastic vow implies that he was writing for some sort of Christian community or proto-monastery. It may well be these brethren who are indicated by the *pauci et valde pauci* – 'few and exceedingly few' – who he exempted from the sins of his own generation in the present.[89] Badon may only have been memorable locally, therefore, much as 'the year of the great flood' of 2004 is in and around Boscastle (Cornwall), but not elsewhere.

Additionally, the year of Badon was Gildas's birth-year and it may well have been this personal milestone that encouraged him to bring the period of mixed fortunes to a close at this point. Had Gildas been born a year earlier, say, would he have opted for that instead so named a different conflict? We do not know but it seems quite possible. Success at Badon was not treated by Gildas as equivalent rhetorically to the victory won by Ambrosius Aurelianus at the start of the war. Rather, its function in Gildas's account is to break up the past into chunks meaningful in terms of the Britons' relationship with God. God's testing His people ended in the year of Badon, giving way to a different period. We should be wary, therefore, of investing Badon with over-much military or political significance. Its prominence in later histories derives in part from its being the only event of this war that was recorded by name by a near-contemporary, in part to its prominence in the *Historia Brittonum*, wherein it is Arthur's final and greatest victory.

What happened after Badon? If God was weighing up His people in this war, as Gildas believed, then His judgement could in theory have gone either way. British victory would mean that the Britons had shown suffi-cient love of the Lord, defeat that they had not. Unfortunately for us, Gildas was not explicit as to how the war ended – he did not need to be, of course, for his audience were perfectly well aware of what had happened across the previous forty-four years. But the year marked by Badon was the point at which Gildas broke off his discourse on the moral and spiritual lessons of the past and shifted from the past tense to the present. He was treating the period that began in that year, therefore, as a single episode in God's rela-tionship with His British people. It was his own generation that he held responsible for everything going wrong:

> when they strayed from the right track God did not spare a people that was peculiarly His own among all nations [i.e. Israel] ... What then will he do with this great black blot on our generation? It has heinous and appalling sins in common with all the wickedness of the world; but beyond that it has as though inborn in it a load of ignorance and folly that cannot be erased or avoided.[90]

Given Gildas's birth in the year of Badon, 'our generation' began then. He considered that those who had experienced the war 'kept to their own stations' thereafter (this equates with his childhood); once the next genera-tion took over, the situation worsened. There was external peace (i.e. with the Saxons) but civil war.[91] Clearly, Gildas considered his contemporaries less virtuous than those whom God had tested in the see-sawing conflicts that ended in the year of Badon.[92] Even the descendants of the noble Ambrosius Aurelianus 'have become greatly inferior to their grandfather's excellence'.[93] Looking back, he referred to 'so desperate a destruction of the island' – the Saxon revolt – 'and unhoped-for mention of assistance',[94] the divine aid which enabled too-little-deserving Britons to win some victories. But there had been a steep falling-away from the qualities which had encouraged a merciful God to weigh-up the previous generation's love for Him and reward them with a degree of success: 'All the controls of truth and justice have been shaken and overthrown, leaving no trace, not even a memory, among the orders I have mentioned.'[95]

Gildas saw his own time as a *lugubris divortio barbarorum* – literally 'a grief-inducing divorce of the barbarians', consequent upon *scelera nostra* – 'our sins'.[96] Winterbottom's translation reads 'the unhappy partition with the barbarians', implying some sort of agreement dividing Britain between the Britons and Saxons. Although this has been widely adopted it does not convey the meaning of the Latin very satisfactorily.[97] To grasp Gildas's intention here we need to recall imagery that he used at the start of his work, depicting Britain as 'a chosen bride arrayed in a variety of jewellery'.[98] The marriage to which he was alluding is the rhetorical one of Britain to the British people, to be understood very much in Old Testament terms.[99] The 'divorce' refers metaphorically to the separation of the Britons from Britain as if a groom from his bride. The Saxons were the agents of this calamity but British sin its cause. That this was Gildas's meaning is made clear by the remainder of this passage, for he lamented the inaccessibility of the graves of Christian martyrs at St Albans and Caerleon to 'our citizens';[100] Britons could not travel freely across substantial parts of southern Britain at the time of writing, because their sins against God had brought the Saxons down upon them.

From Gildas's perspective, it was the immorality of his own age group that characterised the period since the year of Badon. That was both the end-point of the period characterised by victories and defeats and the beginning of 'the ignorance and folly' staining his own generation.[101] Gildas's is explicitly a pastoral message aimed at his own fellow countrymen and centred on their morality and obedience to God, his purpose to urge them to mend their ways. His work is, as he said, a 'complaint on the evils of the age'.[102] But, taking his own theory of history as our guide, his condemnation of the sins of his own peer-group can only mean that God was angry with His people throughout Gildas's lifetime, using the Saxons as His agents (as He had used Israel's enemies to chastise His people for their evil ways).

The inference must be that the war was lost around the time of Badon (though, obviously, not as a direct result of the siege), with control over the British Lowlands passing to the Saxons either then or soon after. It may be that Germanic warriors took over widely scattered territories (as sometimes occurred on the Continent), rather than settling behind (i.e. east of) some specific boundary line. Dispersal of the victorious barbarians would have given them control of many different regions of lowland Britain, so making them a widespread threat to passage along the roads, as Gildas implies. It may also help explain the multiplicity of small-scale kingships that characterised early England.[103]

Moving on to his specific criticisms, Gildas paid particular attention to the British kings of his own times, all of whom he pilloried for their sins. He had five individuals in his sights,[104] Constantine, Aurelius Caninus, Vortipor, Cuneglasus, and the greatest of them, Maglocunus, whom he denounced at greater length. All seem to have been based in western Britain. The first ruled Damnonia, which should almost certainly be understood as Dumnonia, modern-day Devon and Cornwall.[105] Aurelius Caninus is difficult to place.[106] The third was 'the tyrant of the Demetae', in south-west Wales (Map 5). Maglocunus is the king of Gwynedd. It is Cuneglasus, though, who has attracted most interest from Arthurians. Gildas referred to him as: 'bear, rider upon many and driver of the chariot of the Bear's Den ... in the Latin tongue "tawny butcher".[107]

As Jackson pointed out, Gildas was not here translating literally, for in Old Welsh Cuneglasus means 'Grey/Tawny Hound'. His words are pejorative, therefore.[108] Interest has been kindled by the two references to a bear in this passage, since *arth* in Old Welsh means precisely that. However, 'Bear's Den' (*receptaculum ursi*) is best read as a play on the name Dineirth, 'Bear's Fortress', which occurs in both Ceredigion and Rhos (Map 5).[109] The reference to a bear at the start of the line should be understood not as an obscure allusion to the name Arthur,[110] or some personal title,[111] but as part of an extended biblical metaphor that applies to all these kings. Gildas termed Constantine the 'whelp of a filthy lioness', Aurelius Caninus a 'lion-whelp', Vortipor 'like a leopard', Cuneglasus 'a bear', and Maglocunus 'a dragon'. There are two passages in the Bible which this recalls: Daniel's four monstrous animals, of which the second was a bear (Daniel, 7, 1–8), and the Revelation of St John, 13, 2, which describes a dragon with the features of a leopard, a bear and a lion.[112] Gildas was deploying a complex biblical metaphor, therefore, as part of his negative treatment of the British rulers of the present, confident that his audience

5 Britain after Rome: a backdrop to the search for King Arthur.

was sufficiently versed in the Bible to grasp the allusion. This has absolutely nothing to do with Arthur.

In conclusion, therefore, we should recognise that Gildas's text is difficult to pin down as regards both time and space and its purpose makes it ill-suited to serve as a framework for the history of his times. His purpose was rather to persuade his fellow countrymen to mend their ways, return to the Lord and thereby regain His protection. The war between the Britons and their erstwhile Saxon mercenaries is only included as one strand within his moral crusade and its treatment is opaque. Gildas's 'history' breaks off in the year of his own birth, just over forty-three years before the present, but there can be no causal link between British victory at mount Badon and the current peace with the Saxons. Rather, Badon marks what Gildas considered the year in which the war turned, bringing to an end a period of mixed fortunes. The 'divorce' of the present time, by implication of the Britons from their island bride, can only mean that the war went badly. The dangers inherent in travelling to named Christian cult-sites confirms that the enemy controlled the roads over extensive territories. There is reference to the Church paying tribute in the Preface,[113] beside the general sense of British loss and diminution. A great deal was ceded to the Saxons, therefore, as the price of peace.

There is no space in Gildas's account for a lengthy period characterised by British success between Badon and authorship of the De Excidio Britanniae – no space for an 'Age of Arthur' in other words. Gildas did not set out the events of this period, focusing exclusively on the sins of the Britons that conditioned them; he could safely assume that his audience knew what had happened and, in any case, writing contemporary history was not his purpose. It is our misfortune that we do not share their knowledge, but that is no excuse for highly imaginative reconstructions which distort what little we can extract from the De Excidio.

Finally, let us make the key points once more, for they are vital: Arthur is neither named in the De Excidio nor alluded to; nor is there any need for a successful British war-leader other than Ambrosius Aurelianus. Badon was not a great victory that brought the war to an end; it merely marked the year of the closure of a period of mixed fortunes in the war, opening a present epoch coincident with Gildas's own life-span. It was the Saxons who won the war and who were dominant in Britain at the time of writing. The reference to a bear in connection with Cuneglasus forms part of a wider biblical analogy; this has nothing to do with Arthur. Gildas's parsimony when it comes to personal names and events has often been considered a factor capable of lessening the significance of Arthur's omission, and arguments *ex silencio* are necessarily weak. However, that is to invert the logic of history – in order to make the case for an historical Arthur and a period of British victory we need near-contemporary testimony of some kind. Gildas was best placed to offer us that. He did not. That matters.

Y Gododdin

What may be Arthur's earliest appearance in an insular text comes in a collection of eulogistic stanzas of early Welsh poetry collectively known as *Y Gododdin*.[114] This survives in a manuscript written in the second half of the thirteenth century, the *Book of Aneirin*, now in Cardiff Central Library. There are two hands, termed A and B, each of which was responsible for one of the two versions recorded. Hand A wrote eighty-eight stanzas, or verses, plus four *gorchanau* (longer poems dedicated to one of the heroes), copying from a recently modernised text. Hand B was responsible for two sections totalling forty-two verses, copying from two texts, B1 and B2. The section which is today designated B2 – the last nineteen verses – derived from an earlier source than the remainder, dating most probably to the eighth, ninth or tenth centuries.[115]

The *Historia Brittonum* names Aneirin as one of several British poets active in the sixth century, implying that he was a contemporary of King Ida of the Bernicians.[116] Bede dates Ida's reign to 547–59.[117] Aneirin's floruit has traditionally therefore been placed in the mid- to late sixth century. Scholars today date *Y Gododdin* within the period *c.* 540–640,[118] and the attack on Catterick by British warriors from Edinburgh which frames this work to the mid- to late sixth century.[119]

Y Gododdin has been described as 'intricate, witty, skilful and exciting',[120] but it is not a simple text to interpret. Internal evidence suggests that the different versions had contrasting textual histories, reaching the *Book of Aneirin* by routes which we can only conjecture.[121] One verse in A and B1 celebrates the death in battle of Domnall Brecc, king of Dál Riata, in 642, at the hands of warriors serving the lord of Dumbarton Rock, suggesting that these texts derive from one that was added to in the Clyde valley in the mid-seventh century (Map 5). That Aneirin wrote some stanzas earlier is entirely possible,[122] but there remains some scepticism regarding composition of even an archetype before the ninth century.[123] Certainly, the grouping of five British poets as if contemporaries in the *Historia Brittonum* suggests systematisation, so should not necessarily be taken at face value.[124] The emergence in the mid-sixth century of Anglian Bernicia (centred on modern-day Northumberland and County Durham) between Edinburgh and Catterick may mean that we should be looking to an earlier date for the main events on which this poetry is based.[125]

Certainly there is scope to imagine *Y Gododdin* circulating in oral or written form in the 'Northern British Heroic Age', then migrating to Wales in the central Middle Ages, before the end of spoken British (Cumbric) in the north.[126] But even if we accept an archaic original at the core of this corpus, some stanzas identify as later. For example, the so-called 'Reciter's Preface' was almost certainly an addition,[127] there is a cradle song (A87), and a stray verse from the Welsh Llywarch Hen cycle (A44) is likely to have been added in Wales. While several such examples can be picked out and quarantined from potentially original content, it is unclear how many other verses might also be secondary, or contain later material.

The main means of testing the authenticity of any particular verse is the presence or absence of early linguistic and stylistic features. However, no passage is likely to have been entirely unaltered since the sixth century. This makes it very difficult to judge whether or not any one passage is 'authentic', and even what 'authentic' actually means in this context.[128] There is, though, some circumstantial evidence linking the poem to the sixth and seventh centuries, such as the drinking of wine from the glass vessels evidenced in the archaeology of this period but not much later.[129]

We can have most confidence in the authenticity of verses which are common to both the A and B versions, but of the forty-two verses in the B text only fourteen have close variants in A (with five additional partial variants). Of those verses for which only one version is available, the nine present in B2 exhibit the earliest linguistic features so have a claim to have been circulating in their present form by about the ninth century.

Only one stanza makes a passing reference to Arthur, and that occurs only in the B2 text:

> More than three hundred of the finest were slain.
> He struck down at both the centre and the extremities.
> The most generous man was splendid before the host.
> From the herd, he would distribute horses in winter.
> He used to bring black crows down in front of the wall
> Of the fortified town – though he was not Arthur –
> among men mighty in deeds
> in front of the barrier of alder wood – Gorddur.[130]

Should we consider Arthur's appearance here to belong to an archaic common ancestor of the two versions dating from the sixth century? Had this stanza been present in both the A and B versions, then we might have been justified in a degree of confidence that it comes from an early stratum, at least. Without that, some scholars have suggested that Arthur's presence could derive from a late interpolation.[131] However, this stanza is part of the earliest version to survive, and it is probably significant that the four lines of the second half of the stanza all rhyme in the original Old Welsh. Either, therefore, there has been a rewrite of all four lines or Arthur's name is original. Along with various stylistic features which are paralleled in what seem to be other 'early' verses,[132] these factors have encouraged John Koch to judge this part of the archetype.[133] Clearly, there can be no certainty either way, but there is a reasonable possibility that this mention in *Y Gododdin* is our earliest surviving reference in Welsh literature to Arthur.

It is worth stressing, though, that Arthur's appearance here is somewhat odd. Oliver Padel has remarked that Arthur appears in *Y Gododdin* 'only not to appear',[134] in the sense that he is not the subject of one of these eulogies but a figure brought in from outside for purposes of comparison. The allusion is so fleeting that it is not even clear whether or not this Arthur should be understood as human. Looking across *Y Gododdin*, it must be stressed that such parallels are so rare that it is difficult to find examples that might help us to understand better what Arthur's appearance here means. Richard Barber suggested that the poet could have been making a comparison with the Scottish prince Artúr of Dál Riata (see below, pp. 170–1),[135] who died in battle *c.* 596 fighting the Miathi (a southern Pictish people known from classical sources as the Maeatae, whose name survives in place-names near Stirling). The story of this battle is likely to have been familiar to a court writer of the period at Edinburgh. But there is a difficulty here, for as already noted stanza B1.1/A78 celebrates the defeat and beheading of Artúr's nephew Domnall Brecc, the king of Dál Riata, in 642. Such differences of attitude towards the Scottish dynasty between the A/B1 and B2 versions of *Y Gododdin* only seem comprehensible if they were already independent of one another by the 640s, when the A/B1 tradition was attracting fresh material in Strathclyde. Certainly, Edinburgh is unlikely to have been a British stronghold by this date, having probably already fallen to the Bernicians,[136] so the variants of *Y Gododdin* must all descend from versions that were by this date circulating outside its place of original composition. That the Arthur of *Y Gododdin* should be equated with the Dál Riatan Prince Artúr therefore has the advantages of both near-contemporaneity and proximity, but difficulties in establishing the textual histories of different versions must in the last resort leave us short of any real confidence in this identification, for the B2 text also reveals links to Dumbarton, and to the A text in particular.[137] Such observations leave us very unsure just who this Arthur might have been.

There are considerable difficulties, therefore, in the way of under-standing Arthur's presence in this Old Welsh verse. Just how early the corpus originated remains an issue. Whether or not the Gorddur stanza quoted above should be included in the 'original' work is disputed (though the case looks stronger now than two decades ago). While his appearance therein has encouraged some to localise King Arthur in the borderlands of England and Scotland,[138] others have rejected this conclusion,[139] and there seems little hope of a resolution. All that we can say for certain is that an Arthur's reputation as a ferocious warrior was well enough established at some point in time floating between at earliest the sixth century and at latest the tenth for a poet to incorporate the name in the earliest of our surviving versions of *Y Gododdin* without further explanation. But there need be no connection between this Arthur and the hero whose deeds were lauded in Wales.

'The Lament for Cynddylan' (*Marwnad Cynddylan*)

It has been suggested that Arthur plays a similar role in another Welsh elegy, 'The Lament for Cynddylan' (*Marwnad Cynddylan*), celebrating the life of Cynddylan, a seventh-century chieftain associated with Shropshire and neighbouring parts of Wales. This is a poem of seventy lines in nine verses,[140] which addresses the rulers of Gwynedd and laments the death in battle of the poet's erstwhile patron. Cynddylan probably died when the Mercian army was destroyed at the battle of Winwæd in 655 (though that is nowhere explicit),[141] and perhaps earlier fought alongside Penda at the battle of Cogwy (Bede's Maserfelth, 642).[142]

Verse 7 (lines 42 to 51) translates thus:

The enormity of the sword fighting! Do you see this?
My heart burns like a firebrand.
I enjoyed the wealth of their men and their wives. It seemed that they
   could never
pay off my poet's reward! I used to have brothers. It was better when
   they were

the young whelps of great (?)Arthur, the mighty citadel.
For the sake of Caerlwytgoed they brought about
    gore under crows with a bloody onrush.
Lime-washed shields used to break in front of the fair sons of the
    Cyndrwynyn.
I shall lament until I shall be in the land of the graveyard
the burial of Cynddylan, famous among chieftains.[143]

Like *Y Gododdin*, though, this is not a simple text to interpret. John Koch
favours composition soon after 655 and the relationship referred to between
the poet and the dead Cynddylan is certainly consistent with such a date.
However, others have considered it later. There is, therefore, some uncertainty as to when this poem can be called as a witness to Arthur's fame.
Additionally, it is not certain that the poet named Arthur at all, for the
manuscript has *artir* (line 46 reads *canawon artir wras dinas degyn*). Koch
defends the emendation to *artur* on the grounds that *artir* makes no sense
and a name or epithet is required after 'whelps',[144] but Jenny Rowland rejects
this, translating the phrase as '?strong-handed whelps'.[145] But even accepting
the emendation does not entirely clarify the issue: 'Arthur' was the name-
form used consistently in early Welsh texts, such as *Y Gododdin*, *Culhwch
and Olwen* and *Preiddeu Annwn*; Artur occurs only in Irish (as Artúr, Artúir),
or in later works written in French.[146]

Although scholarly opinion has generally favoured the emendation to
Arthur,[147] there can be no certainty that the author of the 'Lament for
Cynddylan' intended this. This poem need, therefore, have no bearing on
the origins of Arthur. It must be set aside as unreliable and potentially
misleading.

Princely Arthurs around the Irish Sea

It has long been recognised that the name Arthur (or the Old Irish forms
Artúr, Artúir) was in use on both sides of the Irish Sea in the late sixth and
seventh centuries, and it has often been suggested that this pattern of
naming may point to an important figure bearing this name one or two
generations earlier. Later use of the name, on this reasoning, could be a
significant strand of evidence pointing back to a Dark Age Arthur.[148]

We have already noted one of these figures, Artúr, son of the powerful
Áedán, king of Dál Riata in and around Argyll and the territories of the
same name in Ulster from *c.* 574 up to *c.* 608. Artúr is named in the

Clonmacnoise Chronicle in an entry for *c.* 596 and as Arturius in Adomnán's *Life of Columba*, where he is said to have died in battle against the Miathi – near neighbours of the Gododdin.[149] He predeceased his father, as Columba had supposedly foretold, so never became king. Artúr's British-originating name presumably stems from this Gaelic-speaking royal family having intermarried with British dynasties.[150] A link with the Cambro-Irish rulers of 'Brecknock' has been suggested,[151] but the surviving genealogy for this family is unhistorical and there seems little advantage in allying with such a distant and minor Welsh dynasty. More likely is a marriage contracted with one of the British royal families of what is now central and southern Scotland, where Áedán was attempting to expand his influence. The name Arthur recurs in the Dál Riatan royal family in the next generation,[152] alongside two other Welsh names (Morgand = Morcant; Rígullón = Rhiwallon[153]), again suggesting links with the 'Northern British Heroic Age'. That *Art-* was a well-established name element in Old Gaelic perhaps facilitated the Irish adoption of Artúr (and similar).[154]

Another Arthur of the period was the son of Peter (Arthur map Petr) in the Harleian genealogy of the kings of Dyfed (earlier Demetia), in southwest Wales.[155] This lineage was composed in its surviving form no earlier than the mid-tenth century, but this section is also found in an Irish text, *The Expulsion of the Déisi*, written most probably *c.* 800.[156] Assuming generations averaging twenty-five years and working back from Owain (Ovein), who came to the throne in the mid-tenth century and was his descendant in the thirteenth generation, this Arthur would seem to belong late in the sixth or the first half of the seventh century.[157]

There are other occurrences of the name at about the same date. 'Artúr, son of Bicoir the Briton' is named in the *Annals of Tigernach* for 625 as the man who killed Mongán, son of the powerful Fiachnae mac Báetáin, king of the Ulaid in north-east Ireland (though this is far from being a contemporary source). One of the signatories of Adomnán's 'Law of the Innocents' in 697 at Birr was Feradoch, grandson of Artúr,[158] perhaps one of the Dál Riatan Arthurs mentioned above.[159] Further examples of the name are known from Leinster (immediately west and south of Dublin), initially within the Uí Máil dynasty, and then the Uí Muiredag as they in turn secured dominance in this region. The latest of these dates to the mid-eleventh century.[160]

Ann Dooley may well be right in her view that Irish use of the name spread via dynastic alliances, initially from 'British' Britain to Argyll and Ulster and then south to Leinster and the valley of the Liffey. An Artúir later appeared in that same vicinity in *Tales of the Elders of Ireland* (*Acallam na Senórach*). This was composed early in the fourteenth century but was in part based on earlier poems of uncertain date, one of which seems to underlie this episode.[161] This Artúir is said to be a son of Benne Brit (a British ally of the Irish saga figure Mac Con in a ninth-century tale[162]) and a member of Fionn's company who absconds with three of his chief's hounds to Wales from Howth at the mouth of the Liffey. Fionn's men pursue him, kill his men, seize his horses and bring them and Artúir back to Fionn (it was acquisition of the horses that supposedly triggered this story's inclusion). That Artúir is here characterised by little other than his Britishness implies an awareness in Ireland that this was a British name.

None of these figures look even remotely like the battle-leader who features in the *Historia Brittonum*, from whom the later Arthurian tradition stems. In particular, none have any connection with conflicts between British and Saxon forces, with which the *Historia*'s Arthur is inextricably linked.[163] Nor, collectively, need they require, or even imply, that there had been an earlier 'great man' after whom they were all named. All that these Arthurs reveal is that the name bank in use around the Irish Sea during this period included this name. How and why it was used is unclear but it was far from unusual, for there were other names of ultimately Roman (and Greek) origin in western Britain in this period, some of which are evidenced in the same genealogies. These princely names do not, therefore, offer us meaningful evidence for a 'real' King Arthur in Britain *c.* 500.

Bede and the Britons

Bede does not, of course, name Arthur, but his *Greater Chronicle*, *c.* 725, and *Ecclesiastical History* (*Historia Ecclesiastica*), completed *c.* 731, were powerful voices in the struggle for the past in which Arthur later came to play a major role. We need not dwell on this work in detail, but it is important that we recognise the nature of Bede's contribution. Across the next few centuries his historical works were well known in Wales, as elsewhere. What Bede said mattered, particularly if you disagreed with him.

In his treatment of Britain's history before the arrival of Augustine, Bede used several continental texts but relied primarily on Gildas's *De Excidio Britanniae*, which became his major source as he moved into the late Roman period.[164] Bede was, however, on the opposite side of the argument regarding which was God's people in Britain. He therefore 'turned' Gildas's comments in such a way as to dismiss the Britons from God's protection:

To other unspeakable crimes, which Gildas their own historian describes in doleful terms, was added this crime, that they never preached the faith to the people of the Saxons or Angles....[165]

At the start of book II, Bede asserted that the Britons' rejection of Augustine and Rome's authority was punished by God at the battle of Chester:

It is said that Augustine, the man of God, warned them [the assembled British clergy] with threats that, if they refused to accept peace with their brethren, they would have to accept war from their enemies; and if they would not preach the way of life to the nation of the English, they would one day suffer the vengeance of death at their hands. This ... came to pass in every particular as he had foretold it.[166]

In the present (731), Bede claimed that:

Though, for the most part, the Britons oppose the English through their inbred hatred, and the whole state of the Catholic Church by their incorrect Easter and their evil customs, yet being opposed by the power of God and man alike, they cannot obtain what they want in either respect.[167]

By 731, Bede could report that the Picts and Irish had been persuaded by his compatriots to accept the Roman dating of Easter, leaving only the Britons (and not even all of them) adhering to their own customs. Within Britain, therefore, the 'Roman' English could dismiss the Britons as heretics. Bede positioned them as if latter-day Jews of the New Testament, a people who would find salvation at the last but for the moment had brought down God's ire on their heads by rejecting the authority of Christ's successors, the bishops of Rome.[168]

Arthur in the British Dark Ages

Our conclusions are necessarily somewhat negative, therefore. There is no indication that Arthur originated as a god or demi-god of the pre-Roman or Roman period; the strong likelihood is that he did not. And we can safely discount each and every claim to have identified King Arthur as an historical figure who is recorded by some other name, such as the fifth-century Riothamus.

It is a fact that all later attempts to write the history of the fifth and early sixth centuries in Britain rest on the only near-contemporary account available, Gildas's *De Excidio*. That Arthur is absent from this work poses intractable problems for anyone attempting to establish him as an historical figure. And there is no wriggle-room here, for no amount of special pleading can argue that away. Nor is there any obviously 'Arthur-shaped' space in Gildas's narrative into which he could be parachuted. But our difficulties do not end there. Gildas was interested in the past primarily as an arena in which to set out his view of the relationship between his people (and their leaders particularly) and God. Though it will have been broadly accurate (as far as it went), his description of the war between the Britons and Saxons (which later becomes the backdrop to Arthur) is brief, anecdotal and opaque. It was offered primarily as evidence that it was British disobedience to the Lord that had allowed the Saxons to establish themselves in Britain, since when moral decline had steepened. The turning point in this highly contrived narrative was the year of Gildas's own birth. British success at the siege of mount Badon marks that year; Gildas abandons the past tense at this point in favour of the present. Badon must have been well-enough remembered forty years later among his intended audience to be used for this purpose, but it was neither a victory by which the war had been brought to a triumphant conclusion nor even the last British success. The peace of the present time conceded extensive power and territory to the Saxons, suggesting that the Britons lost far more than they won; this likewise occurred in or about the year of Badon. The Britons had become 'divorced' from Britain, so had lost control of much of its resources; there is no space here for an 'Age of Arthur' during which a victorious, British, emperor-like figure held back the barbarian hordes. Such portrayals of Arthur have no basis in this text; there is no other capable of making up this deficit.

Gildas's emphasis on British immorality was seized on by Bede, for whom it was the precursor to the present division inside Britain between the virtuous *Romanitas* of the English (and the Scots and Picts under English guidance), and the heretical Britons. In 731 these British 'barbarians' were in Bede's view outside God's protection and impotent rebels against both Him and the English.

We are left, therefore, with various figures named Arthur whom we can identify in Britain and Ireland from the late sixth century onwards, but none of these are known to have fought against the Saxons, let alone triumphed against them on twelve occasions (as Arthur is famously said to have done in the *Historia Brittonum*). Rather, they are very much figures of the Irish Sea world, remote from the main areas of English expansion in the fifth and early sixth centuries and all are too late to be the *Historia*'s Arthur. It seems possible that the early Welsh poem *Y Gododdín* was making reference to one of these 'Irish Sea' figures – most probably the very late sixth-century, Scottish prince, given this work's northern origins. But that is as far as we can take this reasoning; it is not very far.

There are many reasons for choosing a name but reverence for a great British Arthur who defeated Britain's invaders is unlikely to have encouraged leading Irish families on the western fringes of Britain to have adopted this one. The scatter of 'Arthur' names among predominantly Irish families *c*. 600 are not, therefore, likely to have borne witness to a famous champion of the Britons a few generations earlier. We have searched the early post-Roman centuries for Arthur but found virtually nothing capable of supporting his existence.

6

ARTHUR AND THE *HISTORIA BRITTONUM*

... the only direct statement about the wars of Arthur is a document in
Nennius that lists twelve of his battles, evidently victories, the last of
them at Badon.

— John Morris, The Age of Arthur

Beyond all other works written in the early Middle Ages, it is the *Historia
Brittonum* (*History of the Britons*) that establishes Arthur as a great
British hero. This is a work of about 8,500 words,[2] conventionally
divided into seventy-five chapters, the focus of which is the story of Britain
and the Britons from their first arrival down to the late seventh century CE.
Like the *De Excidio Britanniae* and the *Ecclesiastical History*, it is written in
Latin. Its author termed it a *sermo* ('sermon'),[3] and it certainly has a pastoral
and rhetorical content, but it has long been treated as an *historia*, despite being
somewhat disjointed and rather colourful in the material which is included.
Our treatment of it must depend on understanding why it was written, where
the author obtained his information, how he used what he had gleaned and
the ways in which he expected his work to be understood. Only then will we
be in a position to decide the extent to which the *Historia* offers us valid testimony regarding events that supposedly occurred several centuries earlier.

A 'history' in context

The route that we must take is somewhat circuitous, but the religious and
political backdrop to this work is fundamental. Perhaps the most neglected

aspect is the religious. As Bede remarked, in his day the British and Roman Churches had long been in conflict; neither side generally recognised the other as co-religionists.[4] This impasse ended c. 768, when Elfoddw, a bishop in Gwynedd, persuaded the Welsh clergy to adopt the Roman formula for dating Easter.[5] Even so, the Welsh did not go as far as to accept the authority of Rome's representatives in Britain – the archbishops of Canterbury and York, for Elfoddw was himself accorded the status of archbishop in the *Annales Cambriae* entry recording his death c. 809.[6] The Welsh shifted therefore from outright rejection of the Roman Church to a claim to equality alongside others within the Catholic family of churches. No Welsh archdiocese was ever recognised outside Wales,[7] but adoption of the Roman Paschal calendar removed the stigma of heresy, allowing Welsh kings and clergy to operate on the same religious playing field, so to speak, as their neighbours. By the mid-ninth century, senior Welsh figures were visiting Rome and at least one died there.[8] But in the decades after 868, Welsh clerics were having to work through the implications of this reconciliation with the Roman Church and rethinking the British past accordingly. The *Historia Brittonum* is our principal witness to this process.

The political context also matters. Most of the British north and the lowlands of the westerly Roman province (Britannia Prima) fell to English rule across the sixth and seventh centuries, leaving only the Clyde valley, Wales and Cornwall under indigenous rule.[9] These were comparatively minor kingships, frequently dominated by more powerful neighbours. Pressure applied by Offa, king of Mercia (757–96), may well have been a factor in the Welsh acceptance of Roman Easter Tables. Certainly, he exerted considerable influence in the west, his forces campaigned against various Welsh kingdoms,[10] and he is credited with constructing a great dyke – Offa's Dyke – along his border with Powys.[11] King Caradog of Gwynedd was 'murdered among the Saxons' in 798;[12] then between 813 and 822 Mercian armies pushed still deeper into Wales, attacking Dyfed, sacking Degannwy and overrunning Powys.[13] Wales was close to being taken over, therefore, by the Mercians.[14] Gwynedd's resistance was undermined by dynastic infighting; one contender, Cynan ap Rhodri, died c. 816, his rival, Hywel ap Caradog, c. 825.[15] At this point, though, the Mercians also fell victim to internal divisions,[16] their English clients threw off their hegemony and westward expansion collapsed.

On Anglesey, Merfyn Frych ('Merfyn the Freckled') took the throne c. 825. He was not a member of the royal family by male descent but (probably) Cynan's son-in-law. Welsh tradition traces him to Manaw – the Isle of

Man.[17] In England, King Ecgberht of the West Saxons profited most from
Mercia's difficulties, extending his oversight initially to the small Anglo-
Saxon kingdoms of the South East and East Anglia, then Mercia itself in
829 and even Northumbria later that year. A chronicler writing in Alfred's
reign claimed that in 830 he 'led the army among the Welsh, and reduced
them to humble submission'.[18] Merfyn will almost certainly have had to
accept West Saxon overlordship at this juncture. These were dramatic
events. Wessex and its rulers go unmentioned in the *Historia Brittonum*,
perhaps so as to avoid giving offence. It refers instead to the iniquities of
Kentish Saxons, then the Mercians, finally the Northumbrians.

In practice, Ecgberht's hegemony was short-lived and Mercian kingship
was quickly restored but English oversight west of Offa's Dyke fell away as
the Mercians and West Saxons found themselves under attack by the
Vikings. But the *Historia Brittonum* dates to Merfyn's fourth regnal year,
829–30,[19] just as West Saxon power peaked. It seems to have been written in
haste and kept intentionally brief,[20] so was probably not a considered work
with a lengthy gestation. It should be viewed, therefore, as part of the immediate, north Welsh reaction to the sudden advent of West Saxon overlordship. When reading the *Historia* we need to be mindful of the political and
religious backdrop and the sense of a work that belonged to a particular
moment in history.

Establishing the text

We need also to recognise that the *Historia Brittonum* is a difficult work to
pin down, for it was something of a 'living' text across the next few centuries and repeatedly altered. There are nine different recensions in Latin,
with considerable variability even within each of these textual 'families',[21]
plus a Gaelic translation with its own peculiarities.[22] Four different authors
were credited with composition in the different recensions, only one of
whom – Nennius (Ninnius, perhaps originally Nemniuus) – is viable
chronologically. That he is credited in the Gaelic translation confirms that
he was already named in the prologue of the 'Nennian' recension from
which it derives in the eleventh century.[23] The lack of a prologue in every
other recension led David Dumville to dismiss this as a late addition,[24] but
a case for its inclusion in the archetype was made by P.J.C. Field,[25] which has
now been further elaborated by Ben Guy. Their proposal that there
is better reason for its omission from other recensions than for its addition
to just one carries some weight.[26] Nennius's authorship should once again

be accepted as a possibility, therefore, albeit very cautiously; there can be no certainty either way.

Substantial differences between the recensions would matter little if we had the original, but that is sadly lost. The best and most complete of the early versions is that in the British Library, copied *c.* 1100.[27] The Vatican recension stems from a copy made in England *c.* 944, when Wales was subject to England's kings, but this was heavily edited and numerous passages omitted.[28] Another copy of *c.* 900, kept at Chartres until its destruction during the Second World War,[29] broke off mid-sentence part-way through chapter 37 and seems only to have ever comprised excerpts.[30] While passages present in all three have the best claim to represent the archetype, opportunities for comparison are limited, particularly from the point where the Chartres manuscript ended.

Today most readers of the *Historia* use John Morris's handy edition, published posthumously in 1980, but this is in many respects inadequate, containing several textual errors and numerous passages drawn from late recensions, as established by Mommsen in his highly confusing apparatus.[31] Unfortunately, Morris's efforts to differentiate the additions are neither consistent nor particularly effective, resulting in a composite version that is very far from the original. When reading his edition we should bear in mind that the Harleian manuscript lacks the passages marked by daggers or a change of type-face (comprising almost half his text); there are un-marked changes besides.

But our problems go still deeper. The Harleian manuscript contains eight different works within which the *Historia* with its 'appendices' constitute the fourth. Sixty-six chapters of the *Historia* are followed by a collection of thirty-two British genealogies,[32] the *Annales Cambriae* (*Welsh Annals*), a list of twenty-eight *Civitates Brittaniae* (*Cities of Britain*), and finally the *Mirabilia Britanniae* (*Wonders of Britain*).[33] Although the genealogies seem to derive from a north-Welsh genealogical collection, this was then fleshed out and adapted to the needs of Dyfed's court in the 950s; this is the text that we have. Likewise, the *Annales Cambriae* were compiled in their extant form in the south, no earlier than 954, over a century later than the *Historia*. On that basis, the Harleian text is best understood as copied from a manuscript written at St David's in or after the mid-tenth century.[34]

Most recensions of the *Historia* include both *Civitates* and *Mirabilia*, which have therefore been widely accepted as parts of the archetype,[35] but that supposes that the genealogies and *Annales* in the Harleian text had been interpolated into the *Historia*. That is not impossible but it is not easily explained. Furthermore, the *Civitates* and *Mirabilia* are very different in both style and purpose to the first sixty-six chapters of the *Historia*. The *Civitates* provide a gloss to the *De Excidio Britanniae* and *Historia*, offering names equal in number to the *civitates* (literally 'tribal capitals' but better here simply 'cities') that both reference numerically.[36] This is clearly not a reliable list of sub-Roman towns;[37] it is, rather, a mix of Roman-period settlements and places of more recent significance that can only have been compiled in the central Middle Ages. The strong bias in favour of southern Wales and the southern March suggests that it was authored there.[38] The Vatican recension has these names, and a further five, within the main text, implying a Welsh exemplar with that same feature.[39] There is a strong case, therefore, to consider the *Civitates* an addition to the *Historia*, not part of the archetype.

The *Mirabilia* lists *miracula* and *mirabilia* in Wales, the Marches, Scotland and Ireland (Appendix III),[40] their purpose apparently being to demonstrate that God was a positive presence in areas of the British Isles outside (or until recently outside) English control. Such 'wonders' occurred widely in the reading matter of the clergy, in the *Aeneid*,[41] the Bible, hagiographies and various tales in both Old Welsh and Irish. Again, there is a southern Welsh and southern March bias to the main section (Map 6; see below, pp. 26–9; 291–2). Stylistically, these passages are dissimilar to other sections of the *Historia*,[42] and their ordering in the Harleian manuscript, following the British genealogies and the *Annales*, militates against their being original parts of this work, which seems complete in and of itself.[43] Differences in the way that personal names are treated likewise suggest different hands, for Arthur is Latinised and declined in the *Mirabilia* but not in chapter 56.[44] And their southern bias counts against their being part of the original *Historia*, the first sixty-six chapters of which display barely any interest in Wales south of Builth and Gwerthrynion.[45] It seems reasonable to conclude, therefore, that the *Civitates* and *Mirabilia* are very unlikely to have been written by the *Historia*'s author. If it had not come south earlier, then the *Historia Brittonum* may have reached Dyfed with Merfyn's great-grandson, Hywel Dda, when he became king *c.* 904. Both the *Civitates* and *Mirabilia* are likely to have been attached to the *Historia* there and should be treated as independent texts written in southern Wales. It seems very likely that the archetype of the *Historia* was limited to the first sixty-six chapters.[46]

Style, authorship and purpose

Further difficulties result from the *Historia Brittonum*'s style, for the narrative is anecdotal, framing the past in semi-independent sections. But we should not underestimate the authorial input, for the text betrays imagination and intelligence and strives for a high degree of chronological management. The author was, as David Dumville noted, 'a synchronising historian of a type met regularly in medieval Ireland',[47] who pulled together disparate material from a variety of sources to construct a chronologically ordered narrative (a style which began with the early fifth-century Roman writer, Orosius). His synchronisms were frequently inaccurate, his sources were few, far from consistent and of poor quality, he was cavalier in his handling of some of his material and he edited some pieces so lightly that some sections still retain characteristics of their source.[48] Even so, the framework was his own and his achievement was considerable, particularly given the poverty of his materials.

We can infer a little about the author from his work. If the prologue is accepted as original (which remains a big 'if'), then he was a member of the community which had been presided over by Bishop Elfoddw until his death c. 809. In that case he is likely to have been trained at that bishop's principal centre, which Ben Guy has suggested (with even greater caution) was at Abergele.[49] Nennius is otherwise credited with having created a unique British alphabet,[50] though his responsibility is attested on only one of the four surviving manuscripts, added by a third party familiar with the *Historia*'s prologue.[51] A degree of circularity in the argument is inescapable, therefore.

Nennius's responsibility remains problematic, though I will use his name in what follows to relieve over-reliance on such phrases as 'the *Historia Brittonum*'s author'. What else can we say about him? Clearly, he was a native Welsh speaker; his Latin is 'not of much literary merit',[52] competent but far from sophisticated. He had a religious education, obviously, in a monastery or a bishop's household. He also knew a little Old Irish, though perhaps not that much (see below, p. 204). His education gave him knowledge of the Bible, *computus* and sacred number,[53] and he seems to have had an interest in chronology. He had access to a library,[54] had spoken with Irish clerics,[55] and was drawing also on 'the ancient traditions of our elders'.[56] Up to now he has generally been viewed as an incomer from southern Wales or the March,[57] but that rests on his responsibility for the *Mirabilia* and the claim therein that he had personal experience of two of its wonders.[58] If these were by a different hand, though, then that argument falls, leaving the *Historia* more likely to have been the work of a north Walian. If we accept the prologue as part of the archetype then he is perhaps best seen as connected with Elfoddw's principal church, which is likely to have been Gwynedd's leading intellectual centre at this time.

Focusing on the first sixty-six chapters of the *Historia* allows us better to see it as a work written in response to the particular circumstances facing the new king in the late 820s. Its author's purposes are clear enough even without, but the prologue brings them into focus:

> I, Nennius, disciple of the blessed Elfoddw, have been careful to write some excerpts which the ineptitude of the people of Britain threw out, because the scholars of the island of Britain had no skill nor set down any record in books. I have therefore made a heap of all that I have found both from the annals of the Romans and the chronicles of the holy fathers, and from annals of the Irish and Saxons and from our own ancient traditions. Many scholars and copyists have been tempted to write but they have somehow left the subject more obscure, whether through very frequent pestilences or the very numerous destructions wrought by war.[59]

The *Historia*'s author certainly drew on Roman, Irish and English sources, but 'frequent pestilences' and 'destructions wrought by war' point towards the *De Excidio Britanniae*, suggesting an intention to 'improve' on Gildas's version of British history. The new work provides the Britons with a prestigious place in both legendary and providential history, substantiating their claim to be a people of the Lord and the rightful possessors of the island of Britain. Post-768 British writers had the task of reintegrating their own past with the 'Roman' mainstream, even while still opposing the view implicit in Bede's works that the English were God's chosen people within Britain and the Britons heretics.

Our author was well aware of the dangers posed by the *De Excidio*. Whereas Gildas had followed the Old Testament prophets in castigating his fellow countrymen, the *Historia*'s author passes no judgement on the Britons in the present, limiting himself to the period before 700. He does admit to British sins in the early sub-Roman period but these are exclusive to just two kings, Vortigern and Benlli,[60] with heroes equivalent to the Old Testament prophets established alongside. Indeed, the author drew repeatedly on the Old Testament in framing his British past. The scene in which Emrys confronts Vortigern's magi is reminiscent of Daniel interpreting the dream of King Nebuchadnezzar;[61] Bishop Germanus replacing Benlli with Cadell recalls the prophet Samuel's support for David over King Saul,[62] and the destruction wrought on the fortresses of Benlli and Vortigern invokes the fate of Sodom and Gomorrah in Genesis, 24–5.[63]

Like Gildas, therefore, Nennius was writing British history through an Old Testament lens. It was, though, the unfathomable nature of divine will, not the sins of the Britons, that accounted for Britain's loss: 'Britain is occupied by people from outside and its citizens expelled [until] God shall aid them [the Britons].'[64] The Saxons had prevailed by weight of numbers, through wicked trickery,[65] and because it was the will of God, for: 'Who can struggle against God's will, even should he try? For God does whatsoever He wishes and He rules and He steers all nations.'[66]

This is history from a biblical mould, its racial bias embedded in its language. Bede had referred to the non-English peoples of Britain as 'barbarians' (*barbari*),[67] but the *Historia* reverts to Gildas's use of *barbari* and *ambrones* for the Saxons,[68] depicting them as 'like wolves in word and deed'.[69] Following the break with Rome, the *Historia* focuses on the arrival of the first Saxons, commenting on their descent from a son of god: 'but he is not the God of gods, amen, the God of Hosts, but one of their idols, that they worshipped.'[70] And the 'historical' narrative ends with the pagan Mercian king, Penda (died 655) depicted as: 'victorious through diabolical arts, for he was not baptised and never believed in God.'[71]

This emphasis on English paganism offered rhetorical advantages in the present. The problem of course is that Britons who had only accepted the Roman dating of Easter in 768 could be seen by their English neighbours as latecomers to the faith. In response the *Historia* emphasises the paganism, barbarity and treachery of the early Saxons, contrasted with early British conversion to Christianity, their close engagement with continental churchmen and a role in converting their neighbours. Such had some potential to adjust the ideological landscape to the benefit of the Welsh, at least in local, 'British' eyes.

The *Historia Brittonum* was, therefore, a pro-British history written to an extent at least against the English. With his eye very much on Gildas, the author revisited the British–Saxon conflicts of the sub-Roman period that were central to the 'Loss of Britain'. The focus of this section (and arguably of the whole work) is an elaborate prophesy, set out as a struggle between two 'worms,'[72] the red representing the Britons, the white the Saxons, as interpreted by the fatherless child, Emrys (Ambrosius Aurelianus).[73] The two 'worms' are asleep wrapped in a cloth. Once exposed they awake, and three times fight together. Despite long seeming to have the worst of it, at the third attempt the red drives its rival off the cloth (representing Britain) and across the underground lake (the sea). This represents successive struggles between the Britons and Saxons in which the latter long have the upper hand but the former achieve ultimate victory, against the odds. This work is imbued with the same hope for Britain's recovery, therefore, that we find elsewhere in Welsh literature of the central Middle Ages.

The *Historia* is framed chronologically. We begin with 'origins' legends, one purpose of which was to slot the Britons into the historical framework of racial pedigrees set out in the so-called 'Frankish Table of Nations', which was then circulating on the Continent. This seems to have reached Wales from Italy *c*. 800.[74] A Virgilian origin story was adopted by Frankish scholars by the seventh, when the *Chronicle of Fredegar* depicts the Franks as of both Trojan and biblical descent.[75] The *Historia* follows suit, offering a British descent from Aeneas and via a line of Old Testament figures back to Noah's son Japheth,[76] so establishing the Britons as the island's most illustrious race and first inhabitants. These origin-legends extend Gildas's historical sketch, which only begins with the Roman Conquest, providing a past of considerable rhetorical value.

Chapters 19 to 56 then flesh out the historical introduction to the *De Excidio Britanniae*, raising the moral stature of the Britons and contesting Gildas's judgement of them as weak and cowardly in the face of external attacks. Interactions between the Britons and the Romans (chapters 19 to 30) are given a positive twist. That the Britons still had their own kings under the Romans was a reasonable reading of Bede's reference to a British king Lucius in this context.[77] The Roman period was ended not by wicked rebellion, as Gildas,[78] but by the expulsion of timid Romans by warlike Britons.[79]

Then comes the reign of Vortigern (chapters 31 to 49). Gildas had equated his 'proud tyrant' with Pharaoh, responsible for the captivity of the Israelites in Egypt.[80] The *Historia* develops this image, offering a figure who was both pagan and debauched, by inference a latter-day version of both Pharaoh and Nebuchadnezzar – two of the most prominent persecutors of the Israelites in the Old Testament. Alongside this, its author deployed biblical numbering to highlight the Christian virtues of the blessed Germanus, spiritual champion of the Britons under Vortigern's rule, who is compared implicitly not only with Samuel (above) but also Moses and Christ.[81] Vortigern is given a virtuous son, Vortimer, who drives the Saxons from Britain before his death allows their return. As Vortigern's reign closes in scenes reminiscent of Sodom and Gomorrah, Germanus returns home, his work done, and we switch (in chapter 50) to Patrick's captivity in Ireland. His escape from Irish pagans parallels that of the Britons from Vortigern's dark tyranny; Patrick is a British Moses,[82] the greatest of the Old Testament prophets, who led his people out of Egypt.

Nennius was, therefore, reinterpreting Gildas's version of British history and developing a case for the Britons as modern-day Israelites, once again using Old Testament parallels. This was achieved largely through figures whom Gildas had ignored – including Germanus, Vortimer and Patrick.

Arthur in chapter 56 of the *Historia Brittonum*

Following Patrick's death,[83] Nennius introduces another new figure, Arthur, in chapter 56:

> At that time the Saxons were increasing in numbers and growing in Britain. After Hengist's death, Oct[h]a, his son, came from the northern part of Britain to the kingdom of Kent, and from him are descended the Kentish kings. Then in those days Arthur fought with the kings of the Britons against them but he himself was the commander of battles [*dux bellorum*]. The first battle was in the mouth of the river which is called Glein. The second, and third, and fourth, and fifth [were] on another river, which is called Dubglas, and it is in the region of Linnuis. The sixth battle was on a river called Bassas. The seventh battle was in the wood of Caledonia, that is Cat Coit Celidon. The eighth battle [was] in the castle of Guinnion, in which Arthur carried the image of Saint Mary the perpetual virgin on his shoulders, and on that day the pagans were put to flight, and a great slaughter was upon them through the power of our Lord Jesus Christ and the power of Saint Mary his holy virgin mother. The ninth battle was fought in the city of the legion. The tenth battle was waged on the bank of the river called Tribruit. The eleventh battle occurred on the mountain which is called Agned. The twelfth battle was on the mountain of Badon, in which there fell in one day nine hundred and sixty men from one charge [of] Arthur; and no one slew them except him alone, and in all battles he was the victor. And they [the Saxons], when they were overthrown in [these] battles, sought help from Germany, and they were reinforced repeatedly without any break, and they brought [their] kings across from Germany, so that they reigned over them in Britain even up to the time when Ida reigned, who was Eobba's son. He was the first king in Bernicia, that is in Berneich.[84]

If the author intended his audience to understand Vortigern as a British Pharaoh (as Gildas), and Patrick as Moses (this is explicit), then by implication Arthur was a British Joshua, the warrior who succeeded Moses as the Israelites' leader and led them into the Promised Land. The symbolically charged twelve battles and the reference to Arthur as *dux bellorum* will have alerted a biblically literate audience to the parallel.[85] Rejecting this biblical comparison, on the grounds that it is not sufficiently explicit,[86] is to deny the numerous and often quite subtle biblical references throughout this work. Much like both Gildas and Bede, the author of the *Historia* used various techniques by which to anchor his work to sacred text, from explicit identification with biblical characters through to the merest allusion. His purpose here was to flesh out the British–Saxon conflict alluded to by Gildas in chapter 26 of the *De Excidio*, claim victory therein and represent the Britons as a warrior-nation led by Christ's own champion. Instead of Gildas's perception of the war as God finding His people insufficiently obedient to deserve victory, the *Historia* offers a string of battles won by a God-beloved leader. The ultimate success of the English is acknowledged, for that was unavoidable, but it was the result not of victories in war (for such were never admitted) but of fresh migration. The *Historia* thereby lifts the Britons out of the moral relativism (at best) of Gildas's 'war of the Saxon federates' to establish them as a people of the Lord united in victory, in defiance of the 'Englishness' pervading so much of Britain.

Chapter 56 had, therefore, considerable rhetorical value in early ninth-century Wales, but is it in any sense factual? Our answer must depend on the nature and antiquity of any sources that the author may have accessed, for these events were already very far removed in time. In the *Historia*, Vortigern's reign begins *c.* 425 and the Saxons arrive in his fourth regnal year (428–29),[87] though elsewhere the author dated the same event even earlier, 429 years before the present (i.e. *c.* 400).[88] Arthur's battles follow the deaths of Vortigern and Hengist, the Saxon incomers' first leader and Vortigern's supposed father-in-law, and the succession of his son Oct[h]a.[89] On this internal reckoning, the events of chapter 56 should probably be assigned to the quarter century beginning in 450, so the lifetimes of the author's great-great-great-great-great-great-great-great-great-great-great-great-grandparents (give or take a generation or two either way).[90] Let us be quite clear, a work written in 829–30 cannot provide near-contemporary spoken testimony to this much earlier period. There is no room for doubt on this: Nennius did not have reliable oral sources for Arthur.

What, though, if our author was using a written source? After all, he accessed works additional to those of Gildas and Bede for chapters on either side of chapter 56. He referred to a *Book of the Blessed Germanus*;[91] he used Irish texts for Patrick's mission and had access to (and substantially rewrote) a Kentish origins story featuring Hengist.[92] He incorporated both British and Anglian genealogies and chapters 57 and 61 to 65 seem to rest on one or more text – often referred to under the generic titles 'Northern Chronicle' or 'Northern Memorandum'[93] – written (or finalised, at least) in western Northumbria post-687.[94] But the notice of Germanus returning 'to his fatherland' – *patria sua* – at the start of chapter 50 seems to be the last material taken from the *Book of Germanus* and neither the Irish Patrician texts nor what we can recover of the 'Northern Memorandum' mention Arthur.[95]

In practice, it seems reasonably clear which texts were used to frame chapter 56. The general sense of war between the Britons and Saxons leading up to Badon is reminiscent, at least, of chapters 23 to 26 of the *De Excidio*, and increases in the numbers of Saxons (at the beginning and end of the chapter) hark back particularly to 23, 4. The second sentence, noting Hengist's death and Octa's takeover, most probably derives from the Kentish origins story.[96] Material from the 'Northern Memorandum' comes only in the final lines of chapter 56, once Arthur's battle-list has ended, as Nennius sought to bridge the gap separating Gildas's narrative from the English domination characteristic of the late sixth century. Our author was, therefore, in this chapter splicing together the last 'historical' material in the *De Excidio Britanniae* up to the year of Gildas's own birth, the closure of Hengist's story in his Kentish source, and materials reaching Gwynedd from the north, with an eye on the reality of English power in the present (prompting his repeated references to mass migration).

But what of Arthur's battles, which, Badon apart, appear in none of these? Is it possible that the battle-list derives from a much earlier text? This was proposed by Heinrich Zimmer in the 1890s, who argued chapter 56 to be among the earliest passages in the *Historia Brittonum*, based on a text written no later than the 690s.[97] The suggestion that it came from an Old Welsh battle-catalogue poem appeared first in 1932 and has since gathered momentum,[98] even achieving a degree of consensus in the later twentieth century.[99] This rested initially on the assumption that the proper place to carry an emblem into battle is on the shield, not the shoulders (as in the *Historia*'s description of Arthur's eighth battle), in which case a scribe perhaps inadvertently confused Old Welsh *iscuit* ('shield') with *iscuid* ('shoulder') when translating from Welsh into Latin. But use of *humeros suos* ('his shoulders') rather confirms that our ninth-century author was comfortable in depicting this as an appropriate place to display an image, in

which case there seems little reason to suppose mistranslation.[100] The case
for a Welsh poetic source was strengthened, though, when Thomas Jones
pointed out the extent to which Arthur's battle-names rhyme.[101] All of
battles two to six end in –*as* (Dubglas, four times, and Bassas), while Welsh
names for battles seven to nine, eleven and twelve could all have ended
in –*on* (Celidon, Guinnion, Legion, Breguoin,[102] Badon).[103] Such would be
consistent with the rhyming conventions of the *awdl* meter that was used in
praise poetry celebrating sixth-century British leaders;[104] it is unlikely to be
coincidental.

This opens up the possibility that the author of the *Historia* based chapter
56 on a pre-existing poem celebrating Arthur's victories. There are, though,
real difficulties with treating any such work as a credible witness to these
events. Firstly, chapter 56 of the *Historia Brittonum* so little resembles any
extant Old Welsh praise-poem that translation cannot be the appropriate
term;[105] we might think in terms of the borrowing of names but little more.
Secondly, wars neither ancient nor modern feature strings of battles with
rhyming names. Unless Arthur's battles were an exception (which seems
extraordinarily unlikely), we are dealing here not with a record of historical
events but a poet unshackled by what actually occurred, striving for literary
effect. If this was a feature of some earlier poem, then it condemns that work
as unhistorical. Thirdly, the argument involves a degree of special pleading.
Battles two to five are all noted as being on the Dubglas, but successive lines
of poetry ending with the same river-name would be unparalleled. Clearly,
it was the *Historia*'s author who was responsible for there being four battles
on this river, not any source he might have used. Fourthly, the Agned of
the Harleian MS has been dropped by those promoting this theory in favour
of the Breguoin of the Vatican recension – a change which is otherwise
of uncertain merit. Fifthly, there can be no certainty in reconstructing the
endings of Welsh names from the Latin (as *urbs Legionis, mons Badonis*).
Lastly, it is worth noting that in the only place in chapter 56 offering both
Latin and Welsh versions of a battle-name – the seventh, *silva Celidonis*,
the Latin is glossed in Welsh (*Cat Coit Celidon*) rather than the reverse. That
Latin is primary here rather implies that any source was in Latin. Additionally,
Arthur Brodeur was of the view that two irregular hexameter lines of Latin
poetry can be distinguished within chapter 56:

> *Tunc Arthur pugnabat contr' illos in illis diebus*
> *Cum regibus Brittonum, sed ipse dux erat bellorum*
> [Then in those days Arthur fought against them

with the kings of the Britons, but he himself was the commander of battles].[106]

However, the verse which he perhaps identified is external to the battle-list, which, Badon excepted, Brodeur considered 'fantastic'. There are arguments in favour of not just one but two poems, therefore, one each in Latin and Old Welsh, but we are in no position to press either case to a conclusion. And even if the *Historia*'s author did use a battle-listing poem, the rhyming names pretty well rule out this being a near-contemporary work capable of providing reliable information.[107]

So did our ninth-century author have access to near-contemporary written sources for the fifth or early sixth centuries, independent of Gildas, which could potentially underpin the battle-list? Our answer can only be no: this seems highly improbable. Even if he was drawing on a poem, as so often supposed, it was neither near-contemporary nor authoritative.[108] Rather, any such work was of the same time period as the other British works that Nennius used. His knowledge of St Germanus was rooted not in the fifth-century *Life* by Constantius (which seems not to have circulated in Wales) but in a more recent and local one which depended on Irish and English works of the late seventh and eighth centuries. Germanus's mission against British heretics is unlikely to have been viewed favourably by Welsh churchmen pre-768, so it seems unlikely that churches were dedicated to St Harmon/Garman before then.[109] The *Life* used by our author is therefore unlikely to have been written more than a half-century before his own work and can have no independent historical value – what we have of it is a mishmash of biblical parallels, folk tale and crude fabrication.

Patrick's case is similar. His value to the *Historia*'s author rested on his having set out for Rome, trained at Auxerre under Germanus and then, with papal approval, taken over the Roman mission to Ireland,[110] so a British cleric deeply engaged with the continental Church. But this version of Patrick derives not from his own writings (which, again, seem unknown in early Wales) but from Muirchu's *Life*, written *c.* 700,[111] in which Patrick's Roman credentials had been exaggerated so as to advance the ambitions of 'Roman' Armagh. It is this late seventh-century Patrick who we meet in the *Historia*, a missionary sent to Ireland by the pope on the advice of Germanus. Again, the notion of a fifth-century British cleric hand in glove with Rome will only have had much appeal in Wales post-768.

The *Historia*'s portrayals of Germanus and Patrick reflect, therefore, the back-projection of the recent accommodation with Rome onto the sub-Roman period. This had value in early ninth-century Welsh intellectual circles but is without historical merit. In much the same way, the so-called 'Northern Memorandum' cannot date earlier than the late seventh century (though its late sixth- and seventh-century northern 'British' content could derive from materials written somewhat earlier[112]); its historical perspective is similarly late. We have established that Arthur's battle-list is unlikely to derive from any of these, but recognition of how recent such writings were in 829–30 helps us to appreciate the extent to which Nennius's efforts to improve on the *De Excidio Britanniae* rested on late works of little or no historical value.

The same logic applies to Arthur's battles. Only the names could potentially have come from a Welsh poetic source but the better they rhyme the weaker its claims to historicity. Other features of this passage seem late. The cult of the Virgin Mary, which appears in the description of the eighth battle, originated in the Mediterranean world,[113] gained impetus during the Monothelete Controversy in the mid-seventh century,[114] and spread to England and Ireland thereafter at the urging of committed 'Romanists'.[115] This is unlikely to have attracted overmuch interest in Wales before the later eighth century, implying yet again that the battle-list was recent in 829–30.[116] Like Germanus and Patrick, Arthur therefore seems touched by the effort to rewrite the past in such a way that the British, not the English (as Bede), bore the flame of orthodox Christianity in early, post-Roman Britain. The sense in which Arthur's battle-list 'improves' on Gildas's account of the 'war of the Saxon federates' and the prominence given the Virgin both point to this chapter being either based on a recent text or original to the author of the *Historia* himself.[117]

What of the battles? There is unavoidable tension between the chapter's introduction, which implies a war fought by Arthur against the Saxons of Kent,[118] and several of the battle-names that follow, which have northern resonances. This has left scholars divided: some have plumped for a southeastern locus for Arthur and all twelve battles;[119] others have opted for the Highland Zone;[120] others again favour 'correcting' the *Historia*'s account, either by identifying Arthur with Badon and the south and excluding those battles which seem to have occurred elsewhere,[121] or seeing Arthur as a northerner and supposing that Badon is not his.[122] Beyond recognising the ambiguity of the text, there seems little reason to prefer any one of these approaches to the remainder.

Identifying the battles has itself a long and complex history. There were several attempts made in the nineteenth and early twentieth centuries,[123] but

Kenneth Jackson's expert intervention for a long time damped down speculation.[124] It was his opinion that of the eleven sites named in the *Historia*
(including Bregion/Breguoin which replaces Agned in the Vatican recension) and the *Annales Cambriae* (Camlann), few can be identified with much
certainty. The 'wood of Caledonia' must lie in Scotland (though closer identification is highly problematic),[125] and 'the city of the legion' is probably
Chester (less likely Caerleon). Chester's candidacy is strengthened by its
inclusion in the *Civitates* as Cair Legion. Caerleon is here Cair Legion Guar
Usic (incorporating the river-name) and York is Cair Ebrauc (from Roman-
period Eburacum).[126] Doubts arise from the appearance of *Legionum urbs* in
Gildas, which is generally thought to be Caerleon.[127] The 'Vatican' recension
glossed *urbs Leogis* (sic) as, 'in British Cair Lion', but this probably reflects
Bede's naming of Chester as 'Legacaestir or what the British call Caerlegion',[128]
so is again consistent with Chester. Of the remaining names, Jackson considered that the River Glein might refer to the Glen in either modern-day
Northumberland or Lincolnshire, assuming that *ostium* here has the same
meaning as Welsh *aber* (mouth, confluence: as Abergavenny). Linnuis can
safely be identified as Lindsey – the area dependent on Lincoln (Lindum),
but no river Douglas (Dubglas) is known in that region;[129] Breguoin in the
Vatican recension may be the Roman fort at High Rochester (Bremenium).[130]
Since the gloss offered here is Welsh,[131] it seems reasonable to infer that this
was already present in the manuscript used by the English scribe.

Of course, a major problem facing us in seeking to identify Arthur's
battles is the wholesale loss of pre-English and pre-Scandinavian elements
in the place-names of England, and pre-English, pre-Gaelic and pre-
Scandinavian in southern Scotland. Despite efforts to maximise the available data,[132] thousands of place-names in use in the first half of the first
millennium CE are today lost,[133] with (outside Wales and Cornwall) only a
thin scatter still available. Survival has been better among river-names (and
we are helped by the fact that four of our names are of rivers), but many
even of these have been replaced. Additionally, some names (Douglas and
Glen included) are attached to too many different waterways to allow a
confident identification to be made,[134] even supposing the correct attribution still survives. The problem of identifying place with name began early:
as the space characterised by British place-names contracted, so there was
an ever-greater risk of mistakes in locating wide-flung places remembered
in literature with similarly named places still within the shrinking name
pool.[135] In seeking to interpret Arthur's battles, confusion seems extraordinarily likely. We should certainly expect no higher rate of success than

Jackson achieved, and we should share his caution regarding even those identifications that he proposed.

But locating Arthur's battles has become something of a cottage industry in recent years.[136] Rather than rehearse all the identifications on offer, let us focus on Badon, the last and best known of Arthur's battles in the *Historia*, which terms it *mons Badonis*, 'the mountain of Badon'. Geoffrey of Monmouth equated Badon with Bath,[137] and he was followed in this by the scribe responsible for a thirteenth-century recension of the *Historia Brittonum* preserved at Cambridge, who added 'where the Baths of Badon are' (*in quo balnea sunt Badonis*) to the 'miracle' of the 'hot lake which is in the region of the Hwicce'.[138] This appears in italics in Morris's edition, denoting its derivation from the contents list of the Cambridge edition,[139] but that this is a late addition is all too easily overlooked. Several modern writers have followed Geoffrey, imagining Gildas's siege to have occurred on one of the hills (such as Little Solsbury Hill) above the town.[140] But the late Roman name was Aquae Sulis,[141] not Badon, and there is no reason to suppose that an entirely different name was substituted in the fifth century. Anglo-Saxon 'Bath' has a Germanic derivation – 'Bath' = 'bath', it is as simple as that. While it connects with the Romano-British name in terms of its meaning ('waters': 'bath'), it is not a direct translation and is unrelated linguistically. Geoffrey was therefore conflating two quite separate names, the *Historia*'s *mons Badonis* (and behind that Gildas's *Badonicus mons*) and Old English Baðan (Bath),[142] for no better reason than that they sound a bit similar. *Balnea Badonis* is cod-onomastics, therefore, and should be dismissed, along with every study of Arthur which places Badon at or near Bath on those grounds.

There is no greater merit in arguments favouring any of the several hillfort or place-names formed in English which contain the element 'Bad-' (as Badbury Rings), since these are all likelier to be Old English than in some way related to Badon – think Baden-Baden in Germany.[143] Other candidates have included Liddington Castle (above Badbury),[144] a naval engagement on the Clyde,[145] Dumbarton,[146] the vicinity of Dunadd (Argyll),[147] Bowden Hill (Linlithgoe),[148] The Breidden (near Welshpool),[149] Mynydd Baedan near Bridgend,[150] Great Bedwyn (Wiltshire),[151] Baumber (Lincolnshire),[152] either Great Barton (near Bury St Edmunds) or Barton (near Cambridge),[153] Aconbury (Herefordshire),[154] and Braydon Forest (Wiltshire).[155] None of these identifications are sufficiently compelling to merit support (and some are virtually impossible[156]). The twelfth-century identification of Badon with Bath merely demonstrates that writers then already had no better knowledge than we do where *Badonicus mons* actually was. Of course, it may have been a very minor place of relevance only to Gildas and his close circle, less a mountain than a hillock. It does not help that the meaning is obscure. Michael Winterbottom saw it as 'normal Celtic' and compared it to Vaubadon in Normandy,[157] which was *Vallis Badonis* ('valley of Badon') in the Domesday Book.[158] But this too probably derived from a Germanic personal name,[159] so the parallel has no value. There is no obvious root in the Celtic languages;[160] Latin is no more helpful. In Greek, 'Bados' (βάδος) is 'a walk'. While this could have been Latinised and used in the naming of a local eminence by some well-educated, Romano-British estate owner, any such supposition is entirely speculative and the locality long forgotten. We would all be better off today facing up to the fact that Badon is lost, unless and until fresh evidence is forthcoming.

We might usefully just remind ourselves at this point, the *Historia Brittonum* is primarily about the relationship between God, His British people and their English neighbours, and was written predominantly for immediate purposes. The author was a churchman, trained to find literal, allegorical and spiritual truth in the Bible. That all of the second to fifth of Arthur's battle-list were said to have occurred on the same river suggests that it was the spiritual message inherent in the apostolic number, twelve, which mattered to him more than the individual engagements. The only battle of Chester that was certainly remembered in Wales was the defeat inflicted by the Anglian King Æthelfrith on a British army *c.* 615, when numerous monks were slaughtered and a Welsh king killed.[161] This was held up by Bede as God's punishment of the Britons for their refusal to obey Augustine of Canterbury.[162] Inclusion of the same battle here as one of Arthur's victories may well have been intended as a challenge to Bede's interpretation of this event as proof of God's support for the English, even while still pagan, against the Britons.

We should recognise that several other of Arthur's battles are reminiscent, at least, of conflicts mentioned in early Welsh poems.[163] 'Bassas' may recall the (probably) ninth-century Welsh poem, '*Eglwysau Basa*' ('the churches of Basa'). In Welsh 'bas' means 'shallow', which might be appropriate to a minor river-name, but Basa was also an Old English personal name;[164] if this is linked in some sense with Baschurch (Shropshire), as is generally assumed, then it may well be a fully English place-name, formed after the takeover of this area. The poem *Kat Goddeu* (*Battle of the Trees*), which is taken up by a mythological conflict involving a tree-host, perhaps relates in some respect to the battle of Coit Celidon (Coed Celyddon);[165] Traeth Trywruid,[166] one of Arthur's battles in the poem *Pa Gur,* is probably the same conflict as the *Historia*'s battle on the shore of the 'river which is called Tribruit',[167] but Arthur's opponent therein has a Welsh name. Lastly, Breguoin may derive from 'the battle of *Cellawr Brewyn*' ('the cells of Brewyn') in one of the poems attributed to Taliesin praising Urien of Rheged.[168] Both Taliesin and Bede pre-date the *Historia*, making their works potential sources.

These parallels suggest a highly eclectic approach to Arthur's battle-list. What we can be confident of, therefore, is that the list cannot be historical, including as it does battles borrowed from elsewhere fought by a variety of champions against different enemies.

Historical method in early ninth-century Wales

To this point we have been exploring the *Historia Brittonum* in ways characteristic of studies focused on Arthur, with our hero centre-stage. He features, though, in only one of the sixty-six chapters of the original *Historia* (i.e. excluding the *Civitates* and *Mirabilia*). Obviously, Arthur was not its author's principal interest; indeed, the *Historia* should not be considered an 'Arthurian' text as such at all, for it addresses much wider issues. A different approach is needed if we are to better understand its author's methods and, by extension, those underpinning the recent Welsh texts that only survive in short passages excerpted or paraphrased in this work. A wider exploration will enable us to evaluate the nature of the scholarship on display in the *Historia*. To what extent did its author treat his sources respectfully? How much confidence can we have in what he wrote more generally? What did the writing of history mean to the scholarly community to which he belonged? We need to unpick how Nennius presented other characters doing similar things to Arthur. We will focus, therefore, on his presentation of British war-leaders more generally, in the hope that these may lead us to a better understanding of the Arthur of chapter 56 of the *Historia*.

Given that he is the only such figure named by Gildas,[169] Ambrosius Aurelianus might seem our obvious starting point, but his treatment in the *Historia* is more complex than that of Arthur and not that of a British war-leader fighting invaders. He appears first as the boy born of a virgin mother who interprets the conflict between the white and red 'worms' beneath Vortigern's part-built fortress, which was eventually gifted him along with 'all the kingdoms of the western districts of Britain' (see above, pp. 183–4).[170]

This story seems potentially etymological in origin; the strong biblical parallels (cf. Elijah, Daniel and Christ) suggest that it derives from clerical circles,[171] perhaps even from the pen of Nennius himself. In the context of Vortigern's death, Ambrosius is 'the king among all the kings of the British people', the superior of Vortigern's son, Pascent, ruler of Builth and Gwerthrynion.[172] This seems a logical development of the *De Excidio Britanniae*'s treatment of Ambrosius as a national leader of the Britons and stands comparison both with Arthur's role as *dux* in chapter 56 and his later emergence as a quasi-imperial figure, but it has no historical value. More importantly, this story asserts the past existence of a British over-kingship centred on Gwynedd, much to the advantage of Merfyn in the present.

One further episode featuring Ambrosius comes in the chronological summary that ends the 'original' *Historia*: 'And from the reign of Vortigern even to the disagreement of Guitolinus and Ambrosius are 12 years, which is Guoloppum, that is Catguoloph [the battle of Guoloph].'[173] Guoloppum/ Guoloph is generally (though not certainly) identified as Wallop in Hampshire. The place-name's origin is uncertain: Old-English *wælla-hop*, 'valley of the spring/well', is one possibility but a pre-Celtic origin has also been urged.[174] The latter would obviously better suit its occurrence here. Guitolin is the Welsh version of the Roman name Vitolinus (with the ending restored in this Cambro-Latin text), which occurs otherwise in the *Historia* in the genealogy of Teudubir, Vortigern's descendant (and the king of Builth). Here, though, he is Vortigern's grandfather, making interaction with Ambrosius (whose childhood is depicted occurring late in Vortigern's reign) highly implausible. Catguoloph implies an Old Welsh source – possibly a poem, but whether or not this event should be considered historical is impossible to say. Clearly, the *Historia Brittonum*'s treatment of Ambrosius is heavily legendised. His story had been elaborated and fictionalised, taking it far beyond the little that Gildas had offered and in new directions. It here fulfils a very different role to Arthur's. He must therefore be set aside for our purposes, though there are interesting similarities with the *Historia*'s approach to, and then the later development of, Arthur's story.

A closer parallel is Vortimer, who is likewise depicted as a British champion fighting against Saxon incomers:

> Meanwhile Vortimer [Guorthemir], son of Vortigern [Guorthigirn], fought aggressively with Hengist and Horsa and with their people and expelled them even to the aforesaid island, which is called Thanet, there he three times shut up, besieged, struck at, threatened and terrorised

them. And they sent envoys over the sea even to Germany asking for keels with a vast number of men skilled in war. And afterwards they fought against the kings of our people: sometimes they were victorious and extended their borders, sometimes they were defeated and expelled.

And Vortimer keenly fought four battles against them. The first battle [was] on the river Derguentid; the second battle [was] on the ford which is called in their language Episford, in our language however Rithergabail, and there fell Horsa with a son of Vortimer, whose name was Categirn; the third battle [was] in the field by the inscribed stone, which is on the shore of the Gallic sea, and the barbarians were overcome, and he was the victor, and they took flight towards their keels and were drowned clambering aboard like women.[175]

These passages are thought to rest ultimately on an English origins story written in seventh-century Kent,[176] but they have been extensively reworked in the British interest. The English place-names imply that named battles featured in the original,[177] but their presentation here as Vortimer's victories necessarily belong to the 'British' rewrite. That the *Anglo-Saxon Chronicle* names Vortigern as the British leader, not Vortimer, may mean that he featured in the original.[178] If so then Vortimer should be read as a doublet of his putative father (as the close similarity of their names might also imply),[179] introduced to avoid crediting this hate-figure with fighting the Saxons. Like many others in the *Historia*, this passage has a strong 'Gildasian flavour',[180] though whether or not that was already a feature of the Kentish text is unclear. There seems little reason to look beyond our author as the person responsible for the 'British' rewrite.[181] Certainly, similarities with chapter 56 are easiest explained if the author of the *Historia* was responsible for the wording of both Vortimer's and Arthur's victories.[182]

In order to seek out further examples we must broaden our focus beyond the British–Saxon conflict. A central theme of the *Historia Brittonum* is that the Britons were the original (and rightful) inhabitants of Britain in its entirety, having arrived in the 'Third Age of the World'. History thereafter is largely a succession of foreign invasions – by the Picts, the Irish, the Romans and finally the Saxons. The narrative centres on British resistance to incomers, with periods of foreign domination ended by successful expulsions. There are not always names attached to the British cause,[183] however, so several episodes are rather impersonal. It is the Roman period that provides the fullest cycle of invasion, occupation and expulsion, so our best opportunity is to explore this approach.

Gildas's account of the Roman Conquest is brief and dispiriting:

> Crossing the strait, and meeting no resistance, it [the Roman expedi-
> tionary force] brought the laws of obedience to the island. The people,
> unwarlike but untrustworthy, were not subdued like other races, by the
> sword, fire and engines of war, so much as by mere threats and legal
> penalties.[184]

This refers specifically to the Claudian invasion of 43 CE but Gildas was
interested less in events *per se* than the opportunity for negative comment
on the Britons as a people (see above, p. 155). The *Historia* provides a more
positive story, though not a different outcome. Although no British hero is
named, its version is otherwise similar in intent to its depiction of British
resistance to the Saxons; the emperor had to fight 'a great and bloody battle,
not without injury to his troops', before 'he was the victor in Britain'.[185]
Gildas's picture of a bloodless victory derives from Orosius.[186] Nennius is
very unlikely to have based the more positive aspects of his account on an
ancient source. He was, therefore, rewriting this episode to laud the Britons
as a martial race in contradiction to both of his sources.

Gildas's failure to include the earlier expeditions of Julius Caesar left
Nennius freer to paint an uplifting picture:

> Then Julius Caesar, the first to accept and obtain sole rule, ... came to
> Britain with sixty keels, and landed in the Thames Estuary, where his
> ships suffered ship-wreck, while he was himself fighting with Dolabella,
> who was the proconsul of the British king, who was himself called
> Bellinus, and he was the son of Minocannus, who had occupied all the
> islands of the Tyrrhenian Sea, and Julius returned without victory, his
> soldiers killed and his ships broken.[187]

This derives from Orosius's account,[188] which in turn rests on Caesar's,[189]
but our author made significant changes, for example adding his own
location for the Roman landing (which probably occurred between Walmer
and Ramsgate on the Kent coast). Specification of the Thames Estuary had
the effect of placing British resistance to both Roman and Saxon invasions
in the same locality,[190] implying that there were parallels. Gildas's emphasis
on the Thames as a route into Britain perhaps influenced Nennius here.[191]
Similarly, the somewhat incongruous use of the Old English term *ciulis* –
'keels' – for the Roman ships shows that this was written with the *De Excidio*

Britanniae's Saxons in mind.[192] Rhetorical links were being created, therefore, between the Roman and Saxon invasions.

Just as the Saxons returned after Vortimer had expelled them,[193] and
fresh hordes arrived following Arthur's victories, so too did Caesar come
back:

> And again, after the space of three years, he came with a great army and
> three hundred keels, and arrived even at the mouth of the river, which is
> called the Thames. And there they fought a battle and many of his horses
> and soldiers fell, because the aforesaid proconsul [Dolabella] placed
> iron stakes and 'battle seed', that is caltrops, in the ford of the river. This
> unseen strategy proved a great hindrance to the soldiers of the Romans
> and they withdrew without peace on that occasion. The third battle was
> fought near the place called Trinovantum.
>
> And Julius received empire over the British people 47 years before
> the birth of Christ, from the beginning however of the World 5215
> [years].[194]

This likewise rests on Orosius, but it seems to have been rewritten with
an eye on Gildas's account of the coming of the Saxons, which is likely
to have been the source for the repeated use of 'three' (Orosius specified
six hundred ships and Caesar's expeditions were in successive years). As
with the Saxons, the invaders' success in establishing control of Britain
seems out of all proportion to the achievements they were credited with on
the battle field.

How should we read this? At one level we might just dismiss it as a poor-
quality version of Orosius's account which leaves us one stage further adrift
from what actually occurred. But our author's changes were purposeful,
imbuing the Roman Conquest with meaning relevant to the central issue of
the present day – 'foreign' domination of Britain. Nennius developed what
he found in Orosius in ways designed to challenge Gildas's negativity; he
was using these ancient struggles to present the Britons in ways designed to
promote their self-belief as a people in the present.

His approach is particularly revealing when dealing with the British
leadership. Caesar named King Cassivellaunus as the British supreme
commander;[195] Orosius has virtually the same name (Casovellaunus).[196]
The *Historia* disregards this;[197] its 'Bellinus, son of Minocannus' comes
instead from a garbled reading of Orosius's description of events some
eighty years later, when 'Minocynobelinus, son of the king of the Britons'

surrendered to Caligula.[198] One might suppose that Nennius was working from memory here and just made a mistake, but the parachuting in of a figure from a quite different historical context is so characteristic of this work that it seems likely that this was deliberate. And we have the additional detail added, that either Bellinus or his father had 'occupied all the islands of the Tyrrhenian Sea'. Orosius referred repeatedly to the western Mediterranean by this name,[199] but it was Nennius alone who sought to enhance the stature of the British king through this utterly bogus claim.[200] Bellinus – whose name recalls Latin *bellum*, 'battle', 'war' – was thereby elevated to the stature of an imperial figure in his own right, so in some sense Caesar's equal. This was clearly intentional; the representation of Bellinus in the *Historia* reveals an author who was prepared to misrepresent his source and fabricate the past in pursuit of a particular effect.

The role of Bellinus's lieutenant, Dolabella, brings such methods into still sharper focus. Orosius did not name a British leader other than the king, so this character is entirely our author's creation. There are linguistic parallels between Dolabella's achievements and Arthur's, who: 'fought [*pugnabat*] against them [the Saxons] in those days with the kings of the Britons [*regibus Brittonum*] but was himself [*ipse*] the *dux bellorum*.' Arthur is the subject of this sentence but Dolabella is the object when he first appears, with Caesar as subject: 'He [Caesar] himself fought [*ipse pugnabat*] with Dolabella, who was the proconsul of the British king [*regi Brittanico*].'[201] Similarities in the language used and the rather contrived adoption of 'Roman' titles in both instances (*proconsul, dux*) suggest that parallels were intended.

Where did our author find Dolabella? Orosius had referred to a Roman aristocrat of that name (he was an associate of Caesar and Cicero's son-in-law) in the context of the civil war which erupted at Caesar's death,[202] but he neither visited Britain nor commanded a British army against Rome. Additionally, it is worth noting that Nennius changed Orosius's Dolabellam (in the accusative) to Dolabellum, presumably so as to again emphasise Latin *bellum* ('war', 'battle') as a name element.[203] This minor change apart, the name is authentic enough, but Dolabella's role in the *Historia* is pure fiction. Again, this can only have been intentional and rhetorically driven.

Such a cavalier approach to the use of sources is not confined to the *Historia Brittonum* but can also be detected in the works of recent Welsh scholarship that its author was using. In illustration, let us focus on Brutus, the figure after whom the Britons were supposedly named. The Spanish author Bishop Isidore provides our starting point, as he did that of these late eighth- and early ninth-century clerics (see above, p. 129). In his *Etymologies*, he noted that most peoples were named after an eponymous founder – the Romans after Romulus, the Lakedaimonians after Lakedaimon, and so on.[204] Of the Britons, though, he wrote: 'Some suspect that the Britons were so named in Latin because they are *brutus* ['heavy', 'immovable', 'insensible', especially of animals]'.[205] Unsurprisingly, British scholars *c*. 800 CE substituted the proper name Brutus, converting Isidore's slur to an eponym equivalent to those of other peoples of the ancient world.

The problem came, though, in adapting what was all too obviously a name from Roman history to the role of a founder of the pre-Roman Britons. The *Historia* reveals the difficulties experienced by the Welsh cleric on whose work Nennius was drawing. Brutus appears first in chapter 7, the opening section of a geographical description of Britain based very loosely on that of Gildas,[206] but amended to conform to contemporary 'knowledge': 'Britain the island is so-called from a certain Brutus, the Roman consul.'

Jerome's *Chronicle* has an entry against the year 138 BCE that 'Brutus subjugated Hiberiam even to the Ocean'. This refers to D. Junius Brutus's conquests in Hispania ('Further Spain') but *c*. 800 the locale could easily have been mistaken for Ireland (Hibernia).[207] There is also a likelihood of confusion with L. Junius Brutus, who legend had it freed Rome from the rule of Tarquin, the last king, *c*. 509 BCE and served as one of the city's first consuls.[208] This figure was known to early medieval scholars from Orosius and from the early Christian chronicles;[209] that clerics were familiar with him in the Irish Sea region is confirmed by his appearance in one of the Irish origin legends precised in the *Historia*: 'They [the Irish] came to the regions of Dariet [Dál Riata] in the time in which Brutus ruled among the Romans, with whom the consuls began'.[210]

An alternative was to name this founding figure Britto. A text excerpted in the *Historia* wove him into Rome's legendary history:

It is written in the annals of the Romans thus. Aeneas after the Trojan War arrived in Italy with his son Ascanius and, overcoming Turnus, received Lavinia, the daughter of Latinus, son of Faunus, son of Saturn, in marriage and, after the death of Latinus, he obtained the kingship of the Romans or Latins. Aeneas founded Alba [Longa] and afterwards he married a wife, and she gave him a son named Silvius. Silvius married a wife, and she was pregnant, Aeneas learned that his son's wife was pregnant and sent to his son Ascanius that he should send his magus to observe the wife, and discover what she had in [her] womb, whether a boy or a girl. And the magus observed the wife and returned. The magus was killed by Ascanius because of this prophecy, because he said that the woman had a masculine [child] in the womb and he would be the son of death, because he would kill his father and his mother and would be very hateful to all men. Thus it turned out: his mother died giving birth and the son was reared and was called Britto. After a long time, just as the magus prophesied, while he was playing with others, he killed his father with an arrow shot, not intentionally but by accident. And he was expelled from Italy ... And afterwards he [Britto] came to this island, which received its name from his, that is Brittania, and he filled it with his race and dwelt there. From that day, Brittania has been inhabited even to the present time.[211]

These are less 'Roman annals' than a British rewrite of Rome's legendary history designed to establish a more apt eponym for the Britons than Brutus supplied. Nennius found the story in a pre-existing text; he did not make it up himself. But such close intertwining of the origins of the Britons and the Romans is only likely after the Welsh acceptance of Rome's Paschal dating, *c.* 768 (see above, p. 177). Like the *Book of the Blessed Germanus*, therefore, this text is unlikely to have been much more than a generation earlier than the *Historia*. These were Latin texts written by churchmen tasked with repositioning the Britons within a tradition of European history that centred on Rome. The methods used were highly inventive; the results, obviously, have no historical authority.

For our final example we will turn to another British warrior, Cunedda. The *Historia* refers to him twice, first in chapter fourteen:

Last came Damhoctor and there he settled with all his people even to the present in Britain. Istoreth, son of Istorni, held Dalrieta [Dál Riata] with his [followers]; Builc however with his held the Eubonian island [the Isle of Man] and others around; the sons however of Liethan settled in the region of the Demetians and in other regions, that is Guir Cetgueli [Gower, Kidwelly], until they were expelled by Cuned[d]a and his son from all the British regions.

Then in 62:

The great king Maelgwyn reigned among the Britons, that is in the region of Gwynedd, because his ancestor, that is Cunedag, with his sons,

of whom the number was eight, had earlier come from the northern
part, that is from the region which is called Manaw Guotodin [Manaw
Gododdin], 146 years before Maelgwyn ruled, and they expelled the
Scots [Irish] with very great slaughter from those regions, and they
never went back again to live [there].

In the *Historia Brittonum*, therefore, Cunedda is a northern Briton who
comes south, ejects the Irish from Wales and triumphantly establishes
himself and his sons as rulers of Gwynedd.

Thereafter he occurs in Gwynedd's royal pedigree in the tenth-century
Harleian genealogies, and his sons (excepting one who had supposedly
remained behind in the north) are named as eponyms for various regions
of Wales, with the rivers Dee and Teifi set as the limits of their power.[212]
This is thought to rest on a north Welsh genealogy compiled in the
mid-ninth century, perhaps at the same centre where the *Historia* was
composed.[213] The early generations of this genealogy are fictional, opening
with Anna, cousin to the Virgin Mary and wife of 'Beli the Great'.[214] The
lineage should be accepted as potentially historical only from Maelgwyn
onwards, and need not be reliable before 'Catman map Iacob', Cadwallon's
father, *c.* 610. Earlier generations were made up or contrived from unconnected genealogical scraps. That Cunedda's forebears have Celticised
Roman names (Eternus, son of Paternus 'red cloak', son of Tacitus) suggests
that this section was copied from a short northern British genealogy of a
kind that we know to have been circulating in ninth- and tenth-century
Wales;[215] it seems very unlikely that it originally had any connection with
Gwynedd's royal line.

Cunedda was long accepted as historical in this guise,[216] but his story as
set out in the *Historia* cannot be literally true.[217] 146 years prior to
Maelgwyn's reign suggests that Cunedda was evicting Irish incomers from
Wales in the second half of the fourth century,[218] but Roman forces were
still manning Britain's Irish Sea defences then,[219] with or without the aid of
Irish federate troops.[220] And 146 years seems too long between the reigns of
Cunedda and his great-grandson. Depending on which of these 'facts' is
given greater weight, Cunedda swings in modern studies between *c.* 380
and *c.* 440.[221] However, Irish influence in Wales continued through the fifth
and into the sixth centuries, as evidenced by Ogam inscriptions and Irish
names in Welsh genealogies, so these western incomers seem not to have
been expelled before *c.* 550, if they ever were; in reality acculturation seems
more likely.

1 A wine label from Podstrana, Croatia, featuring the sword in the stone. The stone depicted is the longer of the 'Artorius' inscriptions (see Plate 3).

2 St Martin's Church, Podstrana. One of the replica inscribed slabs is visible in the cemetery wall immediately to the left of the church.

3 The larger 'Artorius' inscription, restored and displayed inside St Martin's Church, Podstrana.

4 One of three pieces of the smaller 'Artorius' inscription that was recently re-identified in the Archaeological Museum of Split.

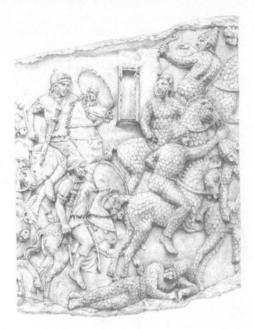

5 A depiction of Sarmatian warriors in flight from Roman cavalry on Trajan's Column. This scene provides a near-contemporary vision of Sarmatian equipment, but may not have been particularly accurate in its execution.

6 'Sarmatian' beads from Chesters Roman fort on Hadrian's Wall: a very rare example of material that has been interpreted as being deposited by Sarmatian warriors serving in Britain.

7 A funerary relief carving of a probable Sarmatian cavalryman found at Chester, perhaps a *draconarius* serving with the legion stationed there.

8 A lead 'tamga' from Ribchester, which has so far been the sole artefact of probable Sarmatian manufacture that has been found at this, the only cavalry fort in Roman Britain known to have had a Sarmatian garrison.

9 The 'Apollo' monument from Ribchester: the inscription refers to 'Gordian's own unit of Sarmatian cavalry'.

10 Three Sarmatian burial mounds at Vaskút, Hungary, reflecting the colonisation of the Carpathian Basin by these Black Sea nomads during the early Principate. No such monuments have ever been found in Britain.

11 Mid-fifth-century Sarmatian pottery from excavations of the brick factory site at Tiszaföldvár, in the Tisza valley, Hungary.

12 Sarmatian beads of the mid-fifth century from excavations of the brick factory site at Tiszaföldvár.

13 Excavation of the fourth- and fifth-century levels at Ribchester in 2016. Both wall-lines and industrial workings are now being uncovered, comparable to many other Roman fort sites in northern Britain.

14 A stone footprint at the Dál Riatan stronghold of Dunadd (Argyll), which may have been used in ceremonies of royal accession by Scottish kings.

15 A sword-in-the-stone motif features on the late medieval crozier of the archbishop of Siena. This derived from the cult of St Galgano, which developed in the late twelfth century at nearby Montesiepi.

16 A mountain village in the Caucasus, with the stone houses and towers characteristic of the area, illustrated in Douglas Freshfield's *Travels in the Central Caucasus and Bashan.*

17 The Mote of Mark, a Celtic, Dark Age defensive site near Dalbeattie, Dumfries and Galloway, Scotland. The name derives from the high medieval French *motte* ('castle-mound') combined with King Mark of far-off Dumnonia, as popularised in literature of the thirteenth century.

18 The Battersea Cauldron, a high-status bronze vessel from *c.* 800–700 BCE found in the River Thames. Such finds illustrate the antiquity of this kind of manufacturing in Atlantic Europe.

19 The Antiochos dedication is a rare instance of Greek lettering on stone in Roman Britain. It is probably significant that this has strong medical associations, as this is a line of work in which knowledge of Greek will have been particularly valued.

20 The 'astronomer' mosaic at Brading Villa is thus far the sole discovery of a mosaic image of an astrologer found in Roman Britain.

21 Part of the archivolt of the Porta della Pescheria in Modena Cathedral showing King Arthur (Artus *de Bretania*) with his supporters attempting the rescue of Winlogee (Guinevere) from a castle defended by Burmaltus.

22 The Winchester Round Table, displayed on the wall of the great hall of Winchester Castle. The table was probably commissioned by Edward I in the thirteenth century (the timbers were likely felled 1250–80) and was refurbished and painted on the orders of Henry VIII early in the 1520s.

23 South Cadbury hillfort, a prominent candidate for the site of King Arthur's Camelot at least since the sixteenth century. It was an Iron Age hillfort that was refortified in the later fifth century, when it was the residence of a powerful member of the elite.

24 The farm of Camlan Uchaf in the small township of Camlan. The road from Aberangell to Dinas Mawddwy runs across the foreground with the River Dovey behind; several passes led from here northwards and north-eastwards into Gwynedd and Powys.

25 Pen-y-Fan, in the Brecon Beacons, viewed from Cribyn. Pen-y-Fan is the highest of the Brecon Beacons and thought to be the Kaerarthur named by Gerald of Wales in the 1190s.

26 Arthur's Stone, a Bronze Age burial site at Llanrhidian Lower on the Gower Peninsula. Folklore has it that this was a stone that lodged in Arthur's shoe on his way to fight the battle of Camlann, which irritated him so much that he threw it 7 miles across the Loughor estuary.

27 'King Arthur's Hall', an enigmatic 47 x 20 metre rectangular setting of massive stones near St Breward, Cornwall, on the north-western edge of Bodmin Moor, which has been dated variously from the Neolithic to the medieval periods.

28 Pendragon Castle, Mallerstang, near Kirkby Stephen, Cumbria. Despite being named for Arthur's legendary father, this is a Norman keep built by Ranulph de Meschines, earl of Chester, probably in the reign of William Rufus (1087–1100).

29 The Maen Huail, a badly degraded slab of limestone set against the half-timbered wall of the rebuilt Exmewe Hall, St Peter's Square, Ruthin, on which Arthur is reputed to have had Huail beheaded.

Maen Huail

Ar y garreg hon dywedir
i'r Brenin Arthur ddienyddio Huail
ei elyn marwol, brawd Gildas yr hanesydd.

On this stone the legendary King Arthur
is said to have beheaded Huail, brother
of Gildas the historian, his rival in
love and war.

30 The more recent of the Maen Huail explanatory plaques, put up by Cadw.

31 Arthur killing Mordred in illuminated medallion 49 from the fifteenth-century French manuscript *Histoire Universelle*. Note the plate armour, which is characteristic of this stage of the Hundred Years War.

32 Tintagel, the Dark Age settlement and later castle site viewed from across the causeway with the haven in the foreground. This has been reputed the site of Arthur's conception since Geoffrey of Monmouth, but he was in fact recycling a far older folkloric story that had been recorded much earlier in Ireland and in the classical world.

In reality the kingdom of Gwynedd only seems to have come into existence *c.* 500, replacing the Roman-period Ordovices. The name is first evidenced in its Latin form, Venedotia, on an inscription of about this date found at Penmachno (near Betws-y-Coed, Gwynedd);[222] it probably derives from the Irish *Féni* (meaning 'Irish'). Its adoption should probably be linked with a dramatic shift in the balance of power in Ireland at this time stemming from the Uí Néill seizure of Brega (central eastern Ireland).[223] In that case Gwynedd's origins must be in some sense Irish, either a result of Irish migration or the establishment of a client, British kingship.

The *Historia's* Cunedda cannot therefore be historical in any strict sense.[224] Nor can his sons, whose names were almost certainly generated retrospectively as eponyms for various regions of Wales (as Ceretic for Ceredigion; Docmail for Dogfeiling, etc.), to support the dynasty's claims to these territories.[225] But Cunedda is also the subject of an Old Welsh elegy, the *Marwnad Cunedda*, supposedly composed by the sixth-century Taliesin but only surviving in a manuscript written in the first half of the fourteenth century.[226] The poem is located by reference to (Dumbarton) Rock, the Lake District(?), an unnamed town on the River Wear, Luguvalium (Carlisle), the Coeling (a British dynasty associated with several pre-Anglian Pennine kingships), and Bryneich (a British form of later Anglian 'Bernicia', which also occurs in the *Historia* as Berneich). The 'Northern British Heroic Age' was clearly this Cunedda's theatre of activities; according to the poem it is here that he lived and campaigned and here too that he died without heirs of his body. Reference to him in the poem as *mab Edern* ('son of Eternus': line 38) ties him to the same genealogy as was incorporated in the lineage of Gwynedd's kings.[227]

Unsurprisingly, given its provenance, this poem was long written off as a work composed in late medieval Wales.[228] However, John Koch points to linguistic reasons to think it early and makes the additional point that a Welsh poet aware of Cunedda's role in Gwynedd's foundation story is unlikely to have produced a work so obviously at variance with the *Historia*.[229] There is a good case, therefore, to suppose that the poem predates the *Historia*, reached Wales from the 'Old North' before 829–30 and there came to the attention of Nennius, but was later 'modernised' and included in a late medieval collection of poems under Taliesin's name.

It is only the *Historia* that has Cunedda coming south to liberate Wales from the Irish, and even this acknowledges his northern origins. Given the degree of overlap, it seems reasonably safe to assume that both texts refer to the same figure; these stories are, though, clearly incompatible. Which offers the more authentic Cunedda? The eulogy is likely to be the earlier by several centuries, so it is this work that we should prefer as a witness. While there can be no certainty, it seems very likely that his appearance in the *Historia* as the scourge of the Irish is another example of a figure given a fictional career by its author, to accord with his own rhetorical needs.

We might also note problems internal to these passages of the *Historia Brittonum*. 'Damhoctor' is offered as a personal name but this is the Old Irish phrase, *dám octair*, 'company of eight'.[230] That there are eight sons credited to Cunedda in the second extract can hardly be coincidental. Our author seems therefore to have been using source material reaching him partly (at least) in Old Irish. T.M. Charles-Edwards dislikes the possibility that the story was 'invented as propaganda for Merfyn',[231] but Cunedda does resemble other of the *Historia*'s fictionalised characters. His significance is threefold. Firstly, by providing a British hero who ejected Irish incomers and restored 'British regions' to British control our author was 'improving' on Gildas's terrified Britons powerless to resist attacks by the Picts and Irish.[232] Secondly, British bravery again won through (just as in the ending of Roman Britain), the Irish were ejected and they stayed ejected – an important point given his interest in the Saxons. Thirdly, the story shows the Britons acting in concert; the 'Old North' came to the aid of the Welsh and established an insular champion on the throne of Gwynedd. Just as Merfyn had recently come from Manaw (the Isle of Man) to take up the kingship of north-west Wales, so too was the founder of the previous dynasty a man from another northern *manaw*, Manaw Gododdin. This is unlikely to be coincidental.[233] In this fictionalised form, therefore, Cunedda provided a useful precedent for Merfyn's takeover, bringing hope for a lasting British victory over 'foreigners' led from a Gwynedd rejuvenated once again by a northerner.[234]

The *Historia Brittonum* names further British leaders who fought the Saxons subsequent to Arthur's time. Chapter 61 notes the killing of King Edwin and his sons 'by the army of Catguollaun [Cadwallon], king of the region of Gwynedd'. This is an episode covered by Bede,[235] but the *Historia* also drew on 'British' sources (for example for the name of the battle). In chapter 62, Outigirn 'in that time was fighting bravely against the people of the English'. The context is Ida's reign, so Nennius apparently thought him a mid-sixth-century figure, but offered no details. This chapter otherwise lists British poets 'all famous at this one time in British poetry', so Outigern may, like Cunedda and Cadwallon, have been a figure commemorated in verse. Given that both Aneirin and Taliesin of those listed were northerners (as was Ida), it seems likely that Outigern was also a figure of the 'Northern British Heroic Age', but his absence from any other surviving text leaves him very much on the edge of history (and there is always the possibility of his being another doublet of Vortigern). The final example is a group of British kings, Urbgen (Urien), Riderchhen (Rhydderch Hen), Guallac (Gwallawg) and Morcant, fighting against the Bernician kings (and Theodoric in particular), who are listed with their regnal years at the beginning of the chapter.[236] Of these Urien and Rhydderch are reasonably well established, one the king of Rheged famed in Taliesin's poetry,[237] the other a ruler of Dumbarton Rock in the late sixth century. Gwallawg was named as Elmet's king in poems ascribed to Taliesin.

These figures all occur within passages which are thought to derive from the so-called 'Northern Memorandum', a text or group of texts written in one of the more 'British' parts of Northumbria,[238] which Nennius used to frame his work from the last sentence and a half of chapter 56 through to 65. It is structured around various English regnal lists and genealogies, which seem already to have been interpolated with pro-British, anti-English comments (quite possibly in the form of marginalia) when they reached our author. This commentary shared our author's prejudices: it was here that the English (*Saxones*) were termed *ambrones*, for example;[239] English characters are critiqued in various ways and British achievements celebrated. Some of this material could have entered the *Historia* virtually verbatim, though the language and phrasing of chapter 63 of the *Historia* is likely to have been influenced by the *De Excidio Britanniae*,[240] and similarities between the deeds of Vortimer (in chapter 43) and the four northern British kings in chapter 63 may mean that this passage, at least, was rewritten in the early ninth century.

The 'Northern Memorandum', though, gave the *Historia*'s author access to a commentary which was comparatively local to most of the issues that it touched on and, in very broad terms, rather closer to contemporary with some at least of these events than the texts with which he had supplemented Gildas's *De Excidio* in passages up to chapter 56.[241] His response seems to have been to rein in his earlier tendency to lace his narrative with invention and adopt a more sober approach. That said, a willingness to reinvent the past in promoting the British cause is still detectable, as in the claim that the British Rhun baptised King Edwin.[242] In the Nennian Recension, this was attributed to the testimony of 'bishop Renchidus and Elvodug [Elfoddw], the holiest of bishops', so was apparently part of the orally transmitted 'traditions of our elders' that Nennius acknowledged in the prologue. The problem is that this claim is totally at odds with Bede's earlier, comparatively detailed and arguably well-founded account of Edwin's conversion.[243] The *Historia*'s reference to Eanflæd's baptism suggests knowledge of chapters 9 and 14 of book II of Bede's *Ecclesiastical History*. The 'twelve days after Pentecost', the twelve thousand men baptised alongside Edwin and the forty days of Rhun's baptising all occur elsewhere in the *Historia* and reflect Nennius's interests in sacred number, but each finds parallels in Bede's account of Paulinus's conversion of the Northumbrians, which this account seems intended to challenge.[244] Despite modern attempts to reconcile the two accounts,[245] this is best interpreted as an attempt to counter Bede's damaging slur on the Britons,[246] by claiming that they had indeed converted Saxons.[247] That this supposedly reached him from senior clerics implies that Nennius's methods were already entrenched in local Church circles.

The passages dealing with Cadwallon, perhaps Outigirn and more certainly Urien and his associates should be treated separately, therefore, from the British heroes featured in the *Historia* up to and including chapter 56; they are more factual and better rooted in identifiable sources. It is exploration of Bellinus, Dolabella, Vortimer, Brutus, Britto and Cunedda that provides insights to Nennius's approach in the passages that rework British history up to the close of Gildas's 'historical' survey. For these, neither our author nor his recent Welsh 'sources' had any fresh, authentic material to set beside Orosius, Gildas and the Christian chronicles. This was a scholarly community prepared to manipulate the distant past, shift individuals around and invent characters to make British history fit for purpose. They amended names to better suit their needs, misquoted from and rode roughshod over earlier testimony, fictionalised historical figures and made up others *de novo*. The harvesting of names from their original setting to be reused in a different context was commonplace.

Outside the *Historia Brittonum*, there is one further example that might perhaps help us understand this approach to the past, for it has been suggested that the omens regarding the Saxon settlers in Gildas's *De Excidio Britanniae*, reportedly from a Saxon source, is interpolated: 'The winds were favourable; favourable also the omens and auguries, which prophesied ... that they would live for three hundred years in the land towards which their prows were directed'.[248]

If this was, indeed, not part of the original *De Excidio*, then its message best fits an addition sometime around the close of this three-hundred-year period, during the reign of Offa, perhaps.[249] The message would seem to be that the English stay in Britain was destined to end and end soon. The composition of prophesies was common in the insular Middle Ages. This may well be an early example from a time when British clerics were revisiting Gildas's text in the hope of coming across some hint of English colonisation ending. There are parallels between this interpolation – if that is what it is – and the effort made in the *Historia Brittonum*, to 'revise' the earlier text so as to produce a 'better' story. Nennius was likewise interested in foreign dominations, the time they endured and the manner of their ending:

> Romans ruled with the Britons 409 years. The Britons however threw off the rule of the Romans: neither did they pay taxes to them nor did they accept kings from them, to rule over them; nor did the Romans dare to come to Britain any more to rule, because the Britons killed their *duces*.[250]

This is not good history in any modern sense, but, once again, it helps us to see what these writers were trying to achieve; there are implicit connections here between the *Historia* and what may be the thought-world of recent scholarship.

So, just as close examination of chapter 56 throws up reasons to be extremely wary of accepting Arthur's battle-list as in any sense historical, extending the discussion to embrace a range of the *Historia Brittonum*'s 'historical' characters reveals just how inventive its author was in constructing the remote past in ways that best suited the present. Clearly, his interests were focused more on the overall effect of his message than the detail on offer, much of which he altered out of all recognition. Let us face facts: the *Historia Brittonum* is in large part a work of historical fiction. While its author seems to have stayed reasonably close to his 'northern' source for the later sixth and seventh centuries, none of his elaborations on or 'corrections' to Orosius's *Seven Histories against the Pagans* or Gildas's *De Excidio Britanniae* stand up to critical scrutiny. Passages in the *Historia* which borrow from slightly earlier 'historical' works reveal a similarly cavalier approach there too, with fictional or fictionalised characters and the past reinvented for present purposes. It may be that the authors of these works were responsible for training Nennius, in which case we should perhaps suppose that all these works were produced by a small group across just two generations, even within a single religious centre. Whether or not, our author clearly had no qualms about using excerpts from these recent works and he adopted the same approach when he set about writing about British resistance to foreign invasion. This begins with Bellinus and Dolabella as British heroes confronting Caesar. Arthur is the last of these figures but there is no better reason to think him historical. The *Historia's* purpose in both passages was much the same, to provide an uplifting story of British warriors confronting aggressors coming from overseas. We can appreciate the ways in which chapter 56 fitted with the overall direction and rhetorical purpose of the *Historia* but its account of war against the Saxons cannot be judged any more historical than Dolabella's battles six centuries earlier.

The northern dimension

That does not, though, quite get rid of Arthur for, as we have seen, Nennius often adopted the names of real people from the past for his fictional characters. However incongruous Dolabella's role in the *Historia Brittonum*, his name is historical, as too is Bellinus's (albeit badly garbled). So are those of Brutus and Cunedda, and we can at least see how and why Welsh scholars came up with Vortimer. We need to ask ourselves, therefore, where might the name Arthur have come from before it was parachuted into the *Historia* to fulfil this particular role? There can be no certain answer to this question but we can at least explore some possibilities.

Firstly, the name Arthur as used in *Historia* is a Welsh form, despite most probably originating as the Roman Artorius. The starting point was therefore probably either the Welsh name or its close Old Irish equivalent, Artúr, not Artoriüs, Artus, Arturus or Arcturus. This pretty well rules out any text written outside the British Isles.

Secondly, there is no reason to expect the name to have occurred in a passage similar to that in which Arthur appears in chapter 56 of the *Historia*. Just as Dolabella and Cunedda (to take just two) were parachuted into scenes in the *Historia Brittonum* which were very different from those from which their names had been taken, so too is this likely to have been the case with Arthur. Each time, though, there was a reason to select a particular name. Brutus became the British eponym because Isidore suggested that the name derived from *brutus*, 'brutish'. Why Dolabella? Perhaps so as to take advantage of the meaning of the second part of the name in the (altered) accusative (Dolabellum; cf. Arthur as *dux bellorum*).

Much like Dolabella and Vortimer, Arthur appears in the *Historia Brittonum* not as a king but as a military leader. There is no reason to think any of his battles to be authentically connected with him (and those for which we have other information all seem to have been 'lifted' from other stories), but the notion of a brave warrior leading a 'national' army may be something which carried over from the 'original' individual of this name. One option is to identify the *Historia*'s character with Arthur, son of Peter in the royal genealogy of Dyfed (see above, p. 171),[251] but as has already been remarked Nennius shows barely any awareness of or interest in southern Wales. A somewhat more attractive possibility is to connect the Arthur of the *Historia* with the enigmatic figure of that name in *Y Gododdin*. As already discussed (see above, p. 167), this collection includes a verse honouring the British hero Gorddur, which notes that, though heroic, he was 'not Arthur'. Like the Arthur of the *Historia*, therefore, this allusion implies a great martial reputation. Given that Arthur appears in the earliest version of *Y Gododdin* now extant, this may pre-date the *Historia. Y Gododdin* passed south from northern Britain to Wales at some point. Though we do not know that this had occurred by 829–30, the possibility is at least there; *Y Gododdin* just might have provided the *Historia*'s author with the name.

In this context it is important to remind ourselves that *Y Gododdin* originated in the Lothians, but one of the surviving versions attracted at least one additional verse in Strathclyde soon after 642.[252] The Arthur of *Y Gododdin* is likely, therefore, to have been a figure of the 'Northern British Heroic Age' who was a famous warrior and leader of warriors in the sixth or early seventh centuries. It is tempting to place this alongside what we know about the patron for whom the *Historia Brittonum* was written, for Merfyn likewise came, in all probability, from the north, from the Isle of Man. Man (Mevania) was considered by Orosius to have been already settled by the Irish when he was writing early in the fifth century,[253] but was considered 'British' by Bede and linked by him with Anglesey in the time of King Edwin.[254] It should therefore be seen as something of a meeting place both culturally and politically, lying as it does at the southern end of the North Channel, between Ulster, Scottish Argyll, British north Wales and Strathclyde, and the more 'British' regions of western Northumbria. It seems likely that influential families based in Gwynedd and Man intermarried at various stages; Merfyn may well have been a scion of just such a union (as in medieval Welsh tradition). There is evidence for a major Christian centre at Maughold on the east coast; the place-name recalls a Scottish saint who was remembered as the patron saint of the island and there is a notable concentration of carved stones of the Celtic period, some of a British type.[255]

Unsurprisingly, we can detect a variety of Irish influences on Merfyn's court, some of which fed into the *Historia Brittonum*. Irish visitors seem to have been common,[256] including the Dubthach who was responsible for a cryptogram that has survived.[257] The *Historia* borrowed from the *Book of the Taking of Ireland* (*Lebor Gabála Érenn*), a biblically inspired pseudo-history of the Gaels that was composed in Ireland,[258] including Irish settlement stories for both Dál Riata and the Isle of Man.[259] That at least one version reached our author from 'very skilful [men] of the Scots' (*peritissimi Scottorum*) implies face-to-face contact with Irish clerics.[260] Likewise, Patrick's treatment in the *Historia* derives from traditions centred on Downpatrick and Armagh and written up there.

This northern material was not, though, all Irish in origin. As already noted, our author used a body of northern British material, the so-called 'Northern Memorandum', from a church community with a long 'British' tradition, probably somewhere in what had earlier been Rheged (Dumfries and Galloway, Cumbria) but was now part of Northumbria (see above, p. 205).[261] Cunedda's story likewise derived from northern Britain; given that his character appears initially in the *Historia* in conjunction with an Irish settlement story referring to Dál Riata and Man, this may have arrived via Irish-speakers. The *Historia* records the names of several British poets, among whom Aneirin and Taliesin were certainly northerners (we know nothing of the others). The only surviving poetry attributed to Aneirin is, of course, *Y Gododdin*, which does refer to Arthur, but Breguoin may well derive from Urien's 'battle of the cells of Brewyn', in verse reputedly by Taliesin.[262]

We can establish, therefore, that Nennius was indebted to both Irish and British literary cultures around North Channel. This perhaps offers our best chance of localising the Arthur whose name appears in his work. That this name was recorded on both sides of the Irish Sea from the later sixth century onwards has been urged both as supportive of the case for an 'historical' Arthur,[263] and for the suggestion that the 'original' Arthur was at least as Irish as British. However, this is rather to miss the point, for all that we are seeking is someone whose name could have been 'borrowed' into the *Historia* for a character developed by its author for his own rhetorical purposes. What we have are fragments of a northern literature with parts at least of which the *Historia*'s author was familiar, and contact with Irish clerics. Arthur's name could have come from either. *Y Gododdin* is one possibility (see above, pp. 167–9). Another is that the name derived from Irish material, be that written or oral.

There are several stories that originated among the Gaels at the northern end of the Irish Sea that left their mark in medieval Wales and which are quite likely to have entered via Merfyn's court. The Scottish King Áedán is one of very few non-British figures from the north whose name lodged in the Welsh narrative tradition.[264] It was his close ally Fiachnae mac Báetáin who fathered that Mongán who was killed by 'Artúr, son of Bicoir' *c.* 625. Who this Artúr was is unclear, though the Demetian king has been suggested, in which case Bicoir should be understood as a variant of Welsh Petr or Irish Petuir (Peter).[265] Mongán was the hero of several seventh-century stories, including one called *The Conception of Mongán* (*Compert Mongáin*) in which he was fathered by the Irish sea-god Manannán (a figure closely associated with the Isle of Man[266]) on Fiachnae's wife while the king was away fighting alongside Áedán. This 'conception of the hero' story parallels the Greek myth of the birth of Hercules,[267] and other early tales from as far afield as India.[268] Interestingly, though, it is virtually the same as the tale later told by Geoffrey of Monmouth of Arthur's conception.[269] Of course, this is a folk tale that was equally applicable to any number of characters but it may just be worth noting its proximity to the name Arthur in the seventh century and then again in the twelfth. This may at least imply that a Welsh 'conception of the hero' folk tale, similar to one known from seventh-century Ulster, underlies Geoffrey's tale of Arthur's conception at Tintagel.

A further parallel from this same northern world is provided by another associate of Áedán, Mael Umai mac Baetán of the Cenél nEogain (around Derry), who was credited in the *Clonmacnois Chronicle* with killing the brother of Æthelfrith of the Northumbrians *c.* 603.[270] Once again he was remembered as a fierce war-leader who died (*c.* 610) without becoming king. Though his story has not survived, his name occurs near the beginning of the catalogue of Arthur's followers in *Culhwch and Olwen* immediately before four Irish names taken from the Ulster Cycle.[271] That Mael Umai (here Maelwys mab Baedan) was grouped with these legendary northern heroes implies that the author appreciated his Irish provenance,[272] and perhaps suggests that something of his tale was then still remembered in Wales.[273]

In the light of such Irish connections, should we be looking to Ireland for the inception of Arthur's story? In practice, this seems unlikely, for the Arthurian tradition only seems to have become established there comparatively late. The *Historia Brittonum* was translated into Gaelic in the late eleventh century (the earliest surviving manuscript dates to *c.* 1200),[274] but this adds little to the Latin original. Outside the *Tales of the Elders*, the name Arthur occurs in Irish literature in only a single translated work before the later Middle Ages. Then just five of the sixty or so 'romantic tales' surviving

from the fifteenth and sixteenth centuries are in any sense 'Arthurian'. That
these are independent of known external sources must allow the possibility
of an ongoing local tradition,[275] but such tales as *The Story of the Crop-
Eared Dog* and *The Story of Eagle-Boy* draw too heavily on continental
Arthurian traditions later than Wace to be considered earlier than the
Historia.[276] We can be reasonably certain, therefore, that Arthur's story did
not begin in Ireland.

But, clearly, much of the material available to the author of the *Historia
Brittonum* came from around the northern Irish Sea. The cluster of northern
Irish names in surviving medieval Welsh literature is at least consistent
with the name Arthur having come from this region. The likeliest candidate that is known to us is Artúr, son of Áedán, the king of Dál Riata whose
name passed into the medieval Welsh tradition; this Artúr might also lie
behind the allusion to Arthur in *Y Gododdin*. This is, though, no more than
a possibility and rests on circumstantial evidence. And even if this were the
case, it would not mean that Arthur's deeds in the *Historia* were in any
meaningful sense based on the career of this 'Scottish' Arthur, or that we
should seek Arthur's alleged battles in this or neighbouring regions of
Scotland,[277] and I really cannot emphasise this enough. All it implies is that
this could have been where Nennius found the name that he would give to
the God-beloved British leader who he depicted as twelve-times defeating
the Saxons in his 'improved' version of Gildas's 'war of the Saxon federates'.

The Arthur of the *Historia Brittonum*

Overall assessment of the *Historia* is hampered by the fluidity of the text
across the manuscript traditions but chapter 56 is not in much doubt.
It offers twelve victories, the last at Badon, won by the ever-victorious
Arthur, *dux bellorum*, as leader of the Britons. Given the length of time
that had elapsed, Nennius clearly did not rely on word-of-mouth testimony
for Arthur. Nor did he have any near-contemporary written testimony
for British history in this period other than Gildas, who cannot have been
his source for the name. That several of his battle-names rhyme may imply
an earlier Welsh poem. Alternatively, the author of the *Historia* may just
have favoured rhyming names when he made up the list. Whichever,
the better the battle-names rhyme the less they should be credited as
historical. That several occur earlier as battles fought by different figures
against various opponents suggests heavy plagiarism. Use of biblical
numbering and emphasis on the Virgin Mary mark it as the work of a

churchman, quite possibly Nennius himself; if not then some other very recent north Welsh cleric.

Chapter 56 should be read less as a 'source' for an historical Arthur, therefore, than as part of a wider rewriting of British history under way in Wales in the decades around 800. Its purposes were highly contemporary, reflective of the Welsh reconciliation with Rome in 768, of rapidly changing relations with the English and of the hope that Britain might, when God saw fit, be restored once again to its rightful, British owners.

While his narrative up to and including all but the closing lines of chapter 56 was framed by the *De Excidio Britanniae* and the Kentish origins story, Nennius was seeking to 'improve' on Gildas, manipulating his sources to fit a very different account and inventing new characters to carry out deeds that had not hitherto been recorded. As a result, the *Historia Brittonum* offers us little of value to our understanding of the fifth and early sixth centuries; rather the contrary, for it reflects an approach to history which is far removed from the ways that we think about the subject today. The characters whom he introduced bear this out. Germanus provides a prophet-like figure through whom the Britons could be equated with the Israelites of Exodus, in opposition to Vortigern (who had already been compared by Gildas with the Old Testament Pharaoh). Patrick appears as a British type of Moses whose Irish mission provides evidence that the fifth-century Britons championed continental Christianity and took the lead in extending its reach to Ireland. In the same vein, the British Rhun was credited with converting King Edwin of the Northumbrians,[278] in defiance of Bede's earlier (and far more credible) account.

Unlike these figures, the *Historia*'s Arthur is a warrior and leader of warriors, the last of a string of British protector-figures stretching forward from Bellinus and Dolabella, via Cunedda and Vortimer. None can be accepted as historical in anything like the form in which he appears, though the names of the first three, at least, derive from reliable sources. What stands out is the systematic fictionalisation of all these figures in the *Historia*. This was an approach to the past that Nennius shared with other, near-contemporary Welsh writers whose works he used or whose orally transmitted 'information' he incorporated. Acceptance of Britto illustrates the manner in which his 'historical' technique built on theirs.

The *Historia*'s presentation of Arthur is, therefore, problematic in many respects. The gap of over three hundred years separating its composition from these 'events', the lack of early sources, suspicion that individual battles were plagiarised from earlier stories featuring quite different characters, recent Christian influences on the text – all these factors count against the *Historia*'s Arthur being historical. Our wider exploration of its author's methods provides an important extra dimension, for we can now see rather more of his approach as an historian. Given his penchant for taking names from other contexts and applying them to fictional characters in his own work, it would be extraordinarily rash to accept Arthur's achievements in chapter 56 as in any sense 'real'. Perhaps Arthur's name was 'borrowed' from that of an historical figure of the past, then redeployed, much as was Dolabella's, or (less certainly) Cunedda's. We have explored the possibility that the name derived from the northern Irish Sea area, either from *Y Gododdin* or from stories circulating in Ulster or Dál Riata, but this can be little more than guesswork. We can neither know where the name came from nor establish with any certainty why it was this particular name that was chosen for the role.

In presenting his warrior-Arthur there are parallels sufficient to suggest that our author had the biblical Joshua in mind, as ever reimagining the British past through an Old Testament lens. What Arthur offered to a ninth-century audience above all else was an example of how a British war-leader might unite the disparate forces of their kings into an army capable of triumphing over their enemies. Since history was the working through of God's will, Nennius was seeking to position the Britons as the Old Testament Israelites and their leaders as types of the figures who guided their establishment in the Promised Land. Even while writing the past, therefore, he was anticipating an upturn in the fortunes of God's own British people. Just so did the Lord long ago, and at times of His own choosing, succour the Israelites and smite their enemies.

In early ninth-century Wales, history was written by men trained as exegetes, whose normal reading material consisted primarily of the Bible, commentaries thereon and saints' lives. It was driven more by present religious, cultural and political needs than a desire to set down accurately what had occurred in the distant past. The truth-claims of the *Historia Brittonum* are of little merit prior to the mid-sixth century; what is on offer is heavily fictionalised. The agenda of this work is more propaganda than history, its purpose to place Gwynedd's king at the forefront of the nationalist cause. It was in Gwynedd that Vortigern was advised by his magi to 'Make a fortress in this place, because it will be for ever the safest against the barbarian people [the English].'[279] Vortigern gifted this stronghold to Ambrosius – Embreis Guletic ('Emrys the Overlord'), 'king among all the kings of the Britons'. Merfyn was Gwynedd's king in the present and (almost certainly) our author's patron; by implication, he was heir to both the 'safest' fortress against the English and Ambrosius's high-kingship. So, too, was Gwynedd the base of 'Maelgwn the great king among the Britons'. One of the *Historia Brittonum*'s main purposes was to serve as political propaganda on behalf of Merfyn, reinforcing his claim on Gwynedd by asserting this ancient right to be recognised as leader of the whole British nation.

7

A BRITISH ARTHUR
Starting the Tradition

> In them [the Welsh Arthurian poems] we find the poets and their audiences
> at play. They help us understand how the Celtic peripheries became the
> focus for marvels and adventures in twelfth-century European literature.
> — Oliver Padel, 'The Early Welsh Arthurian Poems'[1]

Only a few of the characters who first appear in British history in the
Historia Brittonum enjoyed much of an afterlife. Notwithstanding
its stress on his Britishness, Patrick remained primarily a figure of
Irish storytelling throughout the Middle Ages; the *Historia Brittonum*'s
presentation of him as a British Moses never really took off – Geoffrey of
Monmouth barely referenced him in the *History of the Kings of Britain*.[2]
Despite a scatter of church dedications, St Germanus's British 'Book' has
not survived and seems to have spawned no imitations. Geoffrey's longer
passage regarding him drew not on the *Historia Brittonum* but on Bede,[3]
with only a brief appearance otherwise in a passage focused on Vortigern's
Saxon marriage derived from the *Historia*.[4] Vortigern (as Gwrtheyrn, etc.)
occurs in medieval Welsh genealogies but Vortimer does not, though
Geoffrey did include him.[5] Genealogists inserted Cunedda and his immediate forebears into Gwynedd's royal pedigree, and he appears in the *History
of the Kings of Britain* as Cunedagius,[6] but he otherwise made little impression on Welsh storytelling. Dolabella slipped out of British history almost as
bizarrely as he had entered it, when Geoffrey converted this imaginary
general into the fortress Dorobellum oppidum.[7] Obviously, we should not
let this highly imaginative twelfth-century reinterpretation influence our

reading of the ninth-century *Historia Brittonum*,[8] but this brings down the curtain on Dolabella's strange appearance in British history.

A minority of the *Historia*'s characters, though, did very much better. Geoffrey of Monmouth conflated Britto with Brutus, adopting the former's Trojan lineage but the latter's name, and made him central to the *History of the Kings of Britain*'s first book as the founding ancestor of the (entirely fictional) British royal line – Arthur included. *Brut* came to signify the pseudo-historical tradition which Geoffrey began, initially in Wace's French version but later in English and Welsh. Indeed, *Brut* was used in both these languages to describe 'history' more generally, particularly works that were in some sense continuations of the *History of the Kings of Britain*.[9]

Bellinus was another whose stock rose post-1000, appearing as Beli, Geoffrey's twenty-second king (and perhaps also as Heli, the seventy-ninth[10]). His achievements in war against the Romans alongside his putative brother Brennus (based on the Gaulish leader who reputedly sacked Rome in Antiquity[11]) dominate book III of the *History of the Kings of Britain*. Beli Mawr appears in Welsh genealogies as an ancestral figure, and has a significant role in later Welsh Romance and pseudo-history, though whether or not he originated with the *Historia* character is today disputed.[12]

But Arthur was the *Historia Brittonum*'s most successful, most recent and only explicitly Christian leader of national resistance to foreign threats, the most difficult to refute, given his absence from earlier histories,[13] and still very much relevant, for the Saxon threat remained. Arthur was, therefore, always the likeliest of these figures to interest Welsh leaders and their bards. His omission from the tenth-century poem, *Armes Prydein* suggests that his take-up was patchy at first, but Scandinavian, Anglo-Saxon and then Anglo-Norman attacks on Wales can only have encouraged his adoption. Translation of the *History of the Kings of Britain* into Welsh *c.* 1200 provided an additional spur to bards in adopting him as one of the nation's legendary heroes. The eleventh-century takeover of Dyfed by the Gwynedd dynasty is likely to have raised awareness of Arthur in the south (whence come the majority of surviving 'Arthurian' texts). Witnesses are typically late but by the eleventh-century Arthurian stories seem to have been circulating throughout the Celtic world, Brittany included,[14] and pushing outwards to France, Italy and England. William of Malmesbury, writing *c.* 1125, remarked:

> With his [Vortimer's] death the strength of the Britons withered away, their hope dwindled and ebbed; and now in fact they would have collapsed entirely had not Ambrosius, the sole survivor of the Romans,

who was ruler of the kingdom after Vortigern, kept down the barbarian menace along with the exceptional deeds of the warlike Arthur. This is the Arthur concerning whom even today among the Britons they talk nonsense [*nugae*], though plainly he deserves to be the subject of truthful history rather than the false fables they dream, for he long sustained his falling motherland and roused the broken spirit of its citizens to battle, and at length at the siege of Badon mountain, relying on the image of the mother of our Lord which he had sewn on to his arms, he overthrew nine hundred of the enemy single handed, routing them with incredible slaughter.[15]

William's 'truthful history' is, of course, based on the *Historia Brittonum* and has no better claim on reality than his source – indeed less, for he adopted a cut-and-paste approach, transplanting features of the eighth battle to the twelfth (as had the *Annales Cambriae*, of course). Of greater interest today would have been the 'nonsense' that William had come across, but we cannot know anything about these stories beyond his considering them fanciful. These may have been orally transmitted tales, perhaps encountered second-hand.[16] Of course, some of these may survive but obviously we do not know which specific tales William was alluding to. We can, though, explore Arthur's appearances in what survives of Welsh literature composed in or about this period. Much of this material will have been experienced largely if not exclusively as oral performance (written works included[17]), but we can only access the fraction that was both written down and has survived.

Before we begin, though, we should be quite clear about what we are doing and what we are not. It is Arthur whose appearances we are exploring, not such later accretions to the legend as the sword in the stone, Camelot, the Round Table or the Holy Grail. Despite weighty academic opinion in favour of the early inception of each of these elements,[18] it is important to recognise that even the earliest cannot be shown to have entered the tradition before the mid-twelfth century,[19] so can have nothing to tell us about the early development of Arthur himself.

Camelot

To take the only one of these that has not been discussed to this point, there have been innumerable attempts firstly to identify Camelot as a real place and then to argue from that to the whereabouts of King Arthur. But the place-name Camelot appears first (and then only fleetingly) in Chrétien de Troyes's late twelfth-century romance *Lancelot* or *The Knight in the Cart* (*Le Chevalier de la Charrête*).[20] This is an extended reworking of a tale centred on Guinevere's abduction which featured in the Welsh cleric Caradoc of Llancarfan's earlier-twelfth-century *Life of Gildas* and in a scene carved onto the archivolt of the Porta della Pescheria in Modena Cathedral (Plate 21).[21] Chrétien's abductor, Meleaganz, derives from the Welsh Melvas, so we can be confident that he used a Welsh or Breton archetype (this was presumably the source material provided by Marie, Countess of Champagne which he acknowledged at the start of the work). His is a root-and-branch rewrite, though, which replaces Arthur as the queen's deliverer with Lancelot (the 'knight in the cart'), who seems to have been his own creation (he appears earliest, fleetingly, as 'Lancelot of the Lake' in his *Erec and Enide*). There are numerous plot and character changes besides and the story is enormously extended. This is, therefore, in most respects an original work; beyond the bare framework, it owes few debts to its Welsh or Breton source.

It is often supposed that Camelot was the name of a defended site in Britain that Chrétien took from his Celtic source but this is arguably to take too naïve an approach to his work. The Modena inscription does not name the tower in which Guinevere was captive, so we cannot test Chrétien against this earlier witness. Caradoc set Guinevere's captivity and the confrontation between Arthur and Melvas at Glastonbury (Glastonia) but *The Knight in the Cart* ignores this. In fact, the French romance offers very few places that can certainly be identified in Britain. Of these, Engleterre and Londres were common names in contemporary French; Caerleon and Bade (Bath) are both present in Wace's *Brut*.[22] Logres (England) was by this date long-established in the Celtic tradition and was used repeatedly in the *History of the Kings of Britain*.[23] Most names are continental, from France (including Dombes, Amiens, Montpelliers, Poitiers, Limoges, Toulouse, Lyon), the Low Countries (Ghent), Italy (Rome), Spain (Pamplona, Aragon), Greece (Thessaly) or the east (Babylon or Cairo, in different versions).[24] Others are either minor French place-names or made-up names.[25] His place-naming strategy suggests that Chrétien was more concerned to locate the story within a geography with which his French-speaking audience felt comfortable, than adhere to an 'authentic' Celtic archetype.[26]

Where does this leave Camelot (Chamaalot or Camaalot, the manuscripts vary)? Here is William Kibler's English translation: 'On a certain Ascension Day King Arthur was in the region near Caerleon and held his court at Camelot, splendidly and luxuriantly as befitted a king.'[27]

This implies a place within a day's journey, or so, of Caerleon but the absence of other authentic 'British' places beyond those which were both very well known in the twelfth century and prominent already in Arthurian literature counts against this deriving from a Celtic source.[28] It seems likelier that it was made up. One might hypothesise that Chrétien selected the stem, 'Cam-' so as to root a place where Arthur held court within contemporary perceptions of Arthurian place-naming – he could have had Geoffrey's 'Camblan' or Wace's 'Camble' in mind.[29] *Lot* is an unproblematic French word meaning 'lot', 'portion', 'share', or 'fate', selected so as to rhyme with *tenue ot* at the close of the previous line.[30]

Camelot is therefore very unlikely to derive from a Celtic source detailing an authentic sub-Roman, British place-name, let alone from some pre-Roman myth or legend.[31] On the contrary it seems probable that it began with this brief appearance in a highly imaginative French romance written between 1170 and 1190; there is no trace of it in either English or Welsh before the thirteenth century so no local tradition which can have any claim to antiquity.[32] It was often identified as Winchester in the later Middle Ages, for example by Malory, presumably because this was known to have been an early seat of royal power (in the late Anglo-Saxon period) and had featured prominently in the *History of the Kings of Britain* and Wace. Additionally, the Round Table was (and still is) there (Plate 22), suggesting that this identification goes back to the Plantagenet era, when the table was made.[33] Caxton, though, in his preface to the first edition of Malory's work, supposed Camelot to be in Wales.

Unless and until it can be shown that Chrétien took both place and name from a much earlier work, we should therefore reject all attempts to locate Camelot. We must dismiss John Morris's identification of Arthur's capital with Colchester (Roman-period Camulodonum),[34] and Jim Storr's attempt to revive this same theory.[35] Likewise, we should have no truck with the urgings of Simon Keegan and Peter Field in favour of that other Camulodunum – the Roman fort at Slack near Huddersfield;[36] the fort has so far revealed no evidence of occupation later than the second century,[37] though the vicus next to it was in use well into the third.[38] Camelon (near Falkirk) was proposed in the nineteenth century and has since found support from those keen to place Arthur in Scotland,[39] but this is probably Gaelic in origin and very unlikely to have come to Chrétien's attention. Suggestions in favour of an Iron Age hillfort close to Cardiff (Castlefield Camp east of Craig-Llywn) or Roxburgh Castle do not even have a similarity in their names to commend them.[40]

Nor should Camelot be located at any other Roman centre for no better reason than that it might have been inhabited at the right sort of time and suits a particular theory as to Arthur's whereabouts.[41] The best-publicised connection in recent times has been with South Cadbury hillfort (Plate 24), as first noted by John Leland, a keen Arthurian,[42] in the sixteenth century:

> At the very south ende of the chirch of South-Cadbyri standith Camallate, sumtyme a famose toun or castelle, apon a very torre or hille, wunderfully enstrengtheid of nature, to the which be 2 enteringes up by very stepe way . . .
>
> Much gold, sylver and coper of the Romaine coynes hath be found ther yn plouing: and lykewise in the feldes in the roote of this hille, with many other antique thinges. . . .
>
> The people can telle nothing ther but that they have hard say that Arture much resortid to Camalat.[43]

Whether it was Leland himself who made the connection or someone earlier is unclear,[44] but the thinking behind it is pretty transparent, deriving as it must from the similarity of local name elements (as the settlement names Queen Camel, West Camel, named after the River Cam), allied with the site's defensive form and archaeological finds coming from the interior.[45] That South Cadbury hillfort was an elite residence in the later fifth and early sixth centuries is important,[46] but many British forts were in use in that period in the west. Such are found at least as far north as Trusty's Hill (Galloway),[47] the Mote of Mark (Dumfries: Plate 17),[48] and Dumbarton Rock (on the Clyde's north bank). These were the strongholds of British chieftains or kings. But neither the British name of the fort later known as South Cadbury nor of its owner need have come down to us, for the Old Welsh, personal-name element Cad- is one of the few that were absorbed into Old English (as the seventh-century West Saxon king Cædwalla) and the Old English suffix, *burh*, implies a place-name formed in Anglo-Saxon. We can be perfectly clear, therefore: the identification of South Cadbury as Camelot dates no earlier than the later Middle Ages and has nothing to contribute to our understanding of the inception of Arthur's story.[49]

That such warnings are necessary is demonstrated time and again by writers appealing to one or more of these latecomers to the literary tradition to sustain their own arguments regarding the origins of Arthur[50] – and this is of course as much a feature of continental theories as British ones.[51]

We need to be on our guard. Our approach must be to seek out the earliest evidence for the tradition. We will proceed by surveying Arthur's presence in texts written in the central Middle Ages in either Latin or Welsh, attempting to impose a degree of chronological order on these often problematic works.

The *Annales Cambriae*

The earliest ('A') version of the *Annales Cambriae* (*Welsh Annals*) is a comparatively thin set of annals that was one of the Welsh texts copied into Harleian MS 3859.[52] Internal evidence strongly suggests that these were compiled at St David's (Welsh Mynyw, Latin Menevia), in Dyfed, in the reign of Owain (died 988), most probably in or very soon after *c.* 954 (the date of the final entry). The *Annales* were studied closely by Kathleen Hughes, who proposed that the earliest section derived from a now-lost Irish chronicle written at the monastery at Clonmacnoise.[53] That in turn depended on continental chronicles and the 'Chronicle of Ireland', now lost but the archetype of all the Irish chronicles. The tenth-century author used annals written locally from the late 790s onwards and a north Welsh chronicle covering the period *c.* 754–*c.* 858, that may have been written to serve as an appendix to the *Historia Brittonum*.[54] Victorius's Easter Table influenced this work,[55] reflecting Welsh acceptance of the Roman system of calculation of Easter in the third quarter of the eighth century (see above, pp. 176–7).[56] Internally, dates were omitted,[57] but (with occasional exceptions) one line was provided for each year. The framework has therefore to be fixed chronologically by reference to entries covering events dateable externally, which is far easier in later sections than at the beginning. The dates offered here are, therefore, only approximate.[58]

Entries in the first century (*c.* 447–*c.* 546) are particularly thin, occurring only for the nine years corresponding to 453, 454, 457, 468, 501, 516, 521, 537 and 544. Most derived from the Irish exemplar: the birth of the Irish saint Brigid (454), the deaths of Patrick (457) and St Benignus of Armagh (468), and the birth of Iona's founder, St Columba (521), all occur in Irish chronicles (though the dating is variable). The 453 entry, giving Pope Leo responsibility for the calculation of Easter, may reflect familiarity with Bede's *The Reckoning of Time*;[59] inclusion confirms the author's interest in the Paschal issue.[60]

The earliest 'British' material, found in neither Irish annals nor Bede, is a pair of 'Arthurian' entries:

[516]: The battle of Badon, in which Arthur carried the cross of our Lord Jesus Christ for three days and three nights on his shoulders and the Britons were the victors.

[537]: The battle [*Gueith*] of Camlann, in which Arthur and Medraut fell, and there was a mortality [*mortalitas*] in Britain and Ireland.[61]

These have often been considered authoritative,[62] and they have certainly exercised a strong influence on later authors, the second in particular spawning a vast literature centred on Arthur's death. We must ask, though, both where the author of the *Annales* could have found this material, and how he determined where it should sit within his overall framework? The problem, once again, is the lapse of time separating events early in the sixth century from the act of writing-down. Just as we dismissed the possibility of reliable oral sources underlying the *Historia Brittonum*, so too must we set aside any chance that the *Annales*, which were written some five generations later, could derive from word-of-mouth testimony. Our focus must, therefore, be on written material.

Leslie Alcock assured his readers that the *Annales* derived from marginal entries in Easter Tables written in the sixth century.[63] However, a later annalist able to draw on such material would almost certainly have found references to local bishops and abbots, which he would then have drawn into his own work. None occur before 796. Instead, Arthur's battles provide the sole British contributions to this first century of the *Annales*. A royal genealogy which was likewise written in Dyfed in Owain's reign recorded an Arthur as the king's ancestor thirteen generations earlier.[64] Our annalist will almost certainly have been familiar with this (he may even have been its author), so is likely to have considered Arthur a figure of local significance whose activities were worth including.[65] This does not, though, excuse the absence of any other of the Demetian elite within this period. We can surmise, therefore, that access to locally maintained records begins very much later. Clearly, knowledge of Arthur's deeds did not derive from near-contemporary Easter Tables or other forms of annals kept in Dyfed.

It has often been suggested that the 'Badon' entry in the *Annales* was from the same source as underlies chapter 56 of the *Historia*, or one closely related to it, for there is an undeniable similarity. An alternative is to suppose that the author of the *Annales* was here drawing on the *Historia Brittonum* directly.[66] The *Annales*' entries concerning King Edwin's baptism (*c.* 626) and death (*c.* 630), and Oswald's death (*c.* 644) all have some resemblance to passages in the *Historia* (chapters 63, 61 and 65 respectively), suggesting that the *Historia* may have been available to the *Annales*' author. The main difference in the references to Badon in the *Historia* and the *Annales* lies in the manner in which Arthur is characterised. In the *Historia* he is a ferocious warrior slaughtering Saxons in their hundreds; in the *Annales Cambriae* he appears as a Christ-figure carrying the cross to his crucifixion, or a Christ-helper modelled on Simon the Cyrenian, who bore the cross in Luke's Gospel.[67] This entry has echoes not just of the *Historia*'s twelfth battle but also its eighth,[68] at which 'Arthur carried [*portavit*] the image of Saint Mary ... on his shoulders [*super humeros suos*]'. In the *Annales*, Arthur 'carried [*portavit*] the cross of our Lord Jesus Christ for three days and three nights on his shoulders [*in humeros suos*]'.[69] The language used implies a very close connection indeed, but with the *Annales* reworked to fit the very different political conditions facing Dyfed in the mid-tenth century, when its king was reliant on English protection against his north Welsh cousins.[70]

The source of the first 'Arthurian' entry was either the *Historia* or its immediate source, therefore, and the annalist's decision to include Badon probably resulted from its prominence therein. The *Historia* offered no date, though, so he was left juggling its insertion as best he could. He knew from his Irish exemplar that Patrick died *c.* 457 and Gildas *c.* 570, so recognised that Badon belonged in between. He located the date roughly midway in 516. This is contradicted by the *De Excidio Britanniae*'s indication that Maglocunus (Maelgwn) was still alive in the forty-fourth year after Badon. However, the *Annales*' author may well have been unfamiliar with this at first-hand, leaving him to place the death of Mailcun (Maelgwyn) *c.* 547 and Badon *c.* 516, only thirty-one years earlier.[71] Another possibility is that the author knew Bede's *Greater Chronicle*, in which British success under Ambrosius Aurelianus occurred in the period 474–91, then added the forty-four years of Bede's *Ecclesiastical History* (based on the *De Excidio*), giving him the time-frame of 518–35. Entries corresponding to 516 and 537 are close.[72] Whatever the precise method used, it seems clear that the dating adopted for the *Annales Cambriae* was based not on much earlier testimony but on calculations that can bear very little historical weight.

The second 'Arthurian' entry finds no echo in the *Historia Brittonum*. The *mortalitas* may come from the Irish annal; a 'failure of bread' is recorded under both 536 and 539 in surviving versions,[73] presumably reflecting the so-called 'volcanic winter' of the later 530s. This term is more often in medieval chronicles to mean 'epidemic' than 'famine', but its use in the Preface of the *Historia* as something of a catch-all perhaps justifies its sense here of 'a great death'. Old Welsh *gueith* occurs five times for 'battle' in the *Annales* but the other four (*c.* 722, 876, 906 and 921) were probably all recorded within living memory of the event.[74] *Gueith Camlann* ('the battle of Camlann') in 537 seems too early for that to be an option so we are perhaps looking towards an Old Welsh non-annalistic source, such as an elegy or lament. Camlann was long believed to be Camelford in Cornwall but that is now rejected.[75] More recently it has been identified with the Roman fort of Camboglanna on Hadrian's Wall,[76] but this Roman-period name is unlikely to have still been in use in the central Middle Ages,[77] and the *Annales Cambriae* does not in any case otherwise draw on material from northern Britain earlier than the 570s.[78] A more plausible identification is with the small vill of Camlan in the Dovey (Dyfi) valley.[79] The name was recorded before 1600 and it lies on a natural route-way between Ceredigion and Gwynedd (Map 6; Plate 24). It seems quite possible that an Arthur – perhaps the one named in the royal genealogy of Dyfed – was remembered as having been killed here, barely a two-day journey (37 miles) beyond Demetia, at the foot of passes running up the Dovey towards Bala, the Afon Cerist towards Dolgellau (where there is a tributary named Afon Gamlan), and the Afon Dugoed towards Powys.

We must conclude, therefore, that while the *Annales Cambriae* provide entries which date both Badon and Arthur's death, neither is capable of bearing much historical or chronological weight. The Badon entry almost certainly resulted from the author's familiarity with the *Historia Brittonum* or its immediate source, but he toned it down to conform to the political sensibilities of Dyfed's court at this date. Camlann came from a different source, probably local and most likely in Welsh but since lost. Given that the *Annales Cambriae* were written at St David's, this is likelier to have been referring to the Demetian Arthur than the warrior celebrated in the *Historia*. That these entries were included close together in annals which omit all other of Demetia's early kings implies that the author assumed that these two were the same figure, so conflated the *Historia*'s Arthur and the Arthur of the local dynasty. In that he was almost certainly wrong but the mistake is understandable. The dates depended on a rather poor framework of non-contemporary source material of relevance only to the chronology of the *Historia*'s Arthur. If the entry for *c.* 537 does refer to the Demetian Arthur, then counting generations back from *c.* 950 may suggest that this was inserted a couple of generations too early,[80] but once again that is understandable if the author supposed these two Arthurs to be the same individual and guesstimated the dating.

The *Mirabilia Britanniae*

The *Mirabilia Britanniae* (*The Wonders of Britain*) is a collection of miracles (*miracula*) and wonders (*mirabilia*) written in Latin, comprising little more than a thousand words, which appears first in Harleian MS 3859, copied from a south Welsh archetype written no earlier than the mid-950s (as above). It is untitled, but has long been known by this name.[81] Setting aside the first example, at Loch Lumonoy (Leven), which is a distant outlier in modern-day Scotland,[82] what is arguably the primary group numbers twelve, located in south-east Wales, the Severn valley, Ceredigion and the southern March (Map 6: 2–7, 9–14). Among these has been interpolated a miraculous ash tree beside the Wye which bears apples (8).[83] Then four *miracula* in Anglesey have been appended (15–18),[84] rounded off by two stories relating to Ireland (19, 20: see Appendix III).

Although this work has generally been accepted as part of the archetype of the *Historia*, with which it then descended,[85] it is separated from the first sixty-six chapters in the earliest complete text (the Harleian) by a set of British genealogies and the *Annales Cambriae*. It is unlikely, therefore, to be by the same hand as the *Historia* and is better treated as a separate text, which was assimilated to the *Historia* (see above, pp. 179–80).[86] The *Mirabilia* do not occur in the Vatican recension of *c.* 944, so were perhaps absent from the Welsh exemplar used by its English scribe, but it is otherwise a near ubiquitous element of the *Historia* in its later recensions.

It seems fairly clear that the *Mirabilia* began life as several different works. The core passage suggests an author of some learning and who was personally acquainted with southern Wales and the southern March,[87] so a cleric who knew that region well. The two wonders from Ireland seem to have been added very much as an afterthought,[88] perhaps as a result of contact with an Irish visitor (again most probably a cleric). The four relating to Anglesey have their own internal numbering, indicating their origin as a separate text; repeated use of *ibi* ('there') suggests that this group was written somewhere other than Anglesey.

The *Mirabilia* comprises, therefore, a grouping of shorter passages which had originally comprised a separate and independent composite text. All were probably clerical in origin and written in Latin from the outset, despite some stories (the Arthurian pair included) relying on knowledge of the vernacular. Arthur's two appearances occur in the 'core' passage, both providing evidence of his status as a warrior but also connecting him with wild places and marvellous events:

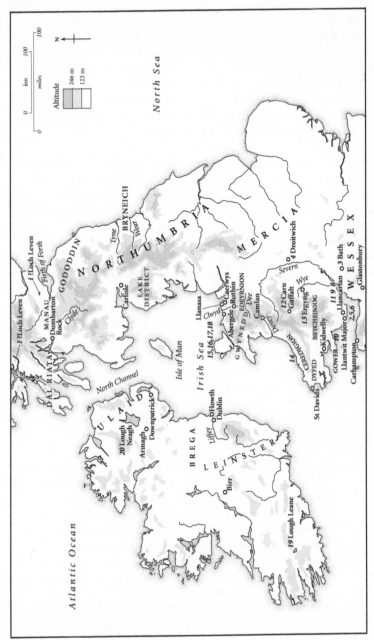

6 Britain and Ireland: the Celtic world in which King Arthur first emerged (numbers refer to those of the *mirabilia* that can be located with any degree of confidence).

There is another wonder in the region which is called Builth. There is a pile of stones there and one stone positioned on top of the heap has the footprint of a dog on it. When he hunted the boar Troynt, Cabal, who was the hound of Arthur the warrior, made an imprint on the stone, and Arthur afterwards collected up the heap of stones under the stone in which was the footprint, and it is called Carn Cabal. And men come and they carry the stone in their hands for the space of a day and a night, and on the next day it has returned to the top of the pile.[89]

This wonder-tale provides our earliest reference to Arthur's great boar hunt, which features in much greater detail in *Culhwch and Olwen* (see below, pp. 237–9).[90] The cairn (probably of the Bronze Age) is Carn Gaffalt, one of several in a group above Rhayader (Powys). The story apparently evolved in order to explain the name of the cairn, relying on Arthur's owning a hound called 'horse' – *cabal* in Welsh (it was perhaps earlier known as 'Horse's Cairn'[91]). This obviously has no etymological value, but it shows Arthur featuring in name-explaining stories in the upper Wye valley by the mid-tenth century.

Much the same can be said of his second appearance:

There is another miracle in the region called Ergyng [Archenfield]. There is there a grave next to a spring, which is called Licat Amr, and the name of the man who is buried in the tumulus is Amr; he was a son of the warrior Arthur, and he himself killed him in that very place and buried him. And men come to measure the grave, which is sometimes six feet long, sometimes nine, sometimes twelve, sometimes fifteen. Whatever length you measure on one occasion, you do not repeat that measurement, and I have tried myself.[92]

Again, this story has evolved to explain a local name in Old Welsh. The spring is the source of the River Gamber,[93] an anglicised form of Amr. This derives from an Old Welsh word meaning 'eye', which as a source of tears denotes a spring. Only once it had been reinterpreted as a personal name was it necessary to add *Llygad*, with the same meaning. The phonetic similarity of Amr and Arthur was presumably what inspired the tale. This grave is either the prehistoric burial mound (and later hundred meeting place) known as Wormelow Tump (destroyed in widening the road in 1896) or the round barrow known as Gamber Head.[94]

The *Mirabilia* name only three individuals, St Illtud, Arthur and Amr. Of those three only St Illtud is certainly historical, though the wonder-tale in which he appears here is obvious fiction. Amr is a back projection from the river-name, so arguably has no claim on history whatsoever. Both the Arthurian tales seem highly contrived; neither need have been particularly old when first written down.

Arthur in the landscape

The *Mirabilia* provide the earliest examples of what would become a wide-spread phenomenon, namely the appearance of Arthur in local folk stories or in names attached to features of the landscape. Sufficient instances can be identified in the Middle Ages to suggest that they then formed a meaningful category of Arthurian evidence in their own right. To the two examples provided by the *Mirabilia* we can add an 'Arthur's Seat' and 'Arthur's Oven' putatively shown to the canons of Laon in 1113 (see below, pp. 243–4),[95] and an 'Arthur's Oon [Oven]' (probably a Roman building near Falkirk destroyed in 1743) reported by Lambert of St Omer in 1120.[96] Gerald of Wales, *c.* 1190, noted a mountain named Kaerarthur (generally identified as Pen-y-Fan in the Brecon Beacons: Plate 25), which he translated as 'Arthur's Seat'.[97] Arthur's Stone, a Neolithic Burial Chamber at Dorstone (Herefordshire), was recorded in the thirteenth century and one of the many examples of Carreg Arthur (Crec Arthur) in 1306.[98]

There was a keen interest in place-name lore in the Celtic world across the central and later Middle Ages. That Arthur featured strongly need reflect nothing more ancient than his gradual acceptance as a British hero stem-ming from the *Historia Brittonum*. Thereafter, other stories centred on Arthur encouraged recourse to his name, particularly once the *Brut* trad-ition entered Welsh in the thirteenth century. Many Arthurian names were noted only after the Middle Ages had closed;[99] of the 158 listed by Scott Lloyd, only twenty-seven were evidenced before 1535.[100] The distribution focuses on Wales (particularly north-east, north-west and south-west Wales) but has numerous outliers in Cornwall, Brittany and northern Britain.[101]

This chronologically disparate but numerically impressive body of evidence has been drawn on to support interpretations of Arthur as folk-loric or mythological in origin (see pp. 149–51).[102] But if the *Mirabilia* is recognised as separate from the *Historia* that became attached to it in southern Wales, then it is probably a later work. In that case there is no evidence that Arthur was present in folk stories prior to composition of the *Historia Brittonum*. It is likely to have been his Christian credentials, martial qualities and role as a national hero therein that launched Arthur in this secondary arena. The *dux* and *victor* of twelve battles, who killed 960 of the enemy with his own hand at Badon, reappears in the *Mirabilia* as *Arthur miles*, 'Arthur the warrior'. In the landscape this Arthur became a giant associated with various large stones and otherwise inexplicable prehistoric monuments – as for example the legend attached to Arthur's Stone in Llanrhidian Lower, on the Gower peninsula (Plate 26),[103] Cegin Arthur in Llanddeiniolan,[104] and the massive standing boulders that form the perimeter of the enigmatic 'King Arthur's Hall', on Bodmin Moor (Plate 27).[105]

Some categories of Arthurian place-names are necessarily late: stories or names referencing the Round Table – such as the Iron Age hillfort of Din Sylwy at Llanfihangel-din-Sylwy (Anglesey),[106] the Roman amphitheatre at Caerleon or the prehistoric henge at Eamont Bridge (Cumbria) – cannot pre-date its first appearance in the mid-twelfth century; *coetan* ('quoit') is a term unlikely to have been in use prior to the sixteenth.[107] Many 'Arthurian' names in northern Britain are likely to be late or post-medieval. Some arguably derive from Clan Arthur (Gaelic *Clann Artair*), a subgroup of the Campbell clan, others from use of Arthur as a personal name.[108] The appearance of other Arthurian characters in local names must also be considered late, as Pendragon Castle (Mallerstang, Cumbria), named for Geoffrey's Uther Pendragon (Plate 28) but not built until the reign of William Rufus (1087–1100); similarly, Mote of Mark combines Norman French 'motte' and the character King Mark of Cornwall who featured in the thirteenth-century French *Prose Tristan* (and later in Malory: Plate 17).[109]

Stories about Arthur found a home as far away as Sicily, which was ruled by close allies of the Angevins; Gervase of Tilbury, who had been in the service of Sicily's king in the 1180s, recorded a tale of Arthur living in a wonderful palace beneath Mount Etna.[110] This owes something to the notion of Avalon, which he included at the close of a resumé of Arthur's career, following the *Brut* tradition.[111]

Stories of a king who was still awaiting his return, asleep in a cave with his army around him, have been told in many different parts of Britain,[112] yet cavers never seem to disturb his slumbers. These can be interpreted as local manifestations of a widespread folk tale featuring a king who will come again to save his people, which occurs right across Europe.[113]

In order to appreciate how this kind of local Arthurian story might develop, it may be helpful to pursue just one somewhat further. On the west side of St Peter's Square in the Welsh market town of Ruthin (Rhuthun) is a badly weathered slab of sandstone some 1.2 metres long and 0.6 metres high and wide (Plate 29).[114] On the wall above there are two plaques. The older reads: 'Maen Huail. On which tradition states "King Arthur beheaded Huail, brother of Gildas the historian". The second, added more recently by CADW (the heritage arm of the Welsh government: Plate 30), reads: 'On this stone the legendary King Arthur is said to have beheaded Huail, brother of Gildas the historian, his rival in love and war.'

Maen Huail means 'Stone of Huail'. 'Tradition', here, is short-hand for the chronicle written by Elis Gruffudd, a member of the Calais garrison during the reign of Henry VIII. This vast manuscript (there are 2,400 large folio pages), written in Welsh,[115] refers to a quarrel between the 'cheeky and wanton' Huail, son of Caw o Brydain, ruler of Edeyrnion,[116] and King Arthur, over one of his mistresses. A fight ensues and Arthur is wounded in the knee, leaving him slightly lame. A condition of the peace negotiated between the pair is that Huail must never refer to the king's wounding. He cannot restrain himself, though, when he recognises Arthur at Ruthin, disguised in women's clothes and dancing with a group of girls. Arthur hears him say 'this dancing was alright if it were not for the knee' and recognises the voice. Huail is brought before him at Caerwys, reproached for his words and beheaded on a stone in Ruthin's marketplace – henceforth Maen Huail.

This is, of course, an elaborate fiction. Arthur long pre-dates the Plantagenet era yet there is no earlier connection with either Ruthin or Caerwys.[117] Ruthin's market square was laid out following erection of its castle and plantation of a borough in 1282 – an earlier Welsh settlement lay further east.[118] The choice of Caerwys as Arthur's seat of justice is likely to have been prompted by its role in hosting the sixteenth-century assizes.[119] The story necessarily postdates the Edwardian conquest of Wales – a time when Arthur was very much in vogue – and was probably still evolving when it was written down in Henry's reign.

Elis's history runs from Adam and Eve up to 1552 and extends to the whole world as he conceived it. He wrote it far from Wales and without access to local materials, relying heavily on non-Welsh sources.[120] He did, though, incorporate Arthurian material from the *History of the Kings of Britain* and various 'Welsh' stories recalled (one supposes) from his youth, thereby writing his own people into history. This is an onomastic tale which probably began with a connection between some individual called Huail (a popular Welsh name) and the stone; this was drawn into Arthur's orbit. We can trace some of the elements back much further. The Latin *Life of Gildas* by Caradoc of Llancarfan, written in the first half of the twelfth century, has the 'most saintly Gildas' as one of the twenty-four sons of 'Nau [otherwise Cau, Caw, Kaw], king of Scotia', and 'a contemporary of Arthur king of the whole of Britain' (see below, p. 242). His eldest brother, Huail, was 'unend-ingly warlike and a famous warrior' who refused to submit to any king, but 'In the hostile pursuit and in a council of war in the Isle of Man [Arthur] killed the young pillager. After that slaying the victorious Arthur returned, rejoicing greatly that he had overcome his bravest enemy.'[121]

The 'connection' between Caw and Gildas goes back still further to the Breton *Life of Gildas*, which has the saint born in *Arecluta regio* – the region dependent on the citadel on Dumbarton Rock,[122] so the valley of the Clyde – one of the five sons of King Caunus (though the eldest is here named Cuillum, not Huail.[123]

This overlay of stories offers valuable lessons as to how Arthur could become associated with specific places. We begin with an imaginative link between Gildas and a fictional northern king (Caw o Brydain means 'giant of Pictland'), made by a monk at Saint-Gildas-de-Rhuys on the Breton coast. He presumably intended to insert the patron saint of his own church into a suitably prestigious lineage in the British motherland but outside Wales (where there were rival claims on Gildas). A British dynasty still ruled the Clyde valley at this date; he merely added fictional names to its royal pedi-gree. But Gildas's lineage was entirely forgotten by this time. There is no reason to connect the fifth/sixth-century Gildas with Clydesdale, far beyond Hadrian's Wall, for his work implies that he came from a Romanised family in southern Roman Britain (see above, p. 155).[124] The connection between Gildas and Dumbarton Rock is a fiction, therefore. Even so, this story was reworked in Wales when British saints were being pressed into service to defend local religious culture against the incoming Normans. Caw features in several Welsh place-names,[125] and in the late Old Welsh text *Culhwch and Olwen*,[126] the author of which trawled very widely indeed in establishing his extraordinarily numerous cast of characters. He was later remembered as the progenitor of one of the 'three saintly lineages of the Island of Britain',[127] presumably largely on the strength of the (false) tradition that he had fathered Gildas. Both were then included in late medieval genealogies which localised them in both Edeyrnion and Anglesey.[128] Huail (otherwise Hywel[l], [H]iguel, Hueil, etc.) likewise occurs in *Culhwch and Olwen*.

It may even have been Elis Gruffudd himself who localised the story, taking note of Caw's supposed link to Edeyrnion and also, one suspects, confusing the Scottish river-name Clyde with the Welsh Clwyd.[129] Elis was from Llanasa (Flintshire), so will have been familiar with Ruthin.[130] On the mistaken assumption, therefore, that Gildas stemmed from a north Welsh dynasty and had a brother named Huail who had fallen foul of Arthur, the

Maen Huail has been drawn into Arthur's orbit, losing whatever independence and local relevance its tale had earlier enjoyed. The stone itself was something of a landmark, being reportedly in the middle of the road in the seventeenth century. Like so many Arthurian tales, once the connection with Arthur had been made it stuck. Some recent writers have accepted the Ruthin connection,[131] and his links with the area have even been the subject of a heated exchange between MPs.[132] The casual passer-by can be excused, therefore, thinking that Arthur did indeed behead Gildas's brother Huail on this very stone, but this is a complete fiction.

There is another twist to this story which is also perhaps worth mentioning. That Gildas and Huail were brothers and Huail was killed by King Arthur has repeatedly been offered as a solution to a difficulty facing those wishing to give Arthur a prominent role in Dark Age history.[133] Why, they puzzle, does Gildas, who provides our only near-contemporary account of sub-Roman Britain, make no mention of so great a king? The answer: of course he doesn't, for what self-respecting writer could be expected to honour the prince who had killed his brother? You can see the logic. At the same time, of course, since the genealogical links between Gildas, Huail and Caw are entirely spurious, this explanation is worthless. And there is something else which such writers generally skate over, for if you read the whole of Caradoc's *Life of Gildas* you find that he gives Arthur a rather poor press. He is referred to as a *tyrannus* ('tyrant'),[134] for example, which was the word which Gildas applied to contemporary kings whose morality he was attacking. This *Life* actually offers very little to those seeking to promote Arthur or to account for his omission from Gildas's *Ruin of Britain*.

Examination of the story of the Maen Huail exposes, therefore, the non-contemporaneity, fluidity, inventiveness and gross inaccuracies characteristic of such tales, built up by successive authors each in pursuit of his or her own agenda. The legend has been (and still is being) moulded by voices eager to reformulate stories for their own purposes. Such tales can be entertaining, they provide local colour and are worth studying as evidence for thought processes at the time of composition, but as evidence for what happened in the Dark Ages they offer us nothing.

What man is the Gate-Keeper?

An incomplete poem, known as *Pa Gur* after its opening words (*Pa gur yv y porthaur?*) and featuring a dialogue between Arthur and the gatekeeper or porter, Glewlwyd, survives in the *Black Book of Carmarthen*,[135] written in the mid-thirteenth century. Arthur is represented as the leader of a war-band, made up of a mix of heroes, each of whom he is required to announce to gain them entry. 'What man is the Gate-Keeper? Gleuluid Mighty-Grip [*Gauaeluaur*]. / What man asks it? Arthur and Cei the Fair (*Guin*). / What [company] goes with thee? The best men in the world. / Into my house you shall not come, unless you reveal them.'[136] Arthur is the spokesman, providing a summary of the individuals concerned and their notable deeds,[137] but the poem then drifts away to the achievements of Arthur and his principal henchmen, Cei and Bedwyr, fighting a variety of mythical foes:

> Though Arthur was laughing, the blood was flowing –
> In the hall of Awarnach, fighting with a hag.
> He smote Cudgel Head [*Pen Palach*] in the settlements of Dissethach,
> On the mountains of Eidyn he fought with the Dog-Heads [*Cinbin*];
> They fell by the hundred, by the hundred they fell
> before Bedwyr of Perfect Sinew [*Bedrydant*] ...
> On the banks of Tryfruid, fighting with Rough Grey [*garvluid*]
> Furious was his nature, with sword and shield,
> A host was futile, compared with Cei in battle ...[138]

This is a thoroughly legendary Arthur, very much in keeping with the folk-loric figure of Arthur evidenced in the *Mirabilia* and still very much a war-leader, not yet a king. These may be the earliest appearances of both Cei (Kay, etc.) and Bedwyr (Bedivere, etc.) in Welsh literature. There are parallels with chapter 56 of the *Historia Brittonum* which are unlikely to be coincidental: the 'banks of Tryfruid' replicate 'the bank of the river called Tribruit' (*in litore fluminis quod vocatur Tribruit*),[139] and the numbers here are too similar to those killed by Arthur at Badon to be coincidental: 'He was a steadfast commander of an army for a country's good; / Bedwyr and Brydlaw [or 'Bedwyr, son of Brydlaw']; / Nine hundred to listen, six hundred to scatter – /His onslaught would be worth.'[140]

The poem has been assigned to a period around 1100,[141] though the possibility remains that it could be earlier,[142] perhaps even from the ninth or tenth centuries.[143] While the large number of separate incidents mentioned may imply earlier tales featuring the main heroes, it is equally possible that the author was manipulating or even inventing legends to bulk up the story. Many of the conflicts attach to his companions, rather than Arthur himself, and there need be comparatively few links to an orally transmitted bank of Arthurian stories. That this poem and Arthur's battle-list in the *Historia*

Brittonum are connected in some sense seems certain, but estimates of the date of *Pa Gur* count against the author of *Historia* having taken anything from the poem. It seems likelier that this poem was building on chapter 56 of the *Historia*, however circuitous the route in between.

Geraint, Son of Erbin

This poem (in Welsh *Geraint fab Erbin*), probably composed in the period 900–1130,[144] survives in a short version in the mid-thirteenth-century *Black Book of Carmarthen* and a longer one in the *Red Book of Hergest* (late fourteenth century).[145] Opinion is divided as to which text should be given primacy; Oliver Padel discusses the Arthurian content primarily on the basis of the earlier, shorter version but Jenny Rowland offers a composite text framed by the longer, with twenty-seven three-line stanzas; this forms the basis of what follows. The style is highly repetitive, with the same phrases and themes occurring in successive stanzas. There are two main foci: the bulk of the work centres on Geraint's heroics at the battle of Llongborth, while stanzas 19–27 focus on his 'long-legged horses'. This binary division and the absence of any clear linkage between the two parts perhaps implies that it originated as two separate poems.[146]

Geraint is the central figure, named in ten stanzas of the first section (including a reference to him as 'son of Erbin') and in all nine of the second. A king of Dumnonia of this name was the addressee of a letter written by the West Saxon abbot (and then bishop) Aldhelm regarding the Paschal contro-versy.[147] The *Anglo-Saxon Chronicle* notes him fighting King Ine of the West Saxons *c*. 710.[148] Later Welsh genealogists keen to establish royal antecedents for early saints may well have transplanted this figure into the sixth century.[149] The hero of the poem is depicted as 'from the region of Dyfnaint' (i.e. Devon) but is best considered a 'composite figure'.[150] Llongborth has not been identi-fied with any certainty: Portsmouth, Llanborth and Langport (Somerset) have all been suggested, but this may be less a place-name than a generic Welsh term for 'sea-port' equivalent to the Irish '*longphort*'.[151]

Arthur appears in only one stanza, which in Rowland's text closes the first section: 'In Llongborth Arthur lost / Brave warriors, they hewed with steel, / The ruler, leader of battle.'[152] Whether or not Arthur is even present is unclear but his warriors are. This stanza does, though, seem intrusive to a text the focus of which is so closely on Geraint. The association with Arthur belongs not to the historical Geraint but to his legendisation, and may simply have been a means of anchoring him to the sub-Roman heroic age. Arthur's description as '*amheradyr llywyawdyr*' ('powerful leader/ruler') has been dismissed as a poetic commonplace,[153] but the literal meaning of *amheradyr* is 'emperor'.[154] Use of such a term reflects the need to make sense of the *Historia's dux bellorum* – leading the warriors of the Welsh kings – within contemporary understandings of the ways that military leadership worked. This process led inexorably to the royal and eventually quasi-imperial Arthur of Geoffrey of Monmouth, among others. Clearly, this reference to Arthur cannot bear any historical weight.[155]

Preiddeu Annwn

As already noted (see above, p. 110), the Old Welsh poem *Preiddeu Annwn* ('The Spoils of Annwn') is preserved in the *Book of Taliesin*, from the early fourteenth century.[156] Composition is generally dated *c*. 850–1250.[157] The poem is made up of sixty lines arranged in eight stanzas of unequal length. It is in the first person, as if in the voice of that legendary Taliesin who had a special status as cultural superman in Welsh vernacular works.[158] It seems to have been intended less as a celebration of Arthur *per se* than a defence of the bardic tradition against clerical critics.[159] Appropriately, there is an intricate web of allusions to tales which the audience was expected to appreciate, many of which are now beyond recall. The poet particularly highlighted the esteem appropriate to Taliesin's own skills (so his own as the true author), beginning stanzas 2 and 3 with: 'I am one who is splendid in (making) fame'. He also adopted the motif of the poet as a survivor of the events described, familiar to us from *Y Gododdin*. We have, therefore, repetition of the phrase 'Apart from seven, none came back from ...' at the close of the first six stanzas, each with a different place of departure. The last two stanzas attack the narrow-mindedness of churchmen, berating monks in particular, though the poet's stance is Christian throughout. This is not just an 'Arthurian' work, therefore, but a contribution, in verse of high quality, to a debate regarding the truth-claims of traditional systems of knowledge alongside Church learning.

Arthur is named only in stanzas 4, 5 and 6 (though his ship, *Prydwen*, occurs elsewhere). Here is stanza 4 in translation:

> I do not deserve readers concerned with the literature of the Lord
> Who had not seen Arthur's valour beyond the Glass Fort.
> Six thousand men were standing on its wall;
> It was difficult to converse with their watchman.

> Three full shiploads of *Prydwen* went with Arthur;
>
> Apart from seven, none came back up from the Fort of Impediment.[160]

The poem seems to allude to an expedition by ship led by Arthur to set free a prisoner who was being held in a fortress in the 'other world'. The 'cauldron of the chieftain of Annwn' was taken as booty. There are parallels with a variety of other vernacular texts, including *Culhwch and Olwen* and *Branwen, Daughter of Llŷr*, which imply a shared pool of motifs which emerge somewhat differently in different works (see above, p. 111).[161] More distantly there are parallels here too with the journeys of Orpheus and Aeneas to the underworld. This stanza invites comparison with the 'glass tower' (*turris vitrea*) which proto-Irish warriors supposedly attacked in the *Historia Brittonum*,[162] again with a terrible loss of life. This was a story which need not have originally been 'Arthurian' at all, but was here attached to him. In its current form it clearly postdates the *Historia Brittonum*, and it is perhaps indebted to some degree to that work.

Culhwch and Olwen

A prose narrative of 1,246 lines in late Old Welsh, the origins of *Culhwch and Olwen* (*Culhwch ac Olwen*) lie in oral composition, but in anything like its current form it is the work of a literate author,[163] probably writing in southern Wales.[164] It survives in the *White Book of Rhydderch* (a partial copy) and the *Red Book of Hergest*.[165] The work seems to have been originally written in the eleventh century,[166] but there were further accretions until the thirteenth.[167] The work's component parts seem earlier; similarities to such stories as Jason and the Argonauts and the Irish saga *Tochmarc Emire* suggest that it bears comparison with various ancient folk tales from around the world.[168]

Arthur's aid is invoked by his young kinsman, Culhwch, to locate Olwen, daughter of Ysbaddaden, chief of the giants (*Ysbaddaden Pen-kawr*), the girl whom he is 'doomed' to marry by his stepmother. Ysbaddaden sets him a series of 'impossible' tasks before the marriage might take place. Most of the story consists of the achievement of some ten of these challenges by members of Arthur's war-band, culminating in the hunting of the magical boar, Twrch Trwyth (literally, the 'essential hog'), which elsewhere was recognised as a former king who had been magically transformed.

An unusual feature is the prominent use of extensive lists. The first we encounter is that offered by Glewlwyd, Arthur's gatekeeper here (rather than the figure of authority who he has to reassure in *Pa Gur*), who reminds Arthur of the many expeditions they have shared. This was an opportunity to introduce exotic settings and portray Arthur as a figure active across the known world: 'I was in Europe, in Africa was I, in the islands of Corsica, and in Caer Brythwch and Brythach and Nerthach. I was there of old when you killed the warband of Gleis, son of Merin, when you killed Mil the Black, son of Dugum.'[169] The dialogue between Culhwch and Ysbaddaden is likewise structured as a list, but of tasks, each separated by Culhwch's recurring response that each would be easily accomplished.[170] On his first entering the court, before even Culhwch claimed his boon of Arthur, he invoked the names of over two hundred individual members of his retinue, starting with Cei and Bedwyr, plus a score of ladies.[171] Among Arthur's following are included six Irish heroes and various kings, one of whom, Gwilenhin, may denote William the Conqueror. Clearly, accretion has occurred, though when any one name was added is very much a matter of conjecture.[172] This is a multi-talented war-band drawn from a wide variety of settings, both historical and traditional, a subset of which undertakes the hazardous enterprises necessary, often in the margins of the 'normal' world. The extreme length of the character list and its motley composition are perhaps best interpreted as ironic and are necessarily features of the latest version.

To a significant extent, *Culhwch and Olwen* is a pastiche of pre-existing tales. At its core lies a traditional folk story of the 'Six Go through the World' type, centred on Culhwch himself and his principal helpers, which has been combined with two others, 'the Jealous Stepmother', and 'the Giant's Daughter'.[173] None need originally have included any reference to Arthur. The work which has come down to us is an ambitious story with multiple segments, in many of which neither Arthur nor the suitor-hero plays any explicit role, but held together by the overarching objective of his intended marriage. This is achieved by undertaking a representative sample of the tasks and then killing Ysbaddaden. The work as we have it is plainly composite but the actual size and shape of the underlying tales can only be a matter of surmise. While some elements find confirmation as Arthurian elsewhere, many are unique, but there is no means of separating with any degree of confidence references to pre-existing but otherwise unknown tales from elements composed by this author.

There is obviously nothing in the slightest bit historical in the figure of Arthur revealed here, but it is important that we note the cross-overs between the vernacular storytelling of *Culhwch and Olwen* and the Latin tradition in, for example, the *Life of Cadog*, the Breton *Life of Gildas*, and the *Life of*

David.[174] Similarly, the hunting of the boar Twrch Trwyth which we encounter in the *Mirabilia* occurs at far greater length in *Culhwch and Olwen*,[175] with a geography which seems to recall Dark Age Demetia and its connections with both Ireland (via St David's Head) and the south-west. In addition we should note Arthur's characterisation herein as 'chief of the princes of this land': 'And then Arthur gathered together what warriors there were in the Three Realms of Britain and its three adjacent islands, and what there were in France and Brittany and Normandy and the Summer Country, and what there were of picked dogs and horses of renown.'[176] Here we have the same tripartite frame-work as in the *Welsh Triads*; parallel motifs occur in the *Legend of Saint Goeznovius* (see below, pp. 242–3) and ultimately, of course, in Geoffrey of Monmouth. Combined with the likely appearance of William the Conqueror in Arthur's retinue,[177] this wider geography reflects the broadening of Welsh and Breton horizons following Norman conquests in Italy and the British Isles and the start of the Crusades.

Earlier texts are uniform in depicting Arthur solely as a warrior or a leader of warriors, whether 'real' or supernatural. His emergence here as a king again suggests interpretation of the *Historia*'s remark that Arthur 'fought with the kings of the Britons . . . but he himself was the commander of battles' (see above, p. 185). In the context of the central Middle Ages, it was a king's role to head the army, leading the forces of subaltern rulers. 'Overkingship' was well known, in Wales as elsewhere. It was a small step therefore from 'commander of battles' to a quasi-imperial figure commanding the Welsh kings as well as their forces. This was to prove a landmark shift within the Arthurian tradition, leading directly to 'King' Arthur. This devel-opment can be observed also in the *Geraint fab Erbin* (see above, pp. 235–6), a group of hagiographies of about the same period, and in Geoffrey's work.

This 'kingly' Arthur is likely, though, to have entered this tale no earlier than the eleventh or early twelfth centuries. In the folkloric stories which we can dimly discern underlying *Culhwch and Olwen*, the participants are wilder characters, associated with the hunt, with giants and with witches – more akin to the figures we find in *Pa Gur*. But there is little cause to see these as originally in any sense Arthurian.

The *Welsh Triads*

The *Welsh Triads* – literally *The Triads of the Island of Britain* (*Trioedd Ynys Prydein*) – provide themed references in groups of three to past figures and events. Their principal foci are legendary or mythological tradition, the sub-Roman period and coming of the Saxons, and the 'Northern British Heroic Age' of the sixth and seventh centuries in western and northern Britain.[178] Rachel Bromwich suggests that they originated as a mnemonic aide memoire to the orally preserved narratives that professionally trained bards were expected to know. That the *De Excidio Britanniae*, *Y Gododdin* and *Historia* all betray an awareness of the triad form implies that it had deep roots, but the earliest surviving collection of triads is that in Peniarth MS 16, of the third quarter of the thirteenth century. This has only forty-six examples; those numbered 47–96 in Bromwich's edition are drawn from later manuscripts. Unsurprisingly given the date, Arthur is already present even in the earliest section, and drawing into his orbit characters such as Geraint, Taliesin and Drystan (Tristan) who were probably earlier quite independent. Arthur was becoming central, therefore, to the inherited traditions valued by the Welsh as a people. He is still more prominent in later-recorded triads, in which his court (*llys Arthur*) frequently replaces the older 'island of Britain' (*Ynys Prydein*). This was clearly influenced by 'translation' of the *History of the Kings of Britain* into Welsh (as the *Brut y Brenhinedd*) in the mid-thirteenth century.

Even the earliest triads reflect Arthur's rising popularity. The first has him holding all three of the 'Three Tribal Thrones of the Island of Britain', based at Mynyw (i.e. St David's),[179] Celliwig (Cornwall), and Pen Rhionydd (unidentified, probably northern Britain), associated with various clerics and counsellors of the early post-Roman period. In triad 2 his name has been appended to those of three men remembered for their generosity (Nudd, Mordaf and Rhydderch) as being even more generous, and in triad 4 Llachau, one of the 'Three Well-Endowed Men of the Island of Britain', is identified as Arthur's son.[180] Triad 9 lists 'The Three Chieftains of Arthur's Court' (Gobrwy, Cadr(i)eith, Fleudur Fflam),[181] and 20 has Arthur as first of the 'Three Red Ravagers of the Island of Britain' (in later versions he is appended as greater than the three named).

There are occasional traces of a Welsh tradition of Arthur's death at Camlan. Triad 30 recalls Alan Fyrgan's war-band, who abandoned Arthur by night leaving him to go on to his death at Camlann with only his household servants around him. Otherwise these hints come from later-recorded triads but the story differs so markedly from that of Geoffrey that an independent tradition seems possible, linking perhaps with whatever source lay behind the entry in the *Annales Cambriae*. So triad 53 has as the second of 'Three Harmful Blows of the Isle of Britain', 'that which Gwenhwyfach struck upon Gwenhwyfar: and for that cause there took place afterward the

Action of the Battle of Camlan (*Weith Kat Gamlan*)'. Triad 84, 'Three Futile Battles', references the same story: 'the third was the worst: that was Camlan, which was brought about because of a quarrel between Gwenhwyfar and Gwenhw[f]ach'.

Arthur's omissions may also be noteworthy. While Cai occurs in triad 21 as one of 'Three Battle-Diademed Men of the Isle of Britain', with Bedwyr appended, Arthur does not (the other two are Drystan, son of Tallwch and Huail, son of Caw, both of whom were of course drawn into Arthur's circle). Nor was Arthur included in triad 25 as one of the 'Three Battle-Leaders of Britain', who are Selyf, son of Cynan Garwyn (a late sixth-century king), Urien, son of Cynfarch (of Rheged) and Afaon, son of Taliesin.[182] He is likewise absent as a leader of one of the 'Three Noble Retinues' in triad 31. Similarly, Merlin was not included among the 'Three Enchanters of the Island of Britain', in triad 27. There is still a sense, therefore, in the earliest strata of this material, of an era when Arthur's story was only just beginning to spread in Wales, before it attracted so much else into its orbit.

The British saints' lives

Arthur is entirely absent from such early hagiographical texts as the *Life of Samson*,[183] and the earliest *Life of Gildas*,[184] but occurs in several works written in the eleventh and early twelfth centuries. He can play a pivotal role in the legendary lives of these early Welsh saints, appearing sometimes as a figure who was 'spoiled, demanding what he fancies, but basically well-meaning',[185] but elsewhere in the 'high-kingly' guise accorded him in *Culhwch and Olwen*.

A *Life of Cadog* (*Vita Sancti Cadoci*) written by Lifris at the saint's main foundation of Llancarfan (Glamorganshire) *c.* 1100 exhibits both types. It opens with the abduction of the saint's mother, witnessed by Arthur, Cei and Bedwyr, 'three valiant heroes' who were sitting on a hilltop playing dice.[186] Arthur lusts after the bride-to-be but is dissuaded from seizing her by his companions, instead attacking the pursuers and putting them to flight. The unintended consequence is the saint's conception, in accordance with God's plan. Later, Arthur is termed the 'most illustrious king of Britain'. His demand for cattle with particular markings as compensation for the killing of three of his men by a warrior under St Cadog's protection is miraculously achieved but they are turned into bundles of ferns, so revealing God's displeasure at the king's unreasonable demand. In the aftermath

Arthur and his army have to undertake penance.[187] Arthur's role here is to serve as the saint's foil, demonstrate his power and illustrate the workings of divine providence; the various guises in which he appears reflect the author's need at each point. As in *Culhwch and Olwen*, Arthur's kingliness is a feature of the narrative but, again, this was a natural reading of Arthur as the overall *dux bellorum* of the forces of the British kings in the *Historia Brittonum* and arguably stems either directly or indirectly from interpretation of that ultimate source.

In the earliest *Life of Carannog* (*Prima Vita Sancti Carantoci*), written in Ceredigion early in the twelfth century, Cadwy and Arthur rule together and Arthur is on the trail of a terrible serpent (*serpens*).[188] He cannot locate it, but the saint summons and tames it. As a reward Arthur returns the saint's miraculous altar, which he had tried without success to use as a table, and also grants him land.[189] That this included Carhampton would seem to place the action in Somerset, from where it moves westwards into Cornwall, suggesting that these were assumed from a southern Welsh perspective to have been a single entity when Carannog was alive,[190] and an appropriate space in which to locate Arthur.

The *Life of Illtud* (*Vita Sancti Illtuti*), written *c.* 1140 at Llantwit Major (Glamorgan), makes its hero a cousin of King Arthur who was drawn by his relative's *magnificentia* to visit the 'court of so great a victor'.[191] It is the *Life of Gildas* (*Vita Gildae*) written by Caradoc of Llancarfan (a correspondent of Geoffrey of Monmouth's[192]) that recounts a contest between Gildas's elder brother, Huail, and King Arthur (to which we have already referred), leading ultimately to Huail's death, Gildas's forgiveness and the king's penance (see above, pp. 231–2).[193] It is this *Life* which includes the story of Guinevere's abduction and violation by Melvas: Glastonia (Glastonbury) is said to be the 'city of glass' (*urbs vitrea*),[194] recalling the *Historia*'s *turris vitrea*;[195] Arthur is here a *tyrannus*, taking us back to Gildas's condemnation of the kings of his own day, and is depicted as leading the armies of Cornwall and Devon (*Cornubia et Dibnenia*). The author was therefore seeking to locate him in the south-west but his terminology postdates separation of these two areas by English conquest.

An outlier to these works is the Breton *Legend of Saint Goeznovius* (Goueznou), a saint commemorated in the area of Brest by William, chaplain to an otherwise undocumented Eudo, bishop of Léon (western Brittany). His account is clearly indebted to the *Historia Brittonum*.[196] In scenes which interpret and develop the *Historia*, the usurper Vortigern is succeeded by King Arthur, who campaigns successfully in both Britain and

Gaul.[197] This perhaps reflects local interest in the British colonisation of Armorica, so laying a claim to Arthur on behalf of overseas 'British' communities. If so then the connection is without historical merit. The internal date of 1019 was challenged by J.S.P. Tatlock but has since received some support. This *Life* confirms that the *Historia Brittonum* was known across the Channel and sustains the view that Arthur became a significant figure of the Dark Ages in Brittany in the central Middle Ages, but its role as a witness reflects a perception of history that belongs to its date of production, not significantly earlier.

Concerning the Miracles of Saint Maria of Laon

The church of Laon, in Picardy, was destroyed by fire in 1112. In response, the canons set out on a grand fund-raising tour carrying the relics of Saint Maria, which eventually featured in an account of her miracles – *Concerning the Miracles of Saint Maria of Laon* (*De Miraculis S. Mariae Laudunensis*) – written by Herman of Laon *c.* 1146.[198] Having crossed the Channel, they travelled westwards into 'Danavexeria' (the south-west generally). En route they were shown the 'chair' (*cathedra*) and 'oven' (*furnus*) of 'that famous King Arthur of the Britons' and told that this was 'Arthur's land'.[199] One of their number got into an argument at Bodmin with a local man who had come seeking a cure for his withered arm, who insisted that Arthur was still alive. The altercation sparked a near riot that was only calmed by the intervention of a local clergyman.

Herman considered that the man's subsequent failure to secure a cure was proof of God's position on this matter and included the story as evidence of his own community's special place in the divine scheme of things. His account, though, postdates Geoffrey of Monmouth's Arthurian blockbuster and seems intended as much as a preaching aid as a 'factual' account. It has recently been suggested that there may have been some embroidery of the original story,[200] but there are no obvious similarities between the 'Arthurian' details herein and the *History of the Kings of Britain*, so any influence can only have been indirect. Cornwall was still at this date very 'British', with Cornish widely spoken,[201] so it seems likely enough that Arthur's story was circulating there.[202] There seems little reason to argue that Bretons took any significant part in this affair, as has been suggested,[203] but Herman did note that the Cornishman's argument was 'akin to the manner in which the inhabitants of Brittany argue with the French over Arthur'.[204] This confirms that Arthur was by this date important to all those whose group identity was invested in a British past, marking out Cornwall and Wales from England and Brittany from France, but how much this was influenced by the *History of the Kings of Britain* is difficult to gauge. This passage also provides the earliest explicit evidence for the belief that Arthur lived still, so was a figure of the present and even the future as much as the past (a view perhaps also witnessed in the Welsh poem, *The Stanzas of the Graves*, the archetype of which long pre-dates its copying into the *Black Book of Carmarthen*[205]).

As has long been recognised, the incident at Bodmin shows us something of Arthur's significance to a community which had not yet let go its distinctive 'Britishness'.[206] Interest in Arthur in the south-west seems certain to have pre-dated Geoffrey's reworking of the legend, which of course made frequent use of this region and 'borrowed' Cornish personal names.

'A certain very old book in the British tongue'

In his prologue, Geoffrey of Monmouth claimed that his *History of the Kings of Britain* was his own translation into Latin of 'a certain very old book in the British tongue' given him by Walter, archdeacon of Oxford, which traced the history of the British kings from Brutus down to Cadwalladr. Certainly, Geoffrey did use (and frequently misuse) earlier texts, most obviously Gildas's *De Excidio Britanniae*, Bede's *Ecclesiastical History* and the *Historia Brittonum*, but these were in Latin, not Old Welsh. While the majority of modern scholars have long dismissed this claim to be a mere translator as a crude and thoroughly dishonest attempt to attach ancient authority to his work, a few have suggested that something may lie behind it.[207] Perhaps the most positive stance is that of Norma Lorre Goodrich, a former professor at Scripps College, California: 'From Geoffrey's account it would seem that Merlin was the original narrator whom Geoffrey was translating into Latin, so that, when we read the English, we are reading ... a translation of a translation'.[208]

This is fantasy. The connection between Arthur and Merlin (earlier Myrddin,[209] but this was probably too close to French *merde* – 'excrement' – for comfort) does not pre-date Geoffrey's own works. Certainly, he made extensive use of Merlin, as a putative source of knowledge and as reader, narrator and author, but this remains firmly within the realm of fiction.[210] Taken in the round, the *History of the Kings of Britain* is self-evidently both a work of its day,[211] and Geoffrey's own creation.[212] Arthur is envisaged as an archetype of the king presiding over the centralised feudal state that was twelfth-century England;[213] the *History of the Kings of Britain*'s social fabric is likewise that of the twelfth century. 'Scotia' and 'Albania' refer to Scotland as that was understood then, not much earlier.[214] 'Normannia' is the Normandy of the late Viking Age and Conquest period (though Geoffrey does on occasion also term this region Neustria), and the other territories of northern France are likewise contemporary, albeit augmented with names taken ultimately from Caesar.[215] Many personal names are current, as Cletus, which probably derives from the antipope Anacletus II (1130–38). Others were constructed in the style of the early Roman Empire, so would have been anachronistic in the sub-Roman period. There are over one hundred British kings, most of whom should be pre-Roman in date according to Geoffrey's time scale, but most names derive from genealogies constructed in the central Middle Ages.[216] There are a few Celtic names in passages refer- ring to Scandinavia, though most here are Viking names with which Geoffrey is likely to have been familiar in England. Otherwise he used French personal names.[217] His African king, Gormond, arguably originated as Guthrum, King Alfred's Danish enemy, with the 'black pagans' of Irish works of that period (referring to Scandinavians) mistaken for Africans.[218]

Clearly, there were no Dark Age archives turning up in the twelfth century, though there is perhaps better reason to agree with Goodrich that 'whoever does not believe Geoffrey of Monmouth cannot believe in the historical King Arthur'.[219] We can have every confidence that Geoffrey did not simply translate a 'certain very old book in the British tongue'.[220] Rather he was lifting names and deeds from pre-existing material, synchronising his borrowings from different sources, mixing them into a new confection and larding them with a generous helping of his own imagination. His approach was a development of that employed in the Historia Brittonum, which was arguably Geoffrey's principal inspiration, but he applied these techniques on an industrial scale. The result was the most ambitious, chronologically structured narrative to be written in medieval Britain and the least reliable, but it belongs firmly within the twelfth century,[221] and cannot be adjudged significantly earlier.

That said, this 'certain very old book' is likely to have existed in some form, for Walter was Geoffrey's close associate and still alive when History of the Kings of Britain was completed. That it was written 'within the spirit of the Welsh tradition' rather suggests that Geoffrey used Celtic texts other than the De Excidio Britanniae, Historia Brittonum, Annales Cambriae and a collection of genealogies.[222] That Walter was reputedly skilled specifically in 'foreign histories' has been read as indicative of a Breton text,[223] but there is insufficient narrative material surviving in either Breton or Cornish from

this period for any such judgement to be made.[224] Even Geoffrey's familiarity with the Celtic languages has been questioned.[225]

Geoffrey is, though, often thought to have been of Breton parentage; he
favoured Breton and Cornish characters (such as Duke Cador and King
Hoel) and was rather dismissive of the Welsh in the *History of the Kings of
Britain* (though less so elsewhere). His 'very old book' is perhaps best imagined as a manuscript containing several works (in some respects comparable to the 'Welsh' texts copied into the Harleian MS 3859), some at least in
Old Welsh, Cornish or Breton. There are various passages in his *Historia*
where a debt to Welsh storytelling seems likely, including references to
characters in *Cyfranc Lludd a Llefelys*,[226] and Maxen's marriage to Helen.[227]
Arthur's fight with Ritho (Welsh Rhita or Rhica) on Mount 'Aravius' (or
'Arvaius'), with its reference to a cloak made from the beards of kings whom
he had slain,[228] has been associated with Snowdon,[229] and is probably folkloric.[230] Other possibilities include the stories of Arthur's conception at
Tintagel and his final departure to Avalon,[231] both of which seem to be of
earlier origin. This is little better than guesswork, of course, and the 'very
old book' may have been very different, but Geoffrey does seem to have had
access to various stories from the Celtic vernacular tradition and it may be
that it was a collection of these that Walter had passed on to him. It was
clearly not, though, a fully developed pseudo-history which he then merely
translated. Such is the mix of source material and invention in his work that
we are today in no position to distinguish what he found in this 'Celtic'
source from other elements of his narrative. That said, it is important to
note that the *History of the Kings of Britain* provides no evidence for an
Arthur earlier than the *Historia Brittonum*. It was that text that provided
him with Brutus, Britto's 'Trojan' descent and Arthur; these were the key
ingredients on which Geoffrey built his grandiose story of the British past.

The Arthurian tradition: beginnings

It seems fair to suppose that Arthur was of increasing interest to the Celtic
intelligentsia, both clerical and lay, from the ninth century onwards. There
is, though, virtually no mention of Arthur in works dated earlier than
composition of the *Historia Brittonum* in 829–30. Only the single, fleeting
allusion in *Y Gododdin* seems likely to pre-date the *Historia*, but this may
be a reference to the near-contemporary prince Artúr of the Dál Riatan
royal family who was killed in battle against southern Pictish opponents in
central Scotland (close to Gododdin) shortly before 600. That the *Mirabilia*

can no longer be assumed to pre-date the *Historia* negates this as evidence for Arthur as a figure of earlier place-naming lore. Since other instances of Arthurian place-naming are not recorded this early, the safer approach is to think in terms of an Arthurian tradition that was only just beginning in the ninth century.

While chapter 56 of the *Historia Brittonum* does seem to have drawn on Old Welsh poetry and other texts for the names of battles, Arthur himself seems likely to have travelled in the opposite direction, taken into both the vernacular and Cambro-Latin traditions from the *Historia*. He gradually emerged as a focus for storytelling in the process. Welsh writers eventually took to Arthur with a degree of enthusiasm, remodelling stories which had centred on quite different characters around him. We find two principal guises, as a king or the king of the Britons, and as the leader of a band of warriors operating on the edge of society and ranging backwards and forwards between the worlds of myth and men. This dual figure became a central feature of, for example, the great prose tale, *Culhwch and Olwen*, and the *Welsh Triads*, but signs of ongoing changes point to his development still being very much in progress when these were first written down. Arthur's career as a literary hero is unlikely, therefore, to reach deep into the oral traditions of the early Middle Ages, let alone beyond them. It should not surprise us that Arthur's role in the *Historia* as a Christian, pan-British leader who displayed great personal valour in fighting off the Saxons (the English) attracted attention from a variety of writers, who developed him as best suited their own needs. Over a century later, a southern Welsh annalist was sufficiently persuaded to accept Arthur as historical, so included his victory at Badon in his own work and conflated him with the Arthur who died at Camlan, who may well have been a separate figure local to Dyfed.

The *Historia Brittonum* apart, most of the surviving early Welsh literature that features Arthur was either written in the south or has only come down to us via a south Welsh archetype. Given the *Historia*'s vagueness regarding his locality, southern writers were free to identify him with southern Wales and the south-west. Geoffrey followed suit, having him conceived at Tintagel then ruling from Caerleon in Gwent – a site that will have been familiar to one born in Monmouth. It was Geoffrey who took the Celtic Arthur of the ninth, tenth and eleventh centuries, reconstructed him as an illustrious descendant of Brutus, all-conquering king and quasi-imperial ruler, and launched him into the stratosphere of international fame.

8

'FIRE', 'SMOKE' AND 'HIGHLAND MIST'

It has been quite common for historians to subscribe to the 'no smoke without fire' theory of Arthur, even though the smoke is very thin, and indistinguishable from highland mist.

— Edward James, *Britain in the First Millennium*[1]

D own the years there have been very many answers offered to the question 'Who was the original King Arthur?' Most scholars who currently specialise in either the early Middle Ages or Arthurian studies prefer to avoid the issue, declaring themselves agnostic on the subject: there may have been an historical Arthur, they suppose, but if so we know nothing very much about him.[2] There are many others, though, as Edward James remarks at the head of this chapter, who argue that Arthur's story is rooted in some 'real' figure of history, however far-fetched the stories that later latched onto him. Some go further still, making a case (tentative or otherwise) for a 'real', historical figure who can be tied down to a specific place and time. Such 'positive' Arthurs have been proposed all over Britain, from Argyll in the north to Cornwall in the south.

In important respects these 'positive' Arthurs belong in a single category. Their authors claim to have unpicked the puzzle of who Arthur 'really' was; it is only in the specifics that they disagree. They mostly work within the same pseudo-historical tradition, 'revealing' Arthurs who are actually much of a kind – insular warlords winning battles in the decades around 500 CE (though his opponents can vary quite wildly). The approach is fairly consistent: they synthesise material from a variety of medieval texts as if all can be allowed equal weight as evidence, cherry-pick whatever 'facts' suit their own theories and find ways to explain away those which do not. And they all rely on the same 'sources', most of which stem ultimately (at however many removes) from chapter 56 of the *Historia Brittonum* – indeed, some barely stray beyond this single 'source'. Grouping these Arthurs together as variants of a single phenomenon does of course ignore the specifics of each solution and the wide range of their intellectual grasp of the issues but it allows us to explore the methods used and the possibility of meaningful outcomes without the need to examine each in detail.

Firstly, though, we need to place all this activity within its historiographical context, for the way Arthur has been viewed has its own history that still impacts today. In judging how we should best think about Arthur, we need first to be aware of his backstory – his fame during the high and later Middle Ages but then his rejection from the Renaissance forward, as more analytical approaches to the past emerged. Many figures suffered this fate: take Prester John for example, who was similarly accepted as historical in the twelfth century but later dismissed as legend.[3] What separates Arthur from Prester John is his remarkable regaining of a place in history, even while others stayed in the shadows. Nobody today thinks in terms of an 'Age of Prester John' (though that has a certain appeal) but 'Arthurian archaeology' and the 'Age of Arthur' are familiar concepts. A grasp of how and why Arthur's stock rose, fell and then rose once more is a necessary preliminary to any attempt to judge how to think about Arthur in the present. We will begin, therefore, with Arthur's meteoric rise and subsequent fall, turning then to the how and why of his extraordinary afterlife. To what extent was this 'second coming' justified? Why did it occur? What should his relationship be with history today?

Arthur's rise and fall

Despite his being, supposedly, a figure of *c.* 500, Arthur goes pretty well unnoticed until the *Historia Brittonum* in 829–30. As we have seen, this was a work written in north-west Wales to 'improve' on Gildas's fleeting and highly dispiriting account of sub-Roman Britain and paint an uplifting picture of valorous Britons fighting off foreign aggressors. Arthur here is a divinely favoured British leader who won twelve victories against Saxon incomers (see above, pp. 185–94).[4] He then appears in the *Annales Cambriae*, written no earlier than the mid-950s (see above, pp. 222–5). There are two 'Arthurian' entries, set against years which approximate to 516 (the battle of

Badon) and 537 (Arthur's death at Camlann). The first of these almost certainly derives either from the *Historia Brittonum* or its immediate source (if such there was). The second is likely to come from a different kind of work, in the vernacular and local to Dyfed, though this is probably not correctly dated and arguably refers to some quite different individual. Both these works are far from contemporary with the events they purport to describe; they are, however the bedrock on which the Arthurian legend later developed.

Arthur was taken up first of all in imaginative tales composed in the Celtic world. A set of marvel-stories, the *Mirabilia*, which became attached to the *Historia*, shows how he was beginning to feature in Welsh place-naming lore (see above, pp. 226–9). Soon there is more evidence of this kind, and Arthur appears in Latin saints' lives, as well as poetry and prose stories written in Old Welsh. Writers sought to rationalise his status as a national war-leader leading the combined forces of the British kings (as in chapter 56 of the *Historia*); given the political realities of the times, this required his elevation to royal status, and even to 'supra-royalty', hence 'King' Arthur and his quasi-imperial persona.[5] At the same time his martial deeds at Badon laid the foundation for the emergence of a warrior-leader credited with fantastical deeds. Arthur was becoming a complex figure, therefore, but one still confined to the Celtic fringe of western Europe.

Local versions of the names Arthur and Gawain (as Artusius and similar, Walwanus) appear in northern Italy by *c.* 1080, probably under the stim-ulus of stories told by Breton raconteurs accompanying the Norman and Breton knights then taking over parts of Italy.[6] An Arthurian scene carved on the archivolt of the Porta della Pescheria in Modena Cathedral reveals interest in his story early in the twelfth century (Plate 21). This is our earliest representation of Arthur.[7] The Norman Conquest of England encouraged an interest in non-English historical traditions in Britain, hence the copying *c.* 1100 of Welsh texts into Harleian MS 3859, probably at Canterbury, alongside various classical works.

Arthur's take-off as a figure of history stemmed from Geoffrey of Monmouth's *History of the Kings of Britain*, finished late in the 1130s. Even despite some scathing (and much-deserved), near-contemporary criti-cism,[8] Geoffrey's *magnum opus* provided the Anglo-Norman elite with a welcome alternative to what had long been the dominant historical tradi-tion in England – of God-sanctioned, Anglo-Saxon power.[9] In a beguiling narrative, Geoffrey shifted attention back beyond the English to a succes-sion of British kings, allowing the English supremacy to come into focus only from the reign of Athelstan (924–39),[10] so the generation of Edward the Confessor's great-grandparents. Geoffrey's grand sweep of earlier British 'history' was grounded in that same (entirely spurious) Trojan ancestry as had been claimed at Rome a millennium earlier, as first noted by Sallust, then developed as a foundation myth by Livy and Virgil. Britain was colonised by Brutus, Aeneas's grandson; his followers, named 'Britons' after their leader, were Trojans by descent. Geoffrey drew heavily on the *Historia Brittonum*, adopting its fictionalising approach and both joining up and elaborating its discrete narrative sections to create an epic story stretching across the reigns of 114 kings. This was a past with considerable appeal to the sons and grandsons of the Norman knights who had brought English power crashing down. It chimed also with the ideological needs of the kings ruling the mid-twelfth-century English state – the present was represented in and justified by the past, as it were.

Arthur was Geoffrey's 106th king and his greatest hero, leading his people at the high point of their success. He was represented as having thrust back Britain's invaders; he then conquered or over-awed his neighbours and rose to dominate Atlantic Europe, even crushing a great army sent against him by the Roman emperor. In the prologue Brutus and Cadwalladr book-end this story; otherwise only Arthur gains a mention here, singled out as its central figure even before the action begins; within the work he was then given more space than any other of Brutus's putative descendants. Time slows; the breadth of his realm, the number, stature and geographic spread of his tributaries, the size of the contingents to his army, the scale of opposing forces that he overcame – in so many ways Arthur's reign dwarfs all others.[11] It is easy to read Geoffrey's *History* as a vehicle conceived to promote Arthur's reputation, an act of homage by an enthusiast who had even adopted his hero's name.

Should we consider Geoffrey's work a history? No, of course not, at least not in any modern sense of the word. It is not even legend; it is better considered 'a hoax', 'one of the greatest romantic novels of all time'.[12] Geoffrey's Arthur is no more historical than his Brutus; both were lifted from pseudo-historical passages in the *Historia Brittonum*. Indeed, to press the point further, neither are significantly more 'real' than the savage giant of Mont St Michel whom Arthur supposedly overthrew in single combat.[13] But – and it is a fundamentally important 'but' – the *History of the Kings of Britain* was widely accepted as true (or 'true-ish', at least) at the time. It served the needs of both author and audience very well. His status as a famous author presumably contributed to Geoffrey's appointment to the

bishopric of St Asaph (though he is not known to have taken up the appointment). His readers seem to have found his work empathetic, uplifting and
entertaining – just what history should be, leading to large numbers of
copies being made. And it aligned closely with the ambitions of the Anglo-
Norman political elite not just in England but throughout the Celtic world
and France as well.[14] Its style conveyed the illusion of an authoritative
narrative, capable of comparison with passages in the Old Testament, the
Aeneid, classical histories and various Norman works.[15]

From this pseudo-historical platform, Arthur shot to prominence, taken
up by writers in Latin, French, German, Dutch, English and pretty well
every other European language. The result was a truly international
'Arthurian' literature across the later Middle Ages. Wace's 'translation' of
Geoffrey's work into French set in train the *Brut* tradition of history (named
for Brutus as the founding figure), which entered English through the work
of Laȝamon. Alongside, Welsh and Breton stories that are absent from
Geoffrey's account continued to spread. The scale, glamour, yet fluidity of
Arthur's court in these several conceptions provided a valued backdrop
for romantic storytelling in both verse and prose. The result was a succession of Arthurian works that built one on another, combining what had
originally been quite separate strands (such as the stories of Joseph of
Arimathea, the legend of Veronica and the Grail). As the Middle Ages
progressed, many of these narratives would be richly illustrated, with
Arthur and his associates represented in contemporary garb and acting out
well-known scenes (Plate 31). The image of rulership projected by Wace,
among others, was one that interested insular kings; Edward I was particularly enthusiastic, seeking to draw on the Arthurian past to support his
ambition to achieve Britain-wide rule.[16] Arthurian stories reveal a strong
interest in the nature of political authority,[17] and they map onto the religious and chivalric interests of the wider political elite, their conceptions of
social class, religion and gender.[18]

Despite the increasing professionalism of warfare in the later Middle
Ages, social and economic power remained largely in the hands of land-
holding aristocracies who still adhered to the values embedded in Arthurian
literature.[19] Arthur was included among the 'nine worthies', a chivalric
device first conceived in an early fourteenth-century romance written by
Jacques de Longuyon. This motif appears repeatedly across the later Middle
Ages and beyond, including in several of Shakespeare's plays. As the medieval epoch closed, Malory's *Le Morte d'Arthur* (in late Middle English,
despite the French title) consolidated Arthur's centrality to insular culture.

This was one of the earliest non-religious works to be printed and so break out of the confines of manuscript-copying.[20] Mass production delivered Arthur to wider audiences. In Britain Arthur was still credited as historical in some quarters across the sixteenth century and into the seventeenth (his historicity was always more equivocal on the Continent). The Yorkist dynasty claimed descent from the 'Brut' kings and Henry VII drew on this connection in naming his eldest son.[21] James I likewise drew on the legend in support of his own pan-Britain kingship. For many, Arthur's story remained central to history; this was the 'Matter of Britain', his story was England's (confusingly enough),[22] as much as Scotland's or Wales's.

But scholars, particularly in Renaissance Italy, were developing new methods by which to underpin history.[23] Practice slowly shifted from the uncritical retelling of a good tale (with or without further elaboration) to investigation of the source of any particular 'fact'. Was this material near-contemporary and from a generally reliable and sober account? Was the author in a position to know what had happened? If not, how did he or she come by it? By such means the past was gradually subjected to interrogation and fact sorted from fiction, to establish a basic chronology of events and cast of characters.[24]

Arthur's place in English history was vulnerable to this process, resting as it did on works no earlier than the twelfth century; Welsh sources could only push this back to the early ninth, still some three hundred years adrift of his supposed floruit. Geoffrey had been criticised already in the twelfth century; by the fifteenth the *Brut* tradition was losing credibility. In 1485, in his prologue to the printed edition of Malory, Caxton came to Arthur's defence, despite his awareness that: 'divers men hold opinion that there was no such Arthur, and that all such books as been made of him, be but feigned and fables, because that some chronicles make of him no mention, nor remember him nothing, nor of his knights.'[25]

Early in the sixteenth century, Henry VII commissioned an Italian scholar, Polydore Vergil, to write a history of his kingdom.[26] Unsurprisingly, he found nothing capable of supporting Geoffrey's version of early British history and rejected his work. Despite Arthur's significance to Henry's claim on the throne, Vergil cut him down to a walk-on part. This work remained unpublished until 1534, when it was printed in distant Basel in Switzerland.[27] In the meantime, John Rastell's *Pastyme of People* (published in 1529) dismissed Arthur in his entirety.[28] Despite several English writers vehemently defending him (including John Leland[29]), scepticism ultimately prevailed. While the *Brut* tradition continued to provide a rich seam for poets and playwrights,[30] by the third decade of the seventeenth century Arthur was barely featuring in history outside antiquarian discussion of specific sites;[31] he was either omitted entirely or appeared as a figure of only local significance – in south-east Wales,[32] the south-west,[33] Argyll,[34] or the Anglo-Scottish Borders.[35]

In the mid-nineteenth century the great Anglo-Saxonist John Mitchell Kemble dismissed Arthurian history as 'a confused mass of traditions borrowed from the most heterogeneous sources, compacted rudely and with little ingenuity, and in which the smallest possible amount of historical truth is involved in a great deal of fable.[36]

His words sum up the dominant opinion of several generations of English historians, fixed as they were on a very 'German' view of the nation's origins; Arthur was in their eyes more-or-less un-historical and the *Historia Brittonum* of little value.[37] Many scholars of the period considered Arthur mythical – a leftover perhaps from the Celtic gods (see above, p. 149).[38] Throughout Victoria's reign, most studies of the insular Middle Ages began with an English Settlement story based on the *Anglo-Saxon Chronicle*. Arthur had no part in this and was consigned instead to the historical fringes or to those 'romantic narratives' that were best left to the poets.[39]

Arthur's return

But even if he was now rarely considered 'real', Arthur remained one of the best-known figures of the British past. Indeed, his fame increased across the nineteenth century and into the twentieth. Following a period of neglect stretching back to 1634, new editions of *Le Mort d'Arthur* began to appear in 1816, influencing writers from Sir Walter Scott onwards. And a few scholars still wished to have Arthur inside their histories; a text-based re-evaluation was published in 1825 favouring Cornwall as his home, an edition of the *Historia Brittonum* came out in 1838,[40] and several scholars sought to establish Arthur as a 'real' figure of the 'Northern British Heroic Age'.[41] His stories featured prominently in the rising tide of medievalism – jousting and all – which swept Britain in the mid-nineteenth century.[42] Arthur was central to Tennyson's work,[43] and attractive too to the Pre-Raphaelites.[44] Starting in 1852, William Dyce carved Arthurian scenes on the wooden panelling of the queen's robing room in the Houses of Parliament;[45] in the late 1850s Dante Gabriel Rossetti and his friends decorated the Oxford Union with episodes from the legend.[46] Arthur's return in the corporeal sense remained a matter of speculation into the twentieth century, with Lord Kitchener mooted as a potential 'reincarnation'.[47] Arthurian notions of chivalry underpinned the codes of gentlemanly behaviour promoted in British public schools in the decades around 1900,[48] when Malory was particularly popular.[49] In 1889 Mark Twain published a semi-comic challenge to Tennyson's reverential treatment of the late medieval tradition, contrasting the industrialised world which he favoured with older notions of slavery and class.[50] The first 'Arthurian' film appeared in 1904; over fifty more were to follow.

Arthur's was a noisy presence, therefore, as the nineteenth century drew to a close. Unsurprisingly, the scepticism of historians was frequently overlooked, for they were few in number and their studies swamped by works more accepting of the king. As literacy levels rose, Arthur was increasingly tailored to the needs of children,[51] with collections of his stories written specifically for a young audience (cleansed of course of the immorality of the late medieval tales[52]).[53] And popular histories consisted largely of just the type of unverifiable, romantic stories that academics disliked; the best-known today is Henrietta Marshall's *Our Island History*,[54] published in 1905. 'The coming of Arthur' (i.e. the sword-in-the-stone episode) was her twelfth chapter and 'the founding of the Round Table' the next, before she moved on to Pope Gregory's encounter with young English slaves (chapter 14), and King Alfred's love of learning but failure as a cake-maker (15, 16). By implication, Arthur was no less historical than Gregory, Alfred and the rest, leaving him a familiar figure within popular perceptions of the nation's story.[55] There was an ongoing presumption in favour of an historical Arthur across the wider public, therefore, despite a general acceptance of, and enthusiasm for, England's Germanic roots.[56]

Ironically, it was in the Germany whose hordes Arthur had supposedly fought against that his scholarly revival began. In 1893, Heinrich Zimmer, then the world's foremost Celticist, published a study of the *Historia Brittonum* entitled *Nennius Vindicatus* ('Nennius Vindicated'), that made the case for several passages deriving from much earlier texts. These included chapter 56, which he believed part of the earliest archetype, written no later than the 690s, raising the possibility that it might provide reliable testimony for events *c.* 500.[57] It was Zimmer who had in 1890 already derived the name Arthur from Roman 'Artorius',[58] so he could pretty well rule out a Celtic mythological origin. He therefore favoured the *Historia Brittonum*'s Arthur being considered historical, potentially at least. Theodor Mommsen accepted the broad outline of this approach when he edited the text, inserting subtitles to distinguish the different sections, including 'Arthuriana' as a heading for chapter 56.[59] As the nineteenth century closed, therefore, Arthur was thrust back into history by two of the giants of German historical scholarship.

Understandably enough, their support encouraged renewed interest in Arthur as potentially historical in the English-speaking world. A study of his battles published in English in 1905 (albeit in a German journal), depicted him as overlord of the Britons of the upland zone, campaigning in an arc from Hereford to the north.[60] In 1923, the American scholar James Douglas Bruce remarked that 'the evidence ... is meagre, relatively late, and almost wholly fantastical',[61] yet accepted that chapter 56 belonged to 'the oldest strata of the work' and that Arthur should be accepted as 'real', 'a man of Roman descent or a Romanized Celt'.[62] In 1927 Sir Edmund Chambers produced what was arguably the best historical analysis of the evidence to date – indeed, he deserves recognition as the first agnostic of the modern era.[63] There was interest in Arthur in France too, with Edmond Faral's production in 1928 of a scholarly, three-volume study and edition of the early texts, like Anscombe favouring battle-sites stretching across the Highland Zone of what had been Roman Britain.[64] In the same year, A.O. Anderson speculated that Gildas's depiction of his contemporary, Cuneglasus, as a bear might be a coded reference to Arthur, in which case there is a nearer-contemporary witness for his existence even than the *Historia Brittonum* (see above, p. 163).[65] In 1932 Hector and Norah Chadwick examined the *Historia* as part of their wide-ranging study of early literature and suggested that the text underlying chapter 56 might have been a Welsh poem. Although they did not suppose that this need be factually based, they thought that widespread occurrence of the name Arthur in the late sixth and seventh centuries 'must have been due to some famous person of that name in the near past'.[66]

Arthur was regaining his ground, therefore, as an historical figure. There were various attempts to date his career.[67] The veteran scholar W.G. Collingwood offered a new analysis of his battles that favoured sites in the south-east;[68] this was the arena preferred likewise by Arthur Brodeur in 1939, who dismissed the *Historia*'s northern-seeming battle-names as apocryphal and concluded that only Badon was fought by the 'real' Arthur.[69] But O.G.S. Crawford defended the *Historia*'s 'northern' setting of Arthur, seeing him as 'plainly a historical personage' whose battle-list was likely to have derived from early annals, since lost.[70] Despite the essays of Collingwood and Crawford representing dramatic departures from their authors' normal interests into a research area for which neither was well-equipped,[71] both encouraged the presumption of Arthur's real existence.

While Zimmer's thesis was necessarily the initial trigger for this renewed scholarly interest,[72] support for Arthur as a figure of history gained momentum in the English-speaking world as a consequence of attitude shifts resulting from the First World War, fuelled in particular by Germanophobia whipped up by governments during the conflict.[73] A heroic British leader who had triumphed over Germans in the distant past provided a symbol of national delivery from the same foe of immediate relevance. We find Arthur surfacing in some surprising places – as, for example, the 'King Arthur' class of steam locomotives, of which seventy-four were built between 1918 and 1926.[74] H.V. Morton's hugely popular *In Search of England*, first published in 1927, called on Arthur as if a spirit of the land in the prefatory poem and in his descriptions of Windsor Castle, Tintagel and Glastonbury.[75] His companion volume on Wales, published in 1932, turned to this same subject in the depths of Snowdonia: 'Surely Arthur was an ex-officer of Rome ... who rose up among the ruins of the crumbling Western Empire and for a little time tried to drive the barbarians towards the sea.'[76]

By far the most influential academic of the war generation was W.G. Collingwood's son, Robin (R.G.), professor of metaphysical philosophy at Oxford and an expert on Roman Britain. In 1936, Collingwood turned to Arthur as he closed his final work on that subject. His Arthur was very like Morton's: 'Through the mist of legend that has surrounded the name of Arthur, it is ... possible to descry something which at least may have happened'. Civilisation was evaporating and the tide of barbarism running in. Only Arthur had the vigour and understanding of what was afoot to make a stand; he gathered together comrades prepared to fight as cavalry in late Roman style and led them to victory in 'a dozen campaigns'. Arthur 'was the last of the Romans: the last to understand Roman ideas and use them for the good of the British people.'[77]

Collingwood was cautiously accepting of the view that a stratum within the *Historia Brittonum* was sufficiently early to provide evidence of Arthur's deeds, he considered the *De Excidio Britanniae*'s mention of Badon supportive and he looked favourably on Anderson's suggestion that, in terming Cuneglasus a bear, Gildas might also have had Arthur in mind (see above, p. 256).[78] It may be that Robin's father influenced his judgement,[79] but their works were very different in scope and both are perhaps best viewed as manifestations of the broader groundswell of support for an historical Arthur, begun by Zimmer but popularised and reinvigorated in the post-war context. The focus on Arthur provided a welcome diversion from the 'Germanist' tradition of English history (a simpler matter for Romanists than medievalists) and a means of focusing the nation's story on insular heroes. As the threat from Germany re-emerged and war clouds gathered once more,[80] R.G. Collingwood threw his weight behind Britain's foremost Dark Age hero.

Collingwood's Arthur was, though, very much his own creation. While others attempted to locate his battles or sought fresh sources of evidence, his was a more broad-brush approach; it was less his specific deeds than what Arthur symbolised that mattered. This was the 'great man' approach to history that was very popular at the time and reflective particularly of Collingwood's own classical perceptions and the high value he attached to Roman civilisation. He considered that Arthur's 'Roman' name suggested that he came from some region where 'romanization was still relatively high';[81] this very 'Roman' Arthur became the leader of a mobile field army of late Roman type, its task to protect Roman civilisation. This was the beginning of Arthur's career as a late-Roman cavalry commander,[82] a figure that Collingwood imposed on the ninth- and tenth-century texts in complete disregard of their 'British' agenda.

Nowell Myres, Collingwood's co-author, was not sufficiently impressed by this to make any reference to Arthur in his portrayal of the Anglo-Saxon settlement (where we might have expected mention of him, at least). Other students of early English history, though, felt obliged to at least take account of Collingwood's judgement.[83] His words were extraordinarily influential – *Roman Britain and the English Settlements* would be the main work of scholarship on Roman Britain and the manner of its ending for the next three decades,[84] and retained considerable influence even thereafter.[85] This was an age of deference in which the opinions of eminent scholars carried great weight; none was more eminent than Collingwood. His conception of Arthur was widely accepted in early post-war Britain,[86] encouraging those supportive of the 'positive' case to push on.

We should also take note of the Nazi inclination to consider the English as fellow Aryans, with all the racist implications that that entailed. Once war had broken out in 1939, widespread discomfort with this ideology combined with fears of German invasion to give further impetus to Arthur as an emblem of British national resistance. RAF pilots fighting the battle of Britain were depicted in the press as modern-day knights of the Round Table; the name Excalibur was borne (unofficially) by a Spitfire flown by

603 Squadron (the RAF's most successful fighter squadron in the battle of Britain), and Arthur surfaces too in war-time poetry.[87] T.H. White had already published *The Sword in the Stone* in 1938, but wrote much of what later became *The Once and Future King* during the war, its darkness reflecting his dismay regarding the conflict. In 1947, John Masefield, the poet laureate (1930–67) and something of a disciple of Tennyson,[88] published his own patriotic Arthurian novel, *Badon Parchment*, featuring an Arthur who was surely modelled on Collingwood's cavalry commander. Sir Winston Churchill in turn accepted this same figure as historical.[89]

This Arthur shifts still further into focus in Shepherd Frere's *Britannia*, a scholarly study of Roman Britain published in 1967: 'The evidence is sufficient to allow belief that he [Arthur] had a real existence and that he was probably the victor of Mount Badon. It is likely that he succeeded Ambrosius in the leadership'. Frere was less circumspect than Collingwood in accepting chapter 56 of the *Historia Brittonum* as historical and even seems to nod in the direction of William of Malmesbury; again Arthur was conceived as a leader engaged in 'a form of warfare in which small numbers of horsemen could rout many times their number of ill-armed barbarian foot-soldiers'.[90]

The positions adopted by Collingwood then Frere encouraged archaeologists, in particular, to accept Arthur as an historical figure. Academe was divided sharply between the Roman and medieval periods at this time, with the Celtic world rather slipping between the two. The response of archaeologists was to frame a new age of British history to bridge the gap – named for its best-known character the 'Age of Arthur' and with the eponymous king a quasi-imperial figure at its centre.[91] Across the summers of 1966–70, with the BBC filming the dig as it happened, the Cardiff-based archaeologist Leslie Alcock excavated South Cadbury hillfort in Somerset with the express intention of exposing Arthur's Camelot (Plate 23).[92] There was widespread support from the archaeological community,[93] and Alcock's initial conclusion was that his capital had indeed been discovered.[94] A multi-authored book stimulated by the project, *The Quest for Arthur's Britain*, published in 1968, rapidly sold out, revealing the public appetite for Arthur and 'his' age.[95] Ralegh Radford adopted this new-found 'Arthurian' period as a unifying theme for his West Country excavations,[96] and, in 1971, Alcock published an overview entitled *Arthur's Britain*. As well as his own field of archaeology, he drew on the ninth- and tenth-century written evidence and urged that it could be relied upon. Alcock's reconstruction looked back to Collingwood's very 'Roman' figure, even offering a glance into his hero's wardrobe: 'Arthur himself when on parade ... would have worn a uniform based on that of a Roman emperor or high-ranking general: a fine, knee-length tunic and breeches, a leather jerkin with metal-studded fringe'.[97]

So Arthur had not only regained his place in Britain's past but history was even reformulated around him. This new status was confirmed in 1973 by John Morris's publication of his own weighty re-examination of the British Isles in the period 400–600, *The Age of Arthur*. Though he paid some attention to the archaeology, Morris was more comfortable working from written evidence. He drew on numerous texts written many hundreds of years after the events they were supposed to 'document', confident that he could make them offer up reliable information regarding sub-Roman Britain. For Morris, Arthur was solidly a figure of history: 'The personality of Arthur is unknown and unknowable. But he was as real as Alfred the Great or William the Conqueror; and his impact upon future ages mattered as much, or more'.[98]

Academe experienced what we might term 'peak Arthur', therefore, in the decade centred on 1970. Alcock and Morris were university academics of high repute, their books engaged with a great variety of evidence and they placed Arthur at the centre of British history. This is an attractive tale, and Arthur's successes against Saxon incomers had a strong appeal following two wars fought against Germany. The Arthurian tradition is extraordinarily rich, stretching back across a millennium, and Arthur's story had by this point been attracting historical support for some eighty years. As Geoffrey Ashe asserted in 1968, the 'stand' so long 'maintained' by 'the unbelievers' seemed to have 'dwindled to a rear-guard action'.[99] Arthur is a figure that a wider public is eager to accept; he has emotional appeal, invoking heroic deeds in the national cause in a golden age long gone. He has romance, too, but in the end his is a tragedy of Shakespearean proportions. It is easy to follow down this road and put Arthur back into our histories; we see this occurring across the later 1970s.[100]

Alcock and Morris met with a damning response, though, from a key section of the scholarly community. Post-Zimmer, a fundamental weakness of Arthur's return to history was its furtherance by scholars with little or no expertise in the central-medieval Welsh texts on which his historicity must ultimately depend. Specialists in this literature now dismissed the arguments of both Alcock and Morris as naïve, highlighting their concerns in specialist reviews.[101] The best-known riposte is David Dumville's in 1977, labelling the literary evidence more 'apparent' than 'real' and accusing both writers of not having understood the nature of the sources that they were using: 'I think we can dispose of him [Arthur] quite briefly. He owes his place in our history books to a 'no smoke without fire' school of thought ... The totality of the evidence ... shows Arthur as a figure of legend (or even ... of mythology).'[102] Dumville showed how recent the *Historia Brittonum*'s 'sources' for late fifth-century Britain were (Gildas excepted) when the *Historia* was written, thereby removing the central plank of Zimmer's case for an historical Arthur.

This scholarly rebuttal divided those with an interest in the period into opposing camps which continue still to the present day. On one side are those who remain committed to the Collingwood–Frere–Alcock–Morris tradition and in some sense still wish to view King Arthur as historical; on the other are those who dismiss their works as irretrievably flawed, take a more critical approach to the literary evidence and urge Arthur's exclusion from history. Alcock accepted the criticism and reinterpreted South Cadbury without reference to Arthur.[103] Morris died in 1977, having been seriously ill for several years so unable to contribute further to the debate.

In his *Roman Britain*, which in 1981 finally replaced Collingwood's contribution to the *Oxford History of England*, Peter Salway gave due weight to the sceptics, commenting that: 'so much doubt has now been thrown on the state of knowledge about the Celtic written sources for Arthur that both his connection with the archaeology and his very existence ... need to be held in abeyance'.[104] A succession of specialists thereafter omit all mention of Arthur as an historical figure,[105] include only the most sceptical remarks,[106] or lend their weight to his debunking.[107] In 1986 Myres updated his earlier collaboration with Collingwood, noting the 'historical insignificance of this enigmatic figure'.[108] John Morris's work, in particular, has attracted widespread criticism. Guy Halsall comments: 'There are essentially two things that you need to know about Morris's *The Age of Arthur*: one is that it is a marvellous, inspiring read; the other is that very little of it can be relied upon.'[109] Andrew Breeze likewise terms it 'a unique blend of insight and blunder'.[110] Much the same can of course be said of the first edition of *Arthur's Britain*, though Alcock's greater reliance on archaeology and his efforts to address the criticisms in a later edition led to its drawing less sustained hostility.

Alongside, though, the 'pro-Arthur' camp is still very much alive. Dumville's comments were written for a learned audience and published in an academic journal. They are not particularly accessible, therefore, and have not always received the attention that they warrant. Since the 1970s, many general histories have overlooked the more critical studies and continue to include Arthur as a figure of history,[111] providing further momentum to his acceptance. The works of both Alcock and Morris remain in print and there have been any number of books and articles written by those accepting of their general approach. Several academics with interests centred on the period are at least sympathetic to this position. Responding to Dumville's comments, Christopher Snyder remarked that 'it must be admitted – even by the skeptics – that there has been an awful lot of smoke blowing around . . . it is hard to see the "fire" as the tale of one creative medieval bard.'[112] The *Historia Brittonum* is hardly the work of a 'bard', but, agreed, the quantity of smoke is indeed impressive.

Others have gone much further. Despite recognising that any battle-catalogue poem underlying Arthur's battle-list is likely to have been both late and unreliable, Bernard Bachrach remains inclined to accept Arthur as historical, even suggesting that the four river-names within the *Historia*'s list means that his wars included naval operations. 'Gildas may have intended to name Arthur,' he supposes, referring once more to the use of *ursus* in chapter 32 of *De Excidio Britanniae*, 'or he may have intentionally omitted any mention of him.'[113] Christopher Gidlow likewise champions an historical figure operating on the wide geographical stage envisaged by Morris.[114] He recently addressed the same basic question as my own but from the opposing perspective: 'Did King Arthur really exist? ... Did Henry VIII exist? Did Queen Victoria? Do history books ... have to start by proving their existence? Arguably Arthur stands equally high in public knowledge of British history'.[115]

'Yes' must be our answer to that last question; we do need to demonstrate the historicity of a figure as problematic as Arthur. Let's face it, Sharpe 'stands equally high in public knowledge' of the Napoleonic Era, but that has no bearing on whether or not he existed (he did not, of course, notwithstanding his close physical resemblance to the actor Sean Bean).[116]

Despite criticising Morris, Breeze also considers the *Historia Brittonum*'s Arthur to be historical, and proposes locations for each of his battles in the *Historia Brittonum* and *Annales Cambriae* (Appendix II), all but one being in southern Scotland and the Anglo-Scottish borders. In his view 'Arthur is a historical figure, and not ... purely one of folklore ... He really existed, as one might think from his Roman name *Artorius*, which is not a native Celtic form.'[117] But while we may agree that a Roman-originating name is unlikely to have become attached to a figure of Celtic folklore, that does not make Arthur historical; there are other options not being considered here. And it is difficult to justify, on the one hand, accepting Arthur's responsibility for the 'northern' battles listed in chapter 56 of the *Historia* yet at the same time dismissing the clear implication at the start of that same chapter that these were fought against the Saxons of the south-east. There is no textual reason to separate Badon from the battles that have gone before; this is a matter of judgement based entirely on external factors. Much like his predecessors,[118] Breeze is confident that his candidates for the battle-names are superior to other candidates on offer, but several are problematic, at best.[119] His essays do, though, demonstrate just how strong the impulse remains to consider Arthur historical, despite all the scholarly energy that has gone into nailing down the lid of this particular coffin across the last half century.

'Positivist' solutions post-Morris

Alongside writing his own study of the period, Morris initiated new editions and translations of key insular texts from the early Middle Ages, publication of which continued beyond his own death. This series, Phillimore's *History from the Sources*, is perhaps his greatest achievement within the sphere of British history, providing highly accessible, well-translated texts. However, neither *The Age of Arthur* nor the introductions to each volume offer sufficient guidance as to how such works are best read, or the questions that can reasonably be asked of them. In particular, Morris took personal responsibility for the *Historia Brittonum*. The lack of an introduction (which he never completed due to ill-health) undermines the reader's ability to grasp just how problematic this work is,[120] and he tended to gloss over its many textual difficulties, including material from different versions. The result is a composite text which is very far from the original. Additionally, it is essential that we take account of the context in which it was written and its author's mindset. Reading a work like the *Historia* as if it were written by someone much like ourselves who just happened to live a long time ago risks misunderstanding it fundamentally.

The ease of access to these texts combined with the positivist thinking championed by Alcock and Morris to open the floodgates to ever more theories. The result is a whole raft of Arthurs, each 'revealed' for 'the very first time' and proclaimed as incontrovertibly 'true' (even though several resemble Arthurs suggested much earlier, apparently unbeknown to their modern-day proponents; see above, p. 254). Type 'King Arthur' into an online search engine today and you will be deluged with contenders,[121] locating him in modern-day South or North Wales, Devon and Cornwall,

Shropshire and Powys, Cumbria, Dumfriesshire and Galloway, Argyll, the Anglo-Scottish borders, Yorkshire, Lincolnshire, Hertfordshire, East Anglia and Essex (Map 7).[122] Many of these writers start from the assumption that Arthur is historical and the ninth- and tenth-century sources reliable – provided they are read 'correctly' (i.e. as these writers propose).

In seeking to evaluate these 'positivist' works as a category, it may help to have a flavour of the sort of arguments on offer. In illustration, let us explore a recent example, Graham Phillips's claim to have identified Arthur's Avalon, so his place of burial. This was not an island in the sea in his view but 'a lake island', for Malory termed the boat that transported Arthur 'a lytyll barge',[123] and 'a barge is not a seafaring boat but one used for inland travel.'[124] Avalon is eventually 'revealed' as The Berth, a prehistoric hillfort near Baschurch in Shropshire.[125] Two surveys have been conducted which reveal anomalies on part of the site. One is a possible pit with metalwork perhaps detected at the centre.[126] Phillps interprets this as the burial place of Cynddylan, a hero of Dark Age poetry connected with the Marches.[127] If Cynddylan is here, then so too is Arthur, on a part of the site not so far surveyed.

This reasoning exhibits some quite extraordinary failings. Firstly, Arthur's vessel. In Malory's day a 'barge' was any small boat, normally oared. The terminology places no obstacle in the way of a sea voyage. Malory depicted Bedivere carrying Arthur on his back to the 'watirs syde' and helping him into the 'lytyll barge'. As the attendant ladies 'rowed fromward the londe', Arthur said to him:

> I [wyll] into the vale of Avylyon to hele me of my grevous wounde ...
> And as sone as sir Bedwere had loste the syght of the barge he wepte and
> wayled, and so toke the foreste and wente all that nyght. And in the
> mornyng he was ware, betwyxte two holtis hore, of a chapell and an
> ermytage.[128]

It was there that he found the hermit (the archbishop of Canterbury as was) and a new grave that he supposed to be Arthur's. But Bedivere travelled overland; the chapel where Arthur was perhaps buried (Malory left the matter uncertain) was a night's journey through the forest. Avalon is not here an island at all but a 'vale' – from a different strand of the tradition.

Agreed, Malory did not actually specify the sea, but the fact that Bedivere waited until the boat passed out of sight rather implies that it was a 'sea-sized' expanse of water that he had in mind. That is certainly sustained by

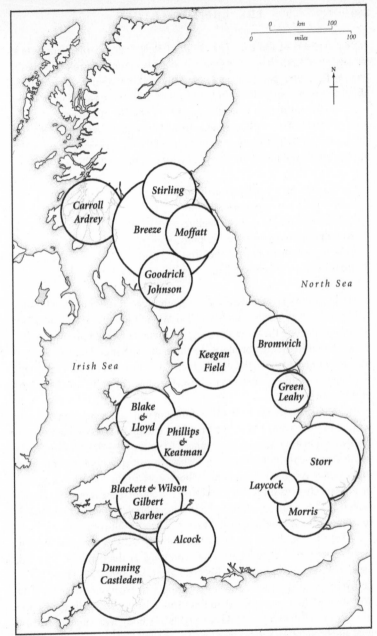

7 Localising Arthur: a map of where selected modern writers have supposed that Arthur was active.

earlier versions of the tale: *The Death of King Arthur*, written in French shortly after 1215, has a *nef* ('vessel'), *pleinne de dames* ('full of ladies'), coming for Arthur *parmi la mer* ('across the sea').[129] Laʒamon's *Brut*, written about the same time, offers (in translation): 'with these words there came moving in from the sea a small boat, driven onward by the waves'.[130] The *Stanzaic Morte Arthur* meanwhile, which Malory knew, has a 'riche' ship on the sea taking Arthur to the 'vale of Aveloun'.[131] But variations abound; the Suffolk monk and poet John Lydgate, writing in the 1430s, has:

> To staunche his woundis & hurtis to recure,
> Bor[n] in a liteer cam into an Ile
> Callid Aualoun; and ther of a venture,
> As seid Gaufrid recordeth be scripture,
> How Kyng Arthour, flour of chevalrie,
> Rit with his Knihtis & lyveth in Fairye.[132]

Arthur's story is offered here as a warning against treachery, but how he was meant to have reached the 'isle called Avalon' on a litter is far from clear. Malory was telling the same story, equally imaginatively, in his own words. This is literature written primarily to entertain, with moral undertones but little imperative to make the details internally consistent. Malory's description can be considered no more authoritative than any of the other versions of this same story.

Behind such issues lurk more fundamental problems. Malory was writing in the second half of the fifteenth century and basing his work on highly imaginative Arthurian romances written post-1200. Obviously, his words do not constitute a source for what happened around one thousand years earlier. Avalon only entered Arthur's story in the 1130s, six hundred or so years after his supposed life; clearly, the entire scene is inadmissible as evidence. This is history of the Indiana Jones school,[133] entertaining enough in its way but with nothing to add to our understanding of the past.

What of Cynddylan? He is a comparatively well-known hero of early Welsh poetry who is thought to have perished at the battle of Winwæd, along with Penda and most of his great army, late in 655.[134] This disaster occurred when the Mercian army attempted to cross the River Went in Yorkshire when it was in flood. In the ensuing battle, Bede tells us,[135] more were drowned than killed.[136] That Cynddylan's body was somehow recovered and brought back to his own lands seems extraordinarily unlikely. Even had he been, there is no reason to think that he had been interred here.

Lastly, let us revisit The Berth. Yes, the fortification was originally surrounded by water, with a causeway beside which a late prehistoric cauldron was recovered,[137] so it might just about be described as an island (though hardly a 'vale'), but that is as far as Arthurian parallels can take us; it is not very far. Interpretation of the survey data cannot be anything more than tentative prior to excavation. The anomaly on which Phillips focuses might be a burial but British–Welsh graves of this period characteristically yield neither weapons nor shields. The possible trace of metalwork is not therefore likely to indicate a Dark Age Celtic burial. Several British cemeteries of the period have been excavated in the region, the largest, at Tandderwen (near Denbigh), revealing almost forty graves characterised by rectangular ditches around what were probably mounds.[138] An anomaly suggestive of a circular ditch, central pit and metalwork is likelier to represent either a Bronze Age or an Anglo-Saxon burial mound (an Anglo-Saxon glass bead found on The Berth might favour the latter).[139]

The frailties of this line of reasoning well illustrate the problems of all such recent, 'positivist' Arthurian works. Snippets are taken from literature that is highly imaginative and far removed in time from the events under discussion and treated as if meaningful evidence, divorced from scholarly understandings of the period. Similar weaknesses characterise other of these studies. Take for example the case for King Arthur ruling the southwest.[140] The stories on which this is based are known only from the twelfth century onwards, far too late to provide evidence of events *c*. 500. While Geoffrey of Monmouth does seem to have drawn on Arthurian stories circulating in Cornwall, there is no reason to think them particularly ancient. Despite its having been an important Dark Age centre,[141] Tintagel is connected with Arthur no earlier than Geoffrey's work.[142] As we have seen, the story of Arthur's conception there is a version of a folk tale already circulating in seventh-century Ulster and traceable back to the ancient world (see above, p. 211); the heroes' names were interchangeable, clearly, so there is no reason to think Arthur's presence in such a story particularly early or in any sense reliable. Even the place-name Tintagel seems late. This may have been the Roman-period Durocornovium ('Purocoronavis' in the *Ravenna Cosmography*),[143] though this is little more than guesswork. Clearly there was an important site here *c*. 500, most probably royal given the quantity of Mediterranean pottery that was broken on site, and certainly with literate clerics present. But Geoffrey's 'Tintagol' is likely to have been his own creation,[144] for the township had a different, Cornish name until that was displaced by the more famous Arthurian one in the nineteenth century. Construction of a medieval castle on the promontory postdated Geoffrey's *magnum opus*; the site had no particular strategic or seigneurial value so its defence was arguably an attempt to benefit from the stronghold's portrayal in the *History of the Kings of Britain* (Plate 32).[145]

Nor do any of the rival locations for Arthur's activities rest on better evidence. Here is a passage from Steve Blake and Scott Lloyd's *The Lost Legend of Arthur*:

> The *Dream of Rhonabwy* describes the route taken by Arthur and his warriors on the way to Caer Faddon, the Welsh name for Badon. 'And then they traversed the great plain of Agryngroeg as far as Rhyd-y-Groes on the Severn. And a mile from the ford, on either side of the roads, they could see the tents and pavilions and the mustering of a great host. And they came to the bank of the ford. They could see Arthur seated on a flat island below the ford.'[146]

The ford of Rhyd-y-Groes lies near Buttington, east of Welshpool, and the 'plain of Agryngroeg' can be identified with Gungrog fawr and Gungrog fach, just north of the same town. If Arthur was in the mid-Severn valley immediately before Badon, the battle-site should lie nearby; Blake and Lloyd therefore propose Breidden Hill (otherwise The Breidden), on which, they tell us, excavation has revealed 'evidence of occupation at this period.'[147]

But *The Dream of Rhonabwy* (*Breuddwyd Rhonabwy*) is a work of fiction. Written in all probability in the decades around 1300,[148] it was framed as a dream experienced by a retainer of the last king of Powys, Madog ap Maredudd (who ruled 1132–60).[149] Arthur and Owain play a game similar to chess but they are repeatedly interrupted by fighting between Arthur's squires and Owain's ravens. The battle of Badon does not even occur, a truce with the Saxons being arranged instead; at the close Arthur leads his men away, purposing to reach Cornwall by nightfall.

The siege of Badon did occur, though (where and when is not the point in this context), it was not deferred; that much we know from Gildas. And Dark Age armies were not made up of squires and ravens, obviously, and you certainly cannot march an army from Welshpool to Cornwall in an afternoon. Faddon was the Welsh name for Bath, which authors were by this date identifying with Badon, so no different location for the battle is even necessary. That events are set close to Mathrafal, a castle built by Madog in 1156 and widely considered thereafter in literary circles to be the ancient centre of Powys,[150] reflects nostalgia for a kingdom which fragmented following his death. It is in this context that criticism of the present-day Welsh is voiced by ancient heroes, with the great Arthur contemptuous of the 'little fellows' who now 'keep this Island'. *The Dream* has something to tell us about Welsh nationalist sentiment *c.* 1300, therefore, but nothing useful to say about a siege that occurred around eight hundred years earlier. Nor have modern-day excavations on The Breidden demonstrated a Dark Age occupation, for, as the excavator Chris Musson put it, 'no convincing evidence of post-Roman activity was encountered.'[151]

Just as suspect is the use made of late medieval genealogies. These were written for contemporary purposes, generally on the basis of very poor source materials for the early generations. Just think of the claim made on Edward IV's behalf to descent from Brutus.[152] A recent instance is the suggestion that we should identify Arthur with Arthwys, a figure named in genealogies known collectively as the 'Lineage of the Saints' (*Bonedd y Saint*).[153] These survive in manuscripts of the late thirteenth century onwards and are unlikely to have been composed before the twelfth.[154] Obviously, genealogies originating this late cannot be relied upon for lineages seven hundred years earlier unless they can be shown to contain much earlier material. Such is not the case here. Additionally, Arthwys is not the same name as Arthur. If we are to consider all the 'Arth-' names that occur in medieval Welsh sources as potential candidates, then there are rather a lot to go at and little reason to prefer one to another.

Nor should we have any truck with the identification of Arthur as Athrwys ap Meurig, a figure of the southern March named in the *Llandaff Charters*.[155] Once again, there is simply no reason to make the connection between King Arthur and any of the 'Arth-' personal names formed in Welsh that crop up in this collection (or any other).[156] A similar approach was tried centuries ago;[157] it did not convince then and does not now. Nor is the suggestion that Arthur's name is in origin Germanic any more helpful, based as it is very crudely on the same 'sounds-a-bit-like' principle that so pervades attempts to locate Arthur's battles. Agreed, a few Anglo-Saxon names were adopted in Wales late in the first millennium CE,[158] but none so far as we know as early as the sixth century. Attempts to derive the name Arthur from Anglo-Saxon Eadhere or the Lombard Authari are far from satisfactory phonetically.[159] The descent of Arthur from Roman Artorius or Greek Arktouros is linguistically seamless; such markedly inferior possibilities can only muddy what is one of the clearer pools of Arthurian water.

As is occasionally acknowledged,[160] academic historians rarely comment on populist Arthurian 'histories'. Their silence plays, though, into the hands of these authors by withholding the guidance that would allow non-specialist readers to come to a balanced assessment of the arguments. To comment meaningfully on any one theory is time-consuming and diverts scholars from the research and teaching that most are employed to do. When they do respond their comments rarely amount to much more than straightforward rejection of a particular theory without explaining why, leaving readers having to make choices in a 'one's word against another's' situation. In such circumstances claims that are backed up by populist arguments may seem preferable to a negative unsupported by any reasoning, leaving the 'siren claims of the pseudo-histories' dominating booksellers' shelves.[161] But despite each claiming to 'reveal' the 'true' Arthur reigning in a 'real' past, all such works should be relocated to fiction. They can be entertaining but they are not 'histories' within any definition of the term that we can recognise today.

Arthur and the agnostics

Despite their many differences, the theories in favour of 'foreign', 'mytho-logical' and 'real, British' Arthurs all share a belief that their authors have discovered the 'true' origin of this ultra-enigmatic king. There remain many, though, who are unconvinced by each and every one of these solu-tions. As already remarked, this is the position which today secures much of the academic vote.[162] As the American Arthurian scholar Alan Lupack puts it, 'the most reasonable position ... is to be an agnostic about the ques-tion of Arthur's historicity.'[163] The early medieval historian Guy Halsall expresses this even more forcefully. While acknowledging the attractions of a 'real' Arthur, he recognises that the evidence is inadequate. It is impos-sible, though, in his view to prove that there is no ' "fire" behind the "smoke" of later myth and legend ... this is the *only* attitude that can seriously be held concerning the historicity of the "once and future king"'.[164]

Is this right? Our answer must be both 'yes' and 'no'. It does seem reason-able on the face of it to accept that the evidence is insufficient to demon-strate that Arthur did specific things in a recognisable historical context, so in that sense fence-sitting makes good sense. Clearly, Arthur is not an historical figure in the same way that William the Conqueror is, or Alfred the Great (the figure with whom he has on occasion been comically confused).[165] There is just not the near-contemporary evidence that we need for Arthur's deeds – the fierceness of the claims and counter-claims is proof enough of that. His existence is at best problematic; there is nothing wrong with saying 'I just do not know'.

But agnosticism may be less defensible than it at first sight appears, and I say this on several counts. This book has tested the more prominent theories currently in circulation, assessing whether or not any one of them is even part-way defensible – and part-way might be considered sufficient, given the poor quality of the evidence on which they all rest. The conclusion, though, is that none are. That alone must tip us towards a less ambivalent stance. Then, just for a moment, let us mass these theories together. As we have seen, writers across all our main categories claim to have identified 'the real King Arthur' but each and every solution conflicts with at least some of the others. He cannot be a 'true' figure of pre-classical Greece and Dark Age Glamorgan, Wales and Dál Riata, Cornwall and Sarmatia, a Celtic deity as well as a Roman soldier buried in Dalmatia. So, accepting King Arthur as historical does not distinguish a group with one broadly unified position. Rather, we are faced by a mass of conflicting theories, with those who accept one necessarily rejecting others. Even the believers are unbelievers, therefore. Given that every theory that we have explored has failed when put to the test, disbelief in Arthur as an historical figure should surely carry the day.

Let us return to Lupack's urging of agnosticism: 'While incontrovertible proof of such a historical figure neither exists nor is likely to be discovered, it is also unlikely that the negative will ever be absolutely proven.'[166] This is a line of reasoning that we encounter repeatedly when dealing with Arthur, as in Halsall's comment (above). But, we may well ask, so what? Surely, there is no requirement on us to prove a negative. The point was made succinctly by Bertrand Russell: 'Many orthodox people speak as though it were the business of sceptics to disprove received dogmas rather than of dogmatists to prove them. This is, of course, a mistake.'[167] He illustrated the point by supposing the existence of a teapot in orbit around the sun that is too small to be visible even through the most powerful telescope. That this assertion cannot be disproved does not mean that it should be allowed to influence our thinking about the solar system. That way only chaos lies, for such speculations are potentially infinite.

The same principle must be applied to every claim to have 'found' King Arthur. Take, for example, the popular historian Alistair Moffat's 'discovery' of Camelot at Roxburgh. Unfortunately, he remarks, 'now no trace whatever remains, nor any ability to find some because no archaeology is permitted by the landowner.'[168] No evidence? Then Russell's teapot must guide us and the theory be discarded. Proponents of any argument in favour of an historical Arthur need to go some way at least towards proving their case. If they cannot do so then their ideas are just speculation. There is nothing wrong with a bit of speculation but a theory which rests on nothing more cannot stand.

Even when claims equivalent to Russell's illusory teapot reach us from a thousand years ago, the same critical processes must apply. To be included in history, an individual and his or her deeds must pass a repeatable set of tests. We should feel confident that we are making a fair and balanced assessment of the evidence in favour of someone having existed in a particular space and time, doing ascertainable things. Of course, people who lived in the early Middle Ages are rarely named by many near-contemporary writers, often by only one. In such cases, we are dependent on the reliability of a single author, so their existence is often a matter of probability rather than certainty. Medieval history is beset by such issues. The fact remains, though, that there is nothing even remotely resembling a near-contemporary account of Arthur and his deeds. Barring a compelling argument for chapter 56 in the *Historia Brittonum* deriving from some reliable and, to an extent, verifiable source written close in time to the events, that alone rules him out of history.

There are other figures in the literature of the Anglo-Norman world who in some respects resemble Arthur. Take Havelok the Dane, whose story first appears at some length in the twelfth century in a French 'history' written by the Anglo-Norman chronicler Geoffrey Gaimar.[169] Perhaps he was based on some earlier Norseman, perhaps not. Similarly, King Horn is a pseudo-historical character known to us from the *Romance of Horn*, written *c.* 1170.[170] Both these figures could have roots in insular storytelling earlier than the Norman Conquest, in which case they have been adapted prior to the earliest form in which they now exist (Horn, for example, repeatedly fights Saracens but his story may have originally featured Vikings). Their stories were popular. Havelok features on the seal of the city of Grimsby, a medieval borough with whose foundation his story became entwined, and he was 'remembered' as an English king in fifteenth-century France. Both these stories appeared in print early in the twentieth century,[171] but they are no more historical for that. There is no room for agnosticism here; significantly, no one has urged it. All are agreed, neither Havelok nor Horn warrant admission to our histories. Obviously, there is far less invested in these figures than in Arthur, but the principle is the same. Given that the witnesses to his activities are even further removed from his supposed time, there is no reason whatsoever to judge Arthur's case differently.

Arthur and British history

We have tested the Dalmatian, Sarmatian, Greek and Ossetian connections claimed for Arthur but examination of the evidence in each instance shows just how speculative these theories are; none offers a viable solution to the puzzle of Arthur's origin. In some sense, therefore, his starting point must lie in Britain – as was widely acknowledged in the Middle Ages. We too must focus there.

Despite the 'mythological' strand in many portrayals of Arthur across the high and later Middle Ages, that the name almost certainly reached Britain from Italy in the Roman period pretty well rules out any origin from within Celtic mythology.[172] Nor was he an imported deity, for Arcturus/Arktouros is not known to have been culted in the classical world. Arthur cannot therefore be explained as a leftover from one of the pre-Christian pantheons. Nor can there be any realistic hope of an archaeological 'discovery' of King Arthur,[173] despite all the efforts made across the twentieth century. Labelling Arthur 'legendary', though, is no more satisfactory, for this just kicks the whole question into the long grass. Every legend must have a starting point, if only we can identify it.

Nor do any of the 'positive' Arthurs work out, for all are based (however distantly) on the assumption that sources for Arthur that are near-contemporary and broadly reliable underlie chapter 56 of the *Historia Brittonum*. As we have seen, this requires so much special pleading as to be highly improbable. In practice, all the 'real, British' Arthurs stem from one, basic, methodological error, which is to read the *De Excidio Britanniae*, the *Historia Brittonum* and the *Annales Cambriae* (and in many cases other later texts as well) as if equally capable of contributing to an account of what actually happened *c.* 500 CE. Take the following, by the keen Arthurian Mike Ashley, as just one example of many: 'Arthur won such a decisive victory over the Saxons at Badon (sometime between AD 495 and 516) that they retreated and left Britain in relative peace for many years'.[174] Of these texts, only the *De Excidio* is sufficiently close in date for it to be considered authoritative but it offers neither dates nor any mention of Arthur. Badon was a siege in Gildas's view, not a battle (as it would be in the *Historia*), and it was in no sense 'decisive'. Nor is there any evidence that the contemporary peace with the Saxons was either consequent upon British victory or characterised by a

Saxon pull-back. Gildas treated Badon as 'pretty well' the last British success, naming it not because it mattered *per se* but as a marker of the year in which the period of mixed fortunes in the 'war of the Saxon federates' came to a close. It was the year that mattered, not the siege. And Badon also marked the start of the present epoch – the time of writing – for it was the year of Gildas's birth. His principal focus throughout was the sin in which his own generation was steeped; the year in which he was born marked the starting point, therefore, of his condemnation of his own times.

Arthur's responsibility for Badon is not 'recorded' until the *Historia Brittonum* but the three-century gap must bar this text from being treated as a source equal in authority to the *De Excidio Britanniae* (the *Annales Cambriae* are a century still further removed and its author seems barely even aware of the conflict). That is unfortunate, of course, for the *De Excidio* tells us frustratingly little about 'the war of the Saxon federates', in which Arthur's battles eventually took root. But no matter; applying modern standards of historical analysis requires that we recognise Gildas's work as the only authentic element of what Ashley termed 'the historical record'.[175] We can surmise nothing about Arthur from the *De Excidio* beyond the fact of his absence. Along with so much else written on the subject, Ashley's words are as fictional as those of Nennius.

That said, we should perhaps be sympathetic towards the early ninth-century cleric who was tasked with working up the distant British past into a narrative suited to the rhetorical needs of his own times in North Wales. This was no easy task. The *De Excidio Britanniae* was the only near-contemporary account that was available, then as now, but Gildas's complex, moralising style, his repeated condemnations of his own people and self-identification with the prophet Jeremiah were real obstacles to a British writer seeking positives in his people's backstory.[176] Yet Gildas's lengthy criticism of Maglocunus (the *Historia Brittonum*'s Maelgwn) meant that there was no real alternative to accepting his version of events as relevant to Gwynedd.[177] The solution adopted in the *Historia* was to 'improve' on Gildas's dispiriting portrayal of his 'fellow countrymen' by providing an account that highlighted the Britons' rights as the first inhabitants of the island. The new work is studded with British heroes courageously resisting incomers and prophet-like religious leaders guiding this latter-day people of the Lord. While Gildas had depicted his own times, particularly, in terms of divine punishment of a disobedient, latter-day Israel, the *Historia*'s Britons better recall the same Old Testament people when struggling bravely against their foes with God at their side – more David and less

Jeremiah, as one might say. The *Historia* was written for a 'British' princeling at a moment of heightened threat from a (briefly) united England; clearly, it was an act of defiance intended only for 'British' consumption, designed to centre the British cause on both Merfyn and Gwynedd. As the modern British historian John Vincent remarks: 'All history [is] inspired by and intent on promoting a set of beliefs.'[178] Such was as true in ninth-century Wales as in the nineteenth and twentieth centuries. Before we take anything factual from old histories, it behoves us to work out just what beliefs the author was attempting to promote.

If criticism of the synthetic approach that Ashley's typifies seems overly harsh, it may help to point out that such reinventions of the past are extraordinarily commonplace. Geoffrey of Monmouth was guiltier still of wholesale 'improvements' to history and the imaginative stitching together of disconnected gobbets into a single narrative. His was a past that certainly never happened, however eagerly it was read and heard. The Arthurian tradition long continued down this path, with the addition of such motifs as the sword in the stone, Camelot, the Holy Grail and the sword in the water (to take just the best-known examples). This is fiction piled on fiction. And history was frequently manipulated in the early Middle Ages by those in power.[179] A work that is well worth comparing with the *Historia Brittonum* is the *Tarikh al-Sudan*, a set of chronicles composed at Timbuktu following the Moroccan conquest of the region. This rewrote the past in highly imaginative ways, in the process fabricating much that later came to be accepted as West Africa's earliest history.[180] Such fictionalising narratives are tailored to immediate needs but they can gain long acceptance where there is a lack of more reliable source material. 'Fake news' is nothing new; we should always be on our guard.

To conclude, therefore, the question whether or not Arthur can reasonably be allowed a role in history can only elicit a negative response. None of the 'foreign' theories stack up. Only if the *Historia Brittonum* can be trusted as an historical source could the 'British' Arthur be even quasi-historical, but when tested it falls far short of what is required. Arthur's battles look to have been pulled together from a variety of sources and individual champions in a style of composition best described as plagiarism. Surveying the great British heroes depicted in the *Historia* underlines its shortcomings as history. Were Brutus or Britto the founders of the British race? Was Bellinus king of Britain (or any part of it) when Caesar invaded? Did he or his father rule the islands of the western Mediterranean, as well? Was Dolabella his general? Did Cunedda expel the Irish from Wales and then found Gwynedd's royal line? Did Vortimer eject the Saxons from Kent? To these questions we can only reply 'no', 'no', 'no', 'no', 'no' and 'no' again, with more or less certainty. These are either fictionalised or make-believe characters, introduced to create the impression of a British people that had a right to Britain, had bravely resisted 'foreigners' across the long durée and hitherto always succeeded in expelling them. All good stuff in 829–30, but this cannot be accepted today as historical evidence in any shape, size or form. Similarly, we must dismiss the *Historia*'s version of 'the war of the Saxon federates' to the extent that it is unsupported by Gildas, dispensing with Arthur and his battles in the process.

The first of the *Annales*' two mentions of Arthur almost certainly derives either from the *Historia Brittonum* or sources very close to it; the second is independent but not likely to refer to the same figure (see above, pp. 223–5). Without the *Historia* as a creditable witness there is no reason to allow Arthur any role in the history of Britain in the fifth or early sixth centuries. On the basis of the evidence that we have, the only safe conclusion must be that he was a fictional or fictionalised character introduced for rhetorical purposes in 829–30. We should cast Arthur out of our histories, therefore,[181] and, in particular, de-couple 'King' from 'Arthur', for even the *Historia*'s Arthur is a war-leader, a *dux*, not a *rex*. His kingship derives from later attempts to make sense of a war-leader who had authority over the forces of several British kings. And Badon ushered in no 'Age of Arthur'; that much is evident from close reading of the *De Excidio Britanniae*. Like all golden ages, Arthur's was back-projected onto a distant and little-known past for present purposes, centuries later. There is no reliable evidence for a successful fight-back by the Britons against their Saxon enemies, despite so many claims to the contrary across the later twentieth century. All this is make-believe.

Focusing on the methods used by the author of the *Historia Brittonum* does, though, allow us some insight into when, how and why Arthur originated. His name may well have come from some quite different context, much as did that of Dolabella (for example), but it is little more than guesswork where the *Historia*'s author found it. I have suggested the north, but there is insufficient evidence to press this home to any sort of satisfactory conclusion. Not knowing where the name came from gives us no reason to consider Arthur legendary, though, for there seems no reason to doubt that he and his victories were brought together for the first time either in the *Historia Brittonum* itself or (less likely) some very recent antecedent text. He was not a character in old stories, the origins of which were already lost in the mists of time by 829–30. Nor did he come from the realm of faerie, though many of the stories which later gathered around him arguably did. Rather, we can be reasonably confident that the Arthur with whom we are familiar was made up by one imaginative clerk early in the ninth century as the last of a string of courageous British war-leaders through whom he was seeking to deliver a vision of British success in warfare against foreign interlopers. These fictitious characters provided exemplars of immediate relevance to the ninth century, sustaining the hope of a 'British' triumph over 'foreigners' (i.e. the Saxons) that was still to come, to be achieved by the union of all their forces under one leader. Arthur was the last of these figures and the most apt for the present time as regards his Christianity, his campaigning against the Saxons (as opposed to the Romans or Irish) and his leadership of the combined forces of the British kings. His meaning lay in the present, therefore, even the near future, not the distant past.

All of this occurred so long ago that today we have no absolute proof that the *Historia*'s Arthur was invented. So should we just sit on the fence? Scholars frequently adopt courtroom analogies when discussing Arthur's existence, suggesting that 'the court is still out' or returning a verdict of 'case unproven'. It would, though, be a very strange court indeed that was prepared to accept testimony from three hundred years later than the events under discussion, that seems to have been based on no near-contemporary sources and which demonstrably invented or fictionalised a whole string of similar characters. This does not mean that everything in the *Historia* is false, for it is not, particularly when it comes to the later sixth- and seventh-century material drawn from northern Britain. The fact remains, though, that the *Historia* was written as a mix of fact, fictionalisation and downright untruth. It defies the normal constraints of history as practised today, subverting even the voices of the few early witnesses that were accessible to its author (such as Orosius, Gildas) in pursuit of broader 'truths' of relevance to the present. Particularly in the earlier periods, the *Historia* is so laced with invention that it cannot be treated as an historical source for any matter for which we lack external, much-nearer-contemporary confirmation. Arthur's battle-list should be seen as the last of these wholly unreliable passages; it is as fictional as Bellinus and Dolabella. Confronted by a half-decent barrister, Nennius would be exposed as an unreliable witness in any modern court of law, his evidence thrown out and his person held on a posthumous charge of perjury.

That is not in any sense to disrespect Nennius and the *Historia Brittonum*, for it is unfair to judge the work of a ninth-century cleric in such black-and-white terms. The type of analysis deployed here is applicable to modern histories, of course, but this is another kind of historical beast entirely, in which a statement should be understood as at the same time both 'real' and entirely unhistorical. John Updike put it as well as anyone in the novel, *Roger's Version*: 'Writing was sympathetic magic, we should remember that'. After giving several examples from first-century Christian works, he continues: '[these fabrications] were simply, for the perpetrators, a way of dressing truth, of presenting the truth in the robes and ornaments *it should have*.'[182] That a 'history' written for a crisis-ridden, early ninth-century Welsh kinglet should have prioritised contemporary, ideological needs over accurate recounting of the distant past should not surprise us one iota. Indeed, that is exactly what we should expect.

The Arthurian tradition rests on what must be judged a ninth-century fiction, therefore, an extraordinarily successful one needless to say, but a fiction nonetheless. Given the obscurity into which several of the *Historia Brittonum*'s heroes fell, Arthur's rise to fame seems in some respects strange, but several of his later characteristics already attach to the *Historia*'s Arthur – his Christian credentials, for example, his role as national war-leader versus the 'Saxon' enemy and his personal prowess. His kingship is a logical development of this role. That Arthur's personal history and his geography were so fluid from the very beginning meant that he could be reimagined in almost any form and used as the backdrop to virtually any story. He passes from one language community to another; he has never died – there is no grave, so he might be imagined coming again (the analogy is with Christ, of course). He became a figure of story, of folklore, of history, of romance, of chivalric ideals and of secular and religious thought, lending himself to uses far distant from his purpose at the moment of creation.

That Arthur has produced extraordinary quantities of 'smoke' is in large part because he is so well suited to be a fulcrum of make-believe. But there is no historical 'fire' underlying the stories that congregated around him, just 'highland mist'. This metaphor is perhaps best approached via the words of another novelist, William Boyd, who depicted a 'pall of smoke converging – arrowing in – on one point, to feed the small, angry conflagration of the fire.'[183] Imaginative writing has license to upend the laws of physics for literary effect; Arthur belongs entirely within that sphere. When all is said and done, all we have are swirling shapes in a fantastical cloud; there is neither flame nor fire beneath. Half-imagined wraiths forming in hill mist are no foundation for our histories.

We could do worse than close with a rhyme first published in the early 1870s, when the 'historical' Arthur had been pretty well expunged from Britain's past:

> When good King Arthur ruled this land, he was a goodly king:
> He stole three pecks of barley meal, to make a bag-pudding.
> A bag-pudding the king did make, and stuffed it well with plums.
> And in it put great lumps of fat, as big as my two thumbs.
> The king and queen did eat thereof, and noblemen beside;
> And what they could not eat that night, the Queen next morning fried.[184]

Gone, here, in all but name and title, is the sovereign lord portrayed by Malory (whose work this author is likely to have known). Instead we have a parody. It is the contrast between the royal dignity, on the one hand, and his petty criminality on the other that makes us smile (although both Arthur and his wife might have been transported for these crimes as late as 1868). In an age in which his claim on history had crumbled, Arthur was metamorphosing once more, this time to become a comic figure for the nursery. For over a millennium Arthur has shifted to accord with the times, ever-changing according to the needs of author and audience, fluid yet resilient, a made-up character in stories full of invention.

Arthur comes down to earth with a thud in this Victorian ditty, yet this version is no less 'true' or 'false' than any other. And it was ever so. Arthur is not historically 'true' today. Nor was he when first dreamed up, when the support of Christ and the Virgin Mary and his twelve victories against the foreigners who had taken over so much of Britain provided much-needed 'truths' in support of an insecure prince ruling one corner of Wales. His ever-changing story provides insights to the world-views and purposes of those who have written him, portrayed him, imagined and reimagined him, loved him and denied him, in the process adding ever more layers to his long, long tale. Therein lies both his fascination and his value to the historian but we can now agree to discount King Arthur as a 'real' figure of the past, leaving him and his deeds to the 'smoke' and 'highland mist' of make-believe and wishful thinking; it is there that he properly belongs.

Appendix I

THE 'ARTORIUS' INSCRIPTIONS

The Inscriptions / Suggested Chronologies

Longer Inscription	Shorter Inscription	Malone	Pflaum	Medini	Malcor	Miletić	Present Suggestion
Centurion in III *Gallica*		132–35			158–62	135–38	146–49
Centurion in VI *Ferrata*					162–66	139–42	149–52
Centurion in II *Adiutrix*					166–70	143–46	152–55
Centurion in V *Macedonica*					170–74	147–50	155–58
Primus pilus of V *Macedonica*	*Primus pilus* of V *Macedonica*				175	151	158
Praepositus classis Misenatium					176–80	152–54	158
Camp Prefect of VI *Victrix*	Camp Prefect of VI *Victrix*				181–84	155–62	159–62
Dux against the Arm----		150–55	183–85		185	162–66	162–66
Procurator of Lib---				184–85	186–	167–74	c. 170

Appendix II

ARTHUR'S BATTLES AS DESCRIBED IN
THE *HISTORIA BRITTONUM* AND
ANNALES CAMBRIAE

Arthur's Battles in the HB and AC	Location according to Jackson	Location according to Littleton and Malcor	Location according to Breeze
'in the mouth of the river which is called *Glein*'	?R. Glen (Northumb. or Lincs.)	R. Glen (Northumb.)	R. Glen (Northumb.)
'another river, which is called *Dubglas*'	Too many possibilities to attempt location	R. Douglas (Lancs.) or Douglas Water (S. Lanark.)	Douglas Water (S. Lanark.)
'the region of *Linnuis*'	?Lindsey	A mistake in the HB	Read as *Clutuis* ('Strathclyders')
'on a river which is called *Bassas*'	Unlocated	Unlocated	Read as *Tarras*; either Mouse Water (S. Lanark.) or Taras Water (D.&G.)
'in the wood of Caledonia, that is *Cat Coit Celidon*'	Scotland	Scotland/ Northumb.	The area around Beattock Summit (S. Lanark.)
'in the castle of *Guinnion*'	Unlocated	*Vinovium* (Binchester)	Carwinning (N. Ayrshire)
'in the city of the legion'	Chester (?or Caerleon)	York	Adopting the Cumbric reading *carrec legion*, identified as 'the cliff by Kinneil House' Falkirk
'on the bank of the river called *Tribruit*'	Somewhere northern	Ribble estuary	Dreva, on the Upper Tweed (Borders)

Arthur's Battles in the HB and AC	Location according to Jackson	Location according to Littleton and Malcor	Location according to Breeze
'the mountain which is called *Agned*'	Unlocated	Unlocated	Reading as *Agheu*, 'death'; Pennango (Newmill, Borders)
'*Breguoin*'	Bremenium (High Rochester)	Bremetennacum (Ribchester)	Bremenium (High Rochester)
'on the mountain of Badon'	Unlocated	Dumbarton Rock	Reading as *Bradon*; Ringsbury Hill, by Braydon Forest (Wilts.)
'*Camlann*'	?Cambolanda (Birdoswald)	Camboglanna (Castlesteads)	Camboglanna (Castlesteads)

Sources: Jackson, 1945, 1949; FSTC, 327–31 and passim; Breeze, 2016.

Appendix III

THE *MIRABILIA*: A LIST OF WONDERS AND MIRACLES THAT BECAME ATTACHED TO THE *HISTORIA BRITTONUM*

Chapters 67–75

Number on Map 6	Designation in the *Mirabilia*	Location and/or Nature of Wonder/Miracle
1	'First *miraculum*'	Loch Leven (*stagnum Lumunoy*); either Fife or Lorn (Scotland)
2	'Second *miraculum*'	Estuary of the River Trahannon, reference to the Bore (*sissa*) suggests a tributary of the Severn
3	'Third *miraculum*'	The hot lake in the country of the Hwicce, so Bath
4	'Fourth *miraculum*'	The salt springs in the same, so Droitwich
5	'Another *miraculum*'	'The two kings of the Severn' (*Duorig Habren*; *Duo reges Sabrinae*), the Severn Bore
6	'Another *miraculum*'	The mouth of Llyn Lliwan (*Linn Liuan*), a tidal lake near Chepstow
Unlocated	'Another *mirabilis*'	A spring called *Finnaun Guur Helic*, in the region of *Cinlipiuc*
8	No designation	Ash-tree bearing apples on a hillside close to the estuary of the Wye (*Guoy*)
9	'Another *mirabilis*'	Cleft in the hill from which the wind always blows called *Vith Guint* (MW *Cwthwym Gwynt*), in Gwent
10	'Another *mirabilis*'	An altar in Gower (*Guhyr*) in a place called Llwynarth (*Loyngarth*), near The Mumbles
11	'Another *mirabilis*'	A spring by the 'wall of Pydew Meurig' (*vallis putei Mouric*) in Gwent (not more closely identified)

Number on Map 6	Designation in the *Mirabilia*	Location and/or Nature of
12	'Another *mirabilis*'	Carn Gaffalt (*Carn Cabal*) in Builth, near Rhayader
13	'Another *miraculum*'	Tomb of Amr beside the spring called Llygad Amr (*Licat Amr*), the head of the River Gamber
14	'Another *mirabilis*'	A tomb on the top of the mountain called Crug Mawr (*Cruc Maur*) in Ceredigion (*Cereticiaun*); Crug Mawr is near Cardigan
15	'First *miraculum*'	'a shore without a sea' (this opens a sub-set of *miracula* located on Anglesey, nos. 15–18)
16	'Second *miraculum*'	'a hill there which turns around three times a year'
17	'Third *miraculum*'	'a ford there which floods when the sea floods and when the sea ebbs it subsides'
18	'Fourth *miraculum*'	'a stone that walks by night in the valley of *Citheinn*' that found its way back from having been thrown into 'the abyss of *Cerews*, which is in the middle of the sea which is called Menai (*Mene*)'
19	'there is a lake'	Lough Leane (*Luchleinn*), near Killarney, Republic of Ireland
20	'there is another lake'	Lough Neagh (*Luch Echach*), Ulster, from the Irish, *Loch nEachach*

ABBREVIATIONS

AC	*Annales Cambriae*, ed. L. Faral, *La Légende Arthurienne*, III (Paris, 1929), reprinted with some additions and translated by J. Morris in *Nennius, British History and the Welsh Annals* (London, 1980), 44–9, 85–91.
Adomnán	*Adomnán's Life of Columba*, ed. and trans. A.O. Anderson and M.O. Anderson, revised by M.O. Anderson (Oxford, 1991); there is also a translation by R. Sharpe: Adomnán of Iona, *Life of St Columba* (London, 1995).
ALITMA	R.S. Loomis (ed.), *Arthurian Literature in the Middle Ages: A Collaborative History* (Oxford, 1959).
AM	Ammianus Marcellinus, *Histories*, trans. J.C. Rolfe, 3 vols (Cambridge, MA, 1939).
Appian	*Appian's Roman History*, ed. G.P. Gould, trans. H. White, 4 vols (Cambridge, MA, 1913).
Aratus	Aratus, *Phaenomena*, ed. D.A. Kidd (Cambridge, 1997).
ASC (A, E)	*The Anglo-Saxon Chronicle: A Collaborative Edition*, general eds D. Dumville, M. Lapidge and S. Keynes: vol. 3, MS A, ed. J.M. Bately (Cambridge, 1986); vol. 7, MS E, ed. S. Irvine (Cambridge, 2004); for a translation, see *The Anglo-Saxon Chronicle*, trans. and ed. M. Swanton (London, 1996).
Avienus	Avienus, *Ora Maritima*, ed. J. P. Murphy (Chicago, 1977).
Bede	Bede, *De Natura Rerum*, in *Corpus Christianorum Series Latina*, 123a, ed. C.W. Jones (Turnhout, 1975); for a translation, see Bede, *On the Nature of Things and On Times*, trans. C.B. Kendall and F. Wallis (Liverpool, 2010).
Bosworth/Toller	*An Anglo-Saxon Dictionary based on the manuscript collections of the late Joseph Bosworth, edited and enlarged by T. Northcote Toller* (Oxford, 1898).
Caesar	Caesar, *The Gallic War*, ed. G.P. Gould, trans. H.J. Edwards (Cambridge, MA, 1917).
CaO	*Culhwch and Olwen: An Edition and Study of the Oldest Arthurian Tale* (Cardiff, 1992), ed. R. Bromwich and D.S. Evans;

an alternative translation is that by G. Jones and T. Jones, *The Mabinogion* (London, revised ed. 1974), 95–136.

Capella   *Martianus Capella and the Seven Liberal Arts*, II, *The Marriage of Philology and Mercury*, trans. W.H. Stahl and R. Johnson (New York, 1977).

CI   *The Chronicle of Ireland*, trans. with introduction and notes by T.M. Charles-Edwards (Liverpool, 2006).

Cicero   Cicero, *De Natura Deorum*, in *Cicero in Twenty-Eight Volumes*, XIX, *De Natura Deorum Academica*, ed. and trans. H. Rackham (Cambridge, MA, 1967).

CIL   *Corpus Inscriptionum Latinarum*, ed. T. Mommsen et al. (Berlin, 1863–).

Claudian   *Claudian*, trans. M. Platnauer, 2 vols (Cambridge, MA, 1932).

DEB   Gildas, *De Excidio Britanniae*, in *Gildas: The Ruin of Britain and Other Works*, ed. and trans. M. Winterbottom (London, 1978), 13–142, based on the edition of T. Mommsen, MGH: AA 13, *Chronica Minora*, 3 (Berlin, 1898), 1–85.

Dio   *Dio's Roman History*, ed. E.H. Warmington, trans. E. Cary based on a version by H.B. Foster, 9 vols (Cambridge, MA, 1970).

Diodorus   Diodorus of Sicily, *Library of History*, ed. T.E. Page, trans. C.H. Oldfather, 10 vols (London, 1933).

EAT   G. Anderson, *The Earliest Arthurian Texts, Greek and Latin Sources of the Medieval Tradition (Texts, Translations, and Commentary)* (Lewiston, NY, 2007).

EDCS   Epigraphik-Datenbank Clauss/Slaby; online at http://db.edcs.eu/epigr/epi.php (accessed 5 June 2018).

EDH   Epigraphic Database Heidelberg; online at http://edh-www.adw.uni-heidelberg.de (accessed 5 June 2018).

EHD, I   *English Historical Documents*, I, ed. D.C. Douglas (2nd ed., London, 1979).

FSTC   C.S. Littleton and L.A. Malcor, *From Scythia to Camelot* (2nd ed., New York, 2000).

Germanicus   *The Aratus Ascribed to Germanicus Caesar*, ed. D.B. Gain (London, 1976).

GoW   *Itinerarium Cambriae*, in *Giraldi Cambrensis opera*, ed. J.F. Dimock, Rolls Series, VI (London, 1868); for a translation see Gerald of Wales, *The Journey through Wales / The Description of Wales*, trans. L. Thorpe (Harmondsworth, 1978).

HB   *Historia Brittonum*; the most accessible version is *Nennius: British History and the Welsh Annals*, ed. and trans. J. Morris (London, 1980), but for the Chartres and Harleian texts see E. Faral, *La Légende Arthurienne: Études et Documents, les plus Anciens Textes*, III (Paris, 1929), 2–62; all modern editions rest ultimately on T. Mommsen (ed.), MGH, *Chronica Minora, IV, V, VI, VII* (Berlin, 1898), vol. 3, 112–222.

HD   The reference system used by EDH

HE   *Historia Ecclesiastica Gentis Anglorum: Bede's Ecclesiastical History of the English People*, ed. B. Colgrave and R.A.B. Mynors (Oxford, 1969).

Herodian   Herodian, *History*, ed. E.H. Warmington, trans. C. R. Whittaker, 2 vols (Cambridge, MA, 1969).

Herodotus   *Herodotus, Books I–II*, ed. G.P. Goold, trans. A.D. Godley (Cambridge, MA, 1920).

Hesiod	'Works and Days', in *Hesiod: Theogony, Works and Days, Testimonia*, ed. and trans. G.W. Most (Cambridge, MA, 2006).
Homer, *Iliad*	Homer, *The Iliad*, trans. R. Fitzgerald (Oxford, 1974).
Homer, *Odyssey*	Homer, *The Odyssey*, ed. and trans. A.T. Murray, 2 vols (London, 1919).
HRB	Geoffrey of Monmouth, *Historia Regum Britanniae*: Geoffrey of Monmouth, *The History of the Kings of Britain*, ed. M.D. Reeve, trans. N. Wright (Woodbridge, 2007).
Isidore	*The Etymologies of Isidore of Seville*, trans. S.A. Barry, W.J. Lewis and J.A. Beach (Cambridge, 2006).
IWMA	*Ireland and Wales in the Middle Ages*, ed. K. Junkulak and J.M. Wooding (Dublin, 2007).
Jordanes	Jordanes, *Getica*, ed. T. Mommsen, MGH AA 5.1 (Berlin, 1882, repr. 1982), 53–138; for a translation, see C.C. Mierow (trans.), Jordanes, *The Origin and Deeds of the Goths* (Princeton, 1908).
Josephus	Josephus, *The Jewish War*, ed. G.P. Goold, trans. H. St J. Thackeráy, 3 vols (Cambridge, MA, 1927).
JRS	*Journal of Roman Studies*.
Juvenal	*Satires*, in *Juvenal and Persius*, ed. S.M. Braund (Cambridge, MA, 2004).
KAIA	G. Anderson, *King Arthur in Antiquity* (London, 2004).
KRSS	J. Davis-Kimball et al. (eds), *Kurgans, Ritual Sites and Settlements of the Eurasian Bronze and Iron Age* (Oxford, 2000).
LAC	N. Cambi and J. Matthews (eds), *Lucius Artorius Castus and the King Arthur Legend* (Split, 2014).
Laȝamon	*Laȝamon's Brut or Hystoria Brutonum*, ed. and trans. W.R.J. Barron and S.C. Weinberg (New York, 1995).
LCdG(P)	*Les Romans de Chrétien de Troyes, V, Le Conte du Graal (Perceval)*, 2 vols (Paris, 1975); for a translation, see Chrétien de Troyes, *Arthurian Romances*, trans. W.W. Kibler (Harmondsworth, 1991), 381–494.
LDC	*Llyfr Du Caerfyrddin*, ed. A.O.H. Jarman (Cardiff, 1982).
LGPN	*A Lexicon of Greek Personal Names*, ed. P.M. Fraser et al., 6 vols (Oxford, 1987–).
Liddell–Scott	*An Intermediate Greek–English Lexicon founded upon the seventh edition of Liddell and Scott's Greek–English Lexicon* (Oxford, 1889).
Livy	Livy, *Ab Urbe Condita*, ed. R.S. Conway and C.F. Walters (Oxford, 1914).
LMLRA	*La Mort le Roi Artu: Roman du XIIIe Siecle*, ed. J. Frappier (Paris, 1936); for a translation, see J. Cable, *The Death of Arthur* (London, 1971).
Lydgate	*Lydgate's Fall of Princes*, III, ed. H. Bergen (London, 1924).
Macrobius, *Commentary*	*Macrobio Commento Al Somnium Scipionis*, I, ed. M. Regali (Pisa, 1983); for a translation see Macrobius, *Commentary on the Dream of Scipio*, trans. W.H. Stahl (New York, 1952).
Malory	*The Works of Sir Thomas Malory*, ed. E. Vinaver, revised P.J.C. Field, 3 vols (3rd ed., Oxford, 1990).
MGH	*Monumenta Germaniae Historica*, ed. G.H. Pertz et al. (Hanover, 1826–).
MIOF	S. Thompson, *Motif Index of Folklore*, 6 vols (Helsinki, 1932–36).
MLLM	J.F. Niermeyer, *Mediae Latinitatis Lexicon Minus* (Leiden, 2001).
Muirchu	Muirchu, *Vita Sancti Patricii*, ed. and trans. A.B.E. Hood, *St Patrick, His Writings and Muirchu's Life* (London, 1978), 61–98.

ND   *Notitia Dignitatum accedunt Notitia Urbis Constantiopolitanae et Laterculi Prouinciarum*, ed. O. Seeck (Berlin, 1876).

NSBA   *Navigatio Sancti Brendani Abbatis*, ed. C. Selmer (Paris, 1959); for a translation, see J.J. O'Meara and J.M. Wooding, 'The Latin Version', in W.R J. Barron and G.S. Burgess (eds), *The Voyage of Saint Brendan: Representative Versions of the Legend in English Translation* (Exeter, 2002), 13–64.

NSFTC   *Nart Sagas from the Caucasus*, assembled, trans. and annotated by J. Colarusso (Princeton, 2002) (the extended, paperback edition is entitled *Nart Sagas, Ancient Myths and Legends of the Circassians and Abkhazians*).

OCI   Anon., *Origo Constantini Imperatoris*, in *Ammianus Marcellinus, Histories*, trans. J.C. Rolfe, vol. 3 (Cambridge, MA, 1939), 506–69.

OPEL   B. Lőrincz and F. Redő (eds), *Onomasticon Provinciarum Europae Latinarum*, 4 vols (Vienna, 1999, 2000, 2002; Budapest, 2005).

Orosius   *Pauli Orosii Historiarum Adversum Paganos Libri VII*, ed. C. Zangemeister (Leipzig, 1889); Orosius, *Seven Histories against the Pagans*, trans. A.T. Fear (Liverpool, 2010).

Ovid, *Fasti*   *Ovid in Six Volumes*, V, *Fasti*, ed. and trans. Sir J.G. Frazer, revised G.P. Goold (2nd ed., Cambridge, MA, 1989).

Ovid, *Tristia*   Ovid, *Tristia: Ex ponto*, ed. and trans. A.L. Wheeler, revised by G.P. Goold (Cambridge, MA, 1988).

PA   Haydock, M., ' "Preiddeu Annwn" and the Figure of Taliesin', *Studia Celtica*, 18 (1983), 52–78.

Pa Gur   *Pa gur yv y pothaur?* The text is edited by B. Roberts in R. Bromwich and R. B. Jones (eds), *Astudiaethau ar yr Hengerdd* (Cardiff, 1978), 296–309; a translation is provided in CaO, xxxv–vi.

Parzival   *Parzival*, ed. K. Lachmann (Berlin, 1926); for a translation see Wolfram von Eschenbach, *Parzival, with Titurel and the Love Lyrics*, trans. C. Edwards (Cambridge, 2004).

Patrick, *Confessio*   Patrick, *Confessio*, in *St Patrick: His Writings and Muirchu's Life*, ed. and trans. A.B.E. Hood (London, 1978), 23–34, 41–54.

Patrick, *Epistola*,   Patrick, *Epistola*, in *St Patrick: His Writings and Muirchu's Life*, ed. and trans. A.B.E. Hood (London, 1978), 35–8, 55–9.

Pausanias   Pausanias, *Description of Greece*, ed. G.P. Goold, trans. W.H.S. Jones et al., 5 vols (Cambridge, MA, 1918–35).

Philostratus   Philostratus, *The Life of Apollonius of Tyana*, trans. F.C. Conybeare, 2 vols (Cambridge, MA, 1969).

PL   *Patrologiae Cursus Completus (Series Latina)*, ed. J.-P. Migne (Paris, 1844–89).

Pliny, *Natural History*   Pliny, *Natural History*, ed. T.E. Page, trans. H. Rackham, 10 vols (Cambridge, MA, 1938).

Plutarch   *Plutarch's Lives*, trans. B. Perrin (London, 1919).

Procopius   Procopius, *History of the Wars*, trans. H.B. Dewing, 6 vols (London, 1914).

Prosper   Prosper, *Chronicle*, ed. T. Mommsen, *Chronica Minora*, 1, MGH, SRM9.

Ptolemy   *Claudii Ptolemaei Geographica*, ed. C.F.A. Nobbe (Leipzig, 1845).

RAP   *The Roman Army in Pannonia: An Archaeological Guide of the Ripa Pannonica*, ed. Z. Visy, trans. G. Bertók (Budapest, 2003).

Ravenna Cosmography	I.A. Richmond and O.G.S. Crawford, 'The British Section of the Ravenna Cosmography', *Archaeologia*, 93 (1949), 1–50.
RIB I	*Roman Inscriptions of Britain*, I, *Inscriptions on Stone*, ed. R.G. Collingwood and R.P. Wright (new ed., Stroud, 1995).
RIB II	*Roman Inscriptions of Britain, Combined Epigraphic Indexes*, ed. S.S. Frere (Stroud, 1995).
RIB III	*Roman Inscriptions of Britain: Inscriptions on Stone Found or Notified between 1 January 1955 and 31 December 2006*, ed. R.S.O. Tomlinson, R.P. Wright and M.W.C. Hassall (Oxford, 2009).
ROF	D.J. Breeze and B. Dobson, *Roman Officers and Frontiers* (Stuttgart, 1993).
S123 etc.	P.H. Sawyer, *Anglo-Saxon Charters: An Annotated List and Bibliography* (London, 1968).
Sallust	'The War with Catiline', in Sallust, *The War with Catiline, The War with Jugurtha*, trans. J.C. Rolfe, revised J.T. Ramsey (Cambridge, MA, 2013).
SHA	*Scriptores Historiae Augustae*, trans. D. Magie (Cambridge, MA, 1989).
SMA	*Le Morte Arthur: A Romance in Stanzas of Eight Lines*, ed. J.D. Bruce (Oxford, 1903); a modernised edition is offered in L.D. Benson (ed.), *King Arthur's Death* (Exeter, 1974), 1–112.
Strabo	Strabo, *Geography*, ed. E.H. Warmington, 8 vols (Cambridge, MA, 1967).
Suetonius	Suetonius, *The Caesars*, trans. D.W. Hurley (London, 2011).
Tacitus, *Germania*	Tacitus, *Germania*, trans. M. Hutton, revised E.H. Warrington (Cambridge, MA, 1970).
Tacitus, *The Histories*	Tacitus, *The Histories*, ed. G.P. Goold, trans. C.H. Moore, 3 vols (Cambridge, MA, 1925).
TAOTW	*The Arthur of the Welsh*, ed. R. Bromwich, A.O.H. Jarman and B.F. Roberts (Cardiff, 1991).
TA-SW	N.J. Higham and M.J. Ryan, *The Anglo-Saxon World* (London, 2013).
The Mabinogion	*The Text of the Mabinogion and other Welsh Tales from the Red Book of Hergest*, ed. J. Rhŷs and J.G. Evans, 2 vols (Oxford, 1887); for a translation, see *The Mabinogion*, trans. G. Jones and T. Jones (revised ed., London, 1974) (page numbers given refer to the translation).
TNAE	*The New Arthurian Encyclopedia*, ed. N.J. Lacy (New York, 1991).
TOTN	*Tales of the Narts: Ancient Myths and Legends of the Ossetians*, trans. W. May, ed. J. Colarusso and T. Salbiev (Princeton, 2016).
TYP	*Trioedd Ynys Prydein: The Welsh Triads*, ed. R. Bromwich (Cardiff, 1978).
Vegetius, *Epitoma*	Vegetius, *Epitoma rei militaris*, ed. M.D. Reeve (Oxford, 2004). For a translation, see N.P. Milner, *Vegetius: Epitome of Military Science* (2nd ed., Liverpool, 2013).
Vegetius, *Mulomedicinae*	*P. Vegeti Renati Digestorum Artis Mulomedicinae Libri*, ed. E. Lommatzsch (Leipzig, 1903).
VG	Constantius, *Vita Germani*, ed. R. Borius, *Constance de Lyon, Vie de Saint Germain d'Auxerre*, Sources Chrétiennes 112 (Paris, 1965); for a translation, see F.H. Hoare (trans.), *The Western Fathers* (London, 1954), 283–320.
VGildae1	The Monk of Ruys, *Vita Gildae*, in H. Williams (ed.), *Gildas: The Ruin of Britain, Fragments from Lost Letters, The Penitential, together with the Lorica of Gildas* (London, 1899), 322–89.

VGildae2   Caradoc of Llancarvan, *Vita Gildae*, in H. Williams (ed.), *Gildas: The Ruin of Britain, Fragments from Lost Letters, The Penitential, together with the Lorica of Gildas* (London, 1899), 394–413.

Virgil, *Aeneid*,   *P. Vergili Maronis Opera*, ed. M. Geymonat (Turin, 1973); for a translation, see Virgil, *The Aeneid*, trans. W.F.J. Knight (Harmondsworth, 1956).

Virgil, *Georgics*   *P. Vergili Maronis Opera*, ed. M. Geymonat (Turin, 1973).

VSB   *Vitae Sanctorum Britanniae et Genealogiae*, ed. A.W. Wade-Evans (Cardiff, 1944).

WATB   T.M. Charles-Edwards, *Wales and the Britons 350–1064* (Oxford, 2013).

Wolfram   Wolfram von Eschenbach, *Parzival*, ed. K. Lachmann, revised E. Nellmann, 2 vols (Frankfurt, 1994).

WoM   William of Malmesbury, *Gesta Regum Anglorum, The History of the English Kings*, ed. R.A.B. Mynors, R.M. Thomson and M. Winterbottom, 2 vols (Oxford, 1998–99).

WRdB   *Wace's Roman de Brut: A History of the British*, ed. J. Weiss (Exeter, 1999).

ENDNOTES

Introduction: Arthur, History and the Storytellers

1. Anon., *English Fairy Tales*, p. 77.
2. Such as the King Arthur Hotel, on the Gower peninsula; King Arthur's School at Wincanton.
3. Tennyson wrote and rewrote *Idylls of the King* across the period 1859–85, dedicating them to Prince Albert.
4. See for example Davis, Tolkien and Gordon (eds and trans.), *Sir Gawain*; Tolkien, *The Fall of Arthur*; *The Hobbit* and *Lord of the Rings* have fairly obvious debts to the Arthurian tradition.
5. See for example, William Morris's 'Queen Guinevere', Henry Justice Ford's 'Guinevere' or Herbert Draper's 'Lancelot and Guinevere'.
6. See for example the 1994 TV movie, *Guinevere*, directed by Jud Taylor.
7. For Lancelot, think of Rossetti's 'Lancelot and Guinevere at King Arthur's Tomb', and such films as *Lancelot and Guinevere* (Cornel Wilde, 1963), *Lancelot du Lac* (Robert Bresson, 1974), and *First Knight* (Jerry Zucker, 1995); Galahad was painted by George Watts, Arthur Hughes and Edward Burne-Jones and his name 'borrowed' for the 1962 film *Kid Galahad*, starring Elvis Presley.
8. 'Jack the Giant Killer' is anonymous and first published in 1711. No references have been discovered to the story prior to 1700. Although clearly set in Cornwall, it does not obviously have roots in the Cornish language: the name Cormoran is best described as 'cod' Cornish, inspired perhaps by Geoffrey of Monmouth's Corineus, similarly of giant-killing fame and who settled in Cornwall; that Arthur was renowned as a giant-slayer (see Grooms, *The Giants of Wales*, xlix–l) may even imply that 'Jack' replaced here the older and more famous name.
9. 'The True History of Tom Thumb', in Anon., *English Fairy Tales*, 203–14; Tom Thumb appeared a century or so earlier than Jack, having been first published in the early seventeenth century, and was already being referenced in the sixteenth; there is no direct evidence that it dates to the Middle Ages but see Green, 'Tom Thumb and Jack the Giant-Killer'.
10. See Schmolke-Hasselmann, *The Evolution*, 44–5.
11. Principally the Macdonalds; Gillies, 'Arthur in Gaelic Tradition'.
12. See for example Eco, *Travels in Hyperreality*, particularly 68–72, the quotation is from p. 71.

13. See, for example, Morton, *In Search of England*, 131: 'if man were looking for the roots of England, this is the place to which he would come'.
14. Bord and Bord, *Mysterious Britain*, 233–4; Bord and Bord, *The Secret Country*, 168; Matthews, *The Arthurian Tradition*; Doel, Doel and Lloyd, *Worlds of Arthur*, passim.
15. Steinbeck, *The Acts of King Arthur*, xi–xiii.
16. Including Jack Whyte, Marion Zimmer Bradley, Diana L. Taxson, Anthony Burgess and Stephen Lawhead; perhaps the most humorous Arthurian novel of recent years is Phillips, *The Table of Less Valued Knights*.
17. Atkinson, 'Unseen Translation', 131.
18. Holt, *The Portable Door*, 72.
19. Walt Disney, *Sword in the Stone*, released Christmas Day 1963.
20. Generally read as the first part of White, *The Once and Future King* (London, 1958), but originally published as a free-standing book in 1938.
21. Malone, 'Artorius'.
22. Nickel, 'The Dawn of Chivalry'.
23. As Bachrach, 'The Alans in Gaul'.
24. Nickel, 'Wer waren König Artus' Ritter?'; Littleton and Thomas, 'The Sarmatian Connection'; FSTC.
25. KAIA; EAT.
26. KAIA.
27. See, for example, Kemble, *The Saxons in England*, I, 27, treating Arthur as a demi-god or mythological hero.
28. Rhŷs, *Studies in the Arthurian Legend*.
29. Malone, 'The Historicity of Arthur'; Van Hamel, 'Aspects of Celtic Mythology'; Chambers, *Arthur of Britain*, 205–32.
30. See particularly, Padel, 'The Nature of Arthur'.

Chapter 1   Lucius Artorius Castus: A 'Dalmatian' King Arthur?

1. Malone, 'Artorius', 374.
2. CIL, III, 1, 303, no. 1919.
3. Zimmer, 'Review'.
4. See, for example, Bruce, *The Evolution of Arthurian Romance*, I, 1–6; Jackson, 'The Arthur of History', 1.
5. Malone, 'Artorius'.
6. As Collingwood and Myres, *Roman Britain*, 320–4; Alcock, *Arthur's Britain*; Morris, *Age of Arthur*; for parallels drawn between Arthur's knights and the RAF, see Laughlin, 'King Arthur in World War Two Poetry', who notes wartime newspapers' parallelling Arthurian knights and RAF pilots and Churchill's use of Tennyson's *Idylls of the King* in his speeches.
7. Particularly at the University of Zadar, where Dr Julijan Medini was lecturing: Kurilić, 'Some Problems', 132.
8. The Kulturno-Šortsko Društvo 'Artorius'.
9. Initially in Littleton and Thomas, 'The Sarmatian Connection'.
10. Dio, LXXII, 6.
11. FSTC, xxviii–xxxi, 62–3.
12. Malcor, 'Lucius Artorius Castus 1'.
13. Malcor, 'Lucius Artorius Castus 2'.
14. See Elliot, 'Lucius Artorius Castus as Global Icon', 147–8, developing arguments in Wadge, 'King Arthur: A British or Sarmatian Tradition?', 204.
15. I am very grateful to Professor Kurilić, who has subjected the longer inscription to detailed epigraphic examination, for her thoughts on the date.
16. Not white marble, as appears in early reports. My thanks to Professor Kurilić for her guidance on this point.

17. Carrara, *De' Scavi di Salona*, 23, no. IX.
18. The slab was slightly in excess of 2.3 metres, with a height of 1.08 metres and thickness of around 0.39 metres; Cambi, 'Lucije Artorije Kast', 30, provides lengths of the fragments as 1.39 metres for the larger, left-hand piece, and 0.91 metres for the smaller, right-hand one.
19. Controlled primarily by the first line, to complete the name ARTORI[US•CA]STUS.
20. CIL, III, 3, 2133, no. 12813.
21. Cambi, 'Lucije Artorije Kast'.
22. CIL, III, 3, 2322, no. 14224.
23. 'L' for Lucius, '7' for centurion (*centurio*), LEGG for legions (*legiones*), and PP for chief centurion (*primus pilus*); Cooley, *The Cambridge Manual*, 359; additionally, there are several ligatures (where two or three letters have been combined into a single letter-space): LE in line 1; LI and TE in 2; ITE, AD and TE in 3; TE in 4; AE in 5; TR in 6; AD and NTE in 7; RO in 8; ET in 9.
24. With ligatures underlined.
25. The ligatures are unmarked; I have retained the original line discipline, with hyphens indicating where words run on; expanded abbreviations are set within standard parentheses; reconstructed text is set within square brackets; where reconstruction is unviable the missing letters are represented by dots.
26. This issue was first explored at any length by Kurilić, 'Some Problems'.
27. As CIL, III, 1, 303, no. 1919.
28. In line 6/7, the mason cut BRITANICIMIARUM when BRITANNICARUM (or similar) was intended.
29. In line 5, [PR]AEFF for [PR]AEF.
30. A common feature of Roman inscriptions of the late Principate; see for example, Pflaum (ed.), *Inscriptiones Latines de L'Algérie*, II, 3, nos 7635, 7645, 7653, 7756.
31. Kurilić, 'Some Problems'.
32. Glavičić, 'Artorii'.
33. Birley, *The Roman Government*, 355.
34. The command structure of a legion following the reforms of first Augustus then Claudius was headed by a legate (*legatus legionis*), beneath whom was the senior tribune (*tribunus laticlavos*) then the camp prefect (*praefectus castrorum*), then five junior tribunes and the senior centurion (*primus pilus*).
35. As EDH HD001067 (15 May 2015), found in Moesia Superior, from the first half of the second century.
36. As EDH HD001949 (15 May 2015), found in Cappadocia, dated 131–230.
37. Smith, 'Dux, Praepositus', 273–7; it was embedded as a standard title only in the late third century; it occurs, for example, in the *Notitia Dignitatum*, e.g. the *dux Britanniarum* in command of the forces of Britannia Inferior; Rivet and Smith, *Place-Names of Roman Britain*, 219.
38. Le Bohec, *The Imperial Roman Army*, 39.
39. See note 27 above.
40. As Birley, *The Roman Government*, 355; Cambi offers *duu? /m*.
41. The feminine genitive plural, from *duo*, 'two', to agree with *legionum*.
42. As EDCS 27500014 (19 June 2015).
43. The convention was that the doubling of the consonant was sufficient, it was less often trebled (though this does occur); again, I am grateful to Professor Kurilić for her advice.
44. As EDH HD053700 (25 June 2015).
45. CIL, III, 1, 303, no. 1919.
46. EDH HD000054; HD000343; HD000346 (25 June 2015).
47. I.e., the genitive plural; my thanks to Professor David Langslow for his advice here.
48. Dobson and Mann, 'The Roman Army'.
49. Smith, 'Dux, Praepositus', 273–6; Kennedy, 'C. Velius Rufus'.
50. Following CIL, III, 1, 303, no. 1919; EDH HD053700 (25 June 2015).

51. A search of the EDH on 18 June 2015 provided only this single example.

52. Caesar, V, 53; VII, 75; inclusion of the *Lemovices* may have been Caesar's mistake, given their apparent distance from both the coast and the other tribes named.

53. As Pliny, *Natural History*, II, 17, 105; it probably derives from Celtic *Aremorio*, meaning 'land next to the sea', referring to the peninsulas of Brittany and Lower Normandy.

54. As Birley, *The Roman Government*, 355; EDCS-27500014 (19 June 2015); EDH HD004074 (15 May 2015); Loriot, 'Un Mythe Historiographique'; Cambi, 'Lucije Artorije Kast', 31; Kurilić, 'Some Problems', 133; I am grateful to Professor Nenad Cambi for his guidance here.

55. Kurilić has suggested to me NI, much as LI in *Gallicae*.

56. Typing 'armeni' into EDCS on 17 July 2015 produced 1,503 inscriptions, split between honorific titles adopted by emperors and references to Armenia as a place.

57. Carrara, *De' Scavi de Salona*, 23.

58. Le Bohec, *The Imperial Roman Army*, 41, lists salaries as 60,000, 100,000, 200,000 and 300,000 sesterces.

59. Dobson, 'The Significance of the Centurion', 402.

60. CIL, III, 1, 1919: Mommsen did not offer a reconstruction, but suggested that Lusitania, Lugdunensis and Lycia might all be considered; the first two are excessively long and the last would require substitution of 'I' for 'y'.

61. I am grateful to Professor Kurilić for her advice.

62. As Pliny, *Natural History*, III, 21–2; Vegetius, *Epitoma*, IV, 33.

63. Once again, I am grateful to Professor Kurilić for her advice.

64. CIL, III, 3, 2322, no. 14224 = 12791.

65. Cambi, 'Lucije Artorije Kast', 39.

66. As, for example, much of the fine work in Hagia Sophia, Istanbul, dating from the early fourth century.

67. CIL, III, 3, 2322, no. 14224 = 12791; Medini, 'Provincia Liburnia', 366; EDCS 32400312 (22 July 2015).

68. Following Cambi, 'Lucije Artorije Kast', 39; EDH HD053922 (19 June 2015) gives a slightly variant reconstruction but the differences are insubstantial as regards the reading, which is unproblematic.

69. The word-ending of the first post is abbreviated so indeterminate.

70. Cooley, *Latin Epigraphy*, 410, 412, 422; this is, though, negative evidence, which makes only for a weak argument.

71. As Petrović, *Inscriptions de la Mésie Supérieure*, III, 2, 46, 59, 65, 66, 77, 81; IV, 44, 81, 83, 94, 96; VI, 45, 158.

72. As ibid., I, 6; Koščević, *Siscia*, plate 8, no. 33, plate 9, no. 38; there are further examples at St Martin's.

73. Bianchi, *Le Stele Funerarie Della Dacia*, passim.

74. And noticeably absent in Italy, Spain and North Africa.

75. Malone, 'Artorius', 371–2.

76. Pflaum, *Les Carrières Procuratoriennes Équestres'*, 535–7, no. 196.

77. SHA, *Commodus*, III, 3–4.

78. Herodian, I, 8, 8.

79. SHA, *Commodus*, VI, 2; Dobson, *Die Primipilares*, 267; Birley, *The Fasti of Roman Britain*, 260.

80. SHA, *Commodus*: VI, 1; XIII, 2.

81. Pflaum, *Les Carriéres Procuratoriennes Equestres*, I, 535–7, followed by Wilkes, *Dalmatia*, 329.

82. Ibid., 328.

83. As Kirigin and Malin, *Archaeological Guide*, 143.

84. Herodian, I, 9, 7–9; writing in Greek, Herodian used the term Illyricum of their command; Illyricum (or Illyria) was the earlier name dating back to the Hellinistic period, which was used somewhat flexibly in this period of Dalmatia with or without the Pannonian provinces, and in the late Empire of the entire Danube frontier region.

85. Medini, 'Provincia Liburnia', 365–81.
86. Birley, *Roman Britain and the Roman Army*, 104–24; Dobson, 'The Significance of the Centurion', 404–5; 'Legionary Centurion or Equestrian Officer?', 193–5.
87. This is the view of Miletić, 'Lucius Artorius Castus I Liburnia'; see Le Bohec, *The Imperial Roman Army*, 43–4, for the context.
88. Hoffman, 'The Quarters of Legionary Centurions', 108.
89. See Roth, 'The Size and Organization of the Roman Imperial Legion'.
90. As Devijver, *The Equestrian Officers*, 139; Dobson, 'The Significance of the Centurion', 404–5; in 'Lucius Artorius Castus 1' Malcor assumed that eighteen was the normal age of recruitment as a centurion, but this was the lower age to join as a legionary (most that we can ascertain were aged between eighteen and twenty-two), and would have been highly exceptional for a centurion.
91. Wilkes, *Dalmatia*, 328; Glavičić, 'Artorii u Rimskoj Provinciji Dalmaciji'.
92. For wider discussion, see Devijver, *The Equestrian Officers*.
93. Cambi, 'Lucije Artorije Kast', 40.
94. After the division of Syria under Septimius Severus, this lay in Syria Phoenice.
95. Pollard and Berry, *The Complete Roman Legions*, 130; the Syrian legions had a reputation for moral degeneracy which may have been ill-founded: Wheeler, 'The Laxity of the Syrian Legions'.
96. Pollard and Berry, *The Complete Roman Legions*, 194.
97. Condurachi and Daicoviciu, *Romania*, 132; Cătăniciu, *Evolution of the System of Defence Works*, 46–7; Wilkes, 'The Danube Provinces', 581–2.
98. Pollard and Berry, *The Complete Roman Legions*, 200–1.
99. Birley, *Roman Britain and the Roman Army*, 153; Dobson, 'The Significance of the Centurion', 404–6.
100. Dobson, 'Legionary Centurion or Equestrian Officer?', 198.
101. Saller, 'Promotion and Patronage in Equestrian Careers', 52.
102. Le Bohec, *The Imperial Roman Army*, 29.
103. In general, see Pitassi, *The Roman Navy*, 45–6; Borriello and D'Ambrosio, *Baiae-Misenum*; Acrudoae, 'Militaries'.
104. Le Bohec, *The Imperial Roman Army*, 41.
105. CIL, VIII, 1446, no. 14854 = 1322.
106. Le Bohec, *The Imperial Roman Army*, 29.
107. Roth, *The Logistics of the Roman Army*, 268, 271.
108. My thanks to Dr Paul Holder for discussion of this point.
109. Malcor's objection in 'Lucius Artorius Castus 1' to identification of this post as *praefectus castrorum* on the grounds that that was a civilian post is misconceived; there are no grounds for reading this as *praefectus alae*, so as the commanding officer of an auxiliary unit; the text clearly identifies it as a legionary post; such was the standard progression for a *primus pilus*.
110. On the basis of the rather imprecise comments in the surviving abridgement of Dio, LXXIII, 2.
111. Pollard and Berry, *The Complete Roman Legions*, 93–4.
112. Roth, *The Logistics of the Roman Army*, 269.
113. Dobson, 'The Significance of the Centurion', 414.
114. An estimation based on an admittedly small sample suggests that service as a centurion averaged three and a half years per posting, implying that Castus had about fifteen years of service when he reached York: Le Bohec, *The Imperial Roman Army*, 43; the youngest known *primus pilus* died aged forty-nine: Dobson, 'The Significance of the Centurion', 411.
115. Pflaum, *Les Carriéres Procuratoriennes Equestres*, I, 535–7; see also Wilkes, *Dalmatia*, 329.
116. Command of military forces in Egypt had always been equestrian, but Severus also gave equestrian officers command of the three new legions he stationed in Mesopotamia: Dio, LXXVIII, 13.

117. As the *dux ripae* commanding on the Euphrates frontier before 240.
118. Southern, *The Roman Army*, 254–5.
119. As Smith, 'Dux, Praepositus', 273.
120. Dobson, *Die Primipilares*, 216–17, no. 94.
121. Though he was not termed *dux*; Jarrett, 'Legio XX Valeria Victrix', 83.
122. See, for example, Millar, *The Roman Near East*; Ball, *Rome in the East*; Chahin, *The Kingdom of Armenia*; Chaumont and Traina, 'Les Arméniens'.
123. Birley, 'Hadrian to the Antonines', 171.
124. Miletić, 'Lucius Artorius Castus I Liburnia', 125–6.
125. Birley, 'Hadrian to the Antonines', 171–2.
126. The Liburni were remembered as a nautical (and piratical) people, after whose ships the light biremes of the Roman fleets were called 'Liburnians': Appian, X, 1, 3.
127. Medini suggested eleven to twelve years but just a handful is at least as likely.
128. Miletić, 'Lucius Artorius Castus I Liburnia', 130.
129. Birley, *The Fasti of Roman Britain*, 118–21.
130. Dobson, 'The Significance of the Centurion', 426.
131. As first proposed by Zimmer, 'Review of Paris, *Histoire Littéraire de la France*', then developed by Malone, 'Artorius', 368–9; my thanks to professors Richard Coates and Peter Schrijver for their correspondence with me in 2002 regarding the Artorius–Arthur phonetic shift.
132. Since the same end results could in theory derive from a very different starting point.
133. A handful of recently noted references to the name makes little difference to the situation overall: e.g. Cornell (ed.), *The Fragments of the Roman Historians*, II, 525, 885; III, 262, 539–41.
134. Syria has three, Asia two, Moesia Inferior, Macedonia, Dacia, Numidia, Lusitania and Hispania one each.
135. One recent estimate has it at about 4 per cent.
136. Malone, 'Artorius', 374.
137. For an overview, see Salway, 'What's in a Name?'.
138. As is implicit in Kurilić, 'Some Problems', though the point is never made explicitly.
139. As Ambrosius Aurelianus, Aurelius Caninus, in DEB, 25, 3; 30, 1.
140. As Patricius, Cualfarnius (?Calpornius) and Potitus, in Patrick, *Confessio*, 1.
141. HB, 56.
142. Malone, 'Artorius', 372.
143. Salway, *Roman Britain*, 199–200; Mattingly, *An Imperial Possession*, 121–2.
144. Dio, LXXIII, 8, 2.
145. Salway, *Roman Britain*, 208.
146. Birley, *The Fasti of Roman Britain*, 135.
147. As a mark of this success Commodus adopted the name Britannicus.
148. Malone, 'Artorius', 373.
149. HRB, IX, 163.
150. Malcor, 'Lucius Artorius Castus 1', 1/11; the inscriptions were not found in Liburnia, as she claimed, but south of Salona, the capital of Dalmatia.
151. Herodian, I, 10.
152. Malcor, 'Lucius Artorius Castus 1', 4/11.
153. Nemeth, 'Roman Dacia and Beyond'.
154. E.g. Kennedy, 'C. Velius Rufus'.
155. Malcor, 'Lucius Artorius Castus 1', 5/11.
156. Ibid., 6/11.
157. Malcor, 'Lucius Artorius Castus 2', 1/11; see also FSTC, 327–31.
158. Though this is not a term which I would use of texts six to ten centuries later than the supposed events.
159. Malcor, 'Lucius Artorius Castus 2', 2/11.
160. Ibid., 11/11.

161. HRB, IX, 158; Malcor, 'Lucius Artorius Castus 2', 2, refers to embassies from Arthur to Rome but the instance referenced here was from the emperor to Arthur at Caerleon.
162. Hiberius does not occur on any Roman inscription and has no obvious meaning in classical Latin; Geoffrey's usage is perhaps rooted in Jerome's mention of Hiberia, meaning Spain.
163. HB, 56; Malcor, 'Lucius Artorius Castus 2'; FSTC, 327–31; for a discussion of this passage, see pp. 185–94.
164. As Gidlow, *The Reign of Arthur*, 14–51; Field, 'Arthur's Battles'; Breeze, 'Arthur's Battles'.

Chapter 2 The 'Sarmatian Connection'

1. Littleton and Thomas, 'The Sarmatian Connection', 512.
2. As ibid.; Littleton, 'The Holy Grail'; Malcor, 'Lucius Artorius Castus 1'; FSTC.
3. Higham, *King Arthur: Myth-Making and History*, 35.
4. Green, *Concepts of Arthur*, 186–7.
5. Halsall, *Worlds of Arthur*, 149–51, at 151.
6. Beginning with Wadge, 'King Arthur: A British or Sarmatian Tradition?'
7. KAIA, 20.
8. Ball, *The Gates of Asia*, 80.
9. Most prominent in Roman texts were the Iazyges and Roxolani; others included the Antes, Aorsi, Basileans, Iaxamatae, Melanastae, Saii, Serboi, Siraces, Spali and Tyrigetae; the Limigantes and Arcaragantes may be the names of subgroups within the Roxolani; in the late fourth century Claudian noted the Massagetes, Alans and Geleni within a mixed hord of Sarmatians and Dacians (Claudian, 'The First Book against Rufinus', 310); Ammianus Marcellinus considered the Alans were in origin Massagetes.
10. Lubotsky, 'Scythian Elements in Old Iranian'; Mayor, Saunders and Colarusso, 'Making Sense of Nonsense Inscriptions'.
11. For modern survivors, see Bailey, 'Ossetia (Nartä)'.
12. Including Peter the Great, Catherine the Great and Nicholas I; the Hermitage has over 20,000 objects of Sarmatian origin; Bespali et al. (eds), *Treasures of the Warrior Tombs*; Aruz et al. (eds), *The Golden Deer of Eurasia*; Haskins, 'Sarmatian Gold Collected by Peter the Great'; an exhibition at the British Museum in 2017–18, 'Scythians: Warriors of Ancient Siberia', offered a selection of the earlier material.
13. Yablonsky, 'New Excavations of the Early Nomadic Burial Ground at Filippouka'; see more generally Sulimirski, *The Sarmatians*, passim.
14. Herodotus, IV, 21, 57. Most scholars assume that the Sauromotae and Sarmatians were identical, with the name represented differently in Greek and Latin, or shifting over time. That Strabo, a Greek writer of the Roman period, used both Sauromatai and Sarmatai could support either theory but Pliny saw Sauromatae as specifically Greek. Today Sauromatae is often used in an archaeological context of the early Sarmatian period, but that is a convention and has no bearing on the original meanings.
15. Ibid., IV, 110–17; Diodorus of Sicily, an historian of the first century BC, offered a rather different origin tale, depicting the Sarmatians as a colony of Scythians drawn from the land of the Medes and planted near Tanais (a Greek city near Rostov-on-Don: Map 2).
16. One recent estimate suggests that 20 per cent of all weapon burials were of young women.
17. Blok, *The Early Amazons*; Ball, *The Gates of Asia*, 74–7.
18. Herodotus, IV, 21, 57.
19. For discussion, see Braund (ed.), *Scythians and Greeks*.
20. As Pliny, *Natural History*, IV, 12, 80, who noted that in his day 'Scythians' was used only of the northernmost rim of these peoples.
21. Ovid, *Tristia*, V, 7, 9–20; quote from translation by Batty, 'On Getic and Sarmatian Shores', 89.
22. Ovid, *Tristia*, I, 2, 82; III, 10, 5; III, 10, 53–86.

23. Strabo, VII, 3, 2; II, 5, 30–1; VII, 3, 17.
24. Though other writers make it clear that they also ate meat, as Pausanias, I, 21, 5.
25. Strabo, VII, 3, 3; VII, 3, 17; II, 6, 2.
26. For a wider discussion, see Hartog, 'Imaginary Scythians: Space and Nomadism'.
27. Herodotus, IV, 5.
28. In a much earlier context, see, for example, Frachetti, *Pastoral Landscapes*; this lifestyle was described as 'migratory nomads' by Ball, *The Gates of Asia*, 11–12; see also Cribb, *Nomads in Archaeology*, 133–61.
29. Kraeva, 'Technological Analysis of Ceramics'.
30. For Scythian royal burial, see Herodotus, IV, 71.
31. See, for example, Kaposhina, 'A Sarmatian Royal Burial'; Bashilov and Moshkova, 'Russo-Italian Computer Assisted Investigations'; Yablonsky, 'New Excavations of the Early Nomadic Burial Ground at Filippouka'; Toshio, 'The Beginning and the Maturity of Nomadic Powers'.
32. For discussion see Sulimirski, *The Sarmatians*, 101.
33. Ibid., 32–3; Kaposhina, 'A Sarmatian Royal Burial at Novocherkassk'.
34. Pausanias, I, 21, 5.
35. Treister, 'Sarmatian Treasures of South Russia'.
36. Raev, *Roman Imports in the Lower Don Basin*, 65ff.
37. Sulimirski, *The Sarmatians*, 151–5; Nickel, 'Tamgas and Runes'.
38. Sulimirski, *The Sarmatians*, 155; Agrigoroaei, 'Vikingi sau Rusi'; tamgas were used by the Avars and then on medieval Polish coats of arms.
39. For the traditional view, see Melyukova, 'The Scythians and Sarmatians'.
40. Strabo, VII, 3, 17.
41. Mordvintseva, 'The Sarmatians'.
42. Going back to Clark, 'The Invasion Hypothesis'.
43. *Contra* Sulimirski and many of his contemporaries.
44. See, for example, Anthony, *The Horse, The Wheel and Language*.
45. E.g. Isaac, 'The Nature and Origin'.
46. Sinor, 'The Hun Period'.
47. See Demkin et al., 'Dynamics of the Properties of Steppe Paleosols'.
48. Sulimirski, *The Sarmatians*, 167.
49. As the Roxolani during Marcus Aurelius' campaigns against the Iazyges: see Zahariade and Gudea, *The Fortification of Lower Moesia*, 60; Braund, *Georgia in Antiquity*, 64.
50. Pliny, *Natural History*, IV, 12, 80; the 'Hungarian Forest' was the mountainous area stretching round Bohemia through Moravia and into Hungary; Carnuntum, capital of Pannonia Superior, lay between Vienna and Bratislava.
51. Vaday, 'Barbarian Peoples'; for numerous ethnic groups in neighbouring Roman territory, see Siscia, *Pannonia Superior*, map 4.
52. Visy, 'Some Notes on the Defence System of Pannonia', 90; Vaday, 'Barbarian Peoples'.
53. Vaday, 'Limes Sarmatiae', 204–5.
54. Josephus, VII, 89.
55. SHA, *Hadrian*, III, 9; V, 2; VI, 6.
56. Cătăniciu, *Evolution of the System*, 11.
57. Eastwards from both Aquincum and Lugio.
58. Although these are predominantly of the third and fourth centuries: Vaday, 'Roman Presence in the Barbaricum'.
59. See, for example, Gabler and Vaday, *Terra Sigillata im Barbaricum*, see particularly illus. 21.
60. Visy, 'The River Line Frontiers'.
61. Vaday, 'Roman Presence in Barbaricum'; for a broader discussion, see Schörner, 'Rom jenseits der Grenze'.
62. CIL, III, 14349; 10505.
63. Birley, 'Hadrian to the Antonines', 161.

64. Verboven, 'Demise and Fall of the Augustan Monetary System'.
65. Birley, 'Hadrian to the Antonines', 165–8.
66. Dio, LXXII, 33, 19; 22, 16.
67. Ibid., 22, 16.
68. Anthony, *The Horse, The Wheel and Language*, 460–2.
69. For a recent survey, see Drews, *Early Riders*.
70. Kulimirski, *The Sarmatians*, 81.
71. Ammianus Marcellinus considered the 'Halani' formerly Massagetae: AM, XXXI, 2, 12.
72. Pausanias, I, 21, 5.
73. Tacitus, *The Histories*, I, 79.
74. AM, XVII, 12, 1.
75. But see discussion of horse size and carrying capacity in Dixon and Southern, *The Roman Cavalry*, 172.
76. Sulimirski, *The Sarmatians*, 32.
77. Tacitus, *The Histories*, I, 79; this episode belongs to *c.* 68 CE.
78. Strabo, VII, 4, 8.
79. Breeze and Dobson, 'Roman Military Deployment in Northern England', 13.
80. Such cavalrymen often even came with their own servants: Goldsworthy, *The Roman Army at War*, 72–3.
81. Southern, 'The Numeri of the Roman Imperial Army'.
82. As was recognised by Richmond, 'Sarmatae'.
83. As the Frisians at Birdoswald and Chesterholm: Gillam, 'Romano-Saxon Pottery'.
84. This idea was first mooted by Richmond, 'Sarmatae', 18; Sulimirski did not reference Richmond, and omitted him from his bibliography, suggesting that he was unfamiliar with this study.
85. Sulimirski, *The Sarmatians*, 175–6.
86. My thanks to Henry Edmunds for sending me an extract from the *Cleveland Bay Stud Book*, published 2015.
87. Dixon and Southern, *The Roman Cavalry*, 161–72.
88. ND, 210 (Oc. XL, 21).
89. Rivet and Smith, *The Place-Names of Roman Britain*, 420, are critical of the earlier identification as Vinovia (Binchester), and suggest Piercebridge or Greta Bridge.
90. Ibid., 220, 442; Praesidium is less an independent place-name than a generic reference to a command building, most probably that at York.
91. Ibid., 329; this command was *praefectus equitum Crispianorum*. If *crispianorum* refers to wavy hair, then this may again point to a particular people as the original recruiting ground.
92. Coole and Mason, *Roman Piercebridge*.
93. Rivet and Smith, *Place-Names of Roman Britain*, 442.
94. From Albis, the River Elbe.
95. Both serving in the east.
96. ND, 65 (Oc. XXXI, 52): *Ala prima Iovia catafractariorum, Pampane*.
97. Ibid., 59 (Or. XXVIII, 26): *Ala septima Sarmatarum, Scenas Mandrorum*.
98. Dixon and Southern, *The Roman Cavalry*, 76.
99. Vegetius, *Epitoma*, III, 23.
100. For German cavalry within the Roman Empire, see Speidel, *Ancient Germanic Warriors*, 135–41.
101. Rostovtzeff et al., *The Excavations at Dura Europos*; Dixon and Southern, *The Roman Cavalry*, 61.
102. The beads are illustrated in Kulimirski, *The Sarmatians*, 176, Map 66; Guido, *Prehistoric and Roman Glass Beads*, 64–5, was doubtful in one instance; Lindsay Allason-Jones is not entirely convinced that the beads are Sarmatian (pers. comm.).
103. Guido, *Prehistoric and Roman Glass Beads*, 97, 234.
104. Allason-Jones, 'Roman Military and Domestic Artefacts', 196 and Map 13, no. 7; my thanks to Lindsey Allason-Jones for alerting me to this find.

308   NOTES to pp. 57–61

105. RIB I, 183, no. 550, now in the Grosvenor Museum, catalogue number 137.
106. Richmond, 'Sarmatae', 17, n. 24, believed he could see scale armour on leg and arm;
     Kulimirski, *The Sarmatians*, 257, wrote in his caption to this image that this was 'a
     mounted Sarmatian chief, clad in scale armour, of possible Roxolanian ancestry'.
107. Dixon and Southern, *The Roman Cavalry*, 61.
108. Carroll, 'The Evidence of Dress and Funerary Portraits'.
109. For discussion of the Roman place-name, see Rivet and Smith, *The Place-Names of
     Roman Britain*, 170–1.
110. Edwards, *The Romans at Ribchester*, 80; for parallels see Sulimirski, *The Sarmatians*,
     151–4, 164, 166, 167, 169–71, 196.
111. Buxton and Howard-Davis, *Bremetenacum*, 247–51.
112. As FSTC, 19: 'A fair number of Sarmatian-type artifacts – pots, tools, and so forth –
     have been found at Ribchester'; Ball, *The Gates of Asia*, 80, identifies the cavalryman on
     a funerary stele found at Ribchester as Sarmatian but this belongs to the Spanish regi-
     ment there in the earlier second century. I can myself recall digging within the fort at
     Ribchester in 1970 and finding nothing which was not characteristically Romano-
     British; see Edwards and Webster, *Ribchester Excavations, Part 3*; my thanks to Patrick
     Tostevin, curator of Ribchester Roman Museum, for confirmation of the general
     absence of 'Sarmatian' material.
113. Shotter, 'The Coinage of Roman Ribchester'; *Roman Coins from North-West England*;
     Edwards, *The Romans at Ribchester*, 46–50.
114. Buxton and Howard-Davis, *Bremetenacum*, 408.
115. Richmond, 'Sarmatae'; his work benefited from access to the work of Collingwood and
     Wright prior to the eventual publication of RIB I, and prior also to Collingwood's death
     in 1943; the seminal study of the 'Apollo' inscription was by Collingwood, in 1924.
116. Ibid., 19, Map 2; RIB I, 196, no. 587; this was gifted to St John's College, Cambridge, and
     since loaned to the Roman Museum, Ribchester.
117. Ibid., 194–5, no. 583; the shaft was initially built into the wall of Salesbury Hall then cut
     out in the nineteenth century and gifted to St John's College, Cambridge; it is likewise
     now in the Roman Museum at Ribchester.
118. Richmond, 'Sarmatae', 26.
119. RIB I, 196, no. 587, from a drawing by Collingwood made in 1927: my line numbering
     assumes two missing lines at the start, though this need not be correct; ligatures and
     abbreviations are extended and missing text reconstructed; diminutive letters were also
     used, particularly I (lines 3, 4, 5) but also O (line 5); the following ligatures are identifi-
     able: line 4, RE, EN, LE, PR; line 5, FL, ID, PR, EP, RE; line 6, EM.
120. Richmond, 'Sarmatae', 27–8, but see the doubts expressed by Edwards, *The Romans at
     Ribchester*, 75; for illustrations, see Richmond, 'Sarmatae', 18, Map 2; RIB I, 194; repro-
     duced in FSTC, 22; the initial drawing was by Collingwood.
121. There are various standard abbreviations: a symbol in line 8 for *centurio*, D for *dominus*,
     N for *noster* and *numerus*, EQQ for *equites* and R for *regio*; ligatures are as follows: line
     2, LLI, MAP; line 3, PRO, TE; line 4, ET; line 5, ME, EN.
122. Rivet and Smith, *Place-Names of Roman Britain*, 208, as *Bresnetenaci Veteranorum*; see
     discussion on 277.
123. For a brief discussion and references, see ibid., 185–215.
124. Referring not to the drink but to the medieval, 'champion' landscapes of much of the
     English Midlands.
125. Richmond, 'Sarmatae', passim, quote from 22–3.
126. RIB I, 199, no. 594, assigned to Ribchester by Camden; see Edwards, *The Romans at
     Ribchester*, 90, for a degree of confirmation.
127. RIB I, 200, no. 595: D(IS) M(ANIBUS) … C(…) AL(AE) SARMATA[RUM. …
     Collingwood and Wright hypothesised DECURIO as the missing word before ALAE.
     For the variation between *numerus* and *ala*, see Southern, 'The Numeri of the Roman
     Imperial Army', 89.

128. ND, 212 (Oc. XL, 54); Rivet and Smith, *Place-Names of Roman Britain*, 221.
129. For discussion of the term, see Rance, 'Drungus', 123–4.
130. Edwards, *The Romans at Ribchester*, 87.
131. My own examination of the inscription, on 24 September 2015, did not enable me to confirm any letters in this lower section, which has been so weathered as to be indecipherable to the naked eye.
132. With the missing letters along the left-hand edge reconstructed, the abbreviations and ligatures extended, words running across two lines hyphenated and space provided between words.
133. Richmond, 'Sarmatae', 15, assumed that it should be dated 238–44; Collingwood and Wright supposed that it belonged to Gordian's reign or later; Rivet and Smith, *Place-Names of Roman Britain*, have 'dated to AD 238–44, perhaps later.'
134. As accepted by Olivier, 'Postscript', 123.
135. A possibility raised by Breeze and Dobson, 'Roman Military Deployment in North England', 13; Buxton and Howard-Davis, *Bremetenacum*, 8.
136. Edwards, *The Romans at Ribchester*, 49.
137. Stephens, 'A Severan Vexillation'; Speidel, 'The Chattan War'.
138. Named herein *Camuloduno colonia*.
139. Exeter (Isca Dumnoniorum); Winchester (Venta Belgarum); Chichester (Noviomago Reginorum); Caerwent (Venta Silurum); Leintwardine (Brano Genium); Cirencester (Corinium Dobunnorum); Silchester (Calleva Atrebatum); Canterbury (Duroverno Cantiacorum); Wroxeter (Viriconium Cornoviorum); Leicester (Rate Coritanorum); Caistor St Edmund (Venta Icenorum) and Corbridge (Corie Lopocarium). While Corbridge was not a fort it was a very 'military' site, unlike the others; except Corbridge, these are corrected names.
140. Rivet and Smith, *Place-Names of Roman Britain*, 191–2, flag up the numerous errors made by the Cosmographer.
141. Rivet and Smith list over twenty in *Place-Names of Roman Britain*.
142. Buxton and Howard-Davis, *Bremetenacum*, 6–8.
143. Philpott, 'The Romano-British Period Resource Assessment', 79.
144. Though that could be a result of site-invisibility resulting from post-Roman land-use as much as a lack of settlement; see Olivier, 'Postscript', 124.
145. Edwards, *The Romans at Ribchester*, 51, noted the complete lack of evidence for Sarmatians breeding heavy horses in the Fylde, but still considered it 'an attractive scenario'.
146. For a flavour of the issues involved, see Middleton, Wells and Huckleby, *The Wetlands of North Lancashire*, 70–1, 118; Higham, *A Frontier Landscape*, 13–16; Watson, 'Viking-Age Amounderness'.
147. Southern, 'The Numeri of the Imperial Roman Army', 89.
148. Cătăniciu, *Evolution of the System of Defence Works in Roman Dacia*, 48.
149. Vaday, 'Barbarian Peoples', 225.
150. Nemeth, 'Roman Dacia and Beyond'.
151. Vaday, 'Barbarian Peoples', 226–7.
152. Kulcsár, 'Kazar Settlement', 233; Vaday, 'Limes Sarmatiae'; Visy, 'Mapping'.
153. See the papers in Curta (ed.), *Borders, Barriers and Ethnogenesis* and Hekster and Kaizer (eds), *Frontiers in the Roman World*, for parallels.
154. OCI, VI, 1, 32.
155. AM, XVII, 12, 1–4.
156. AM, XXVI, 4, 5; XXIX, 6, 15.
157. Prosper, *Chronicle*, 1230.
158. VG, VI, 28.
159. Jordanes, XXXVI, 191; XLV, 236.
160. Jones, *Later Roman Empire*, I, passim; Sulimirski, *The Sarmatians*, 183–203; more generally, see Geary, 'Ethnic Identity as a Situational Construct'; Pohl, 'Introduction:

The Empire and the Integration of Barbarians'; Wolfram, 'Neglected Evidence on the Accommodation of Barbarians'.

161. Procopius, II, 29, 15; VIII, 1, 4; 3, 4.
162. Procopius, III, 3, 1; V, 1, 3, actually referred to the Alans in the west as Goths, but noted a joint kingship of the Vandals and Alans in Africa: III, 24, 3.
163. My thanks to Duncan Sayer, for a conducted tour of his excavations in 2016.
164. As Collins, *Hadrian's Wall and the End of Empire*, passim.
165. Buxton and Howard-Davis, *Bremetenacum*, 421.
166. RIB I, 194–5, no. 583.
167. Ibid., 199–200, nos 594, 595.
168. For parallels see Hodgson and Bidwell, 'Auxiliary Barracks in a New Light', who suggest perhaps three hundred men.
169. As Ehala and Niglas, 'Empirical Evaluation of a Mathematical Model of Ethnolinguistic Vitality'.
170. Jones, *Later Roman Empire*, vol. 2, 619.
171. ND, 218–19 (Oc. XLII, 46–70).
172. See, for example, Sulimirski, *The Sarmatians*, 186–7; Kazanski, 'La Diffusion de la Mode Danubienne en Gaul'; Kazanski, 'Un Témoignage de la Présence des Alano-Sarmates en Gaule'.
173. See, for example, Bachrach, 'The Alans in Gaul'; FSTC, 233–4.
174. The case is argued in ibid., 93–9.
175. Lancelot first appears in a list in Chrétien's *Erec*, which was presumably intended as preparatory to his starring role in 'The Knight of the Cart'; this may be a Celtic name in origin, which reached him from a Breton story (Bruce, *The Evolution*, I, 193, suggested Breton Lancelin; Loomis, *Wales and the Arthurian Legend*, 21, 218, preferred the Irish god Lugh Loinnbhéimionach or Welsh Llauynnawc/Llenlleawc, contaminated by French Lancelin); however, that *launce* meant 'spear' in medieval French, and *lot* 'fate' (which was in origin Old Germanic/English), means that it could be his own construct, in French.
176. Halsall, *Worlds of Arthur*, 151; for this name in Roman Gaul, see EDH HD022019.
177. My thanks to Fiona Edmunds, who confirms finding no place-names in Lancashire which might derive from a 'Sarmatian' root.
178. For the upland–lowland divide, see Schrijver, 'What Britons Spoke around 400 AD'.
179. HB, 42: the word often translated as 'dragon' is *vermis*, used variously in the Middle Ages for 'the serpent', so Satan, as well as the humble earthworm; the Gaelic translation has 'maggot'.
180. HRB, VIII, 132.
181. Vegetius, *Epitoma*, II, 13.
182. Dixon and Southern, *The Roman Cavalry*, 61.
183. *Parzival*, verse 278.
184. As argued in FSTC, 195–205.
185. Jordanes, L; the translation is from Mierow (trans.), *Origins and Deeds*; for discussion, see Pohl, 'Telling the Difference', 27, footnote 45.
186. Ibid., 27–40; at Nedao, the contrast is with Goths fighting with long spears, Gepids raging with swords, Rugi breaking off spears in their own wounds, Suebi fighting on foot, Huns with bows and Heruli as light-armed warriors.
187. See in particular Nickel, 'The Dawn of Chivalry'; FSTC, 195.
188. See Dixon and Southern, *The Roman Cavalry*, 76–7.
189. Setting aside the mounted warriors in Welsh poetry and on the Aberlemno stone in Fife, Scotland as outside the tradition of mailed knights.
190. Claudian, 'On Stilicho's Consulship', 111.
191. FSTC, 18–48.
192. AM, XXXI, 2, 23.
193. Herodotus, IV, 62.
194. Ibid., IV, 70.

195. Ibid., IV, 5.
196. MIOF, motifs H31.1 and D1654.4.1.
197. Micha (ed.), *Robert de Boron: Merlin*, 83ff.; for the ascription, see Gowans, 'What did Robert de Boron really write?'.
198. Dutton, 'The Staff in the Stone', 3–5.
199. My thanks to Luca Larpi for discussion of this parallel; Dutton, ibid., 6, points out that Galgano's sword could easily be removed from the rock until the aperture was sealed with lead in 1924.
200. See Appendix I.
201. Malcor, 'Lucius Artorius Castus Part 2'.

Chapter 3 King Arthur and the Narts

1. Littleton, 'The Holy Grail', 326
2. Grisward, 'Le Motif de l'Épée Jetée au Lac', 89.
3. Dumézil, *Romans de Scythie*, 86ff.; Nickel, 'Wer waren König Arthur Ritter?'.
4. Tales are also told among emigrants from the region, particularly in Turkey; South Ossetia seceded from Georgia in 2008 with the aid of overwhelming Russian military support.
5. Bailey, 'Ossetic (Nartä)', suggested five; several sagas specify three.
6. As the Marakwa warrior who rides a rabbit: NSFTC, saga 74.
7. As, for example, the giant that aided Shoshlan in TOTN, saga 21, or when the Narts Urizmag and Khamis accept an invitation from the giant Afsharon and are entertained by him: ibid., sagas 61, 62; I am extremely grateful to John Colarusso for his generous provision of a draft of this work prior to publication.
8. Though the character Shainag, who features particularly in the story of Batraz, is invariably termed 'chief', he has no 'chiefly' duties in the tales.
9. Ibid., saga 1.
10. The appearance of male twins in an origin myth has numerous parallels.
11. This magical apple tree recurs elsewhere in the Nart sagas; apples originated in Kazakstan, so this topos is consistent with a story cycle originating on the Steppe.
12. Otherwise Dzerashsha.
13. Otherwise Satana, Setayana.
14. One who is not named was fostered by the Donbettir beneath the waves but killed accidentally by Urizhmag, unaware that the boy was his own.
15. Abaev, 'Introduction', liii, endnote 21.
16. As Dumézil has suggested repeatedly; see also Abaev, 'Introduction'.
17. NSFTC, 5; there is a lengthy debate concerning the divine origins of the Narts, for which see particularly Dumézil, *Légendes sur les Nartes*, passim, but also Colarusso, 'The Functions Revisited'.
18. 'Iron' is cognate with 'Iran'.
19. Nasidze, 'Genetic Evidence'.
20. Including Warkhag ('wolf-like'), Akhshar ('brave'), Akhshartag ('kingly') and Urizhmag ('wild boar'): TOTN, liii, lxv, 429–36.
21. Bailey, 'Ossetic (Nartä)', 236–7.
22. Lesser perhaps only because we have much less written about the Alans than the Scythians.
23. NSFTC, 5–6.
24. TOTN, saga 20; the name Shoshlan recalls the Alans.
25. Herodotus, IV, 5.
26. Washtirji is St George; Wasilla is Elijah; Donbettir is 'River-Peter'.
27. For women, see NSFTC, sagas 3, 45; TOTN, saga 51; Shirdon is the most prominent male shape-shifter, becoming both male and female figures at will and even on one occasion an old hat.

28. Swallows occur in several stories as messengers with whom the Akhshartaggata can converse; some heroes can understand their horses, which on occasion offer good advice.
29. Bailey, 'Ossetic (Nartä)', 260, 266.
30. NSFTC, sagas 34, 35, 36, 37; Charachidzé, 'Prometheus among the Circassians'.
31. Homer, *Odyssey*, IX, 331–3.
32. TOTN, saga 11, though here the Nart Urizhmag is without companions; another version appears in NSFTC, saga 52, with Sosruquo as the hero.
33. Hansen, *Ariadne's Thread*, 289–301.
34. NSFTC, saga 76; TOTN, sagas 19, 56.
35. Here Bataraz and Satayana
36. NSFTC, saga 48.
37. See Kadare's novel, *The File on H*, for an entertaining riff on the problems of researching such a corpus.
38. The task was initially undertaken largely by Russian scholars, followed from the 1930s onwards by the French scholar Georges Dumézil (Mayor, 'Introduction', xxi); more recently, John Colarusso has published ninety-two stories collected from the Circassians, Abazas, Abkhaz and Ubykhs of the western Caucasus (NSFTC) and has jointly edited a volume of Ossetian material (TOTN).
39. NSFTC, saga 73.
40. Ibid., saga 77.
41. As Shainag-Aldar, 'Chief Shainag': Abaev, 'Introduction'; depiction of Warzameg as 'ruler and law-giver of the Narts' in the Circassian corpus (ibid., saga 10) apparently reflects this later development.
42. Ibid., 6.
43. This is most noticeable within the Ossetian material.
44. See TOTN, saga 27, where Urizhmag travels on a cart due to his old age, while Shoshlan is on horseback.
45. In NSFTC, saga 13, Shatana carries off her drunken husband in a wagon.
46. As ibid., saga 67.
47. Jenkins and Westerlink, *Nicholas I*, letters 46, 51, 52, 133, 134, 135; today communities in this region variously practice Christianity, Islam and forms of the earlier, polytheistic religion.
48. TOTN, saga 7.
49. Ibid., saga 10.
50. Ibid., 432.
51. Including ibid., sagas 10, 11, 13, 14, 15, 22, 26, 32, 33, 34, 65, though there is a certain ambiguity inherent in this formula.
52. Ibid., saga 24.
53. Ibid., saga 13.
54. Ibid., saga 31.
55. Ibid., saga 72.
56. Ibid., saga 21.
57. Ibid., saga 17.
58. John, VI, 5–21.
59. TOTN, sagas 14, 31.
60. Exodus, II, 1–10.
61. TOTN, saga 11.
62. As ibid., saga 34, when Shatana took her cakes to the spot on the river bank where Shoshlan had been born.
63. Ibid., saga 65.
64. Or Movses Khorenatsi; Bailey, 'Ossetic (Nartä)', 237, noting the Alan princess, Tikin Sat'inik; the name is a combination of Iranian and Circassian elements, TOTN, lxvii, 434.
65. I have used the term 'sword in the water' rather than the more familiar 'sword in the lake' to accommodate instances where the sword is thrown into the sea rather than a lake, as in the Nart saga and a minority of late medieval Arthurian texts.

66. Ibid., sagas 50–72, 81, 84, 89.
67. Ibid., sagas 31, 37, 41.
68. Including NSFTC, sagas 34, 48, 74; he is Pataraz in Circassian; for discussion of the name, see NSFTC, 182.
69. TOTN, saga 50.
70. Ibid., saga 52.
71. Ibid., sagas 53, 54.
72. Ibid., saga 55.
73. Ibid., saga 56.
74. Ibid., sagas 57, 58.
75. Ibid., saga 59.
76. Ibid., sagas 60, 61.
77. Ibid., sagas 62, 63.
78. Ibid., saga 66.
79. Ibid., saga 68.
80. Ibid., saga 69.
81. Torturing a mother-figure to speak truth recurs in NSFTC, sagas 39, 72.
82. TOTN, sagas 71, 72.
83. From Greek, Roman, Indian, German, Scandinavian and Celtic mythology respectively.
84. Grisward, 'Le Motif de l'Épée Jetée au Lac', 300–2, referring back to the earlier work of Dumézil; see the parallels with Greek, Nordic and Indian mythology discussed in NSFTC.
85. NSFTC, saga 8; it has been suggested that Sawseruquo (elsewhere Sasruquo or Sosruquo) is the same hero-figure as Shoshlan; Abaev, 'Introduction', xxxvi; for the tempering of Shoshlan, see TOTN, saga 19.
86. NSFTC, saga 34.
87. Ibid., saga 33; TOTN, saga 69.
88. Shoshlan's death, fighting 'Oinon's Wheel', is likewise probably a metaphor for the conflict between traditional paganism and Christianity; Abaev, 'Introduction', xxviii.
89. NSFTC, saga 74; in this story the magical nature of the giant's property is much reduced and the old Nart who was rescued was Batraz's father-in-law, Wazarmis, but marriage still contextualises the tale.
90. Ibid., 319, note 6.
91. Khamis is here Khmish.
92. Ibid., saga 30.
93. Ibid., 150.
94. Ibid., saga 74; a quite different version of his death is mentioned in NSFTC, saga 18.
95. Sheehan, 'Giants, Boar-Hunts and Barbering'.
96. Tacitus, Germania, 31.
97. Nickel, 'The Fight about King Arthur's Beard', though his proposal that this was introduced to Britain by Sarmatians in the Roman period goes far beyond the evidence.
98. TOTN, saga 57.
99. Ibid., sagas 58, 65; compare Herodotus, IV, 62.
100. Ibid., saga 70.
101. Dumézil, Romans de Scythie, 21, followed by Abaev, 'Introduction', liii, suggests Turkic or Mongolian; Colarusso, NSFTC, saga 33, note 1 on p. 158 argues for East Circassian from Proto-Northwest Caucasian, which he reaffirms in endnote 6 in TOTN, lxv.
102. TOTN, saga 67.
103. Dumézil, Légendes sur les Nartes, 69.
104. TOTN, saga 88.
105. Malory, 1238–40.
106. Dumézil, Légendes sur les Nartes, 30.
107. FSTC, 68.
108. Malory, 1238, lines 32–4; 1239, lines 1–4; 1240, lines 3–9.
109. FSTC, 69.

110. Dumézil, *Romans de Scythie*, 30.
111. NSFTC, saga 11; Urizhmag is here Warzameg.
112. Dumézil considered it early but offered evidence only as far back as the nineteenth century, by which point the 'redness' of the Black Sea was enshrined in local folklore: *Romans de Scythie*, 87.
113. TOTN, saga 72.
114. Similarly, Colarusso suggests a late origin for a story featuring modern weaponry in NSFTC, 152.
115. As Littleton and Thomas, 'The Sarmatian Connection'; FSTC, 61–71.
116. See, generally, Fitzpatrick, 'The Deposition'; for the last, in particular, see Bradley et al., '"Where Water Wells up from the Earth"'.
117. Raffield, '"A River of Knives and Swords"'.
118. Orosius, V, 16, 5–6.
119. See, for example, the papers collected in Jørgensen et al. (eds), *The Spoils of Victory*.
120. LCdG(P), line 4164ff.
121. Though this story postdates the first appearance of the sword-in-the-water motif in French romance, at least in its current form.
122. Including the struggle between the red and white 'dragons' in HB, 42, versions of which reappear in French romances.
123. John, XVIII, 25–7.
124. Ibid., XIII, 38.
125. AC, 537; the earlier HB leaves Arthur very much alive having triumphed over the Saxons in all his twelve battles.
126. See Tatlock, *The Legendary History*, 183.
127. HRB, X–XI; the quotation comes from XI, line 10.
128. As his use of Cornish personal names, such as Gorlois; there is no good reason to follow Geoffrey in this identification, which is generally rejected by modern scholars.
129. Ibid., XI, lines 81–4.
130. Ibid., vii.
131. Some copies name alternative dedicatees but it is generally agreed that Robert was primary; for efforts to see contemporary events in HRB, see Tolhurst, 'The Britons and Hebrews'.
132. Parry, 'The *Vita Merlini*', lines 908ff.
133. Ibid., line 929.
134. Geoffrey's description is reminiscent of the relevant passage in Isidore's *Etymologies*, for which see Throop, *Isidore of Seville's Etymologies*, XIV, 6, 8.
135. NSBA; O'Meara and Wooding, 'The Latin Version'; this was even rewritten in Anglo-Norman; see Short and Merrilees (eds), *Benedeit*, 5; for recent discussion see Byrne, *Otherworlds*, 123.
136. As noted by Selmer in his introduction to the NSBA, xxi; for the debate regarding Christian influence on this work, see Mac Cana, 'Mongán Mac Fiachna and Immram Brain'; Carey, 'The Location of the Otherworld in Irish Tradition'; Egeler, *Islands in the West*; Byrne, *Otherworlds*, 119–29.
137. NSBA, I, lines 18–19, et al., *insulam deliciosam*; *deliciosa* also carries the meaning 'luxurious', in the sense of 'good returns from little work', mirroring the classical concept of the 'Isles of the Blessed'.
138. NSBA, I, 34; IX, 39; XII, 128.
139. NSBA, XII; XXVI; XXVIII.
140. Bennett, 'Britain among the Fortunate Isles'.
141. Pliny, *Natural History*, IV, 22, 120–2; note the use of the same term by Geoffrey.
142. Pliny implied the Azores but Isidore the Canaries; the Hereford *Mappa Mundi* of *c.* 1300 associates St Brendan's Isles with the 'Fortunate Isles', and seems to favour the Canaries; Burgess, 'Introduction', 9.
143. Plutarch, *Life of Sertorius*, VIII, 2–3; the reference is to Homer, *Odyssey*, IV, 563–8.
144. Tatlock, *The Legendary History*, 77–8, 203; though William of Malmesbury's *De Antiquitate*, written *c.* 1129, makes frequent reference to Avalon as an early name for

Glastonbury, this was clearly interpolated after Arthur's grave was 'discovered' there in 1190–91: Scott, *The Early History of Glastonbury*, 29, 34.

145. Byrne, *Otherworlds*, 147; including *Emhain Abhlach*, an island paradise in Irish mythology sometimes associated with either the Isle of Man or Arran.

146. Presumably as the result of a misunderstanding, perhaps consequential on a damaged manuscript, but the similarity between *appell-* and *aball* are unlikely to be coincidental.

147. Rivet and Smith, *Place-Names of Roman Britain*, 238.

148. Romer (trans.), Pomponius Mela, *Description of the World*, III, 6; he seems to have derived this from Strabo (see below).

149. See, for example, Baswell and Sharpe, 'Introduction: Rex Quondam Rexque Futurus', xiii.

150. See Parry, 'The *Vita Merlini*', line 916: 'nine sisters rule by a pleasing set of laws those who come to them from our country', recalling Strabo, IV, 198, which will have reached him via Pomponius, above.

151. HRB, IX, line 107ff.

152. We find the same root appearing in Old Irish in the name of a warrior's sword, Caladbolg; Tatlock, *The Legendary History*, 202; again, this will have derived ultimately from Greek via Latin.

153. NSBA, XXIII; this may well be a representation of Iceland, with its volcanoes; alternatively the Canaries are volcanic in origin.

154. WRdB, lines 13275–93.

155. Ewart (ed.), *Marie de France, Lais*, V, *Lanval*, 58–74, lines 641–3: *Od li s'en vait en Avalun / Ceo nus recontent li Bretun / En un isle que mut est beaus*, probably written in the 1160s or 1180s.

156. Mann, *From Aesop to Reynard*, 309–11.

157. Marie's references to Caerleon, Caerwent, Carlisle, Totnes, Exeter and Tintagel could all derive from Wace.

158. Laʒamon, xii; the final reference to Arthur in this work, in Merlin's prophesy 'that an Arthur should come again to aid the people of England' (line 14296–7), may refer to Arthur of Brittany, the acknowledged heir of Richard I, in which case the work was completed prior to his death in 1203.

159. Laʒamon, line 7; note the *Brut* tradition has jumped the ethnic and language barrier, from Welsh/British to English, via French.

160. Laʒamon, line 14277ff.; the name Argante probably derives from the French version of Morgan, Morgant, perhaps influenced by medieval Latin *argentum*, 'silver'; there is more emphasis on the possibility of Arthur's return here than in either Geoffrey or Wace.

161. LMLRA, 192–3.

162. SMA, lines 3448ff.; for a summary see Lupack, *Oxford Guide*, 104–13.

163. WRdB, lines 9009–12.

164. See Schmolke-Hasselmann, *The Evolution of Arthurian Romance*, 246–9.

165. Though Geoffrey's style of royal inheritance does persist within the Arthurian tradition, for example, in the English *Alliterative Morte Arthure* (ed. Hamel), lines 4316–17: 'Constantyn, my cosyn, I sall þe corown bere / Alls becommys hym of kynde, ʒife Criste will hym thole'; for the shifting attitudes of the English aristocracy post-1190, see Schmolke-Hasselmann, *The Evolution of Arthurian Romance*, 246–50.

166. As CaO, lines 64–5; HRB, IX, 106ff.

167. There has been some attempt to identify this scene with the London Stone (normally sited in Cannon Street but presently removed for safety during redevelopment), as reported by Higgins, *Under Another Sky*, 55–6, but this 'legend' seems to have been twentieth century in inception.

168. That a sword shared its basic shape with the cross obviously helped with this imagery.

169. Micha (ed.), Robert de Boron, *Merlin*, 83–8.

170. Ibid., 91.

171. The scene has since been central to numerous portrayals of Arthur, as Disney, *The Sword in the Stone* (1963); Crossley-Holland, *Arthur The Seeing Stone*; Burgess, *Any Old*

Iron, 325, has it re-enacted in a twentieth-century setting; it is less prominent, though still present, in Ritchie, *King Arthur: Legend of the Sword* (2017).

172. One can read all sorts of psychology into the sword in the stone; see, for example, Cavendish, *King Arthur and the Grail*, 47.

173. LMLRA, 193; the alternative, that Arthur might eventually 'return', was a predominantly English form of the tale; see Flood, 'Arthur's Return'.

174. LMLRA, 192; Bogdanow, 'The Evolution of the Theme', 93–4.

175. CdTP, lines 4160ff.; Girflet originates here as one of Arthur's knights.

176. The Welsh text, *Peredur, Son of Efrawg*, uses a closely comparable device, with Peredur twice ignoring the command of the empress of Constantinople before finally coming in to talk with her, but this was later than LMLRA and this motif was presumably borrowed from it.

177. Micha (ed.), Robert de Boron, *Merlin*, 85–91.

178. LMLRA, 196–204; indeed, this work was termed the 'Story of Lancelot' in the final chapter.

179. See Greene, *Le Sujet et la Mort*.

180. Littleton, 'Georges Dumézil and the Rebirth of the Genetic Model', 175–6.

181. West, *Indo-European Poetry and Myth*, 1–22.

182. As in *Math, Son of Mathonwy: The Mabinogion*, 64; compare for example NSFTC, saga 50.

183. Though giants are far more common in the Nart sagas than in Arthurian literature.

184. After Jones and Mason, *Wace and Layamon*, v–vi. For the false attribution to Alain de Lille and the dating, see Raynaud de Lage, *Alain de Lille*, 13–15; another candidate as author is Alan of Tewkesbury, died *c.* 1202.

185. As do other near contemporaries, including Wolfram von Eschenbach, in *Parzival*; curiously, some modern scholars have treated this passage as evidence for the widespread dissemination of Arthurian legends on the Continent, independent of Britain.

186. As KAIA, 13–14; Louis IX of France did not campaign in Egypt until 1248, far too late for this author.

187. Specifically, the kingdom of Jerusalem, principality of Antioch and counties of Tripoli and Edessa.

188. See Loomis, 'Oral Diffusion', 62. I am not persuaded by the criticism of his interpretation in KAIA, 14.

189. As Chrétien's 'Story of the Grail', which refers to Beirut in line 3406; in the early thirteenth-century *Queste del Saint Graal*, the quest ends in Egypt, whence Bors returns via 'a short voyage' to Arthur's kingdom.

190. Littleton, 'The Holy Grail'; FSTC, xxvii, xxix–xxx, 209–80; various other 'ritual' theories circulating *c.* 1900 were countered by Bruce, *The Evolution*, I, 277–89.

191. The case was made originally by Nutt, *Studies on the Legend*; Marx, *La Légende Arthurienne*, and Loomis, *The Grail*; *Wales and the Arthurian Legend*, 19–41.

192. As Bruce, *The Evolution*, I, 219–68; D'Arcy, *Wisdom and the Grail*; Barber, *The Holy Grail*; Goering, *The Virgin and the Grail*.

193. Evans, *In Quest*; Weston, *The Quest*; Waite, *The Holy Grail*; Ashe, *King Arthur's Avalon*.

194. As confirmed in the text at line 66, though 'Perceval' is often substituted as the title.

195. See, for example, Simons, 'Pattern and Process of Education'; Ullyot, 'Molloy'.

196. Equipped here with Excalibur; it has been suggested that Chrétien learned at this point of his patron's death and redesigned his work accordingly.

197. Gawain takes up 3942 of the remaining lines, as opposed to 283 lines for Perceval.

198. Lines 6009–92.

199. The ultimate derivation is probably from Greek *krater*, a wine-mixing bowl, via Latin *gradalis/cratalis*; Goering, *The Virgin and the Grail*, 156, suggests that it entered French from Catalan.

200. O'Gorman, 'Grail'.

201. *The Mabinogion*, 14, 94.

202. Ibid., 192.

203. Over, 'Transcultural Change'; for parallels, see Carey, *Ireland and the Grail*, 246–7.

204. *Parzival*, verses 238–9.
205. Bruce, *The Evolution*, I, 237–9.
206. Goering, *The Virgin and the Grail*, passim.
207. Ibid., 146–51.
208. Benton, 'The Court of Champagne', depicts her court as a place rich in literature of many different kinds.
209. Though she is not well evidenced as a patron; see Broadhurst, 'Henry II', 71–84.
210. John, XIX, 34; for the symbolism of this passage more generally, see Jung and Von Franz, *The Grail Legend*, 66–78.
211. Several western relics were considered 'the holy lance', including one at Rome in the sixth century, and another associated with the Ottonians in the tenth.
212. The parallels are discussed by Diverres, 'The Grail and the Third Crusade'.
213. Strictly it is not the grail of itself which gives off light but the grail carried by the maiden, which equates with the Virgin's association with the Holy Ghost.
214. O'Gorman, 'Joseph of Arimathie'.
215. As John, XIX, 34–42; the anonymous soldier responsible becomes a centurion named Longinus in the *Gospel of Nicodemus*, an apocryphal construct from Greek *longkhé* (λόγχη), meaning 'lance', which held the field throughout the Middle Ages: Klauck, *Apocryphal Gospels*, 97.
216. James (trans.), *The Apocryphal New Testament*, 94–146; Klauck, *Apocryphal Gospels*, 88–98.
217. See O'Gorman, 'The Gospel of Nicodemus'.
218. Goering, *The Virgin and the Grail*, 112–39.
219. Roach, *Didot Perceval*, lines 1850–2; Bryant, *Merlin and the Grail*, 155.
220. *Contra* the suggestion that this in some sense relates to the magic qualities of Wasamonga, below.
221. Bullock-Davies, 'Chretien de Troyes and England'.
222. For discussion, see Crawford, 'St Joseph and Britain'.
223. See Robinson, *Two Glastonbury Legends*; Lagorio, 'The Evolving Legend'; Stout, 'Savaric, Glastonbury and the Making of Myths' for development of the 'Glastonbury tradition'.
224. For recent discussion, see Murphy, *Gemstone of Paradise*; Goering, *The Virgin and the Grail*, 16–39.
225. There is no need to take seriously Wolfram's claim that he had additional written sources; none have ever been identified and this was a common means of asserting the authority of what was in fact a work of fiction; the fabulous 'prequel' he provided in setting out the career of Perceval's putative father, Gahmuret, in books 1 and 2, sets the tone; books 15 and 16, which conclude Perceval's quest, should similarly be read as his own highly imaginative work.
226. Aberystwyth, National Library of Wales, MS Peniarth 2; the title is written in a fourteenth-century hand but not directly evidenced within the text.
227. PA, 53, 57.
228. PA, 54; TYP, 509–11.
229. Only one bears Taliesin's name in the title, the poem numbered 36 in *The Black Book of Caernarvon*; LDC, 75.
230. Though reference in line 4 to 'the story concerning Pwyll and Pryderi' is arguably a version of *Pwyll Prince of Dyfed*; see Loomis, *Wales and the Arthurian Legend*, 131–78.
231. PA, 60, translation, 62.
232. Parry, 'The *Vita Merlini*', lines 737–940; see also Loomis, *Wales and the Arthurian Legend*, 154–6; TYP, triad 87, implies a connection.
233. Strabo, IV, 198; for the suggestion that the Celtic concept of Annwn had Greek antecedents, see Mees and Nicholas, 'Greek Curses'.
234. *The Mabinogion*, 29, 37.
235. Padel, 'The Early Welsh Arthurian Poems', 56.
236. In general, see Gerloff, *Atlantic Cauldrons*.

237. Goldberg, 'Vernacular Religion in Northern Britain', 208.
238. Though these were not cooking vessels, the hanging bowls of Celtic manufacture which are found in Anglo-Saxon graves *c*. 600 are from a similar tradition of manufacture; Bruce-Mitford, *Late Celtic Hanging-Bowls*; Geake, *The Use of Grave-Goods*, 85.
239. *Parzival*, verse 206.
240. With the meaning 'holy-indicator'; TOTN, 435; the earlier name is Nartamongaê.
241. Ibid., the opening lines of saga 66.
242. NSFTC, saga 69.
243. Ibid., saga 31.
244. For a storytelling contest, see ibid., saga 14.
245. Herodotus, IV, 66.
246. From Athenaeus, *The Deipnosophists*, 152; see Kidd, *Posidonius*, 67.
247. For the dominance of right forelimbs of pigs in a large midden of the early Iron Age discovered at Llanmaes (South Wales), see Madgwick and Mulville, 'Feasting on Fore-Limbs'.
248. See, for example, Virtanen, *Finnish Folklore*.
249. As Philostratus, VII, 26.
250. Plutarch, *Sertorius*, I, 1–2.

Chapter 4 King Arthur and the Greeks

1. EAT, 15–16.
2. KAIA, 13–26.
3. I am extremely grateful to Graham Anderson for providing me with a copy following my difficulties in sourcing this volume.
4. As West, *Indo-European Poetry*, 4, referring back to the work of Dumézil.
5. Tatlock, *The Legendary History*, 220–5.
6. EAT, 7.
7. KAIA, 28; EAT, 7; Liddell–Scott, 117; on the assumption that many readers will not be conversant with the Greek language or its alphabet, I have generally rendered Greek phonetically into the Latin alphabet, including Greek lettering in parentheses as necessary.
8. KAIA, 28; EAT, 7.
9. With the 't' predictably thickening to Welsh 'th'; see Jackson, *Language and History*, 399.
10. As encountered in HB, 56, 73; AC, 516, 537; *Gododdín*, B2.38.
11. Zimmer, 'Review'; Malone, 'Artorius'; Jackson, *Language and History*, 272, 399; Breeze, 'The Name of King Arthur'.
12. *Contra* Chocheyras, 'Sur le Nom d'Arthur'; my thanks to Professor Peter Schrijver for his advice on the phonological issues.
13. Malone, 'Artorius', 467.
14. For Roman examples, see p. 150; for the early Middle Ages, see Davies, *The Llandaff Charters*, which has Arthan, Arthbleid, Arthcumanu, Arthmail, Artuail and Arthuo, as well as Arthur, or Sims-Williams, *The Celtic Inscriptions*, offering Artbeu, Arthi, Arthmail, Artmali and Artognov.
15. See, for example, Pliny's comment in *Natural History*, II, 41, 110, where he notes that the heavens were divided into 'seventy-two signs' according to 'the shapes of things or of animals into which the learned have mapped out the sky.'
16. As Ptolemy, *Almagest*.
17. Homer, *Odyssey*, V, 269–75.
18. Homer, *Iliad*, XVIII, 484–90; Evans, *The History and Practice of Ancient Astronomy*, 3.
19. Mallory and Adams, *Oxford Introduction*, 131; the Wikipedia site for Ursa Major is useful: see https://en.wikipedia.org/wiki/Ursa_Major (accessed 5 June 2018). Scherer, *Gestirnnamen bei den indogermanischen Völkern*, 131, suggests that Indo-European constellation names were typically plural, and that the star Arktouros would originally have been part of the same complex as the Bear.

20. As Gibbon, 'Asiatic Parallels in North American Star Lore'; Berezkin, 'Southern Siberian–North-American Links in Mythology'; bears are also prominent in Finnish mythology.
21. Schaefer, 'The Origin of the Greek Constellations'; genetic divergence in Asia and America began *c.* 25,000 years ago.
22. *Contra* Kidd's commentary, in Aratus, 213, which supposes that Boötes pre-dates Arctophylax.
23. Mallory and Adams, *Oxford Introduction*, 138, specify Latin, Greek and Sanskrit.
24. The earliest records, on clay tablets, date to the second millennium BC and are known as MUL.APIN; there are excellent illustrations in Sachs, 'Babylonian Observational Astronomy'.
25. Hesiod is variously described as Homer's contemporary or up to fifty years later.
26. Hesiod, lines 566, 610.
27. Pliny, *Natural History*, II, 71, 178.
28. The period stretching from the reign of Augustus through to the third quarter of the third century.
29. Hyginus, *De Astronomia*, 2, 1; the Latin text is extracted in EAT, 42, with a translation at 123–4.
30. Hyginus, *De Astronomia*, 2, 4; the Latin text is extracted in EAT, 44–5, with a translation at 126; Hyginus seems to have based this on *Catasterisms* (EAT, 40–1, 121–2), which may also have been the source for other of his passages.
31. Hyginus, *Fabulae*, 84.
32. Pausanias, VIII, 4, extracted in EAT, 57, with a translation at 136–7; Phlegyas was the mythical king of the Lapiths.
33. Hyginus, *Fabulae*, 130, extracted in EAT, 43, with a translation at 125.
34. Aratus, lines 91–5 (based on the lost work of the fourth-century-BCE astronomer, Eudoxus of Cnidos).
35. Maas, *Commentarium*, 355.
36. KAIA, 33–4; EAT, 70, 146.
37. As opposed to the Greeks, who generally used Ursa Major as a navigational guide;
38. Both the 'virgin' and 'ear of corn' are the names of constellations; Cicero, II, 105–10.
39. Ovid, *Fasti*, II, lines 188–90.
40. Ibid., VI, lines 235–6.
41. Virgil, *Georgics*, I, 138, 245–6, 744; cf. *Aeneid* III, 516.
42. Virgil, *Aeneid*, I, 740ff.
43. Ibid., III, 514ff.
44. And it may be a mistake to limit possible attribution to these two; see Baldwin, 'The Authorship'.
45. Germanicus, lines 227ff.
46. Ibid., lines 25ff.
47. Ibid., lines 90ff.
48. Ibid., line 624.
49. Evans, *The History and Practice of Ancient Astronomy*, 23.
50. Pliny, *Natural History*, II, 41, 110; 69, 178; 74, 185.
51. Ibid., II, 47, 124; 71, 178.
52. Hutton, 'Describing Greece', 317–18.
53. Habicht, *Pausanias' Guide to Ancient Greece*, 1–26.
54. As Guilmet, 'The Survival of Pausanias' Text'.
55. Pausanias, VIII, 4, 5–6; X, 9, 6; Habicht, *Pausanias' Guide to Ancient Greece*, 68ff.
56. Macrobius, *Commentary*, I, 12–15; 17–18.
57. Ibid., I, 18, 19; V, 17.
58. Powell, *Cicero*, 124ff.
59. Macrobius, *Commentary*, XVIII, 5.
60. Capella, VIII, 808; 838.
61. Isidore, III, 71, 6–9.

62. As Tobias, bishop of Rochester, HE, V, 8; note the Greek influence in the name he adopted.

63. Ibid., IV, 2.

64. Bischoff and Lapidge, *Biblical Commentaries*, 61, noting that Aldhelm learned astrology at Canterbury.

65. Bede, 201–3.

66. Omitting only further comments concerning links between the stars and the weather.

67. Laistner, 'The Library of the Venerable Bede', 239–45, quote at 242.

68. Eastwood, *Ordering the Heavens*.

69. The *Vita Hludovici*, in Noble, *Charlemagne and Louis the Pious*; the author is dubbed an 'expert in astronomical affairs' in cap. 58 (meaning 'astrological'); see also caps 31, 37, 37, 41, 42, 43, 59, 62.

70. See Pryce (ed.), *Literacy in Medieval Celtic Societies*.

71. For discussion, see Needham et al. (eds), *The Ringlemere Cup*.

72. Frere, *Britannia*, 30, reports a 'wide scatter of Greek coins in southern Britain'; the number of finds has increased in recent years, mainly due to the Portable Antiquities Scheme.

73. As Mays (ed.), *Catalogue of the Celtic Coins in the British Museum*, III; bulls are also more common than bears; a winged lion and a 'crocodile-type' animal also feature, demonstrating influences from the Near East.

74. Allen, *Coins of the Ancient Celts*, 53, 141.

75. Nash, *Coinage in the Celtic World*, 128.

76. Toynbee, *Art in Roman Britain*, 2.

77. The 'Grain-Ear' could refer to the star Stachys, Latin Spica, an 'ear of wheat'; the star-rays are necessarily astronomical; Centaurus is a constellation, but in the southern hemisphere; the Sphinx was an Egyptian constellation.

78. Scheers, 'Celtic coin types'.

79. Avienus, lines 108ff.

80. Strabo, I, 4, 2; II, 3, 5; IV, 5, 5; Pliny, *Natural History*, IV, 16.

81. Strabo, II, 4, 1; 40,000 stadia is *c.* 4597 miles; the British Cartographic Society calculates the coastline of the British mainland as 11,073 miles.

82. See Holder, *The Roman Army*, 104–33; not all these units entered Britain in the first century but the evidence is overwhelming.

83. RIB I, 1065.

84. See, for example, Biddulph, 'What's in a Name?'; Mullen, 'Linguistic Evidence for "Romanization"'.

85. RIB III, 3151; RIB I, 461.

86. Ibid., 1072; the dedication is to Aesculapius, the Greek god of medicine, commissioned by a Roman-named tribune in the 170s CE.

87. Ling, 'Inscriptions on Romano-British Mosaics', 87, noting just two on the Continent, at Autun and Cologne.

88. RIB II, 2448.5.

89. Ibid., 2408.2, 2501.71, 2423.1, 2408.2.

90. Tomlin, 'The Curse Tablets'; 'The Inscribed Lead Tablets'; several other sites have produced small numbers in addition.

91. Mullen, 'Evidence for Written Celtic'.

92. Hanson and Conolly, 'Language and Literacy'.

93. Tomlin, 'Writing to the Gods in Britain', 175.

94. Woolf, 'How the Latin West was Won'.

95. As Collingwood and Myres, *Roman Britain and the English Settlements*, 194.

96. For discussion, see Mullen, 'Latin and Other Languages'.

97. Hood (ed.), *St Patrick*; there are precious few Latin texts referenced either, other than the Bible.

98. Lapidge, 'Gildas's Education'.

99. As Jackson, 'Varia II'.
100. DEB, 23, 3: *cyulis* ('keels'), though it has been suggested that this passage was a later interpolation: see p. 206.
101. Cosh and Neal, *Roman Mosaics of Britain*, IV, mosaic 483.30; Witts, *Mosaics in Roman Britain*, 91.
102. Cosh and Neal, *Roman Mosaics of Britain*, IV, 10.
103. Price and Price, *A Description*.
104. Scott, *Art and Society*, 99–100, 114–17; the alternative is that this is a representation of an individual author, such as Aratus.
105. Witts, *Mosaics in Roman Britain*, 88–90, plate 39.
106. Though these include what were later recognised as asterisms (i.e. star clusters) rather than individual stars.
107. Evans, *The History and Practice of Ancient Astronomy*, 42; Latin names are in brackets where significantly different.
108. Searches in OPEL and on EDH, 18 March 2016.
109. RIB I, inscriptions numbered 1558, 1602, 1726, 1860, 1862.
110. LGPN, Va, Vb.
111. See Thompson, *Saint Germanus*, 9.
112. EAT, 7–8.
113. Cornell (ed.), *Fragments of the Roman Historians*, II, 523; III, 539–41.
114. Juvenal, *Satire 3*, line 26.
115. DEB, 20, 1.
116. Ibid., 25, 3.
117. Ibid., 30, 1.
118. Sims-Williams, *The Celtic Inscriptions of Britain*, 33–4.
119. As RIB III.
120. NSBA, X.
121. As CaO, lines 64–5; Davies, 'A Welsh Version of the Birth of Arthur'.
122. KAIA, 33–4; EAT, 70, 146.
123. Ibid., 257–8.
124. Liddell–Scott, 881.
125. EAT, 40–1, 121–2.
126. Liddell–Scott, 815.
127. See Schmolke-Hasselmann, 'The Round Table', 43–5.
128. For his sources, see WRdB, xvii–xxii.
129. HRB, IX, 154.
130. Wace, lines 9740ff.
131. Ibid., lines 9747ff.
132. *Pace* Bruce, *The Evolution*, I, 87.
133. Foulon, 'Wace', 100.
134. Einhard, *Life of Charlemagne*, XX, in Noble, *Charlemagne and Louis*; Walters, 'Re-examining Wace's Round Table'.
135. Schmolke-Hasselmann, 'The Round Table'.
136. Putter, 'The Twelfth-Century Arthur', 43.
137. Job, XXXVIII, 32.

Chapter 5 A Dark Age King Arthur

1. Collingwood, *An Autobiography*, 93.
2. As Loomis, 'King Arthur and the Saints', picking out his 'low tastes' and 'brutal manners'.
3. Fulton, 'Magic and the Supernatural', 1.
4. Padel, 'The Nature of Arthur'.
5. Grooms, *The Giants of Wales*, 113–28.
6. Lloyd, *The Arthurian Place-Names*, 166, maps 5, 6, for the distribution of Arthurian place-names in Wales.

7. Van Hamel, 'Aspects of Celtic Mythology', 219–33.

8. As Dillon, *Early Irish Literature*, 36–40; Knott and Murphy, *Early Irish Literature*, 147–9; see for example the Fenian Gaelic prose tale, *The Pursuit of Diarmaid and Gráinne*.

9. Ross, *Pagan Celtic Britain*, 349.

10. As *Y Gododdín*, B2.41.

11. Green, *Dictionary*, 34–5; Greene, *Animals in Celtic Life and Myths*, 45; the place-name Bern has also long been linked etymologically with a word meaning 'bear', though there are other possibilities.

12. Ibid., 218.

13. As the rivers Artogna in Piedmont (Italy), l'Artaby in Haute-Provence (France), and Arth in west Wales.

14. RIB I, 409; 410.

15. The name occurs elsewhere, as in EDH HD073076 (15 June 2015) at Carnuntum (Austria); our Artius was probably from the legionary fortress at Caerleon, drafted in to captain this garrison of auxiliaries.

16. Thornhill, 'The Origin', 236.

17. Chocheyras, 'Sur le Nom d'Arthur'.

18. For recent discussion, see ibid., though I cannot support the conclusion that the Roman name Artorius originated in Greek.

19. Bromwich, Jarman and Roberts, 'Introduction', 6, referencing Marcale, *Le Roi Arthur*.

20. As Belatucadrus (and its several variants), Cocidius, Vitris/Huitris, Viridius, Vinotonus, Brigantia, Antenociticus, Coventina, Nodens, Verbeia, Condatis and Sulis; the point is made by Breeze, 'The Name of King Arthur', 33.

21. For discussion of Arthur's appearances in the *Mirabilia*, see pp. 228–9.

22. Initially in Ashe, ' "A Certain Very Ancient Book" '; this theory is dismissed by Halsall, *Worlds of Arthur*, 265–6; see also, Adams, 'Sidonius'.

23. Ibid.

24. Ashe, *The Discovery of King Arthur*, 100–5.

25. Dalton (ed.), *The Letters*, I, 76.

26. As supposed by Adams, 'Sidonius'.

27. The survival of numerous letters allows us an unusual degree of insight into his circle of contacts.

28. Jordanes, XLV, 237; Mierow (trans.), *Origins and Deeds*, 237–8; Cassiodorus had first-hand experience of the Gothic kings, having served Theodoric, then Athalric, who died c. 634.

29. Innes, *Introduction to Early Medieval Western Europe*, 116–17.

30. For a wider discussion, see Wood, *The Merovingian Kingdoms*, 16–19; 'The End of Roman Britain', 21.

31. The emphasis of the brief account of the *Gallic Chronicle of 511* is on the emperor's retaining Arles in the face of Gothic manoeuvres; it was lost soon after he was killed in the civil war that ended his reign.

32. Think of such figures as Vercingetorix in the classical period. For the fifth century, think of Cantiorix (Nash-Williams, *Early Christian Monuments*, 92–3) or Vortigern; see Jackson, 'Varia II'; more recently, Sims-Williams, *The Celtic Inscriptions of Britain*, passim.

33. A thesis promoted by Marilyn Floyde in her *King Arthur's French Odyssey*, a fanciful account of little historical merit written very much under Ashe's influence.

34. It has even migrated to the New World, occurring as an island name off Los Angeles and as a peninsula in Newfoundland.

35. Including the tale 'Merlin and the Forest of Brocéliande', the roots of which lie in the works of Geoffrey of Monmouth, Wace, Chrétien and Robert de Boron.

36. See Nash-Williams, *Early Christian Monuments*; Sims-Williams, *The Celtic Inscriptions*.

37. Patrick, *Confessio*; *Epistola*; DEB.

38. Ibid., 37, 1: *flebilis . . . historia*.

39. So Bede in HE, I, 22, though he did term Gildas an 'historian'; see also Wulfstan's reference to Gildas as a 'prophet' in his 'Sermon of the Wolf to the English': Whitelock (ed.), *Sermo Lupi ad Anglos*, line 184; for a translation, see EHD, I, 929–34, at 933.

40. As O'Loughlin, *Gildas and the Scriptures*.

41. DEB, 1, 1.

42. Higham, *English Conquest*, 13.

43. He is generally assumed to have been in minor orders and may eventually have become a monk; even his name is obscure, with no clear root in Brittonic or Latin (though Gildan (Γιλδαν) occurs on a Greek inscription in the Eastern Roman Empire); see Larpi, *Prolegomena*, 5–7.

44. Sims-Williams, 'Gildas and the Anglo-Saxons', 3–5.

45. As Thompson, 'Gildas', 216–18.

46. Higham, *English Conquest*, 90–117; Dark, *Civitas to Kingdom*, 266.

47. Smyth, 'The Earliest Irish Annals', 9–11; Charles-Edwards, 'Introduction', 8; WATB, 215.

48. Adomnán, II, 1; Vinniau is thought to have been active across the mid-sixth century and died c. 589.

49. Walker (ed.), *Sancti Columbani Opera*, 'Letter 1', 7, line 33.

50. As DEB, 6; Winterbottom, 'Columbanus and Gildas', 311; WATB, 216.

51. DEB, 13, 1.

52. Ibid., 4, 4.

53. As placing construction of both walls and the Saxon Shore forts later than the revolt of Magnus Maximus (in 383); in reality the walls were second century and the forts all predate the 380s.

54. Acts, VII; Bede's commentary on Acts makes it clear that Stephen's approach was well understood in the early Middle Ages; Martin (trans.), *The Venerable Bede*, 72.

55. Gardner, 'Gildas's New Testament Models'.

56. DEB, 93, 3; identification of this event rests on Mike Baillie's work on dendrochronology; current thinking favours a volcanic eruption but Baillie, *Exodus to Arthur*, preferred a meteor strike; now see Oppenheimer, *Eruptions that Shook the World*, 253–60; Büntgen et al., 'Cooling and Societal Change'.

57. DEB, 1, 2, for the ten years.

58. As acknowledged by Wood, 'Gildas and the Mystery Cloud'.

59. DEB, 93, 2: 'You are the light of the world ... nor does one light a lamp and place it under a bushel ... Who then among the priests of today, plunged as they are in the blindness of ignorance'.

60. Lapidge, 'Gildas's Education'.

61. Wright, 'Gildas's Prose Style'.

62. DEB, 1, 14.

63. Ibid., 36, 1.

64. For this translation see Higham, *The English Conquest*, 137.

65. Muhlberger, 'The Gallic Chronicle', 33, considered this testimony one that should 'not be lightly dismissed'.

66. As Dumville, 'The Chronology', 83, offering c. 545.

67. As O'Sullivan, *The De Excidio of Gildas*, 180, suggesting 505–30; Stancliffe, 'The Thirteen Sermons', 179–81, argued for c. 513 as the earliest possible date, and c. 588 as the latest; for a recent overview see George, *Gildas's De Excidio Britonum*, 2–4.

68. *Contra* Morris, *The Age of Arthur*, who structures his account by reference to sections of DEB.

69. As Gidlow, *Revealing King Arthur*, 33.

70. Based on Mommsen's edition, published in 1898.

71. HE, I, 14; he may have taken the name from the Kentish origin story: see p. 196.

72. Larpi, *Prolegomena*, 45–52.

73. Jackson, 'Varia: II', 30; Halsall, *Worlds of Arthur*, 191–4, suggested instead that the 'proud tyrant' may have been Maximus, but the record of his death in DEB, 13, 2 makes it unlikely that he was intended as the figure of authority referred to in 23, 1.

74. DEB, 26, 1; *Badonicus* is adjectival.
75. HB, 56.
76. London, British Library, Cotton MS Vitellius A vi; Larpi, *Prolegomena*, 22–4.
77. Wood, *In Search of England*, 34–41.
78. Following Winterbottom, but see Wood, 'The End of Roman Britain', 23, for an alternative reading of the relative dating; Bede, HE, I, 16, interpreted it as meaning that Badon occurred about forty-four years after the Saxon 'arrival' in Britain; he is our earliest witness and may have had a superior text but it seems unlikely that Gildas would have legitimised the Saxon arrival by dating a British victory by reference to it.
79. Padel, 'The Nature of Arthur', 16; Wood, *In Search of England*, 38.
80. DEB, 24, 3–4.
81. This useful term was coined by Thompson, 'Gildas', 216–19.
82. The quotations are from Jackson, *Language and History*, 199, Morris, *Age of Arthur*, 114, Goodrich, *King Arthur*, 76, Jankulak, *Geoffrey of Monmouth*, 69, and Storr, *King Arthur's Wars*, 93, but there are elements of this in most other modern works, as Collingwood and Myres, *Roman Britain and the English Settlements*, 324; Salway, *Roman Britain*, 498; Dumville, 'The Chronology of *De Excidio Britanniae*', 76; Sims-Williams, 'Gildas and the Anglo-Saxons', 25–6; Gidlow, *The Reign of Arthur*, 51; Field, 'Arthur's Battles', 4.
83. Higham, *The English Conquest*, 47–50.
84. Conflating DEB, 24–5; the destruction of the island is explicitly compared with the Assyrian assault on Israel; the imagery of the sack of British cities is suggestive of Troy's fall; these passages should be understood as rhetorical, not literal.
85. Ibid., 25, 2; use of *domum* here can only mean the places where they had previously been stationed in Britain, not their Continental homelands.
86. Ibid., 25, 3.
87. *Novissimaeque ferme de furciferis non minimae stragis*; that Bede placed the 'Alleluia Victory' after Badon implies that he appreciated this: HE, I, 22.
88. DEB, 2.
89. Ibid., 26, 3.
90. Ibid., 1, 13.
91. Ibid., 26, 2: 'External wars may have stopped ...'
92. Ibid., 26, 1.
93. Ibid., 25, 3.
94. Ibid., 26, 2: *tam desperati insulae excidii insperatique mentio auxilii*; Winterbottom's translation of *auxilii* by 'recovery' is potentially misleading; I prefer the more literal 'assistance', or 'aid' here.
95. Ibid., 26, 3; the 'very few' probably refers to his immediate circle whom he expected to share his own level of education and sympathise with his diagnosis of the present situation.
96. Ibid., 10, 2.
97. For a recent critique see Garcia, 'Gildas and the "Grievous Divorce"'; Garcia's solution, though, that the *divortio* of chapter 10 relates to the Saxon revolt of chapter 23, is ruled out by Gildas's use of *nunc*, 'now' in 10; the *divortio* is in the present, not the distant past.
98. DEB, 3, 3: *electa veluti sponsa monilibus diversis ornate*.
99. See Higham, 'Old Light', for Britain as a land of milk and honey; there are numerous Old Testament parallels, including Exodus, II, 8 and Jeremiah's portrayal of Jerusalem as 'solitary', 'a widow': Lamentations, I, 1.
100. See discussion by Sharpe, 'Martyrs and Local Saints', 106–20.
101. Jeremiah similarly considered his own 'the generation of God's wrath' (as Jeremiah, VII, 29).
102. DEB, 37, 1.
103. Bassett, 'In Search of the Origins'.
104. DEB, 28–36.
105. Ptolemy located the Damnonioi in the Clyde valley (the first element survives in the place-name Dumbarton); however, given Gildas's penchant for punning, this is probably best understood as word-play on *damnatio/damnare* ('damnation'/'to damn').

106. Though if we follow the geographical logic of these Romano-British *civitates* he belongs to south-east Wales among the Silures.
107. DEB, 32, 1.
108. Jackson, 'Varia II', 32–3.
109. Castell Dineirth, near Aberarth (Ceredigion), or Bryneuryn Dinarth near Llandudno; the first name is that of a twelfth-century Norman castle.
110. Anderson, 'Varia', in 1928, was the first to speculate on this.
111. A misunderstanding that led Phillips and Keatman, *King Arthur*, into the farce of identifying Arthur as Owain Ddantgwyn, putative uncle of Maelgwyn of Gwynedd and claiming Wroxeter as Camelot; this misconception was profiled in the TV programme 'In Search of the Real King Arthur', transmitted by *Yesterday* on 8 April 2016.
112. Sims-Williams, 'Gildas and Vernacular Poetry', 187.
113. DEB, 1, 5: 'as Jeremiah had lamented [*defleverat*], "the city (representing the church) ... had been full of peoples, mistress of races, ruler of provinces: now it had become tributary [*sub tribute*]"' (quoting from Lamentations, I, 1).
114. The seminal edition is that of Williams, *Canu Aneirin*, followed by a translation with notes in Jackson, *The Gododdin*, and parallel texts in Jarman, *Aneirin*, and Koch (ed.), *The Gododdin*. Technically, the title only applies to the A text: Hehir, 'What is the Gododdin?', 43.
115. Jackson, *The Gododdin*, 42ff.; Charles-Edwards, 'The Authenticity of the *Gododdin*', 51; Dumville, 'Early Welsh Poetry', 4; Koch (ed.), *The Gododdin*, 2–25.
116. HB, 62.
117. HE, V, 24.
118. As Jackson, *The Gododdin*, 24–5; Cessford, 'Northern England and the Gododdin Poem', 218; Dumville, 'Early Welsh Poetry'; Dunshea, 'The Meaning of *Catraeth*'; for a balanced discussion see WATB, 374.
119. Assuming that Eiden here is Edinburgh, and Catraeth Catterick.
120. Hehir, 'What is the Gododdin?', 79.
121. See Jackson, *The Gododdin*, 42ff.; Charles-Edwards, 'The Authenticity of the *Gododdin*'; Koch (ed.), *The Gododdin*, 'Introduction', but see the critique of Jackson's theory of transmission by Dumville, 'Early Welsh Poetry', 7, and of Koch's by Padel, 'A New Study of the *Gododdin*'.
122. As Charles-Edwards, 'The Authenticity'; Koch (ed.), *The Gododdin*, li.
123. As Padel, 'A New Study of the *Gododdin*', and 'Aneirin and Taliesin'; Isaac, 'Readings in the History and Transmission of the *Gododdin*'.
124. Koch (ed.), *The Gododdin*, liv, sees Aneirin as potentially seventh century.
125. Dumville, 'Early Welsh Poetry', 2–3; there is no mention of Bernicia in the B2 text.
126. Cumbric (i.e. northern British) is generally considered to have died out in the twelfth century.
127. Charles-Edwards, 'The Authenticity', 65, suggests in the eighth century.
128. For discussion, see Koch, 'Waiting for Gododdin'.
129. Dark, 'A Famous Arthur', 78; Campbell, *Continental and Mediterranean Imports*, 73.
130. Jarman, *Aneirin*, 64; Koch (ed.), *The Gododdin*, 23; the translation offered here is based on Koch's but note that his text is an attempt to reconstruct an authentic sixth-century version, it is not the later medieval text.
131. As Charles-Edwards, 'The Arthur of History', 15.
132. As naming of the hero only at the end of the final line.
133. Koch (ed.), *The Gododdin*, 147–8.
134. Padel, 'The Nature of Arthur', 14; Padel, *Arthur in Medieval Welsh Literature*, 6.
135. Barber, *The Figure of Arthur*, 29–38.
136. Jackson, 'Edinburgh'; WATB, 392; Higham, *Ecgfrith*, 69.
137. See for example B2.32 = A 70; Koch (ed.), *The Gododdin*, 12–13.
138. As TYP, 275; in her 'Concepts of Arthur' Bromwich preferred Yorkshire; Moffat, *Arthur and the Lost Kingdoms*; Johnson, *Evidence of Arthur*; Breeze, 'The Historical Arthur'.
139. As Jackson, *The Gododdin*, 112.

140. The earliest surviving exemplar is National Library of Wales 4973 of the early 1630s, perhaps taken (with considerable modernisation) from a text of around the thirteenth century.
141. Rowland, *Early Welsh Saga Poetry*, 135.
142. Koch, *Cunedda, Cynan, Cadwallon, Cynddylan*, 231–92, with the text at 267–72.
143. Following ibid., 270–1.
144. Ibid., 290.
145. Rowland, *Early Welsh Saga Poetry*, 483–4.
146. As Short (ed.), Geffrei Gaimar, *Estoire des Engleis*, which uses 'Artur' throughout with the exception of 'Arthur' in line 410, so revealing that he was aware of the original name.
147. As Green, *Arthuriana*, 60.
148. A line of reasoning first put forward by Chadwick and Chadwick, *The Growth of Literature*, I, 162.
149. Adomnán, I, 8–9; CI, 596; there is little likelihood of a direct borrowing from Adomnán's text since it does not seem to have circulated in Wales.
150. As TYP, 264; Fraser, *From Caledonia to Pictland*, 122.
151. Dooley, 'Arthur of the Irish', 17, meaning Brycheiniog.
152. Though it is sometimes suggested that one name may be a doublet of the other.
153. TYP, 264.
154. As such names as Artbran, Artgal, Artlabar, Artríl in CI; *Art* meant 'bear' in Old Irish.
155. Faral, *La Légende Arthurienne*, I, 51.
156. Meyer, 'The Expulsion of the Dessi'.
157. Miller, 'Date-Guessing', suggests the very late sixth century.
158. Dhonnchadha, 'The Guarantor List'.
159. Mac Shamhráin, *Church and Polity*, 68; Dooley, 'Arthur of the Irish', 19.
160. Ibid., 19–20.
161. Dooley and Roe, *Tales of the Elders*, xvii; for the story see pp. 7–11.
162. Ibid., 226–7, footnote 8.
163. Despite special pleading going back in the modern period to Skene, *The Four Ancient Books*, 50–1.
164. HE, I, 7 (last paragraph); I, 8; I, 12; I, 13 (middle third); I, 14; I, 15 (excluding the opening sentence and the central interpolation); I, 16; I, 22.
165. Ibid., I, 22.
166. Ibid., II, 2.
167. Ibid., V, 23.
168. Foley and Higham, 'Bede on the Britons'.

Chapter 6 Arthur and the *Historia Brittonum*

1. Morris, *The Age of Arthur*, 111.
2. A ball-park figure, for reasons that will become obvious, pp. 179–80.
3. HB, 55.
4. See, for example, HE, II, 4; Aldhelm, 'Letter to Gerontius', in Lapidge and Herren (eds), *Aldhelm: The Prose Works*, 155–60 (and see commentary, 140–3).
5. AC, 768.
6. This is arguably taken from a ninth-century chronicle written in north Wales.
7. For the Welsh 'archdioceses', see Brooke, *The Church and the Welsh Border*, 16–18, 97–9.
8. AC, 854.
9. Alongside the Picts further north, though the HB's author considered them to be immigrants who arrived later than the Britons.
10. AC, 760, 778, 784.
11. Offa's Dyke was first assigned to Offa's reign by the Welsh scholar, Asser, in the late ninth century; for the focus on Powys see Hill and Worthington, *Offa's Dyke*, 113–28.

12. AC, 798: *apud Saxones jugulatur.*
13. Ibid., 822; Maund, *The Welsh Kings*, 37–9.
14. Ryan, 'The Mercian Supremacies', in TA-SW, 179–217.
15. AC, 814, 816.
16. See ASC(A), 821 [823], 823 [825], 825 [827].
17. See discussion in Sims-Williams, 'Historical Need and Literary Narrative', 13–18.
18. ASC(A), 827 [829], 828 [830].
19. HB, 16; for the dating strategies used in HB, see Dumville, 'Some Aspects of the Chronology'.
20. See HB, 55: *sed tamen pro compendio sermonis volui breviare* ('but nevertheless I wish to shorten [my] sermon for the sake of brevity').
21. Dumville, *The* Historia Brittonum, 3, *The 'Vatican' Recension*, xx, 3, provides the essential framework.
22. The Gaelic version (Todd, *The Irish Version of Nennius*), has only thirty-three chapters.
23. Gransden, *Historical Writings*, I, 5–6.
24. Dumville, '"Nennius" and the *Historia Brittonum*'.
25. Field, 'Nennius and his History'.
26. Guy, 'The Origins of the Compilation', 45–53.
27. Harleian MS 3859; MGH, *Chronica Minora, IV, V, VIO, VII*, 3, 115; Faral, *La Légende Arthurienne*, I, 188.
28. Dumville, *The* Historia Brittonum, 3, *The 'Vatican' Recension*, 4–5.
29. Chartres 98, designated text Z by Mommsen; Faral, *La Légende Arthurienne*, III, 4–29 offers it in parallel with the Harleian.
30. Ibid., I, 188; Chartres was missing the Trojan origins of the Britons (10–11), the origins of the Picts and Scots (12–15), various synchronisms (16) and the Roman emperors in Britain (20–30).
31. An apparatus described as 'absurd' by Dumville, *The* Historia Brittonum, 3, *The 'Vatican' Recension*, 7–8.
32. Using the term rather loosely; there is a mix of genealogies and notes about kinship, the last is a brief account of Cunedda's sons.
33. Although neither the *Civitates* nor the *Mirabilia* are titled in the Harleian MS.
34. Dumville, 'The Welsh Latin Annals'; Guy, 'The Origins'.
35. MGH, *Chronica Minora, IV, V, VI, VII*, 3, 115.
36. DEB, 3, 2; HB, 7; Bede took this same number from Gildas: HE, I, 1.
37. For which see Speed, *Towns in the Dark*.
38. Taking the identifications offered by Fitzpatrick-Matthews, 'The XXVIII Civitates Brittanniae', and Breeze, '"Historia Brittonum" and Britain's Twenty-Eight Cities'.
39. Dumville, *The* Historia Brittonum, 3, *The 'Vatican' Recension*, 4; the 'cities' list occurs in chapter 2 of the Gaelic version.
40. The Gaelic version, 26, places the miracles allotted to Anglesey on the Isle of Man.
41. Virgil, *Aeneid*, II, 174; III, 26; VII, 78.
42. Although numerous passages in the historical sections read as glosses on DEB, the tabulated format of *Civitates* is unique in this context; both are a poor fit with the otherwise broadly chronological, narrative framework of the HB.
43. The chronological summation in HB, 66 provides a fitting end to the original work, mirroring the outline of the ages of the world in chapters 1 to 6 and its various interim calculations of dates and time (as HB, 28, 30, 31).
44. HB, 56 uses 'Arthur' consistently, even where a genitive is obligatory; in contrast HB, 73 twice offers the genitive (Arthuri); similarly, in HB, 71, Illtud becomes Iltutus.
45. In HB, 49; other than the spurious claim that Cunedda drove the Irish from Dyfed, Gower and Kidwelly, south Wales is not mentioned; nor is Cornwall; the only reference to Brittany is to its foundation.
46. As Lloyd, *The Arthurian Place-Names*, 15; to avoid unnecessary complications, though, for references to *Civitates* and *Mirabilia* I will still use the chapter numbering 66a–75 as used in editions of HB.

328 NOTES to pp. 181–186

47. Dumville, 'Sub-Roman Britain', 177.
48. As Hanning, *Vision of History*, 91–3; Davies, *Wales in the Early Middle Ages*, 205–6.
49. Guy, 'The Origins', 42–5.
50. Derolez, *Runica Manuscripta*, 157–9.
51. Guy, 'The Origins', 51.
52. Lloyd, *A History of Wales*, I, 223.
53. In general, see Hopper, *Medieval Number Symbolism*.
54. He used Gildas, Bede's HE and *Greater Chronicle*, Orosius, Virgil's *Georgics* and *Aeneid*, and works by Prosper, Jerome, Victorius of Aquitaine and Isidore, various 'Patrician' works written in Ireland, a British *Life of Germanus* and a version of the Kentish English origin legend; reference to 'old books of our elders' (HB, 17) confirms his use of a library.
55. HB, 15.
56. HB, 27; probably in this context the oral culture of his own religious circle.
57. Comparable with Asser, two generations later, journeying from St David's to Wessex.
58. As Dumville, 'The Historical Value', 21; Higham, *King Arthur: Myth-Making and History*, 122.
59. This is based on the MGH; Morris introduced slightly different wording.
60. Satan had entered Vortigern's heart in HB, 37; see HB, 32 for the 'wicked king Benlli'; Higham, *King Arthur: Myth-Making and History*, 128–36.
61. Compare HB, 41–2 with Daniel, II, 1–5; WATB, 443.
62. HB, 32–5; I Samuel, XVI; WATB, 451.
63. HB, 34, 47; these are assumed to be Moel Fenlli (or Foel Fenlli), on the Clwydians and Craig Gwrtheyrn in Ceredigion; Woolf, 'Fire from Heaven', sees these passages as evidence for lightning strikes but the non-contemporaneity of this account rather undermines its value as a witness; for use of heavily burned material in building a hill-fort rampart neighbouring Moel Fenlli, see Karl and Butler, *Moel y Gaer*; recognition of similar material might have contributed to such stories; while place-names featuring Benlli are commonest in north-east Wales, there are two also in Monmouthshire, Caerfenlli and Ffynnon Gaer: Grooms, *The Giants of Wales*, 131–9.
64. HB, 27.
65. Ibid., 36, 37, 46.
66. Ibid., 45.
67. As HE, IV, 2.
68. As HB, 36, 57, 63; Larpi, *Prolegomena*, 73; *ambrones* has a dual meaning, as a tribal people of Gaul and (in the singular) in classical Latin as a 'glutton' or 'spendthrift'.
69. HB, 46; see the parallels with DEB, 23, 1.
70. HB, 31, alluding perhaps to the Anglo-Saxon custom of claiming gods as ancestral to their royal families.
71. HB, 65.
72. Here with the sense of 'dragons'.
73. HB, 40–2; that he is 'Christ-like' in this respect is significant.
74. Goffart, 'The Supposedly "Frankish" Table of Nations', 141–4.
75. See Gerberding, *The Rise of the Carolingians*, 13–20.
76. HB, 10–18.
77. Ibid, 22, triggered perhaps by Bede's mistaken depiction of Lucius as a British king in HE, I, 4.
78. DEB, 13.
79. HB, 28.
80. DEB, 23, 2.
81. As HB, 47: Germanus stands on a rock for forty days and nights, then fasts for three days and nights; for parallels see Exodus, XXXIV, 30; Matthew, IV, 2.
82. HB, 55.
83. Ibid., 54.
84. The translation is from Higham, *King Arthur: Myth-Making and History*, 144–5.
85. Ibid., 141–4; Book of Judges, opening lines, terms Joshua *dux bellum*; the 'Vatican' recension of HB has *dux belli*.

86. Gidlow, *Revealing King Arthur*, 147–8.
87. HB, 66.
88. Ibid., 16; this discrepancy arguably resulted from confusion between different dating schemes.
89. For Octa, see Brooks, 'The Creation and Structure of the Kingdom of Kent', 63–4.
90. Counting generations at twenty-five years gives *c.* 14–15, at twenty years gives 18–19.
91. On which he seems to have based chapters 32 to 35, 39 and 47.
92. Brooks, 'The Creation and Structure of the Kingdom of Kent', and 'The English Origin Myth'; Bede had also accessed this story, HE, I, 15; inclusion of the topos of treachery at a banquet in both HB, 46 and Mierow (trans.), *Origins and Deeds*, 135, suggests that this legend was common to barbarian communities across Europe.
93. Hughes, *Celtic Britain in the Early Middle Ages*, 91–100; Dumville, 'On the North British Section'; for recent reappraisal see WATB, 347–58.
94. Ecgfrith's death (in 685) and Cuthbert's (in 687) are the latest 'Northumbrian' events included; chapters 58–60 comprise Kentish, East Anglian and Mercian genealogies which similarly betray the influence of British phonetics but seem to date a generation or so later than the 'northern' materials.
95. Muirchu's *Life* in Hood (ed.), *St Patrick*; Tirechan's *Memorandum*, in Bieler (ed.), *The Patrician Texts*; for the use of later texts, see Dumville, 'The Historical Value', 13.
96. Though Bede (HE, II, 5), working apparently from a version of the same source, made Oct[h]a Hengist's grandson, rather than his son.
97. Zimmer, *Nennius Vindicatus*, 59ff.
98. As proposed first by Chadwick and Chadwick, *The Growth of Literature*, I, 154–5; for the poems, see Koch, *Cunedda, Cynan, Cadwallon, Cynddylan*, 145–8, 188–94.
99. Koch, 'The Celtic Lands', 248.
100. Higham, *King Arthur: Myth-Making and History*, 146; Gidlow, *The Reign of Arthur*, 25.
101. Jones, 'The Early Evolution'.
102. The alternative for Agned in the Vatican recension.
103. Koch, 'The Celtic Lands', 248, adds that battle ten might have read initially Tribruit Abon 'the River Tribruit'.
104. Ibid., 249.
105. The comparator poems do not feature rhyming battle-names ending successive lines, or anything close.
106. Brodeur, 'Arthur, dux bellorum', 253–4.
107. As recognised by Chadwick and Chadwick; see Pearce, *The Kingdom of Dumnonia*, 144, who supposed a 'poem of the kind which were composed from a miscellany of available material probably well after the time of their subject'.
108. For parallels, see Dumville, 'Historia Brittonum', 419.
109. Nine dedications to Garman have been identified, including St Harmon in Gwastedyn (Swansea), and St Garman at Llanarmon Dyffryn Ceiriog (Wrexham) and Llanfechain-ym-Mochnant (Powys); Dumville, 'Sub-Roman Britain', 186, argued that this was an independent Powysian saint, but his 'returning *sua patria*' in HB is easier reconciled with the lost *Life* recognising him as a Gaulish visitor.
110. HB, 50–1.
111. Muirchu's *Life* in Hood (ed.), *St Patrick*, 5–9.
112. WATB, 358.
113. See Maunder (ed.), *The Origins of the Cult of the Virgin Mary*.
114. Ó Carragáin and Thacker, 'Wilfrid in Rome'.
115. Early evidence for the Marian cult in Ireland comes in a hymn written at Iona in the first half of the eighth century; Breeze, *Mary and the Celts*, 1–3.
116. Field, 'Arthur's Battles', 15–17, suggests that this should be read as an interpolation, but it seems integral to the passage; that the issue of translation of *scuit/scuid* comes at precisely the point where we can be most confident of late composition underlines the problems of that line of argument.

117. As Halsall, *Worlds of Arthur*, 168, who also offers a numerical analysis of the text leading to the same conclusion.

118. See Faral, *La Légende Arthurienne*, I, 147–51; Brodeur, 'Arthur, dux bellorum', 250.

119. As Collingwood, 'Arthur's Battles'.

120. As Anscombe, 'Local Names'; Crawford, 'Arthur and his Battles'.

121. Brodeur, 'Arthur, dux bellorum', 250.

122. See, for example, Breeze, 'Arthur's Battle of Badon' and 'The Historical Arthur'.

123. As Skene, *The Four Ancient Books of Wales*, 50; Anscombe, 'Local Names'; Collingwood, 'Arthur's Battles'; Crawford, 'Arthur and his Battles'.

124. Jackson, 'Once Again Arthur's Battles'; Jackson, 'Arthur's Battle of Breguoin'; Jackson, 'The Arthur of History'.

125. HB's *silva Celidonis* is likely to derive, whether directly or indirectly, from Pliny, *Natural History*, IV, 102, which offers *silvae Calidoniae*; Rivet and Smith, *The Place-Names of Roman Britain*, 290, suggest that its geographical meaning was already very loose indeed in the classical period.

126. HB, 66a; Field, 'Gildas and the City of the Legions' proposes York, but this is incompatible with the consistent application to that centre of names derived from *Eburacum*.

127. DEB, 10, 2.

128. HE, II, 2.

129. The nearest river Douglas is a tributary of the Ribble in Lancashire (also called the Asland); Morris, *Age of Arthur*, 112, supposes that Lincolnshire's largest river, the Witham, might have been called Douglas, on the grounds that its ancient name is not known, but this is unalloyed speculation.

130. Jackson, 'Arthur's Battle of Breguoin'; for discussion of the name, see Rivet and Smith, *Place-Names of Roman Britain*, 276–7.

131. Dumville (ed.), *The* Historia Brittonum, 3, *The 'Vatican' Recension*, 27, has *in monte qui nominatur Breguoin ubi illos in fugam uertit, quem nos cat Bregion appellamus* ('on the mountain which is called Breguoin where he turned them in flight, which we call "*cat Bregion*"'); *cat* is modern Welsh *cad*, 'a battle'.

132. See particularly Coates and Breeze, *Celtic Voices: English Places*.

133. Though see ibid., 4, for words of caution, suggesting that many places will not have had 'true' names.

134. As well as the Douglas in West Lancashire, Douglas Water occurs in Scotland as a tributary of the Clyde and in Argyll as a burn flowing into Loch Fyne, and Douglas occurs as a settlement name in Strathclyde, Strathmore and the Isle of Man; apart from the two examples of Glen that Jackson noted, a river Glen is also a tributary of the Welland and there is another in Ireland.

135. As Koch, *Cunedda, Cynan, Cadwallon, Cynddylan*, 176.

136. Perhaps in part in response to the invitation offered by Koch, 'The Celtic Lands', 251; for some of these see Appendix II.

137. HRB, II, 30, 125; III, 115, 143; IX, 146, 81.

138. HB, 67.

139. White, 'Introductory Note'.

140. Alcock, *Arthur's Britain*, 69–71; Morris, *The Age of Arthur*, 112–13; Phillips and Keatman, *King Arthur*, 88; Moffat, *Arthur and the Lost Kingdoms*, 229; Castleden, *King Arthur*, 95; Barber, *King Arthur*, 181–2.

141. See Rivet and Smith, *Place-Names of Roman Britain*, 255–6.

142. Recorded as Baðanceaster in ASC(A,E), 577, and similarly in Anglo-Saxon charters, the earliest being S51 (676 but unreliable), S265 (808 for 757 x 758, authentic).

143. *Bad-* occurs as a personal-name element, as well as a common noun in Old English, meaning a 'pledge'.

144. Ashe, *Camelot and the Vision of Albion*, 81.

145. Goodrich, *King Arthur*, 76, wrongly assuming a linguistic correlation between Badon and Dumbarton.

146. FSTC, 329, on the basis of nothing earlier or more convincing than HRB, IX, 148–9.

147. Ardrey, *Finding Arthur*, 254, noting the presence of the Badden Burn.
148. 'Arthur's 12 Battles in Scotland' (2013), *King Arthur in Scotland* blog; online at https://arthurianscotland.wordpress.com/2013/06/12/arthurs-12-battles-in-Scotland (accessed 5 June 2018).
149. Blake and Lloyd, *The Lost Legend*, 158.
150. Gilbert, *The Holy Kingdom*, 236–42, this low hill (251m) lacks any trace of defences and the name is almost certainly post-medieval.
151. Gidlow, *The Reign of Arthur*, 60–1.
152. Green, *Arthuriana*, 123, noting the Domesday Book name Badeburg.
153. Storr, *King Arthur's Wars*, 94.
154. Anscombe, 'Local Names', 116.
155. Breeze, 'Arthur's Battle of Badon'.
156. Most obviously those based on Dumbarton and in Argyll.
157. DEB, note to 26, 1, on p. 151.
158. E.g. Morris (ed.), *Domesday Book, Hertfordshire*, I, 13.
159. Lepelly, *Dictionnaire Étomologique*, 264: '*suivi du nom de personne germanique*'.
160. Guessing at what copying error has become incorporated (as Anscombe, 'Local Names'; Breeze, 'Arthur's Battle of Badon') opens the door to any number of lines of speculation.
161. For which now see Davies, 'The Battle of Chester'.
162. HE, II, 2, as above; see also AC, 613.
163. Most recently, see Padel, *Arthur in Medieval Welsh Literature*, 4; Green, *Concepts of Arthur*, 62–7.
164. Rowland, *Early Welsh Saga Poetry*, 139, 487; Watts, *Cambridge Dictionary*, 40.
165. The poem is preserved in the fourteenth-century *Book of Taliesin*; Jones, 'The Early Evolution', 3; TYP, 218–19; Green, *Concepts of Arthur*, 62–7, *Arthuriana*, 67–70.
166. Line 49, 'On the strands of Trywruid'.
167. Jackson, 'The Arthur of History', 11; Sims-Williams, 'The Early Welsh Arthurian Poems', 38–46; Green, *Arthuriana*, 60–3.
168. *Book of Taliesin*, XXXVI, line 22.
169. DEB, 25, 3.
170. HB, 41–2.
171. Muirchu, 20, features a similar contest between Patrick and a magician at Tara.
172. HB, 48.
173. HB, 66.
174. *Domesday Book*, 38c, has *Wallope*, which is consistent with an Old English derivation, but see Coates and Breeze, *Celtic Voices*, 272.
175. HB, 43–4
176. Now known only from the HE, the HB and the ASC; Brooks, 'The English Origin Myth'.
177. Derguentid is presumably the River Dart; Episford is generally identified as Aylesford; the ASC likewise offers English-named battles, albeit different ones.
178. ASC(A, E), 455; Bede had already named him and linked him with Hengist but had not characterised him as a general.
179. As Brodeur, 'Arthur, dux bellorum', 243; Halsall, *Worlds of Arthur*, 213.
180. HB, 43 glosses DEB, 23, 4; in HB, 44 *ciulas suas* mirrors DEB, 26 and *muliebriter* reflects ibid., 6, 2; for a general discussion, see Larpi, *Prolegomena*, 70–7; fortunes of war that ebb and flow look back to DEB, 26, 1.
181. The Welsh names appear to be ninth-century rather than earlier; the HB's author failed to realise that the name Thanet is in origin pre-Roman, suggesting that there had been a break in the name-tradition.
182. In common: *contra illos*; *primum bellum*; *flumen*; *secundum bellum*; *quod dicitur*; *tertium bellum*.
183. As during the Irish and Pictish attacks depicted in the pre-Roman period in HB, 15.
184. DEB, 5, 2.
185. HB, 21; note use of the same term, *victor*, of both Claudius and Arthur.
186. Orosius, VII, 6, 10;

187. HB, 19.
188. Orosius, VI, 9, 2–8.
189. Caesar, IV, 21–36; V, 8–23, though Orosius, VI, 7, 2 names Suetonius as his source.
190. For the Saxons on Thanet, see HB, 43.
191. DEB, 3, 1, one of two rivers by which 'luxuries used to come' from the Continent.
192. DEB, 23, 3.
193. HB, 44.
194. HB, 20; the dating should be compared with Jerome, *Chronicon*, 155, 19, Bede, *Greater Chronicle*, 3903, 3952.
195. Caesar, V, 11, 18, 19, 21.
196. Orosius, VI, 9, 6.
197. *Casabellaunus, rex Britannicus*, was interpolated into the Chartres MS, in a chapter that Faral designated [0] (p. 8).
198. Orosius, VII, 5, 5, which was in turn a garbled reading of Suetonius, IV, 44: *Adminio Cynobellini Britannorum regis filio*.
199. Orosius, I, 2, 7, 61, 67, 100, 102.
200. Orosius did not specify any islands by this nomenclature, which seems entirely fabricated.
201. As in Orosius.
202. Ibid., VI, 18, 6–13, based directly or indirectly on Plutarch, IX, *Antony*, 9, 1; 10, 1; 11, 2–3; Dio, XLII, 29, 1; XLIII, 51, 8; Orosius also referred to two earlier men of this name, in III, 22, 12 and V, 17, 10.
203. Unless this is merely an accident of copying.
204. Isidore, IX, 2, 2ff.
205. Ibid., IX, 2, 101; Latin *brutescere* means 'to become brutish'.
206. DEB, 3.
207. His achievements also appear in Orosius, V, 5, 12; the identification was made by Duchesne, 'Nennius Retractatus', 181.
208. As Livy, I, 56.
209. Orosius, II, 5, 1; Jerome, *Chronicon*, 106, 13–19; Bede, *Greater Chronicle*, 3468.
210. HB, 15.
211. HB, 10; Bruce, *The Evolution*, II, 51–3, suggested that it was a mistaken interpretation of the *reges Albanorum* in Italy as relevant to Albion (Britain) that lay behind this.
212. Bartrum, *Early Welsh Genealogical Tracts*, 9, 1, in which Cunedda is Mailcun's (Maelgwyn's) great-grandfather; 10, 3; 13, 32–3; the districts connected with his sons' names are mapped in Koch, *An Atlas for Celtic Studies*, 34.
213. Gunn, 'The Origins', 25.
214. There is perhaps a connection here with Bellinus; see above pp. 197–8.
215. The Harleian genealogies contain several similar, short, northern genealogies: Bartrum, *Early Welsh Genealogical Tracts*, 10, 6–9.
216. See, for example, Lloyd, *History of Wales*, I, 100, 102, 116–20; Collingwood and Myres, *Roman Britain*, 289–90; Alcock, *Arthur's Britain*, 125–9; more recently, see Gruffydd, 'From Gododdin to Gwynedd'; Koch, *Cunedda, Cynan, Cadwallon, Cynddylan*, 70.
217. Chadwick, Studies in the Early British Church, 32–4; Dumville, 'Sub-Roman Britain', 182; Higham, *King Arthur: Myth-Making and History*, 125–6; WATB, 181.
218. Given that Maelgwyn/Maglocunus was a contemporary of Gildas.
219. E.g White, *Britannia Prima*, 57–72; Caernavon was certainly garrisoned into the late fourth century and various coastal installations were constructed and manned during the late Roman period, though not necessarily quite as late as Caernavon.
220. As Mattingly, *An Imperial Possession*, 451; federate Irish settlements in Dyfed and Gwynedd seem at least plausible.
221. As Lloyd, *History of Wales*, I, 116, opting for the beginning of the fifth century; Alcock, *Arthur's Britain*, 127, preferred 383.
222. Nash-Williams, *The Early Christian Monuments*, 92–3, inscription 103, plate IX.
223. WATB, 178–80.

224. Even Lloyd, *History of Wales*, I, 118, considered Cunedda's driving out of the Irish from south Wales 'an unwarranted extension of the original narrative'.
225. As Ibid., 116–17; Kirby, 'British Dynstic History', 92.
226. Aberystwyth, National Library of Wales, Peniarth MS 2; see Koch, *Cunedda, Cynan, Cadwallon, Cynddylan*, 52–95.
227. Suggesting that the genealogist was aware of both the HB and the elegy, and also had access to a short northern genealogy which ended with Cunedda, which he incorporated in its totality in Gwynedd's royal line.
228. As Lloyd, *History of Wales*, I, 118.
229. Koch, *Cunedda, Cynan, Cadwallon, Cynddylan*, 84–9.
230. Carey, *A New Introduction*, 4; see also Todd, *The Irish Version of Nennius*, 10; this is recognised without discussion in Morris's translation.
231. WATB, 181.
232. DEB, 19–21.
233. Sims-Williams, 'Historical Need', 13–14.
234. Higham, *King Arthur: Myth-Making and History*, 125.
235. HE, II, 20.
236. HB, 63; these regnal years are flawed in detail but the list is probably broadly historical: Dumville, 'The Anglian Collection'; Higham, *King Ecgfrith*, 42.
237. See Sims-Williams, 'The Death of Urien'.
238. The obvious candidate is perhaps Whithorn, which was raised to the status of an English diocesan centre shortly before Bede wrote the HE.
239. HB, 57.
240. Compare the opening line of DEB, 26 and HB, 63, third sentence.
241. See Dumville, 'On the North British Section'.
242. HB, 63: 'If anyone wishes to know who baptized them [Edwin, his family and his people], Rum map Urbgen baptized them, and for forty days he did not cease to baptize all the people of the *ambrones* and through his preaching many believed in Christ.'
243. HE, II, 14.
244. Bede, HE, II, 9, has twelve baptised at Pentecost; in HE, II, 14, Paulinus then baptised 'a vast number of the common people' (*plebe perplurima*) over thirty-six days; the numerical correlations are inexact but close enough not to be coincidental.
245. Chadwick, 'The Conversion'; Corning, 'The Baptism'.
246. HE, I, 22.
247. Higham, *King Ecgfrith*, 59–61; that this was a 'Roman' conversion may have added to its significance to the HB's audience.
248. DEB, 23, 3; Woolf, 'An Interpolation'.
249. Bede's dating of the *adventus* to the mid-fifth century might suggest that this was added to the text *c.* 750, though the HB's chronology might favour a closing date closer to 728; Woolf argued for the envelope 672–747.
250. However inaccurately; HB, 28.
251. The preferred option of Dark, 'A Famous Arthur'.
252. I.e. text B1, Koch (ed.), *The Gododdin*, 26–7.
253. Orosius, I, 82.
254. HE, II, 9; Woolf, 'The Early History', 332, assumes 'a thriving Christian community among the Britons' on early medieval Man.
255. One has the name Guriat carved on the side; Merfyn's father is thought to have born that name but this carving dates *c.* 1100, so is unlikely to refer to the ninth-century figure; see Kermode, *Manx Crosses*, 75, 121–3; my thanks to Dr Ross Trench-Jellicoe for his advice on the dating.
256. See Mac Cana, 'Ireland and Wales in the Middle Ages'.
257. Derolez, 'Dubthach's Cryptogram'; Sims-Williams, *Irish Influence*, 29; a cryptogram is a simple substitution cypher.
258. Scowcroft, 'Leabhar Gabhála – Part II'; Carey, *A New Introduction*, 3.

259. HB, 14.
260. Although this contact could have been earlier than 825–6 so could have occurred outside north Wales.
261. HB, 57, 61–5.
262. Jackson, 'Arthur's Battle of Breguoin'.
263. As Alcock, *Arthur's Britain*, 73; Bromwich, Jarman and Roberts, 'Introduction', 5; Breeze, 'The Historical Arthur'.
264. Mac Cana, 'Ireland and Wales in the Middle Ages', 36; TYP, 264.
265. Dooley, 'Arthur of the Irish', 18.
266. Green, *Dictionary*, 139; for further parallels between Irish and Welsh literature of relevance to Arthur, see Carey, 'Bran Son of Febal'.
267. ÓBroin, 'Classical Source'.
268. Mac Cana, 'Mongán Mac Fiachna', 125–38.
269. Cavendish, *King Arthur and the Grail*, 31; Nagy, 'Arthur and the Irish', 118.
270. CI, 600, naming the brother erroneously as Eanfrith (the name of Æthelfrith's eldest son); HE, I, 34, names the battle as Degsastan and the brother as Theobald, but not his killer.
271. Chnychwr, son of Nes (Conchobar mac Nesa), Fercos, son of Poch (Fergus mac Róich), Lluber Beuthach (Lóegaire Búedach) and Chonul Bernach (Conall Cernach); another, Chubert, son of Naere (Cú Roí Dáiri) was Munster-based.
272. CaO, lines 178–80; see Mac Cana, 'Ireland and Wales in the Middle Ages', 34–6, for discussion.
273. Though Sims-Williams, *Irish Influence*, 185–7, is probably right to see these heroes as late additions.
274. Todd, *The Irish Version*.
275. Nagy, 'Arthur and the Irish', 117.
276. Macalister (ed.), *Two Irish Arthurian Romances*.
277. As Ardery, *Finding Arthur*; Moffatt, *Arthur and the Lost Kingdoms*; Breeze, 'The Historical Arthur and Sixth-Century Scotland'.
278. HB, 63.
279. Ibid., 40.

Chapter 7 A British Arthur: Starting the Tradition

1. Padel, 'The Early Welsh Arthurian Poems', 61.
2. HRB, XI, line 92.
3. Ibid., VI, lines 369–414; HE, I, 17.
4. HB, 37; HRB, VI, lines 339–68.
5. Ibid., lines 399–433.
6. Ibid., II, lines 262–86.
7. Ibid., IV, line 37.
8. *Contra* Russell, *Arthur*, 38, who goes on to postulate that this was an alternative form of the Roman name of Canterbury, but Geoffrey used Dorobernia of that (IX, line 337), from the Romano-British Durovernum Cantiacorum; Russell's theory that HB and HRB reflect rival traditions derived from the Catuvellauni and Trinovantes of Caesar's time is as implausible as it is unprovable and should be set aside.
9. As Jones (ed.), *Brut y Tywysogyon*, 1, which opens in 681 with Cadwaladr's retirement to Rome and 'the Britons lost the crown of kingship, and the Saxons obtained it, as Myrddin had prophesied ...'
10. HRB, III, line 367; Heli is the father of Cassibellaunus, placing him in the same historical period as the HB's Bellinus.
11. Orosius, II, 19, based on Livy, V, 38.
12. See, for example, Koch, 'The Celtic Lands', 288–91.
13. Compare with Dolabella, for example, whose 'British' incarnation was vulnerable to the simple test of reading Orosius.

14. As Loomis, *Wales and the Arthurian Legend*, 179–220.
15. WoM, I, I, 8; the translation is based on that of Mynors, Thomson and Winterbottom, but is more literal.
16. It is unclear whether or not William had the fluency in Welsh to allow him access to such tales without an interpreter, but on balance this seems improbable; my thanks to Professor Rod Thomson for his advice.
17. See, for example, Davies, 'Performing Culhwch ac Olwen'.
18. As, for example, Loomis, *The Grail*.
19. See pp. 218–22 (below) and 142–3 and 104–9 (above) respectively.
20. Chrétien de Troyes, *Lancelot*, line 32.
21. The Modena inscription, dated *c.* 1120–40, names Winlogee (Guinevere), Mardoc (possibly Melwas) and Burmaltus (obscure, but perhaps from the same stem as Chrétien's Bademaguiz) inside a tower besieged by Artus *de Bretania* (Arthur) and Isdernus (obscure but perhaps originating as Aeternus, or similar), while Carrado (Caradoc) fights Galvaginus (Gawain), Galvariun (perhaps a doublet of Gawain) and Che (Kay/Cei); the ultimate source is likely to have been Breton.
22. Roques, *Les Romans*, line 6235; WRdB, lines 9232; 8828, 9130, 9136; 9253; 10205ff.
23. As Loegria, which occurs eleven times in all; for its origin see Coates, 'Welsh *Loegr* "England"'.
24. Roques, *Les Romans*, lines 1858, 1986, 3485, 3504, 5804, 5808, 5811, 6721, 2480, 1859, 5780, 968, 6721, respectively.
25. As, for example, *Disnadaron* (line 2751), probably from Welsh *dinas* and 'd'Aron', so 'Aaron's Castle'; LCdG(P), English translation, 518, footnote 13.
26. In general, see West, *An Index*.
27. LCdG(P), translation, 207; Kibler's edition of the text offers *Li rois Artus et tenut ot / cort molt riche a Chamaalot*; it should be noted, though, that Camelot does not occur in every manuscript, casting some doubt even on its place in the archetype.
28. Bullock-Davies, 'Chrétien de Troyes and England', 58–9; Morris, 'Aspects of Time and Place'.
29. HRB, XI, line 46; WRdB, line 13253; see discussion in Lacy, 'Camelot', in TNAE, 66–7.
30. This is, of course, additionally the second element of the name Lancelot, for which Chrétien was also responsible.
31. As, for example, Darrah, *The Real Camelot*.
32. Lloyd, *The Arthurian Place-Names*, 43, very properly considers it 'unlocatable'.
33. Biddle, 'The Making of the Round Table', suggests the early thirteenth century for its manufacture.
34. Morris, *The Age of Arthur*, 138.
35. Storr, *King Arthur's Wars*, 29, 92, though he later (p. 95) suggests that it may have been Cambridge, attracted presumably by the first syllable.
36. At SE085175; Keegan, *Pennine Dragon*, 66–9, and see report in *The Times*, 20 December 2016.
37. Hunter, Manby and Spaul, 'Recent Excavations'.
38. Hobson, Clay and Brown, *The Romans in Huddersfield*.
39. Including Ardrey, *Finding Arthur* (though he is more interested in Camelon as the site of Camlann), Carroll, *Arturius*, Stirling, *The King Arthur Conspiracy*.
40. Gilbert, *The Holy Kingdom*, 228–9; Moffat, *Arthur and the Lost Kingdoms*, 235.
41. Viroconium (Wroxeter) was proposed by Phillips and Keatman, *King Arthur* and accommodated in the 2017 film *King Arthur: Excalibur Rising*; the place-name is utterly dissimilar and evidence for reoccupation at Wroxeter is now considered less clear-cut than this thesis requires – see Fulford, 'Wroxeter'.
42. As his *Assertio Inclytissimi Arturii*, published in 1544, in answer to Polydore Vergil's critique; Hay (ed.), *The Anglica Historia*, xxix.
43. Smith (ed.), *The Itinerary of John Leland*, I, 151.
44. Alcock, *Cadbury Castle, Somerset*, 5.

45. See Alcock, *'By South Cadbury is that Camelot...'*; there is another river Cam at Cambridge, and the Camel in Cornwall which Geoffrey and Wace apparently had in mind when locating Camlann there.
46. As ibid.; Gidlow, *Revealing King Arthur*, 61–73.
47. Toolis and Bowles, *The Lost Dark Age Kingdom of Rheged*.
48. 'Mote of Mark', National Record of the Historic Environment: Canmore; online at https://canmore.org.uk/site/64911/mote-of-mark (accessed 5 June 2018); the appearance here of the Cornish name Mark is a good example of the geographical fluidity characteristic of the Arthurian legend.
49. The approach adopted by Chambers, *Arthur of Britain*, 184–5, remains among the more sensible; see also Adams, *In the Land of Giants*, 212–19; Lloyd, *The Arthurian Place-Names*, 92–3.
50. As Goodrich, *King Arthur*, 35, equating Camelot with Carlisle; Moffat, *Arthur and the Lost Kingdoms*, 235, *The Sea Kingdoms*, 176, preferred Roxburgh; Ardrey, *Finding Arthur*, 189–99, suggests Dunadd.
51. The Holy Grail, for example, plays a prominent role in FSTC; Anderson, in KAIA, 137–40, suggests that Camelot originated in Greek literature.
52. Faral, *La Légende Arthurienne*, III, 44–50; the 'B' and 'C' versions are thirteenth century; for these and others, Dumville, 'The Welsh Latin Annals'; *Annales Cambriae*.
53. Hughes, 'The Welsh Latin Chronicles'; for the Clonmacnoise Annals, see Grabowski and Dumville, *Chronicles and Annals*.
54. Guy, 'The Origins', 27; that its author probably knew the HB was pointed out by Brodeur, 'Arthur, dux bellorum', 252.
55. For discussion, see Wallis, *Bede: The Reckoning of Time*, xlix–lv.
56. Dumville, 'The Welsh Latin Annals'.
57. Though such may have resulted from copying as opposed to original compilation.
58. I have used Morris's schema for the dates since that is widely accepted.
59. Wallis, *Bede: The Reckoning of Time*, 121–2, 333–4; Leo's papacy is recorded in Irish chronicles.
60. Guy, 'The Origins', 38–9.
61. AC, 516, *Bellum Badonis, in quo Arthur portavit crucem Domini nostril Jhesu Christi tribus diebus et tribus noctibus in humeros suos et Brittones victores sunt*; 537, *Gueith Camlann, in qua Arthur et Medraut corruerunt, et mortalitas in Brittannia et in Hibernia fuit*; the translations are from Higham, *King Arthur: Myth-Making and History*, 198–9.
62. See, for example, Alcock, *Arthur's Britain*, 48ff.; Ashe, 'Annales Cambriae'; Breeze, 'Arthur's Battles'.
63. Alcock, *Arthur's Britain*, 40; unfortunately this has often been repeated, as Adams, *In the Land of Giants*, 214.
64. Faral, *La Légende Arthurienne*, III, 51; Bartram, *Early Welsh Genealogical Tracts*, 10, 2.
65. See discussion in Higham, *King Arthur: Myth-Making and History*, 213.
66. Faral, *La Légende Arthurienne*, I, 222; Higham, *King Arthur: Myth-Making and History*, 201; Koch, 'The Celtic Lands', 252–3.
67. Luke, XXIII, 26.
68. Which may, of course, have influenced William of Malmesbury, above, though he is not otherwise known to have had access to the AC.
69. 'Three days and three nights' derives ultimately from Jonah, I, 17, but was used in HB, 63.
70. Owain and his brother lost the battle of Carno in 951 to the armies of Gwynedd and were thereafter vulnerable to northern Welsh campaigning.
71. For discussion, see Jones, 'The Early Evolution', 5; Dumville, 'Gildas and Maelgwyn: Problems of Dating'.
72. As suggested by Wiseman, 'The Derivation of the Date of the Badon Entry'.
73. Charles-Edwards suggests that one may be a doublet of the other: CI, 536, footnote 6.
74. In the earliest instance a gap of seventy-plus years could imply knowledge passed on via a grandparent.

75. As Breeze, 'The Battle of Camlan and Camelford, Cornwall', though the Cornish location remains popular with novelists, as Morpurgo, *Arthur High King of Britain*.
76. As Crawford, 'Arthur and his Battles', 289–90; Jackson, 'Once again Arthur's Battles'; Breeze, 'The Historical Arthur'; early scholars identified Camboglanna with Birdoswald but Castlesteads is now preferred: Rivet and Smith, *Place-Names of Roman Britain*, 261–2, 293–4; Wilmott, *Birdoswald*, 14.
77. The name of this Hadrianic Wall fort is known today from the Rudge Cup, the Amiens *Patera* and *Ravenna Cosmography*, none of which are likely to have been accessible in tenth-century Britain.
78. *Bellum Armterid, c.* 573 ('The battle of Arfderydd'), generally identified as Arthuret (Cumbria), is the earliest; see Miller, 'The Commanders at Arthuret'; Phythian-Adams, *Land of the Cumbrians*, 49.
79. At SH854121; today there are two settlements, Camlan-uchaf and Camlan Isaf ('Higher-Camlan' and 'Lower Camlan'); Sims-Williams, 'The Early Welsh Arthurian Poems', 51; Gidlow, *The Reign of Arthur*, 81; Lloyd, *Arthurian Place-Names*, 193.
80. Miller, 'Date-Guessing and Pedigrees', suggested the last quarter of the sixth century; counting back twenty-five-year generations from 954 might suggest a date nearer 625.
81. Faral, *La Légende Arthurienne*, III, 58–62; the first six (Levens included) are *miracula*, giving way to *mirabilia* for the next five; the second 'Arthurian' wonder is then introduced as a *miraculum* with the next, in Ceredigion, a *mirabilis*. Those set in Anglesey are then *miracula*, while the Irish pair at the close use neither formula.
82. There are today two lochs named Leven, one in Fife, one in Lorn; if this was not part of the original text then it was perhaps inserted at the top of the opening page, then incorporated by a copyist. However, it begins with the same formula as the remaining miracles and starts the numbered sequence, suggesting that its inclusion occurred before the core of the text became set in its current format.
83. HB, 70; unlike the remainder, this employs neither of the formuli *aliud miraculum/mirabile est* ... and its brevity, consisting of only seventeen words, suggests a late marginal or interlinear gloss which has become incorporated into the text in the process of copying.
84. Which were relocated to the Isle of Man in the Gaelic translation; Todd (ed.), *The Irish Version*, 25.
85. Morris follows Mommsen in treating the *Mirabilia* as section VII of the *Historia*, so as chapters 67–76; likewise, Guy, 'The Origins', 21, sees the AC and genealogies as interpolations.
86. Padel, *Arthur in Medieval Welsh Literature*, 7, termed it 'an appendix'; Lloyd, *The Arthurian Place-Names*, 15, argues for a different author.
87. He was familiar with a miracle of St Illtud and claimed to have tested two of his stories personally, one in Gwent (HB, 72) and another in Archenfield (ibid., 73).
88. Relating to Lough Leane and Lough Neagh respectively; these probably derived from a separate source which has not been thoroughly accommodated.
89. HB, 73; translation from Higham, *King Arthur: Myth-Making and History*, 87.
90. CaO, lines 1057–204.
91. CaO, lxvii.
92. Translation from Higham, *King Arthur: Myth-Making and History*, 89; Faral read Anir for Amr.
93. A tributary of the Wye.
94. At SO495301 and SO494296 respectively; Padel, 'The Nature of Arthur', 3–4.
95. Tatlock, 'The English Journey of the Laon Canons', 4–6, 8–10.
96. See Dumville, 'The *Liber Floridus*', 107; Padel, 'The Nature of Arthur', 4–7.
97. See Padel, *Arthur in Medieval Welsh Literature*, 67, who points out that this should probably have been Kadair Arthur; Caer Arthur translates as 'Arthur's castle'.
98. Roberts, 'Safle Cerrig Arthur', 7, 53.
99. As Chambers, *Arthur of Britain*, 183–93

100. Lloyd, *The Arthurian Place-Names*, 159–63.
101. Grooms, *The Giants of Wales*, 114–28, offers around sixty-five examples; see also Green, *Arthuriana*, 101–15.
102. As Padel, 'The Nature of Arthur'; Green, *Arthuriana*, 91–105.
103. At SS49139055; Grooms, *The Giants of Wales*, 115; Lloyd, *The Arthurian Place-Names*, 190; this is an early Bronze Age tomb.
104. At SH555648; Grooms, *The Giants of Wales*, 127; this is, again, an early Bronze Age burial site.
105. At SX12987765; suggested dates run from the Neolithic to the Middle Ages.
106. Lloyd, *The Arthurian Place-Names*, 171.
107. Grooms, *The Giants of Wales*, 118–26, listing thirty-one examples.
108. Such are likely to include Loch Arthur (Dumfriesshire), Arthur's Craigs (Lanarkshire) and Arthurshiels Farm (Biggar).
109. Curtis, *The Romance of Tristan*.
110. Banks and Binns (eds and trans.), *Gervase of Tilbury*, II, 12.
111. Ibid., 17.
112. Perhaps the best-known example today is associated with the ancient copper mines on Alderley Edge (Cheshire), popularised by Alan Garner in *The Weirdstone of Brisingamen* but known from the late eighteenth century (the king is very 'Arthur-like' but not explicitly named in the earliest version extant); comparable stories are associated *inter alia* with South Cadbury, Eildon Hill (Scottish Borders) and Craig-y-Dinas (Snowdonia).
113. Evans, *The Death of Kings*, 147–73; the kings involved include such famous names as Charlemagne, Frederick Barbarossa and Frederick II.
114. It stands outside the rebuilt Exmewe Hall, currently a branch of Barclays Bank, and on present evidence is used mostly to stub out cigarettes and discard drinks cans.
115. There is an English summary of this passage in TYP, 409–10, which is the source of my quotations; see also Lloyd, *The Arthurian Place-Names*, 94–8.
116. The area around Corwen in the upper Dee valley.
117. I have assumed that it was the Caerwys in Clwyd (formerly Flintshire) that was intended, not that in Powys (formerly Montgomeryshire), which was unrecognisable as a town by the sixteenth century (Soulsby, *The Towns*, 93–5).
118. Ibid., 232, identifies the earlier settlement as around Well Street (formerly Welsh Street, now Stryd-Y-Ffynnon).
119. That it was the site of an *eisteddfod* in 1523 may also have attracted Elis's attention.
120. Hunter, 'Taliesin at the Court of Henry VIII'.
121. VGildae2, 1, 5.
122. Named *Alcluith* by Bede; HE, I, 1; 12.
123. VGildae1, 1–2.
124. Higham, *The English Conquest*, 90–117; Dark, *Civitas to Kingdom*, 258–66; for the alternative identification of Arecluta as Arclid (Cheshire), see Breeze, 'Where was Gildas Born?', but Arclid is very unlikely ever to have been the capital of a 'region' in the central Middle Ages (it certainly was not in 1066) and is otherwise explicable by reference to the Old Scandinavian personal name Arnkell/Arnketill: Dodgson, *The Place-Names of Cheshire*, II, 264–5; there can be no real doubt that this Breton author intended the Clyde valley.
125. Grooms, *The Giants of Wales*, 150–1, though these may have originated in the generic term rather than the personal name.
126. CaO, lines 647, 1016, 1018, 1228, 1232; his sons are also listed, lines 206–13.
127. TYP, 201, triad 81.
128. As *Bonedd y Saint*, in Bartrum, *Early Welsh Genealogical Tracts*, 51–67, at 63; three other sons of Caunus were also considered holy, Mailocus, Allecus and Egreas: VGildae1, 2.
129. These rivers are indistinguishable in early texts.

130. *Contra* Morris's attempt to reconcile the evidence, supposing, in *The Age of Arthur*, 124, that King Caw was 'transported [from the north] to Powys, in his son's early childhood, about 500'.

131. Blake and Lloyd, *The Lost Legend of Arthur*, 235–6.

132. As claims made by Martyn Jones, MP for Clwyd South, reported on the BBC, 26 July 2002.

133. A problem raised repeatedly from the late twelfth century through to the twentieth.

134. VGildae2, 10.

135. National Library of Wales Peniarth 1; LDC; damage limits the number of lines which are extant.

136. *Pa Gur*, lines 1–4.

137. Sims-Williams, 'The Early Welsh Arthurian Poems', 38.

138. *Pa Gur*, lines 20–28.

139. Ibid., line 47.

140. Ibid., lines 30–33; compare the 960 men in HB, 56; 'nine score' also occurs in the last line of surviving text.

141. Padel, *Arthur in Medieval Welsh Literature*, 15.

142. Bromwich, 'Celtic Elements in Arthurian Romance', 45.

143. Green, *Arthuriana*, 61.

144. Bollard, 'Arthur in the Early Welsh Tradition'; Rowland, *Early Welsh Saga Poetry*, 241, suggests the ninth to the eleventh century, Padel, 'The Early Welsh Arthurian Poems', 46, offers 'early twelfth century or before'.

145. Roberts, 'Rhai o Gerddi'; Rowland, *Early Welsh Saga Poetry*, 240–2, 457–61, 504–5.

146. Ibid., 240.

147. Lapidge and Herren, *Aldhelm: the Prose Works*, 140–3, 155–60; Yorke, *Wessex*, 16; Probert, 'New Light'.

148. ASC(A), 710.

149. Bartrum, *Early Welsh Genealogical Tracts*, 45; the name also occurs in TYP, 14.

150. Padel, 'The Early Welsh Arthurian Poems', 46; *Arthur in Medieval Welsh Literature*, 47.

151. Padel, 'The Early Welsh Arthurian Poems', 47; Lloyd, *The Arthurian Place-Names*, 63.

152. Padel, 'The Early Welsh Arthurian Poems', 47, offers a slightly different translation, with detailed discussion.

153. Rowland, *Early Welsh Saga Poetry*, 242.

154. Padel, 'The Early Welsh Arthurian Poems', 47; a parallel is provided by the *Moliant Cadwallon*, where Cadwallon is termed *ymher*.

155. *Contra* Morris, *The Age of Arthur*, 104–5.

156. Aberystwyth, National Library of Wales, MS Peniarth 2; the title is written in a fourteenth-century hand but not directly evidenced within the text.

157. PA, 53, 57; Padel, *Arthur in Medieval Welsh Literature*, 34; Haycock, *Legendary Poems*, 434, favours a late date.

158. Padel, *Arthur in Medieval Welsh Literature*, 34.

159. See, for example, Carey, 'A British Myth of Origins?', 37; Higley, 'The Spoils of Annwn: Taliesin and Material Poetry'.

160. PA, 62, lines 29–34.

161. Sims-Williams, 'The Early Welsh Arthurian Poems'.

162. HB, 13.

163. Koch, 'The Celtic Lands', 257.

164. CaO, xviiff.

165. Ibid.; the texts date to *c.* 1350 and 1382–1410, respectively.

166. Ibid., lxxvii–lxxii; Sims-Williams, *Irish Influence*, 2; Green, *Arthuriana*, 63; for the suggestion that its inception belongs to the early tenth century, see Knight, *Arthurian Literature*, 31–5; Sturzer, 'The Purpose' prefers a date pre-1150.

167. CaO, xxvi, lxxxi–ii.

168. Ibid., xxvi.

169. Bromwich and Evans suggest that this may owe something to Geoffrey of Monmouth: CaO, xxvii; the translation here is that of Jones and Jones.
170. The list has clearly grown in the telling; Bromwich and Evans suggest that there could originally have been as few as three.
171. Padel, *Arthur in Medieval Welsh Literature*, 17.
172. E.g., Sims-Williams, *Irish Influence*, 167–73.
173. CaO, xxvi; Piquemal, '"Culhwch and Olwen": A Structured Portrayal of Arthur?'.
174. CaO, lxxixff.
175. HB, 73; the story is also paralleled in Irish.
176. CaO, lines 1057–60.
177. CaO, line 294: Gwilenhin.
178. TYP, lxvii; Bromwich's introduction provides by far the best available insight to the Triads; what follows is little more than a summary.
179. The later triad 85 substitutes Caerleon, presumably under the influence of the Galfridian tradition.
180. The name occurs also in *Pa Gur*, line 76.
181. This is the only one of the triads in Peniarth MS 16 to have substituted *llys Arthur* for *Ynys Preidein*.
182. Figures of the fifth and sixth centuries.
183. Variously dated to the seventh or eighth centuries; Taylor (ed.), *The Life of St Samson of Dol*; Flobert, *La Vie Ancienne de Saint Samson*, 111, suggests the mid-eighth century.
184. Written at Ruys, in southern Brittany; Williams (ed.), *Gildas*, 322, dated it to the late ninth century though it is dated internally to 1008.
185. Henken, *Traditions of the Welsh Saints*, 301–6.
186. *Vita Sancti Cadoci*, in VSB, XI, 24–141, preface.
187. Ibid., 22.
188. *Serpens* can mean a snake, a devil, or the devil.
189. *Vita Prima Sancti Carantoci*, in VSB, XL, 142–7, chapters 4–5.
190. Padel, 'The Nature of Arthur', 8.
191. *Vita Sancti Illtuti*, in VSB, XII, 194–233, chapter 2.
192. HRB, XI, line 601.
193. Williams (ed.), *Gildas*, 390–413, chapters 5–6.
194. VGildae2, 10, 14; this is yet another false etymology: the Welsh *Ynisgutrin* derives from *ynys* (island) and the personal name Gutrin, earlier Vitrinus.
195. HB, 13.
196. Which is almost certainly the *Historia Britannica* to which it refers, *contra* Pace, 'Athelstan "Twist-Beard"'.
197. De La Borderie, *Histoire de Bretagne*, II, 525, excerpted by Chambers, *Arthur of Britain*, 241–3.
198. PL, CLVI, 983: *De Miraculis S. Mariae Laudunensis*, II, 15–16; for a discussion, see Yarrow, *Saints and their Communities*, 75–99.
199. The 'oven' may be that noted in 1240 on Dartmoor and since interpreted as an early tin-smelting furnace; Padel, 'The Nature of Arthur', 5.
200. Berard, 'King Arthur'.
201. Padel, 'Where was Middle Cornish Spoken?'.
202. Padel, 'Evidence for Oral Tales', 130.
203. Ditmas, 'Breton Settlers in Cornwall', 35.
204. See more generally, Loomis, 'The Oral Diffusion'; Padel, 'The Nature of Arthur', 11.
205. For discussion, see Padel, 'The Early Welsh Arthurian Poems', 49–51.
206. Tatlock, 'The English Journey of the Laon Canons'.
207. As Ashe, 'A Certain Very Ancient Book'.
208. Goodrich, *King Arthur*, 41.
209. Who seems to have taken over a body of tales earlier centred on a northern figure called Lailoken, following this material reaching Wales and entering the common pool of Welsh storytelling in the central Middle Ages.

210. Bell, 'Merlin as Historian'.
211. As Chambers, *Arthur of Britain*, 57: 'We are in the environment of a Norman ecclesiastic, rather than that of a remote Celt.'
212. As in the prominence of Caerleon, which had been central to the Welsh kingdom of Gwent but was now in a region dominated by the Normans and their castles; Howell, 'Roman Past'; Rouse, 'Reading Ruins'.
213. Knight, *Arthurian Literature*, 38–67.
214. See, for example, Evans, 'Cultural Contacts'.
215. Tatlock, *The Legendary History of Britain*, 7–84, 91.
216. Pace, 'Geoffrey of Monmouth', 47–8.
217. Tatlock, *The Legendary History of Britain*, 117, 124–5, 132, 143, 146.
218. Pace, 'Geoffrey of Monmouth', 53.
219. Goodrich, *King Arthur*, 6, 67, 57, 42, respectively.
220. Despite the case made by Pace, 'Athelstan "Twist-Beard"' for a tenth-century Breton original.
221. For an excellent discussion, see Echard, *Arthurian Narrative*, 31–67.
222. Jankulak, *Geoffrey of Monmouth*, 4; for his use of Gildas and the HB, see Wright, 'Geoffrey of Monmouth'.
223. Williams, 'Brittany and the Arthurian Legend', 262; Fulton, 'History and Myth', 50.
224. Dumville, 'Writers, Scribes and Readers in Brittany'; McKenna, 'The Breton Literary Tradition'; Gwara, 'A Possible Arthurian Epitome'.
225. Bruce, *The Evolution*, I, 20.
226. Jankulak, *Geoffrey of Monmouth*, 36; this work, later included in *The Mabinogion*, was probably circulating prior to HRB's translation into Welsh.
227. Here 'Maximianus'; HRB, V, line 202ff.
228. Ibid., X, lines 95ff.
229. CaO, xxviii.
230. Grooms, *The Giants of Wales*, 214–18.
231. HRB, VIII, lines 441–536; XI, lines 81–4.

Chapter 8 'Fire', 'Smoke' and 'Highland Mist'

1. James, *Britain in the First Millennium*, 100
2. Summarising views expressed by Chambers, *Arthur of Britain*; Jackson, *Language and History*, 116; Jackson, 'The Arthur of History'; Jones, 'The Early Evolution'; Charles-Edwards, 'The Arthur of History'; Halsall, *Worlds of Arthur*, viii; Lupack, *The Oxford Guide*, 5; for its inception, see Freeman, *Old English History*, 35–6: 'Most likely there was such a man, but we can tell nothing about him for certain'.
3. See Silverberg, *The Realm of Prester John*.
4. HB, 56.
5. The same thought processes were arguably at work as had propelled Ambrosius Aurelianus into a form of high-kingship already in the HB.
6. Loomis, *Wales and the Arthurian Legend*, 208–13; for a recent survey of Norman penetration, see Brown, *Mercenaries to Conquerors*.
7. The second, in a floor mosaic within Otranto Cathedral (Italy), dates to the 1160s, when this area lay within the Norman Kingdom of Naples.
8. From Ailred of Rievaulx in rather coded terms, very openly from William of Newburgh, who Gransden, *Historical Writing*, I, 264–5, notes had 'mastered the principles of historical criticism'; for Gerald of Wales's mockery of the HRB's truth claims, see GoW, I, 5.
9. As ASC; WoM, both looking back to HE.
10. HRB, XI, line 597.
11. Fulton, 'History and Myth'.
12. Bruce, *The Evolution*, I, 23; Dumville, 'Sub-Roman Britain', 175.
13. HRB, X, lines 74–104.
14. See, for example, Faletra, *Wales and the Medieval Colonial Imagination*.

15. See, for example, Marx (ed.), *Gesta Normannorum Ducum*.
16. Gransden, *Historical Writing*, I, 477–8, 453.
17. As Knight, *Arthurian Literature*, xiv.
18. As Maier, *The Celts*, 211.
19. As Green, *Edward the Black Prince*, 81.
20. In 1485; Spisak and Matthews (eds), *Caxton's Malory*; Caxton was an Arthurian enthusiast who had already printed the HRB and a version of the *Brut* in *The Chronicles of England*.
21. Gairdner (ed.), *Memorials of King Henry VII*, 9–11; Anglo, *Images*, 40–53; Higham, *King Arthur, Myth-Making and History*, 234–5; the prince pre-deceased his father, dying in 1502.
22. For the merging of the 'Matter of Britain' and the 'Matter of England', see Davies, *The Matter of Britain*.
23. See, for example, Ianziti, *Writing History in Renaissance Italy*.
24. The culmination of this process is generally identified with the work of Leopold von Ranke in nineteenth-century Germany.
25. William Caxton, 'Preface', Malory, I; the quote is from the modernised text offered by Strachey, *Le Morte Darthur*, 1; for the original, see Spisak and Matthews (eds), *Caxton's Malory*, 1, lines 31–4.
26. The *Anglica Historia*, written 1512–13; Hay (ed.), *The Anglica Historia*.
27. See discussion by Carley, 'Polydore Vergil'.
28. Rastell, *The Pastyme of People*, ed. Dibdin.
29. Hay (ed.), *The Anglica Historia*, xxxv; Lloyd, *The Arthurian Place-Names*, 91–2.
30. Including Thomas Hughes, *The Misfortunes of Arthur* (1587), Edmund Spenser, *Faerie Queen* (1590), Shakespeare's *King Lear* (1606) and *Cymbeline* (*c.* 1609) and John Dryden's *King Arthur or the British Worthy* (1691).
31. For a more detailed discussion, see Higham, *King Arthur: Myth-Making and History*, 239–66.
32. See, for example, Hume, *The History of England*, I, 20, proposing a 'prince of the Silures'; Turner, *History of the Anglo-Saxons*, III, chapter 3, similarly opted for Glamorganshire.
33. Ritson, *The Life of King Arthur*; Dickinson, *King Arthur in Cornwall*.
34. For the Campbells's interest in Arthur, see Gillies, 'Arthur in Gaelic Tradition'.
35. Stuart-Glennie, *Arthurian Localities*; Skene, *The Four Ancient Books*, 50–1.
36. Kemble, *The Saxons in England*, I, 3.
37. See, for example, De la Borderie, *L'Historia Britonum*.
38. As Macaulay, *History of England*, I, 3; Wright, *The Celt*, 393; Rhŷs, *Studies in the Arthurian Legend*.
39. As Freeman, 'The Mythical and Romantic Elements'.
40. Ritson, *The Life of King Arthur*; Stevenson, *Nennii Historia Brittonum*.
41. As Stuart-Glennie, *Arthurian Localities*, Skene, *Celtic Scotland*.
42. Bryden, 'All Dressed Up'.
43. Simpson, *Camelot Regained*.
44. The starting point is Poulson, 'Arthurian Legend in Fine and Applied Art'.
45. The sequence was still ongoing at his death in 1864.
46. Including William Morris and Edward Burnes-Jones.
47. Morris, ' "Recalled to Life" '.
48. Girould, *The Return to Camelot*.
49. New editions were published in 1893–94 (illustrated by Aubrey Beardsley), 1897 and 1903.
50. Twain, *A Connecticut Yankee*.
51. As Dickens, *A Child's History*, originally serialised in *Household Words*, 1851–53.
52. In particular converting Guinevere's infidelity with Lancelot to a 'pure' (i.e. non-sexual) affection.
53. As Richmond, 'King Arthur'.
54. Worryingly, this was identified by David Cameron in 2010 as his favourite book as a child.

55. Collections of stories extracted from Malory were also popular, as Macleod, *The Book*, published in 1908 and reprinted for the ninth time in 1946.

56. Seen in its most extreme form in the works of Houston Stewart Chamberlain.

57. Zimmer, *Nennius Vindicatus*, 59ff; for a contemporary critique, see Duchesne, 'Nennius Retractus'.

58. Zimmer, 'Review'.

59. MGH, *Chronica Minora, IV, V, VI, VII*, 3, 199–201; this was the first edition since that of Stevenson in 1838, and the first to take systematic account of the numerous different recensions, though the result is highly confusing.

60. Anscombe, 'Local Names'; he proposed that Badon should be identified as Aconbury (Herefordshire).

61. Bruce, *The Evolution*, I, 3.

62. Ibid., I, 4, 9–10.

63. Chambers, *Arthur of Britain*, 169; this well-researched, thoughtful work represented a dramatic departure from his normal interests.

64. Faral, *La Légende Arthurienne*, III, I; he retained Mommsen's sub-headings for his edition of the Harleian text, including [IV. ARTHURIANA]; see also Loth, ' "L'Historia Britonum" Dite "de Nennius" '.

65. Anderson, 'Varia', 404–6; DEB, 32, 1.

66. Chadwick and Chadwick, *The Growth of Literature*, I, 146–62, quote from 162.

67. See, for example, 'Notes and News', *Antiquity*, 5 (1931), 236–9.

68. Collingwood, 'Arthur's Battles'.

69. Brodeur, 'Arthur, dux bellorum'.

70. Crawford, 'Arthur and his battles', 278, 279; on p. 290 he also flirted with a south Welsh Arthur, suggesting that the northern bias of the battle-list might be unrealistic.

71. Collingwood had long been working on Anglian and Viking Age sculpture, culminating in 1927 in his magnificent *Northumbrian Crosses*; Crawford, a geography graduate, was a prehistorian and pioneer of aerial photography; neither had much expertise in Celtic place-names.

72. His influence seems pervasive despite his work only very rarely being referenced in works published in English.

73. Crawford, for example, had seen active service with the infantry in 1914–18, been wounded and, returning to the trenches, was captured by the Germans in 1918.

74. Used by LSWR, then Southern Rail, to head up express services between London and the West Country; only 'Sir Lamiel' survives, now based in the East Midlands and used for 'steam' specials.

75. Morton, *In Search of England*, v, 16, 100–1, 130.

76. Morton, *In Search of Wales*, 145.

77. Collingwood and Myers, *Roman Britain and the English Settlements*, 324.

78. Ibid., 320.

79. Burnham, 'The Willing Suspension of Disbelief'; there seems little doubt that they will have discussed Arthur.

80. Hitler became Führer in 1934 and began supporting Franco in 1936.

81. Collingwood and Myers, *Roman Britain and the English Settlements*, 321; Bruce's influence is detectable here.

82. Later taken up by those promoting the 'Sarmatian connection', as well as in the Dark Age British context.

83. As the third edition, published in 1952, of Hodgkin, *A History of the Anglo-Saxons*, 122–5; Stenton, *Anglo-Saxon England*, 3–4, was equally prepared to consider Arthur historical, though less willing to make much of his achievements.

84. Frere's *Britannia*, which could be considered a worthy replacement of Collingwood's contribution, was published in 1967.

85. This volume was only replaced in the Oxford series in 1981 and was still prominent on university reading lists in the 1970s.

86. See, for example, Lindsay, *Arthur and his Times*.

87. Laughlin, 'King Arthur in World War Two Poetry'.

88. See Dodds, *Arthurian Poets: John Masefield*; Masefield's *Box of Delights* (1935) had already referred to 'King Arthur's Camp' where an 'Arthur-like' knight was depicted defending his people and their stock from 'wolves' (a term which Gildas, of course, several times applied to the Saxons).

89. Churchill, *A History*, I, 46.

90. Frere, *Britannia*, 427.

91. As Ashe, *Caesar to Arthur*, depicting him as the last emperor in the West.

92. Alcock, 'By South Cadbury is that Camelot...'; the identification was first recorded in the reign of Henry VIII; see p. 221.

93. Sir Mortimer Wheeler was president of the steering committee, which included Radford, Frere and Philip Rahtz; Ashe was its secretary.

94. Alcock, 'By South Cadbury is that Camelot...'

95. First published in 1968 it was reprinted in 1971, twice in 1972 then again in 1973, 1975 and 1976; contributors included Ashe himself, Radford, Alcock and Rahtz.

96. Radford, *Arthurian Sites in the West*.

97. Alcock, *Arthur's Britain*, 360.

98. Morris, *The Age of Arthur*, xiii.

99. Ashe, 'Introduction', vii.

100. See, for example, Wacher, *Roman Britain*, 107, 299; Cavendish, *King Arthur and the Grail*, 5–10; Marcale, *Le Roi Arthur*.

101. As Kirby and Williams, 'Review of *The Age of Arthur*', 454, dismissing Morris's book as 'a tangled tissue of fact and fantasy which is both misleading and misguided'; a more polite but equally critical response was Campbell, 'The Age of Arthur'.

102. Dumville, 'Sub-Roman Britain', 173, 174, 187.

103. See Alcock, 'Cadbury–Camelot, a Fifteen-Year Perspective'; Alcock, *Cadbury Castle, Somerset*; the 1989 edition of *Arthur's Britain*, 387–409, likewise seeks to explain his shift closer to the agnostic camp, despite some criticism of Dumville's approach.

104. Salway, *Roman Britain*, 485.

105. As Davies, *Wales in the Early Middle Ages*; Fleming, *Britain after Rome*; WATB.

106. As Branigan, *Roman Britain*, 284; Johnson, *Later Roman Britain*, 123; Mattingly, *An Imperial Possession*, 536; Jones, *The End of Roman Britain*, 64, 67, treats Arthur as 'real' but barely mentions him.

107. Higham, *The English Conquest*, 203–12; Higham, *King Arthur: Myth-Making and History*; Green, *Concepts of Arthur*; Halsall, *Worlds of Arthur*.

108. Myres, *The English Settlements*, 15–16.

109. Halsall, *Worlds of Arthur*, 8.

110. Breeze, 'The Historical Arthur', 166.

111. Bryant, *Set in a Silver Sea*, 45; Roberts, *The Pelican History of the World*, 296; Mellersh, *The Ancient and Medieval World*, 213–14; Ó hÓgáin, *The Celts*, 216; Davies, *The Isles*, 194; Morgan, *A Brief History of Wales*, 14.

112. Snyder, *An Age of Tyrants*, 254–5; see also his *Exploring the World of King Arthur*.

113. Bachrach, 'The Questions', 16, 26.

114. Gidlow, *The Reign of Arthur*.

115. Gidlow, *Revealing King Arthur*, 10–11.

116. The books, by Bernard Cornwell, began to be published in 1980; the ITV series, starring Sean Bean, ran initially from 1993 to 1997.

117. Breeze, 'The Historical Arthur', 177; the exception is Badon; his reasoning is not unlike Crawford's.

118. Including Anscombe, W.G. Collingwood and Crawford.

119. For example, there is near-contemporary evidence that *urbs Legionis* would have been understood as Chester in 829–30, but none supportive of its identification as Falkirk; likewise it is difficult to justify locating *regio Linnuis* anywhere other than early medieval

Lindsey; if we suppose that Badon and other problematic names should be 'corrected' in their reading (see Appendix III), there is an almost limitless range of possibilities (as Anscombe, 'Local Names', 103, offering *hagonis*).

120. See White, 'Introductory Note'.

121. I searched for 'King Arthur history' on the Amazon Books website on 23 January 2016 and was offered 1,899 pages of results.

122. As Blackett and Wilson, *Artorius Rex Discovered*; Gilbert, *The Holy Kingdom*; Barber, *King Arthur*; Blake and Lloyd, *The Lost Legend*; Dunning, *Arthur*; Castleden, *King Arthur*; Phillips and Keatman, *King Arthur*; Goodrich, *King Arthur*; Johnson, *Evidence of Arthur*; Ardrey, *Finding Arthur*; Moffatt, *Arthur and the Lost Kingdoms*; Keegan, *Pennine Dragon*; Green, *Britons and Saxons*; and Leahy, *The Anglo-Saxon Kingdom of Lindsey*, 107–10 (though these two are both very cautious in making the local case for Arthur); Laycock, *Warlords*, 146–50; Storr, *King Arthur's Wars*.

123. Malory, 1240, line 14.

124. Phillips, *The Lost Tomb*, 67.

125. Ibid., 222–44; located at SJ430236.

126. Ibid., 236–7; I take his words to mean a possible ditched barrow.

127. As Koch, *Cunedda, Cynan, Cadwallon, Cynddylan*, 234–59.

128. Malory, 1240, line 32–1241, line 6; in modern English: 'I must go into the vale of Avillon to enable my grievous wound to heal ... And as soon as Sir Bedivere had lost sight of the barge, he wept and wailed, and so took to the forest; and he went all that night, and in the morning he was aware between two grey woods of a chapel and a hermitage'.

129. LMLRA, 193, lines 39ff.

130. Laȝamon, lines 14277–82.

131. SMA, lines 3500–17.

132. Lydgate, lines 3096–101.

133. Phillips actually promotes himself as 'a real-life Indiana Jones': see his personal website at http://www.grahamphillips.net (accessed 5 June 2018).

134. As Rowland, *Early Welsh Saga Poetry*, 135; Koch, *Cunedda, Cynan, Cadwallon, Cynddylan*, 251.

135. HE, III, 24.

136. For the battle, see Higham, *King Ecgfrith*, 101–2.

137. White, *Britannia Prima*, 170; the cauldron was initially thought to be of a later date.

138. Brassil, Owen and Britnell, 'Prehistoric and Early Medieval Cemeteries at Tandderwen'.

139. For the broad context see Lucy, *The Anglo-Saxon Way of Death*; locally, see Gelling, *The West Midlands*.

140. As Castleden, *King Arthur*.

141. See Barrowman, Batey and Morris, *Excavations at Tintagel Castle*.

142. Padel, 'Tintagel'.

143. Rivet and Smith, *The Place-Names of Roman Britain*, 350.

144. HRB, VIII, passim; it is recorded nowhere earlier and may well derive from Norman French.

145. The castle seems to have been constructed in a consciously 'ancient' style, presumably to assist in this purpose.

146. Blake and Lloyd, *The Lost Legend*, 157–8, quoting from Jones and Jones, *The Mabinogion*, 141.

147. Blake and Lloyd, *The Lost Legend*, 158.

148. Stephenson, *Medieval Powys*, 306–10.

149. For whose reign, see ibid., 39–57; for an example of poetry written to commemorate him post mortem, see Gruffydd, 'Cynddelw Brydydd Mawr'.

150. Stephenson, *Medieval Powys*, 51.

151. Musson, *The Breiddin Hillfort*, 54.

152. Anglo, *Images*, 43–6.

153. Keegan, *Pennine Dragon*; he even claims to be Arthur's direct descendant.

154. Bartrum, *Early Welsh Genealogical Tracts*, 51.
155. Barber, *King Arthur*, 24–5; Davies, *Llandaff Charters*, 75.
156. Barber, *King Arthur*, 23–4 also proposes Arthmael.
157. See note 32, above.
158. Most frequently evidenced is Edwin (Eadwine), in its Anglo-Latin form.
159. *Contra* the kite flown by Laycock, *Warlords*, 145–6.
160. Halsall, *Worlds of Arthur*, viii, but even he fails to name the book which so disappointed him on the previous page.
161. Ibid.
162. Exceptions include Field, 'Arthur's Battles'; Breeze, 'The Historical Arthur'; Breeze, 'The Name of King Arthur'.
163. Lupack, *The Oxford Guide*, 5.
164. Halsall, *Worlds of Arthur*, viii; the same sentiment was voiced long since by Jackson, 'The Arthur of History', 1.
165. *Contra* Morris, *The Age of Arthur*, xiii; Breeze, 'The Historical Arthur', 166; Arthur and Alfred were comically blended together by Sellar and Yeatman, *1066 and All That*, chapter 5; unfortunately, undergraduates sometimes still follow in their track.
166. As Halsall, *Worlds of Arthur*, viii.
167. Initially in an article, 'Is there a God?', written in 1952 but only published in 1977 in *The Collected Papers, Last Philosophical Testament*, 547–8; this argument has been widely used since, e.g. Dawkins, *The God Delusion*, 74–5; Garvey, 'Absence of Evidence', 9–22.
168. Moffat, *Arthur and the Lost Kingdoms*, 232–54, quotes at 235, 233.
169. Bell (ed.), *L'Estoire des Engleis by Geffrei Gaimar*, lines 37–818.
170. Pope (ed.), Thomas, *The Romance of Horn*.
171. Ebbutt, *Hero-Myths and Legends*, chapters V, XIV.
172. Despite this view being allowed by Dumville, 'Sub-Roman Britain', 187, promoted by Padel, 'The Nature of Arthur', and since favoured by Laycock, *Warlords*, 139, 151–2, and Green, *Britons and Anglo-Saxons*, 91; that the best alternative, linguistically, is Greek, hardly assists the Celtic mythological solution.
173. As was recognised by Alcock, *Arthur's Britain*, 404.
174. Ashley (ed.), *Arthurian Legends*, the quote comes from his introduction to Steinbeck, 'The Knight with Two Swords', 46.
175. Ashley (ed.), *Arthurian Legends*, 46.
176. DEB, 1, 4–5; Higham, *The English Conquest*, 67–89.
177. DEB, 33–6; HB, 62.
178. Vincent, *An Intelligent Person's Guide to History*, 83.
179. As McKitterrick, 'Constructing the Past'; Innes, 'Teutons or Trojans?'.
180. See Farias, *Arabic Medieval Inscriptions*; I would urge reading this work on anyone who remains willing to accept the HB as a reliable source for Arthur, Dolabella, et al.
181. As Dumville, 'Sub-Roman Britain', 187.
182. Updike, *Roger's Version*, 83.
183. Boyd, *Waiting for Sunrise*, 311.
184. The words can vary somewhat: for a modernised version see Jack, *Pop Goes the Weasel*, 48.

BIBLIOGRAPHY

Abaev, V.I., 'Introduction', in TOTN, xxix–lxviii.

Acrudoae, I., 'Militaries from Pannonia in the Imperial Fleet at Misenum and Ravenna (First–Third Centuries) – Prosopographical Aspects', *Studia Antiqua et Archaeologia*, 18 (2012), 127–60.

Adams, J. du Q., 'Sidonius and Riothamus: A Glimpse of the Historical Arthur', *Arthurian Literature*, 12 (1993), 157–64.

Adams, M., *In the Land of Giants: Journeys through the Dark Ages* (London, 2015).

Agrigoroaei, V., 'Vikingi say Rusi. Noi Cercetări asupra Complexului de la Basarabi-Mufatlar', *Apulum*, 43.2 (2006), 25–49.

Alcock, L., '*By South Cadbury is that Camelot . . .': Excavations at Cadbury Castle 1966–70* (London, 1972).

— 'Cadbury-Camelot, a Fifteen-Year Perspective', *Proceedings of the British Academy*, 68 (1982), 355–88.

— *Arthur's Britain: History and Archaeology AD 367–634* (2nd ed., Harmondsworth, 1989).

— *Cadbury Castle, Somerset: The Early Medieval Archaeology* (Cardiff, 1995).

Alföldy, G., *Die Römischen Inschriften von Tarraco* (Berlin, 1975).

Allason-Jones, L., 'Roman Military and Domestic Artefacts from Great Chesters', *Archaeologia Aeliana*, 5th series, 24 (1996), 187–214.

Allen, D.F., *The Coins of the Ancient Celts*, ed. D. Nash (Edinburgh, 1980).

Amodio, M.C., *Writing the Oral Tradition: Oral Poetics and Literative Culture in Medieval England* (Notre-Dame, IN, 2004).

Anderson, A.O., 'Varia [1. The dating passing in Gildas's Excidium; 2. Gildas and Arthur]', *Zeitschrift für Celtische Philologie*, 17 (1928), 403–6.

Anderson, A.O. and M.O. Anderson (eds. and trans.), *Adomnán's Life of Columba* (London, 1961).

Anderson, G., *The Novel in the Ancient World* (Leiden, 1996).

— *Fairytale in the Ancient World* (London, 2000).

Anglo, S., *Images of Tudor Kingship* (London, 1992).

Anon., *English Fairy Tales* (Ware, 1994).

Anscombe, A., 'Local Names in the "Arthuriana" in the *Historia Brittonum*', *Zeitschrift für Celtische Philologie*, 5 (1905), 103–23.

Anthony, D.W., *The Horse, The Wheel and Language: How Bronze-Age Riders from the Eurasian Steppes Shaped the Modern World* (Princeton, 2007).

Ardrey, A., *Finding Arthur: The True Origins of the Once and Future King* (London, 2013).
Aruz, J. et al. (eds), *The Golden Deer of Eurasia: Scythian and Sarmatian Treasures from the Russian Steppes* (New York, 2000).
Ashe, G., *King Arthur's Avalon* (London, 1957).
— *From Caesar to Arthur* (London, 1960).
— 'Introduction', in G. Ashe (ed.), *The Quest for Arthur's Britain*, vii–xi.
— *Camelot and the Vision of Albion* (London, 1971).
— 'A Certain Very Ancient Book: Traces of an Arthurian Source in Geoffrey of Monmouth's History', *Speculum*, 56.2 (1981), 301–23.
— 'Annales Cambriae', TNAE, 8–9.
— 'Arthur, Origins of Legend', TNAE, 17–21.
— 'Avalon', TNAE, 25–6.
— 'Legenda Sancti Goeznovii', TNAE, 204–5.
— *The Discovery of King Arthur* (2nd ed., Stroud, 2003).
Ashe, G. (ed.), *The Quest for Arthur's Britain* (London, 1968).
Ashley, M. (ed.), *Arthurian Legends* (Edison, NJ, 2002).
Atkinson, K., 'Unseen Translation', in K. Atkinson, *Not the End of the World* (London, 2002), 125–50.
Aurell, M., *La Légende du Roi Arthur, 550–1250* (Paris, 2007).
Bachrach, B.S., 'The Alans in Gaul', *Traditio*, 23 (1967), 476–89.
— 'The Questions of King Arthur's Existence and of Romano-British Naval Operations', *The Haskins Society Journal*, 2 (1991), 13–28.
Bailey, H.W., 'Ossetia (Nartä)', in A.T. Hatto (ed.), *Traditions of Heroic and Epic Poetry*, I, *The Traditions* (London, 1980), 236–67.
Baillie, M., *Exodus to Arthur: Catastrophic Encounters with Comets* (London, 1999).
Baldwin, B., 'The Authorship of the *Aratus* ascribed to Germanicus', *Quaderni Urbinati di Cultura Classica*, NS, 7 (1981), 163–72.
Ball, W., *Rome in the East: The Transformation of an Empire* (London, 2000).
— *The Gates of Asia: The Eurasian Steppe and the Limits of Europe* (London, 2015).
Banks, S.E. and J.W. Binns (eds and trans.), *Gervase of Tilbury: Otia Imperialia* (Oxford, 2002).
Barber, C., *King Arthur: The Mystery Unravelled* (Barnsley, 2016).
Barber, R., *Arthur of Albion* (London, 1961).
— *The Figure of Arthur* (London, 1972).
— *The Holy Grail: Imagination and Belief* (Cambridge, MA, 2004).
Barratt, A.R., 'St Germanus and the British Missions', *Britannia*, 40 (2009), 197–217.
Barrowman, R., C. Batey and C. Morris, *Excavations at Tintagel Castle, 1990–1999* (London, 2007).
Bartrum, P.C., *Welsh Genealogies: AD 300–1400* (Aberystwyth, 1983).
Bartrum, P.C. (ed.), *Early Welsh Genealogical Tracts* (Cardiff, 1966).
Bashilov, V.A., and M.G. Moshkova, 'Russian–Italian Computer Assisted Investigations in Sarmatian Archaeology', *Ancient Civilizations from Scythia to Siberia*, 3.1 (1996), 123–8.
Bassett, S., 'In Search of the Origins of Anglo-Saxon Kingdoms', in S. Bassett (ed.), *The Origins of Anglo-Saxon Kingdoms* (London, 1989), 3–27.
— 'Church and Diocese in the West Midlands: The Transition from British to Anglo-Saxon Control', in J. Blaire and R. Sharpe (eds), *Pastoral Care before the Parish* (Leicester, 1992), 13–40.
Baswell, C. and W. Sharpe, 'Introduction: Rex Quondam Rexque Futurus', in C. Baswell and W. Sharpe (eds), *The Passing of Arthur: New Essays in Arthurian Tradition* (New York, 1988).
Batty, R.M., 'On Getic and Sarmatian Shores: Ovid's Account of the Danube Lands', *Historia: Zeitschrift für Alte Geschichte*, 43.1 (1994), 88–111.
Bell, A. (ed.), *L'Estoire des Engleis by Geffrei Gaimar* (Oxford, 1960).
Bell, K., 'Merlin as Historian in "Historia Regum Britannie"', *Arthuriana*, 10.1 (2000), 14–26.

Bennett, J.W., 'Britain and the Fortunate Isles', *Studies in Philology*, 53 (1956), 114–40.

Benton, J., 'The Court of Champagne as a Literary Center', *Speculum*, 36 (1961), 551–91.

Berard, C.M., 'King Arthur and the Canons of Laon', *Arthuriana*, 26.3 (2016), 91–119.

Berezkin, Y.E., 'Southern Siberian–North-American Links in Mythology', *Archaeology, Ethnology and Anthropology of Eurasia*, 2.14 (2003), 94–105.

Bespali, E. et al. (eds), *Treasures of the Warrior Tombs* (Glasgow, 1996).

Bianchi, L., *Le Stele Funerarie Della Dacia* (Rome, 1985).

Biddle, M., 'The Making of the Round Table', in M. Biddle (ed.), *King Arthur's Round Table* (Woodbridge, 2000), 335–92.

Biddulph, E., 'What's in a Name? Graffiti on Funerary Pottery', *Britannia*, 37 (2006), 355–9.

Bieler, L. (ed.), *The Patrician Texts in the Book of Armagh* (Dublin, 1979).

Birley, A.R., *The Fasti of Roman Britain* (Oxford, 1981).

— 'Hadrian to the Antonines', in A.K. Bowman, P. Garnsey and D. Rathbone (eds), *The Cambridge Ancient History*, XI, *The High Empire, AD 70–192* (2nd ed., Cambridge, 2000), 132–94.

— 'The Commissioning of Equestrian Officers', *Bulletin of the Institute of Classical Studies*, 46 (2003), 1–18.

— *The Roman Government of Britain* (Oxford, 2005).

Birley, E., *Roman Britain and the Roman Army* (Kendal, 1953).

Bischoff, B. and M. Lapidge (eds), *Biblical Commentaries from the Canterbury School of Theodore and Hadrian* (Cambridge, 1994).

Bishop, M.C. and J.C.N. Coulston, *Roman Military Equipment from the Punic Wars to the Fall of Rome* (Princes Risborough, 2006).

Blackett, B. and A. Wilson, *Artorius Rex Discovered* (Cardiff, 1986).

Blake, S. and S. Lloyd, *The Key to Avalon: The True Location of Arthur's Kingdom Revealed* (London, 2003).

— *The Lost Legend of Arthur: The Untold Story of Britain's Greatest Warrior* (London, 2004).

Blok, J., *The Early Amazons. Modern and Ancient Perspectives on a Persistent Myth* (Leiden, 1996).

Bogdanow, F., 'The Evolution of the Theme of the Fall of Arthur's Kingdom', in E.D. Kennedy (ed.), *King Arthur: A Casebook* (London, 2002), 91–103 (originally published in French in 1986).

Bokovenko, N.A., 'The Origins of Horse Riding and the Development of Ancient Central Asian Nomadic Riding Harnesses', KRSS, 304–10.

Bollard, J.K., 'Arthur in the Early Welsh Tradition', in J.J. Wilhelm (ed.), *The Romance of Arthur: An Anthology of Medieval Texts in Translation* (London, 1994), 11–23.

Bord, J. and C. Bord, *Mysterious Britain: Ancient Secrets of the United Kingdom* (London, 1972).

— *The Secret Country* (London, 1976).

Borriello, M. and A. D'Ambrosio, *Baiae-Misenum* (Florence, 1979).

Boyd, W., *Waiting for Sunrise* (London, 2012).

Bradley, R., J. Lewis, D. Mullin and N. Branch, '"Where Water Wells up from the Earth": Excavations at the Findspot of the Late Bronze Age Hoard from Broadward, Shropshire', *The Antiquaries Journal*, 95 (2015), 21–64.

Branigan, K., *Roman Britain* (London, 1980).

Brasil, K., W. Owen and W. Britnell, 'Prehistoric and Early Medieval Cemeteries at Tandderwen near Denbigh', *Archaeological Journal*, 148 (1991), 46–97.

Braund, D., *Georgia in Antiquity: A History of Colchis and Transcausian Iberia* (Oxford, 1994).

Braund, D. (ed.), *Scythians and Greeks: Cultural Interactions in Scythia, Athens and the Early Roman Empire (Sixth Century BC–First Century AD)* (Exeter, 2005).

Breeze, A., 'The battle of Camlann and Camelford, Cornwall', *Arthuriana*, 15.3 (2005), 75–90.

— *The Mary of the Celts* (Leominster, 2008).

— 'Where was Gildas Born?', *Northern History*, 45 (2008), 347–50.

— 'Gildas and the Schools of Cirencester', *The Antiquaries Journal*, 90 (2010), 131–8.

— 'Arthur's Battle of Badon and Braydon Forest, Wiltshire', *Journal of Onomastics*, 4 (2015), 20–30.

— 'The Historical Arthur and Sixth-Century Scotland', *Northern History*, 52 (2015), 158–61.

— 'The Name of King Arthur', *Mediaevistik*, 28 (2015), 23–35.

— 'Arthur's Battles and the Volcanic Winter of 536–7', *Northern History*, 53 (2016), 155–66.

— '"Historia Brittonum" and Britain's Twenty-Eight Cities', *Journal of Literary Onomastics*, 5.1 (2016), 1–16.

Breeze, D.J., 'Cavalry on Frontiers', in ROF, 288–97.

— 'The Abandonment of the Antonine Wall: Its Date and Implications', in ROF, 351–64.

— 'The Roman Army in Cumbria', in ROF, 317–30.

— *The Frontiers of Imperial Rome* (Barnsley, 2011).

Breeze, D.J. and B. Dobson, 'Roman Military Deployment in Northern England', in ROF, 298–316.

Broadhurst, F., 'Henry II of England and Eleanor of Aquitaine: Patrons of Literature in French?', *Viator*, 27 (1996), 53–84.

Brodeur, A.G., 'Arthur, dux bellorum', *University of California Publications in English*, 3 (1939), 237–84.

Bromwich, R., *Trioedd Ynys Prydein: The Welsh Triads* (Cardiff, 1961).

— 'Concepts of Arthur', *Studia Celtica*, 10–11 (1975–76), 163–81.

— 'Celtic Elements in Arthurian Romance: A General Survey', in P.B. Grout et al. (eds), *The Legend of Arthur in the Middle Ages: Studies Presented to A.H. Diverres* (Cambridge, 1983), 41–55.

Bromwich, R., A.O.H. Jarman and B.F. Roberts, 'Introduction', in TAOTW, 1–14.

Brooke, C.N.L., *The Church and the Welsh Border in the Central Middle Ages* (Woodbridge, 1986).

Brooks, N., 'The Creation and Early Structure of the Kingdom of Kent', in S. Bassett (ed.), *The Origins of Anglo-Saxon Kingdoms* (London, 1989), 55–74.

— 'The English Origin Myth', in N. Brooks, *Anglo-Saxon Myths, State and Church 400–1066* (London, 2000), 79–89.

Brown, P., *Mercenaries to Conquerors: Norman Warfare in the Eleventh and Twelfth-Century Mediterranean* (Barnsley, 2016).

Bruce, C.W., *The Arthurian Name Dictionary* (London, 1998).

Bruce, J.D., 'Some Proper Names in Layamon's *Brut* not represented in Wace or Geoffrey of Monmouth', *Modern Language Notes*, 26 (1911), 65–9.

— *The Evolution of Arthurian Romance: From the Beginnings down to the Year 1300*, 2 vols (Baltimore, 1923).

Bruce-Mitford, R., *Late Celtic Hanging-Bowls* (Oxford, 2005).

Bryant, A., *Set in a Silver Sea* (London, 1984).

Bryden, I., 'All Dressed Up: Revivalism and the Fashion for Arthur in Victorian Culture', *Arthuriana*, 21.3 (2011), 28–41.

Bullock-Davies, C., 'Chrétien de Troyes and England', *Arthurian Literature*, 1 (1981), 1–61.

Büntgen, U. et al. 'Cooling and Societal Change during the Late Antique Little Ice Age from 536 to around 660 AD', *Nature Geoscience*, 9 (2016), 231–6.

Burgess, A., *Any Old Iron* (London, 1989).

Burgess, G.S., 'Introduction: The Life and Legend of Saint Brendan', in W.R.J. Barron and G.S. Burgess (eds), *The Voyage of Saint Brendan: Representative Versions of the Legend in English Translation* (Exeter, 2002), 1–11.

Burnham, D., 'The Willing Suspension of Disbelief: R.G. Collingwood and the Historical Arthur', *The Historian* (Autumn 2004), 36–42.

Burns, T.S., 'The Battle of Adrianople: A Reconsideration', *Historia*, 22 (1973), 336–45.

Busby, K. (ed.), *Chrétien de Troyes, Le Roman de Perceval on Le Conte du Graal: edition critique d'après tout les manuscripts* (Tübingen, 1993).

Buxton, K. and C. Howard-Davies, with contributions from J. Carrott et al., *Bremetenacum: Excavations at Roman Ribchester 1980, 1989–1990* (Lancaster, 2000).

Byrne, A., *Otherworlds: Fantasy and History in Medieval Literature* (Oxford, 2016).

Caldwell, C.H., 'The Balkans', in S.F. Johnson (ed.), *The Oxford Handbook of Late Antiquity* (Oxford, 2012), 92–114.

Cambi, N., 'Lucije Artorije Kast: Njegovi Grobišni Areal I Sarkofag u Podstrani (Sveti Martin) kod Splita', in LAC, 29–40.

Campbell, B., *The Roman Army: A Sourcebook* (London, 1994).

Campbell, E., *Continental and Mediterranean Imports to Atlantic Britain and Ireland, AD 400–800* (York, 2007).

Campbell, J., 'The Age of Arthur', *Studia Hibernica*, 15 (1975), 177–85.

Carey, J., 'A British Myth of Origins?', *History of Religions*, 31.1 (1991), 24–38.

— *A New Introduction to Lebor Gabála Érenn* (London, 1993).

— 'The Location of the Otherworld in Irish Tradition', in J.M. Wooding (ed.), *The Otherworld in Early Irish Literature* (Dublin, 2000), 113–19.

— *Ireland and the Grail* (Aberystwyth, 2007).

— 'Bran Son of Febal and Brân Son of Llŷr', in IWMA, 168–79.

Carley, J.P., 'Polydore Vergil and John Leyland on King Arthur: The Battle of the Books', in E.D. Kennedy (ed.), *King Arthur: A Casebook* (London, 2002), 185–204.

— 'England' in N. J. Norris (ed.), *Medieval Arthurian Literature: A Guide to Recent Research* (2nd ed., Abingdon, 2015), 1–82.

Carrara, F., *De' Scavi di Salona nel 1850* (Prague, 1852).

Carroll, D.F., *Arturius: A Quest for Camelot* (Goxhill, 1996).

Carroll, M., 'The Evidence of Dress and Funerary Portraits', in D.J. Breeze et al. (eds), *Understanding Roman Frontiers: A Celebration for Professor Bill Hanson* (Edinburgh, 2015), 154–66.

Castleden, R., *King Arthur: The Truth behind the Legend* (London, 2000).

Cătăniciu, I.B., *Evolution of the System of Defence Works in Roman Dacia*, trans. E. Dumitrescu (Oxford, 1981).

Cavendish, R., *King Arthur and the Grail* (London, 1978).

Cessford, C., 'Northern England and the Gododdin Poem', *Northern History*, 33 (1997), 218–22.

Chadwick, H. M. and N.K. Chadwick, *The Growth of Literature*, I (Cambridge, 1932).

Chadwick, N.K., *Studies in the Early British Church* (Cambridge, 1958).

— 'The Conversion of Northumbria: A Comparison of Sources', in N.K. Chadwick (ed.), *Celt and Saxon: Studies in the Early British Border* (Cambridge, 1963), 138–66.

Chahin, M., *The Kingdom of Armenia* (London, 1987).

Chambers, E.K., *Arthur of Britain* (London, 1927).

Charachidzé, G., 'Prometheus among the Circassians', *The World and I* (1989), 644–51.

Charles-Edwards, T.M., 'The Authenticity of the Gododdin: An Historian's View', in R. Bromwich and R.B. Jones (eds), *Astudiaethau Ar Yr Hengerdd* (Cardiff, 1978), 44–71.

— 'The Arthur of History', in TAOTW, 15–32.

— 'Introduction', in CI, 1–59.

— 'Rome and the Britons, 400–664', in T.M. Charles-Edwards and R.J.W. Evans (eds), *Wales and the Wider World: Welsh History in an International Context* (Donington, 2010), 9–27.

— 'Wilfrid and the Celts', in N.J. Higham (ed.), *Wilfrid: Abbot, Bishop, Saint* (Donington, 2013), 243–59.

Chaumont, M.-L. and G. Traina, 'Les Arméniens entre L'Iran et le Monde Gréco-Romain (Ve Siècle au J.-C., vers 300 ap. J.-C.)', in G. Dédéyan (ed.), *Histoire du Peuple Arménien* (Lisbonne, 2007), 101–62.

Chocheyras, J., 'Sur le Nom d'Arthur', *Bibliographical Bulletin of the International Arthurian Society*, 53 (2001), 371–7.

Chrétien de Troyes, *Lancelot or The Knight in the Cart (Le Chevalier de la Charrête)*, ed. W.W. Kibler (New York, 1981).

— *Arthurian Romances*, trans. W.W. Kibler (Harmondsworth, 1991).

Churchill, Sir W., *A History of the English Speaking Peoples*, 4 vols (London, 1956).

Ciggaar, K.N., 'Robert de Boron en Outremer? Le Culte de Joseph d'Arimathie dans la Monde Byzantin et en Outremer', in H. Hokwerda, E.R. Smits and M.M. Woesthuius (eds), *Polyphonia Byzanita* (Groningen, 1993), 145–59.

Clark, J.G.D., 'The Invasion Hypothesis in British Archaeology', *Antiquity*, 40 (1966), 172–89.

Coates, R., 'Welsh Loegr "England"', *Cambrian Medieval Celtic Studies*, 74 (2017), 41–6.

Coates, R. and A. Breeze, *Celtic Voices English Places: Studies of the Celtic Impact on Place-Names in England* (Stamford, 2000).

Colarusso, J., 'The Functions Revisited, a Nart God of War and Three Nart Heroes', *Journal of Indo-European Studies*, 34.1–2 (2006), 27–54.

Colgrave, B. (ed.), *The Life of Bishop Wilfrid by Eddius Stephanus* (Cambridge, 1927).

Collingwood, R.G., *An Autobiography* (Harmondsworth, 1944: first published 1939).

Collingwood, R.G. and J.N.L. Myres, *Roman Britain and the English Settlements* (Oxford, 1936).

Collingwood, W.G., *Northumbrian Crosses of the Pre-Norman Age* (London, 1927).

— 'Arthur's Battles', *Antiquity*, 3 (1929), 292–8.

Collins, R., *Hadrian's Wall and the End of Empire* (London, 2012).

Condurachi, E. and C. Daicoviciu, *Romania*, trans. J. Hogarth (London, 1971).

Cool, H.E.M. and D.J.P. Mason, *Roman Piercebridge: Excavations by D.W. Harding and Peter Scott 1969–1981* (Durham, 2008).

Cooley, A.E., *The Cambridge Manual of Latin Epigraphy* (Cambridge, 2012).

Cornell, T.J. (ed.), *The Fragments of the Roman Historians*, 3 vols (Oxford, 2013).

Corning, C., 'The Baptism of Edwin, King of Northumbria: A New Analysis of the British Tradition', *Northern History*, 36.1 (2000), 5–16.

Cosh, S.R. and D.S. Neal, *Roman Mosaics of Britain*, IV, *Western Britain* (London, 2010).

Crawford, D.K.E., 'St Joseph and Britain: The Old French Origins', *Arthuriana*, 11.3 (2001), 1–20.

Crawford, O.G.S. 'Arthur and his Battles', *Antiquity*, 9 (1935), 277–91.

Cribb, R., *Nomads in Archaeology* (Cambridge, 1991).

Crick, J., *The Historia Regum Britannie of Geoffrey of Monmouth* (Cambridge, 1991).

Crossley-Holland, K., *King Arthur's World* (London, 1998).

— *The Seeing Stone* (London, 2000).

Curta, F. (ed.), *Borders, Barriers, and Ethnogenesis: Frontiers in Late Antiquity and the Middle Ages* (Turnhout, 2005).

Curtis, R.L., *The Romance of Tristan: The Thirteenth-Century Old French 'Prose Tristan'* (Oxford, 1994).

Dąbrowa, E., 'The Commanders of Syrian Legions', in D.L. Kennedy (ed.), *The Roman Army in the East* (Ann Arbor, MI, 1996), 277–96.

Dalton, O.M. (ed. and trans.), *The Letters of Sidonius*, I (Oxford, 1915).

D'Arcy, A.M., *Wisdom and the Grail: The Image of the Vessel in the 'Queste del Saint Graal' and Malory's 'Tale of the Sankgreal'* (Dublin, 2000).

Dark, K.R., *Civitas to Kingdom: British Political Continuity 300–800* (London, 1994).

— 'A Famous Arthur in the Sixth Century?', *Reading Medieval Studies*, 26 (2000), 77–95.

Darrah, J., *The Real Camelot: Paganism and the Arthurian Romances* (London, 1981).

Davidson, R., 'The "Reel" Arthur: Politics and Truth Claims in Camelot, Excalibur and King Arthur', *Arthuriana*, 17.2 (2007), 62–84.

Davies, J.H., 'A Welsh Version of the Birth of Arthur', *Y Cymmrodor*, 24 (1913), 247–64.

Davies, N., *The Isles: A History* (London, 1999).

Davies, P.V. (trans.), *Macrobius, The Saturnalia* (New York, 1969).

Davies, R., *The Matter of Britain and the Matter of England* (Oxford, 1996).

Davies, S., 'Performing Culhwch ac Olwen', in C. Lloyd-Morgan, K. Busby and R. Dalrymple (eds), *Arthurian Literature XXI* (Woodbridge, 2004), 29–52.

Davies, S. 'The Battle of Chester and Warfare in Post-Roman Britain', *History*, 95 (2010), 143–58.

Davies, W., *The Llandaff Charters* (Aberystwyth, 1979).

— *Wales in the Early Middle Ages* (Leicester, 1982).

Davis, N., J.R.R. Tolkien and E.V. Gordon (eds and trans.), *Sir Gawain and the Green Knight* (Oxford, 1967).

Davis-Kimball, J. et al. (eds), *Kurgans, Ritual Sites and Settlements: The Eurasian Bronze and Iron Age, Papers from the European Association of Archaeologists 4th and 5th Annual Meetings* (Oxford, 2000).

Dawkins, R., *The God Delusion* (London, 2006).

De La Bédoyère, G., *Roman Britain: A New History* (London, 2006).

De La Borderie, A., *L'Historia Britonum Attribueé a Nennius et l'Historia Britannica avant Geoffroi de Monmouth* (London, 1883).

— *Histoire de Bretagne* (Rennes, 1905–14).

Demkin, V. A. et al. 'Dynamics of the Properties of Steppe Paleosols of the Sarmatian Time (2nd century BC–4th century AD) in Relation to Secular Variations in Climatic Humidity', *Eurasian Soil Science*, 45.2 (2012), 119–31.

Derolez, R., 'Dubthach's Cryptogram: Some Notes in Connexion with Brussels MS 9565-9566', *L'Antiquité Classique*, 21 (1952), 359–75.

— *Runica Manuscripta: The English Tradition* (Bruges, 1954).

Devijver, H., *The Equestrian Officers of the Imperial Roman Army* (Amsterdam, 1989).

Dickinson, W.H., *King Arthur in Cornwall* (London, 1900).

Dillon, M., *Early Irish Literature* (Chicago, 1948).

— *Stories from the Acallam* (Dublin, 1970).

Ditmas, E.M.R., 'A Reappraisal of Geoffrey of Monmouth's Allusions to Cornwall', *Speculum*, 48 (1973), 510–24.

— 'Breton Settlers in Cornwall after the Norman Conquest', *Transactions of the Honourable Society of Cymmrodorion* (1978), 11–39.

Diverres, A., 'The Grail and the Third Crusade: Thoughts on Le Conte del Graal by Chrétien de Troyes', *Arthurian Literature*, 10 (1991), 13–109.

Dixon, K.R. and P. Southern, *The Roman Cavalry from the First to the Third Century AD* (London, 1992).

Dobson, B., 'Legionary Centurion or Equestrian Officer? A Comparison of Pay and Prospects', *Ancient Society*, 3 (1972), 193–207.

— *Die Primipilares: Entwicklung und Bedeeutung, Laufbahnen und Persönlichkeiten eines römischen Offiziersranges* (Bonn, 1978).

— 'The Significance of the Centurion and Primipilaris in the Roman Army and Administration', in ROF, 143–85.

Dobson, B. and J.C. Mann, 'The Roman Army in Britain: Britons in the Roman Army', in ROF, 511–25.

Dodds, D.L., *Arthurian Poets: John Masefield* (Woodbridge, 1994).

Doel, F., G. Doel and T. Lloyd, *Worlds of Arthur: King Arthur in History, Legend and Culture* (Stroud, 1998).

Dooley, A., 'Arthur of the Irish: A Viable Concept?', in C. Lloyd-Morgan, K. Busby and R. Dalrymple (eds), *Arthurian Literature XXI* (Cambridge, 2004), 9–28.

Drews, R., *Early Riders: The Beginnings of Mounted Warfare in Asia and Europe* (London, 2004).

Duchesne, L., 'Nennius Retractatus', *Revue Celtique*, 15 (1894), 174–97.

Dumézil, G., *Légendes sur les Nartes* (Paris, 1930).

— *Romans de Scythie et d'Alentour* (Paris, 1978).

Dumville, D.N., 'Some Aspects of the Chronology of the *Historia Brittonum*', *Bulletin of the Board of Celtic Studies*, 25 (1974), 439–45.

— 'The *Liber Floridus* of Lambert of Saint-Omer and the *Historia Brittonum*', *Bulletin of the Board of Celtic Studies*, 26 (1974–76), 103–22.

— '"Nennius" and the *Historia Brittonum*', *Studia Celtica*, 10/11 (1976), 78–95.
— 'On the North British section of the *Historia Brittonum*', *Welsh History Review*, 8 (1976–77), 345–54.
— 'Sub-Roman Britain: History and Legend', *History*, 62 (1977), 173–92.
— 'The Welsh Latin Annals', *Studia Celtica*, 12/13 (1977–78), 461–7.
— 'Gildas and Maelgwyn: Problems of Dating', in M. Lapidge and D.N. Dumville (eds), *Gildas: New Approaches* (Woodbridge, 1984), 51–9.
— 'The Chronology of De Excidio Britainniae, Book I', in M. Lapidge and D.N. Dumville (eds), *Gildas: New Approaches* (Woodbridge, 1984), 61–84.
— *The* Historia Brittonum, 3, *The 'Vatican' Recension* (Cambridge, 1985).
— 'The Historical Value of the *Histora Brittonum*', *Arthurian Literature*, 6 (1986), 1–26.
— 'Early Welsh Poetry: Problems of Historicity', in B.F. Roberts (ed.), *Early Welsh Poetry* (Aberystwyth, 1988), 1–16.
— '*Historia Brittonum*: An Insular History from the Carolingian Age', in A. Scharer and G. Scheibelreiter (eds), *Historiographie im frühen Mittelalter* (Wien/München, 1994), 406–34.
— 'Writers, Scribes and Readers in Brittany, AD 800–1100: The Evidence of Manuscripts', in H. Fulton (ed.), *Medieval Celtic Literature and Society* (Dublin, 2005), 49–64.
Dunshea, P.M., 'The Meaning of *Catraeth*: A Revised Early Context for *Y Gododdin*', in A. Woolf (ed.), *Beyond the Gododdin: Dark-Age Scotland in Medieval Wales* (St Andrews, 2013), 81–114.
Dutton, M.L., 'The Staff in the Stone: Finding Arthur's Sword in the *Vita Sancti Edwardi* of Aelred of Rievaulx', *Arthuriana*, 17.3 (2007), 3–30.
Eastwood, B.S., *Ordering the Heavens: Roman Astronomy and Cosmology in the Carolingian Renaissance* (Leiden, 2007).
Ebbutt, M.I., *Hero-Myths and Legends of the British Race* (London, 1910).
Echard, S., *Arthurian Narrative in the Latin Tradition* (Cambridge, 1998).
Eco, U., *Travels in Hyperreality*, trans. W. Weaver (Orlando, FL, 1986).
Edwards, B.J.N., *The Romans at Ribchester: Discovery and Excavation* (Lancaster, 2000).
Edwards, B.J.N. and P.V. Webster (eds), *Ribchester Excavations, Part 1: Excavations within the Roman Fort* (Cardiff, 1985).
— *Ribchester Excavations, Part 2: Excavations in the Civil Settlement: A. The Structures* (Cardiff, 1987).
— *Ribchester Excavations, Part 3: Excavations in the Civil Settlement: B. Pottery and Coins* (Cardiff, 1988).
Ehala, M., and K. Niglas, 'Empirical Evaluation of a Mathematical Model of Ethnolinguistic Vitality: The Case of Voro', *Journal of Multilingual and Multicultural Development*, 28.6 (2007), 427–44.
Elliott, A.B.R., 'Lucius Artorius Castus as Global Icon: The Modern Uses of Arthurian Legend', in LAC, 145–58.
Evans, J., *The History and Practice of Ancient Astronomy* (Oxford, 1998).
Evans, J.G., *Facsimile & Text of the Book of Taliesin* (Llanbedrog, 1910).
Evans, M., *The Death of Kings: Royal Deaths in Medieval England* (London, 2003).
Evans, N.J., 'Cultural Contacts and Ethnic Origins in Viking Age Wales and Northern Britain: The Case of Albanus, Britain's First Inhabitant and Scottish Ancestor', *Journal of Medieval History*, 41.2 (2015), 1–24.
Evans, S., *In Quest of the Holy Grail* (London, 1898).
Ewart, A. (ed.), *Marie de France Lais* (Oxford, 1978).
Faletra, M.A. (trans. and ed.), *The History of the Kings of Britain* (Peterborough, Ontario, 2008).
Faletra, M.A., *Wales and the Medieval Colonial Imagination: The Matter of Britain in the Twelfth Century* (London, 2014).
Faral, E., *La Légende Arthurienne: Études et Documents, Les Plus Anciens Textes*, 3 vols (Paris, 1929).

Farias, P.F. de Moraes, *Arabic Medieval Inscriptions from the Republic of Mali: Epigraphy, Chronicles and Songhay-Tuareg History* (Oxford, 2003).

Field, P.J.C., 'Gildas and the City of Legions', *The Heroic Age*, I (unpaginated).

— 'Nennius and his History', *Studia Celtica*, 30 (1996), 159–65.

— 'Arthur's Battles', *Arthuriana*, 18.4 (2008), 3–32.

Fitzpatrick, A.P., 'The Deposition of La Tène Iron Age Metalwork in Watery Contexts in Southern England', in B. Cunliffe and D. Miles (eds), *Aspects of the Iron Age in Central Southern Britain* (Oxford, 1984), 178–90.

Fitzpatrick-Matthews, K.J., 'The XXVIII Civitates Brittaniae of the Historia Brittonum: Antiquarian Speculation in Early Medieval Wales', *Journal of Literary Onomastics*, 4 (2015), 1–19.

Fleming, R., *Britain after Rome: The Fall and Rise, 400 to 1070* (London, 2010).

Flobert, P. (ed.), *La Vie Ancienne de Saint Samson de Dol* (Paris, 1997).

Flood, V., 'Arthur's Return from Avalon: Geoffrey of Monmouth and the Development of the Legend', *Arthuriana*, 25.2 (2015), 84–110.

Floyde, M., *King Arthur's French Odyssey: Avallon in Burgundy* (self-published 2009, rev. ed. 2016).

Foley, W.T. and N.J. Higham, 'Bede on the Britons', *Early Medieval Europe*, 17.2 (2009), 154–85.

Frachetti, M.D., *Pastoral Landscapes and Social Interaction in Bronze Age Eurasia* (Los Angeles, 2009).

Frank, R., 'Germanic Legend in Old-English Literature', in M. Godden and M. Lapidge (eds), *The Cambridge Companion to Old English Literature* (Cambridge, 1991), 88–106.

— *The Search for the Anglo-Saxon Oral Poet* (Manchester, 1993).

Fraser, J.E., *From Caledonia to Pictland, Scotland to 795* (Edinburgh, 2009).

Freeman, E.A., 'The Mythical and Romantic Elements in Early English History', *Fortnightly Review* (May, 1866), 641–68.

— *Old English History for Children* (London, 1869).

— *Old English History* (London, 1878).

Frere, S.S., *Britannia: A History of Roman Britain* (revised ed., London, 1978).

Frye, R.N., 'Parthia and Sasanid Persia', in F. Millar (ed.), *The Roman Empire and Its Neighbours* (2nd ed., London, 1981), 249–69.

Fulford, M., 'Wroxeter: Legionary Fortress, Baths, and the "Great Rebuilding" of *c.* AD 450–550', *Journal of Roman Archaeology*, 15.2 (2002), 639–45.

Fulton, H., 'Arthur and Merlin in Early Welsh Literature: Fantasy and Magic Naturalism', in H. Fulton (ed.), *A Companion to Arthurian Literature* (Oxford, 2009), 84–101.

— 'History and Myth: Geoffrey of Monmouth's *Historia Regum Britanniae*', in H. Fulton (ed.), *A Companion to Arthurian Literature* (Oxford, 2009), 44–57.

— 'Magic and the Supernatural in Early Welsh Arthurian Narrative: Culhwch ac Olwen and Breuddwyd Rhonabwy', *Arthurian Literature*, 30 (2013), 1–26.

Gabler, D. and A.H. Vaday, *Terra Sigillata im Barbaricum Zwischen Pannonien und Dazien* (Budapest, 1986).

Gairdner, J. (ed.), *Memorials of King Henry VII* (London, 1858).

Garcia, M., 'Gildas and the "Grievous Divorce" from the Barbarians', *Early Medieval Europe*, 21.3 (2013), 243–53.

Gardner, R., 'Gildas's New Testament Models', *Cambrian Medieval Celtic Studies*, 30 (1995), 1–12.

Garner, A. *The Wierdstone of Brisingamen* (London, 1960).

Garvey, B., 'Absence of Evidence, Evidence of Absence and the Atheist's Teapot', *Ars Disputandi*, 10 (2010), 9–22.

Geake, H., *The Use of Grave-Goods in Conversion-Period England, c. 600–c. 850* (Oxford, 1997).

Geary, P.J., 'Ethnic Identity as a Situational Construct in the Early Middle Ages', *Mitteilungen der Anthropologischen Gesellschaft in Wien*, 113 (1983), 15–26.

George, K., *Gildas's De Excidio Britonum and the Early British Church* (Woodbridge, 2009).

Gerberding, R.A., *The Rise of the Carolingians and the* Liber Historiae Francorum (Oxford, 1987).

Gerloff, S., *Atlantic Cauldrons and Buckets of the Late Bronze and Early Iron Ages in Western Europe* (Munich, 2010).

Gibbon, W.B., 'Asiatic Parallels in North American Star Lore: Ursa Major', *Journal of American Folklore*, 77 (1964), 236–50.

Gidlow, C., *The Reign of Arthur: From History to Legend* (Stroud, 2004).

— *Revealing King Arthur* (Stroud, 2010).

Gilbert, A., *The Holy Kingdom* (London, 1998).

Gillam, J.P., 'Romano-Saxon Pottery: An Alternative Explanation', in J. Casey (ed.), *The End of Roman Britain* (Oxford, 1979), 103–18.

Gillies, W., 'Arthur in Gaelic Tradition. Part II: Romances and Learned Lore', *Cambridge Medieval Celtic Studies*, 3 (1982), 41–75.

Girould, M., *The Return to Camelot: Chivalry and the English Gentleman* (London, 1981).

Glavičić, M., 'Artorii Rimskoj Provinciji Dalmaciji', in LAC, 59–70.

Goering, J., *The Virgin and the Grail: Origin of a Legend* (New Haven, 2005).

Goffart, W., 'The Supposedly "Frankish" Table of Nations: An Edition and Study', in W. Goffart, *Rome's Fall and After* (London, 1989), 133–65.

Goldberg, M., 'Vernacular Religion in Northern Britain', in D.J. Breeze et al. (eds), *Understanding Roman Frontiers, a Celebration for Professor Bill Hanson* (Edinburgh, 2015), 196–211.

Goldsworthy, A.K., *The Roman Army at War 100 BC–AD 200* (Oxford, 1996).

Goodrich, N.L., *King Arthur* (New York, 1986).

Gowans, L., 'The Grail in the West: Prose, Verse and Geography in the *Joseph* of Robert de Boron', *Nottingham French Studies*, 35.2 (1996), 1–17.

— 'What did Robert de Boron Really Write?', in B. Wheeler (ed.), *Arthurian Studies in Honour of P.J.C. Field* (Cambridge, 2004), 15–28.

Grabowski, K. and D.N. Dumville, *Chronicles and Annals of Medieval Ireland and Wales: The Clonmacnoise-Group* (Woodbridge, 1984).

Gransden, A., *Historical Writing in England c. 550 to 1307*, I (London, 1974).

Green, C. (writing as Green, T.), *Concepts of Arthur* (Stroud, 2007).

— 'Tom Thumb and Jack the Giant-Killer: Two Arthurian Fairy Tales?', *Folklore*, 118.2 (2007), 123–40.

— *Arthuriana: Early Arthurian Tradition and the Origins of the Legend* (Louth, 2009).

— *Britons and Anglo-Saxons: Lincolnshire AD 400–650* (Lincoln, 2012).

Green, D., *Edward the Black Prince: Power in Medieval Europe* (Harlow, 2007).

Green, J.R., *The Making of England* (London, 1881).

Green, M.J., *Dictionary of Celtic Myth and Legend* (London, 1992).

— *Animals in Celtic Life and Myths* (London, 2002).

Greene, V., *Le Sujet et la Mort dans 'La mort Artu'* (Saint-Genouph, 2002).

Griffin, C., 'Perceptions of the Past in the Early Middle Ages', *Journal of American Folklore*, 124 (2011), 237–40.

Grisward, J., 'Le Motif de l'Épée Jetée au Lac: La Mort d'Artur et la Mort de Batraz', *Romania*, 9 (1969), 289–340.

Grooms, C., *The Giants of Wales: Cewri Cymru* (Lampeter, 1993).

Gruffydd, R.G., 'From Gododdin to Gwynedd: Reflections on the Story of Cunedda', *Studia Celtica*, 24/25 (1989–90), 1–14.

— 'Cynddelw Brydydd Mawr and the Partition of Powys', *Studia Celtica*, 38 (2004), 97–106.

Guilmet, C., 'The Survival of Pausanias' Text', in M. Georgopoulou et al. (eds), *Following Pausanias: The Quest for Greek Antiquity* (Kotinos, 2007), 52–73.

Guy, B., 'The Origins of the Compilation of Welsh Historical Texts in Harley 3859', *Studia Celtica*, 49 (2015), 21–56.

Gwara, S., 'A Possible Arthurian Epitome in a Tenth-Century Manuscript from Cornwall', *Arthuriana*, 17.2 (2007), 3–9.

Habicht, C., *Pausanias' Guide to Ancient Greece* (Berkeley, 1985).

Halsall, G., *Barbarian Migrations and the Roman West 376–568* (Cambridge, 2007).

— *Worlds of Arthur: Facts and Fictions of the Dark Ages* (Oxford, 2013).

Hamel, M. (ed.), *Morte Arthure: A Critical Edition* (New York, 1984).

Hammer, J., *Les Sources de Geoffrey de Monmouth Historia Regum* (Brussels, 1946).

— *Historia Regum Britanniae* (Cambridge, MA, 1951).

Hanning, R.W., *The Vision of History in Early Britain* (New York, 1966).

Hansen, W., *Ariadne's Thread: A Guide to International Tales found in Classical Literature* (New York, 2002).

Hanson, W.S. and R. Conolly, 'Language and Literacy in Roman Britain: Some Archaeological Considerations', in A.E. Cooley (ed.), *Becoming Roman, Writing Latin? Literacy and Epigraphy in the Roman West* (Portsmouth, RI, 2002), 151–64.

Hartnett, C.P., *Irish Arthurian Literature*, 2 vols (PhD thesis, University of Michigan, 1973).

Hartog, F., 'Imaginary Scythians: Space and Nomadism', in R.V. Munson (ed.), *Herodotus: Volume 2 – Herodotus and the World* (Oxford, 2013), 245–66.

Harty, K.J., '*King Arthur* directed by Antoine Fuqua from a screenplay by David Franzoni. A Buena Vista release of a Touchstone Pictures/Jerry Bruckheimer Films Presentation, 2004', *Arthuriana*, 14.3 (2004), 121–3.

Haskins, J.F., 'Sarmatian Gold Collected by Peter the Great: VII – The Demidov Gift and Conclusions', *Artibus Asiae*, 22 (1959), 64–7, 69–78.

Hay, D. (ed.), *The Anglica Historia of Polydore Vergil* (London, 1950).

Haycock, M. (ed. and trans.), *Legendary Poems in the Book of Taliesin* (Aberystwyth, 2007).

Heather, P., *Empire and Barbarians* (London, 2010).

Hehir, B.O., 'What is the Gododdin?', in B.F. Roberts (ed.), *Early Welsh Poetry* (Aberystwyth, 1988), 57–95.

Hekster, O. and T. Kaizer (eds), *Frontiers in the Roman World* (Leiden, 2011).

Henken, E.R., *Traditions of the Welsh Saints* (Woodbridge, 1987).

Higgins, C., *Under Another Sky: Journeys in Roman Britain* (London, 2013).

Higham, N.J., 'Old Light on the Dark Age Landscape: The Description of Britain in the *De Excidio Britanniae* of Gildas', *Journal of Historical Geography*, 17 (1991), 363–72.

— 'Gildas and "Agitius": A comment on *De Excidio* x, 1', *Bulletin of the Board for Celtic Studies*, 40 (1993), 123–34.

— *The English Conquest* (Manchester, 1994).

— *King Arthur: Myth-Making and History* (London, 2002).

— *Bede as an Oral Historian* (Jarrow, 2011).

— 'Constantius, St Germanus and Fifth-Century Britain', *Early Medieval Europe*, 22.2 (2014), 113–37.

— *King Arthur* (Stroud, 2015).

— *Ecgfrith: King of the Northumbrians, High-King of Britain* (Donington, 2015).

Higham, N.J. and G.D.B. Jones, *The Carvetii* (Stroud, 1985).

Higley, S., 'The Spoils of Annwn: Taliesin and Material Poetry', in K.A. Klar, E.E. Sweetser and C. Thomas (eds), *A Celtic Florilegium: Studies in Memory of Brendan O Hehir* (Lawrence, MA, 1966), 43–53.

Hill, D. and M. Worthington, *Offa's Dyke: History and Guide* (Stroud, 2003).

Hines, J. and A. Bayliss (eds), *Anglo-Saxon Graves and Grave Goods of the 6th and 7th Centuries AD: A Chronological Framework* (London, 2013).

Hoare, F.R., *The Western Fathers* (London, 1954).

Hobson, B., G. Clay and G. Brown, *The Romans in Huddersfield: A New Assessment: Huddersfield and District Archaeological Society Excavations in the Vicus of Slack Fort, 2007, 2008 and 2009* (Oxford, 2015).

Hodgkin, R.H., *A History of the Anglo-Saxons*, 2 vols (3rd ed., Oxford, 1952).

Hodgson, N. and P.T. Bidwell, 'Auxiliary Barracks in a New Light: Recent Discoveries on Hadrian's Wall', *Britannia*, 35 (2004), 121–57.

Hoffmann, B., 'The Quarters of Legionary Centurions of the Principate', *Britannia*, 26 (1995), 107–51.

Holder, P.A., *Studies in the Auxilia of the Roman Army from Augustus to Trajan* (Oxford, 1980).

— *The Roman Army in Britain* (London, 1982).

Holt, T., *The Portable Door* (London, 2003).

Hood, A.B.E. (ed. and trans.), *St Patrick: His Writings and Muirchu's Life* (London, 1978).

Hopper, V.F., *Medieval Number Symbolism: Its Sources, Meaning and Influence on Thought and Expression* (New York, 1939).

Howell, R., 'Roman Past and Medieval Present: Caerleon as a Focus for Continuity and Conflict in the Middle Ages', *Studia Celtica*, 46 (2012), 11–22.

Hughes, K., 'The Welsh Latin Chronicles; Annales Cambriae and Related Texts', *Proceedings of the British Academy*, 59 (1973), 233–58.

— *Celtic Britain in the Early Middle Ages* (Woodbridge, 1980).

Hume, D., *The History of England*, 6 vols (London, 1754–62).

Hunter, J., 'Taliesin at the Court of Henry VIII: Aspects of the Writings of Elis Gruffydd', *Transactions of the Honorary Society of Cymmrodorion*, NS, 10 (2004), 41–56.

Hunter, J., T.G. Manby, and J.E.H. Spaul, 'Recent Excavations at the Slack Roman Fort near Huddersfield', *Yorkshire Archaeological Journal*, 42 (1971), 74–97.

Hutton, R., 'The Early Arthur: History and Myth', in E. Archibald and A. Putter (eds), *The Cambridge Companion to the Arthurian Legend* (Cambridge, 2009), 21–35.

Hutton, W., 'Describing Greece: Landscape and Literature in the Periegesis of Pausanias', in M. Georgoulou et al. (eds), *Following Pausanias: The Quest for Greek Antiquity* (Kotinos, 2007).

Ianziti, A.G., *Writing History in Renaissance Italy: Leonardo Bruni and the Uses of the Past* (London, 2012).

Innes, M., *Introduction to Early Medieval Western Europe, 300–900* (London, 2007).

— 'Teutons or Trojans? The Carolingians and the Germanic Past', in Y. Hen and M. Innes (eds), *The Uses of the Past in the Early Middle Ages* (Cambridge, 2009), 227–49.

Isaac, G.R., '*Gweith Gwen Ystrat* and the Northern Heroic Age of the Sixth Century', *Cambrian Medieval Celtic Studies*, 36 (1998), 61–70.

— 'Readings in the History and Transmission of the *Gododdin*', *Cambrian Medieval Celtic Studies*, 37 (1999), 55–78.

— 'The Nature and Origin of Celtic Languages: Atlantic Seaways, Italo-Celtic and other Paralinguistic Misapprehensions', *Studia Celtica*, 38 (2004), 49–58.

Ishiguro, K., *The Buried Giant* (London, 2015).

Ivantchik, A., 'Roman Troops in the Bosporus: Old Problem in the Light of a New Inscription found in Tanais', *Ancient Civilizations from Scythia to Siberia*, 20.2 (2014), 165–94.

Jack, A., *Pop Goes the Weasel: The Secret Meanings of Nursery Rhymes* (London, 2008).

Jackson, K.H., 'Once Again Arthur's Battles', *Modern Philology*, 43.1 (1945), 44–57.

— 'Arthur's Battle of Breguoin', *Antiquity*, 23 (1949), 48–9.

— *Language and History in Early Britain* (Edinburgh, 1953).

— 'Edinburgh and the Anglian Occupation of Lothian', in P. Clemoes (ed.), *The Anglo-Saxons: Studies Presented to Bruce Dickins* (London, 1959), 35–47.

— 'The Arthur of History', in R. S. Loomis (ed.), *Arthurian Literature in the Middle Ages* (Oxford, 1959), 1–11.

— *The Gododdin, The Oldest Scottish Poem* (Edinburgh, 1969).

— '*Varia* II: Gildas and the Names of the British Princes', *Cambridge Medieval Celtic Studies*, 3 (1982), 30–40.

James, E., *Britain in the First Millennium* (London, 2001).

James, M.R., *The Apocryphal New Testament* (Oxford, 1924).

Jankulak, K., *Geoffrey of Monmouth* (Cardiff, 2010).

Jarman, A. O. H., *Aneirin: Y Gododdin, Britain's Oldest Heroic Poem* (Llandysul, 1988).

Jarman, A.O.H. (ed.), *Llyfr Du Caerfyrddin* (Cardiff, 1982).

Jarrett, M.G., 'Legio II Augusta in Britain', *Archaeologia Cambrensis*, 113 (1964), 47–63.

— 'Legio XX Valeria Victrix in Britain', *Archaeologia Cambrensis*, 117 (1968), 77–91.

Jaski, B., 'Early Irish Examples of the name "Arthur"', *Zeitschrift für Celtische Philologie*, 56 (2008), 89–105.

Jenkins, R.J.H. and L.G. Westerlink, *Nicholas I Patriarch of Constantinople, Letters* (Washington, 1973).

Johnson, F., *Evidence of Arthur* (Madison, 2014).

Johnson, S., *Later Roman Britain* (London, 1980).

Jones, A.H.M., *The Later Roman Empire*, 2 vols (Oxford, 1964).

Jones, G. (intro.) and E. Mason (trans.), *Wace and Layamon, Arthurian Chronicles* (London, 1912).

Jones, G.D.B. and D. Mattingly, *An Atlas of Roman Britain* (London, 1990).

Jones, M.E., *The End of Roman Britain* (London, 1996).

Jones, T., 'The Early Evolution of the Legend of Arthur', *Nottingham Medieval Studies*, 8 (1964), 3–21.

Jones, T. (ed.), *Brut y Tywysogyon or The Chronicle of the Princes, Peniarth MS 20 Version* (Cardiff, 1952).

Jørgensen, L., B. Storgaad and L.G. Thomsen (eds), *The Spoils of Victory: The North in the Shadow of the Roman Empire* (Copenhagen, 2003).

Jung, E. and M.-L. Von Franz, *The Grail Legend*, trans. A. Dykes (2nd ed., Princeton, 1998).

Kadare, I., *The File on H*, trans. D. Bellos (London, 1997).

Kaposhina, S., 'A Sarmatian Royal Burial at Novocherkassk', *Antiquity*, 37 (1963), 256–8.

Karl, R. and H. Butler, *Moel y Gaer Llanbedr Dyffryn Clwyd, Excavations Summer 2009, Preliminary Report* (Bangor, 2009).

Kazanski, M., 'Un Témoignage de la Présence des Alano-Sarmates en Gaule: La Sepulture de la Fosse Jean-Fat à Reims', *Archéologie Médiévale*, 16 (1986), 33–9.

— 'La Diffusion de la Mode Danubienne en Gaul (Fin du IV Siècle–Debut du VI Siècle): Essai d'Interpretation Historique', *Antiquités Nationales*, 21 (1990), 59–73.

Kemble, J.M., *The Saxons in England*, 8 vols (London, 1849).

Kennedy, D., 'C. Velius Rufus', *Britannia*, 14 (1983), 183–96.

Keppie, L., *The Making of the Roman Army, from Republic to Empire* (London, 1984).

Kerlouégan, F., *Le De Excidio Britanniae de Gildas: Les Destinées de la Culture Latine dans Île de Bretagne au VIe Siècle* (Paris, 1987).

Kidd, I.G., *Posidonius*, 3, *The Translation of the Fragments* (Cambridge, 1999).

Kirby, D.P., 'British Dynastic History in the Pre-Viking Period', *Bulletin of the Board of Celtic Studies*, 27 (1976), 81–114.

Kirby, D.P. and J.E.C. Williams, 'Review of *The Age of Arthur*, J. Morris', *Studia Celtica*, 10/11 (1976), 454–86.

Kirigin, B. and E. Maris, *The Archaeological Guide to Central Dalmatia* (Split, 1989).

Klauck, H.-J., *Apocryphal Gospels. An Introduction* (London, 2003).

Knight, S., *Arthurian Literature and Society* (London, 1983).

Knott, E. and G. Murphy, *Early Irish Literature* (London, 1966).

Koch, J.T., 'When Was Welsh Literature First Written Down?', *Studia Celtica*, 20/21 (1986), 43–66.

— (ed.), *The Gododdín of Aneírín: Text and Context from Dark-Age Britain* (Cardiff, 1997).

— 'Why Was Welsh Literature Written Down?', in H. Fulton (ed.), *Medieval Celtic Literature and Society* (Dublin, 2005), 15–31.

— *Cunedda, Cynan, Cadwallon, Cynddylan: Four Welsh Poems and Britain 383–655* (Aberystwyth, 2013).

— 'Waiting for Gododdin: Thoughts on Taliesin and Iudic-Hael, Catraeth and Unripe Times in Celtic Studies', in A. Woolf (ed.), *Beyond the Gododdin: Dark-Age Scotland in Medieval Wales* (St Andrews, 2013), 177–204.

— 'The Celtic Lands' in N. J. Lacy (ed.), *Medieval Arthurian Literature: A Guide to Recent Research* (2nd ed., Abingdon, 2015), 239–322.

Koščević, R., *Siscia, Pannonia Superior: Finds and Metalwork Production* (Oxford, 1995).

Kraeva, L.A., 'Technological Analysis of Ceramics from Early Sarmatian Burials in the South-Western Urals', *Archaeology, Ethnology and Anthropology of Eurasia*, 39.4 (2011), 51–60.

Kulcsár, V., 'Vacszentlászló Harminchányás Cemetery', in Z. Visy (ed.), *The Roman Army in Pannonia* (Budapest, 2003), 231–3.

Kurilić, A., 'Some Problems Concerning the Reading of the CIL 3, 12813', in LAC, 131–43.

Kuzmina, E., 'The Eurasian Steppes: The Transition from Early Urbanism to Nomadism', in KRSS, 118–25.

Lacy, N.J., 'Camelot', in TNAE, 66–7.

Lagorio, V.M., 'The Evolving Legend of St Joseph', *Speculum*, 46 (1971), 209–31.

Laistner, M.L.W., 'The Library of the Venerable Bede', in A.H. Thompson (ed.), *Bede: His Life, Times and Writings* (Oxford, 1935), 237–66.

Lapidge, M., 'Gildas's Education and the Latin Culture of Sub-Roman Britain', in M. Lapidge and D. Dumville (eds), *Gildas: New Approaches* (Woodbridge, 1984), 27–50.

Lapidge, M. and M. Herren (eds), *Aldhelm: The Prose Works* (Ipswich, 1979).

Larpi, L., *Prolegomena to a New Edition of Gildas Sapiens 'De Excidio Britanniae'* (Firenze, 2012).

Laughlin, I., 'King Arthur in World War Two Poetry: His Finest Hour?', *Arthuriana*, 13.1 (2003), 66–91.

Laycock, S., *Warlords: The Struggle for Power in Post-Roman Britain* (Stroud, 2009).

Leahy, K., *The Anglo-Saxon Kingdom of Lindsey* (Stroud, 2007).

Le Bohec, Y., *The Imperial Roman Army*, trans. R. Bate (London, 1994).

Leland, J., *Assertio Inclytissimi Arturii* (London, 1544).

Lepelly, R., *Dictionnaire Étomologique des Noms de Communes de Normandie* (Caen, 1996).

Lindsay, J., *Arthur and His Times* (London, 1958).

Ling, R., *Romano-British Wall Painting* (Aylesbury, 1985).

— 'Brading, Brantingham and York: A New Look at Some Fourth-Century Mosaics', *Britannia*, 22 (1991), 147–57.

— 'The Iconography of the Brading Mosaics', *Mosaic*, 18 (1991), 14–20.

— 'Inscriptions on Romano-British Mosaics and Wall-Paintings', *Britannia*, 38 (2007), 63–91.

Littleton, C.S., 'Georges Dumézil and the Rebirth of the Genetic Model: An Anthropological Appreciation', in G.J. Larson (ed.), *Myth in Indo-European Antiquity* (Berkeley, 1974), 169–79.

— 'The Holy Grail, the Cauldron of Annwn, and the Nartyamongas: A Further Note on the Sarmatian Connection', *Journal of American Folklore*, 92 (1979), 326–33.

Littleton, C.S. and A.C. Thomas, 'The Sarmatian Connection: New Light on the Origin of the Arthurian and Holy Grail Legends', *Journal of American Folklore*, 91 (1978), 512–27.

Lloyd, J.E., *A History of Wales*, 2 vols (London, 1911).

Lloyd, S., *The Arthurian Place-Names of Wales* (Cardiff, 2017).

Loomis, R.S., 'King Arthur and the Saints', *Speculum*, 8 (1933), 478–82.

— *Wales and the Arthurian Legend* (Cardiff, 1956).

— 'The Oral Diffusion of the Arthurian Legend', in ALITMA, 52–63.

— *The Grail from Celtic Myth to Christian Symbol* (Cardiff, 1963).

Loriot, X., 'Un Mythe Historographique: L'Expédition de L. Artorius Castus contre Les Armoricains', *Bulletin de la Societé Nationale des Antiquaries de France* (1997), 85–7.

Loth, J., ' "L'Historia Britonum" dite "de Nennius" ', *Revue Celtique*, 51 (1930), 1–31.

Lubotsky, A., 'Scythian Elements in Old Iranian', *Proceedings of the British Academy*, 116 (2002), 189–202.

Lucy, S., *The Anglo-Saxon Way of Death* (Stroud, 2000).

Lupack, A., '*King Arthur* directed by Antoine Fuqua from a screenplay by David Franzoni. A Buena Vista release of a Touchstone Pictures/Jerry Bruckheimer Films Presentation, 2004', *Arthuriana*, 14.3 (2004), 123–5.

— *Oxford Guide to Arthurian Literature and Legend* (Oxford, 2005).

Maas, E., *Commentarium in Aratum Reliquiae* (Berlin, 1958).

Macalister, R.A.S., *Two Irish Arthurian Romances* (London, 1908).

— *Corpus Inscriptiorum Insularum Celticum*, 2 vols (Dublin, 1958–59).

Macaulay, T.B., *The History of England from the Succession of James the Second*, 2 vols (London, 1867).

Mac Cana, P., 'Mongán Mac Fiachna and Immram Brain', *Ériu*, 23 (1972), 102–42.

— 'Ireland and Wales in the Middle Ages: An Overview', in IWMA, 17–45.

Mac Shamhráin, A., *Church and Polity in Pre-Norman Ireland: The Case of Glendalough* (Maynooth, 1996).

Macleod, M., *The Book of King Arthur and His Noble Knights* (London, 1908).

Madgwick, R. and J. Mulville, 'Feasting on Fore-Limbs: Conspicuous Consumption and Identity in Later Prehistoric Britain', *Antiquity*, 89 (2015), 629–44.

Maier, B., *The Celts: A History from Earliest Times to the Present*, trans. K. Windle (2nd ed., Edinburgh, 2018).

Malcor, L.A., 'Lucius Artorius Castus Part 1: An Officer and an Equestrian', *The Heroic Age*, 1 (1999).

— 'Lucius Artorius Castus Part 2: The Battles in Britain', *The Heroic Age*, 2 (1999).

— 'Merlin and Pendragon: King Arthur's *Draconius*', *Arthuriana*, 10.1 (2000), 3–13.

Mallory, J.P. and D.Q. Adams, *Oxford Introduction to Proto-Indo-European and the Proto-Indo-European World* (Oxford, 2006).

Malone, K., 'The Historicity of Arthur', *The Journal of English and Germanic Philology*, 23.4 (1924), 463–91.

— 'Artorius', *Modern Philology*, 22.4 (1925), 367–74.

Malyshev, A.A. and M.J. Treister, 'A Warrior's Burial from the Asiatic Bosporus in the Augustan Age', *Expedition*, 36.2 (1994), 29–37.

Mann, J., *From Aesop to Reynard: Beast Literature in Medieval Britain* (Oxford, 2009).

Marcale, J., *Le Roi Arthur et la Societé Celtique* (Paris, 1981).

Marshall, H.E., *Our Island Story: A History of Britain for Boys and Girls* (London, 1905).

Maršić, D., 'Antički Profil Podstrane I Okolice', in LAC, 187–230.

Martin, L.T. (trans.), *The Venerable Bede: Commentary on the Acts of the Apostles* (Kalamazoo, MI, 1989).

Marx, J., *La Légende Arthurienne et le Graal* (Paris, 1952).

Marx, J. (ed.), Guillaume de Jumiège, *Gesta Normannorm Ducum* (Rouen, 1914).

Masefield, J., *The Box of Delights* (London, 1935).

— *Badon Parchments* (London, 1947).

Matthews, J., *The Arthurian Tradition* (Shaftesbury, 1994).

— 'A Knightly Endeavour: The Making of Jerry Bruckheimer's "King Arthur"', *Arthuriana*, 14.3 (2004), 112–15.

Mattingly, D., *An Imperial Possession: Britain in the Roman Empire* (London, 2006).

Maund, K., *The Welsh Kings: The Medieval Rulers of Wales* (Stroud, 2000).

Maunder, C. (ed.), *The Origins of the Cult of the Virgin Mary* (London, 2008).

May, W., 'A Guide to the Names', TOTN, xxi–xxvii.

Mayor, A., ' 'Introduction to the Paperback Edition', in J. Colarusso, *Nart Sagas* (Princeton, 2016), xix–xxiv (this is the paperback edition of NSFTC).

Mayor, A., D. Saunders and J. Colarusso, 'Making Sense of Nonsense Inscriptions Associated with Amazons and Scythians on Athenian Vases', *Hesperia*, 83.3 (2014), 447–93.

Mays, M. (ed.), *Catalogue of the Celtic Coins in the British Museum*, III, *Bronze Coins of Gaul* (London, 1995).

McCarthy, D.P. and D.Ó. Croínín, 'The "Lost" Irish 84-Year Easter Table Rediscovered', *Peritia*, 6/7 (1987–88), 227–42.

McCone, K., *Pagan Past and Christian Present in Early Irish Literature* (Maynooth, 2000).

McKenna, M., 'The Breton Literary Tradition', *Celtica*, 16 (1984), 35–51.

McKitterick, R., 'Constructing the Past in the Early Middle Ages: The Case of the Royal Frankish Annals', *Transactions of the Royal Historical Society*, 7 (1997), 101–29.

Medini, J., 'Provincia Liburnia', *Diadora*, 9 (1980), 363–441.

Mees, B. and N. Nicholas, 'Greek Curses and the Celtic Underworld', *Studia Celtica*, 46 (2012), 23–38.

Mehl, A., *Roman Historiography*, trans. H.-F. Mueller (Oxford, 2014).

Mellersh, H.E.L., *The Ancient and Medieval World, Prehistory–AD 1491* (2nd ed., Oxford, 1999).

Melyukova, A.I., 'The Scythians and Sarmatians', in D. Sinor (ed.), *The Cambridge History of Early Inner Asia* (Cambridge, 1990), 97–117.

Meyer, K. (ed.), 'The Expulsion of the Dessi', *Y Cymmrodor*, 14 (1901), 101–35.

Micha, A. (ed.), *Robert de Boron: Merlin, Roman du XIII Siècle* (Droz, 2000).

Middleton, R., C. Wells and E. Huckerby, *The Wetlands of North Lancashire* (Lancaster, 1995).

Miletić, Ž., 'Lucius Artorius Castus I Liburnia', in LAC, 111–30.

Millar, F., *The Roman Empire and Its Neighbours* (2nd ed., London, 1981).

— *The Roman Near East 31 BC–AD 337* (3rd ed., Cambridge, MA, 1996).

Miller, M., 'The Commanders at Arthuret', *Cumberland and Westmorland Antiquarian and Archaeological Society Transactions*, NS, 75 (1975), 96–118.

— 'Date-Guessing and Pedigrees', *Studia Celtica*, 12/13 (1975–76), 96–109.

Miller, V.F., *Osetinsko-Russko-Nemtskij-Slovar*, 3 vols (The Hague, 1927).

Millett, M., *The Romanization of Britain* (Cambridge, 1990).

Moffat, A., *Arthur and the Lost Kingdoms* (London, 1999).

Mordvintseva, V., 'The Sarmatians: The Creation of Archaeological Evidence', *Oxford Journal of Archaeology*, 32.2 (2013), 203–19.

Morgan, P., 'From a Death to a View: The Hunt for the Welsh Past in the Romantic Period', in E. Hobsbawm and T. Ranger (eds), *The Invention of Tradition* (Cambridge, 1983), 43–100.

Morpurgo, M., *Arthur High King of Britain* (London, 1994).

Morris, J., *The Age of Arthur* (London, 1973).

Morris, J. (ed.), *Domesday Book, Hertfordshire* (London, 1976).

Morris, M.L., '"Recalled to Life": King Arthur's Return and the Body of the Past in Nineteenth-Century England', *Arthuriana*, 21.2 (2011), 5–27.

Morris, R., 'Aspects of Time and Place in the French Arthurian Verse Romances', *French Studies*, 42 (1988), 257–77.

Morton, H.V., *In Search of England* (London, 1927).

— *In Search of Wales* (London, 1932).

Muhlberger, S., 'The Gallic Chronicle of 452 and Its Authority for British Events', *Britannia*, 14 (1983), 23–33.

Mullen, A., 'Evidence for Written Celtic in Roman Britain: A Linguistic Analysis of *Tabellae Sulis* 14 and 18', *Studia Celtica*, 41 (2007), 31–46.

— 'Linguistic Evidence for "Romanization": Continuity and Change in Romano-British Onomastics: A Study of the Epigraphic Record with Particular Reference to Bath', *Britannia*, 38 (2007), 35–61.

— 'Latin and Other Languages: Societal and Individual Bilingualism', in J. Clackson (ed.), *A Companion to the Latin Language* (Oxford, 2011), 527–48.

Murphy, G.R., *Gemstone of Paradise: The Holy Grail in Wolfram's Parzival* (Oxford, 2006).

Musson, C.R. with W.J. Britnell and A.G. Smith, *The Breidden Hillfort: A Later Prehistoric Settlement in the Welsh Marches* (London, 1991).

Myres, J.N.L., *Anglo-Saxon Pottery and the Settlement of England* (Oxford, 1969).

— *The English Settlements* (Oxford, 1986).

Nagy, J.F., 'Arthur and the Irish', in H. Fulton (ed.), *A Companion to Arthurian Literature* (Oxford, 2009), 117–27.

Nash, D., *Coinage in the Celtic World* (London, 1987).

Nash-Williams, V.E., *The Early Christian Monuments of Wales* (Cardiff, 1950).

Nasidze, I. et al., 'Genetic Evidence Concerning the Origins of South and North Ossetians', *Annals of Human Genetics*, 68.6 (2004), 588–99.

Nastali, D. and P. Boardman, 'Searching for Arthur: Literary Highways, Electronic Byways and Cultural Back Roads', *Arthuriana*, 11.4 (2001), 108–22.

Needham, S., K. Parfitt and G. Varndell (eds), *The Ringlemere Cup: Precious Cups and the Beginning of the Channel Bronze Age* (London, 2006).

Nemeth, E., 'Roman Dacia and Beyond: New Surveys and Excavations', *Journal of Ancient History and Archaeology*, 1.4 (2014), 28–36.

Newell, W.W., 'William of Malmesbury and the Antiquity of Glastonbury', *Proceedings of the Modern Language Association*, 18 (1903), 459–512.

Nickel, H., 'Tamgas and Runes, Magic Numbers and Magic Symbols', *Metropolitan Museum Journal*, 8 (1973), 165–73.

— 'The Dawn of Chivalry', *Metropolitan Museum of Art Bulletin*, 32 (1975), 150–2.

— 'Wer waren König Artus' Ritter? Über die geschichtliche Grundlage Artussagen', *Waffen- und Kostümkunde: Zeitschrift der Gesellschaft für historische Waffen- und Kostümkunde*, 3.17.1 (1975), 1–27.

— 'The Fight about King Arthur's Beard and for the Cloak of Kings' Beards', *Interpretations*, 16.1 (1985), 1–7.

— 'About the Saxon Rebellion and the Massacre at Amesbury', *Arthuriana*, 16.1 (2006), 65–70.

Ní Dhonnchadha, M., 'The Guarantor List of *Cáin Adomnán*, 697 AD', *Peritia*, 1 (1984), 178–215.

Noble, T.F.X., *Charlemagne and Louis the Pious, Lives by Einhard, Notker, Emoldus, Thegan and the Astronomer* (Pennsylvania, 2009).

Nutt, A., *Studies on the Legend of the Holy Grail* (London, 1888).

Ó Broin, T., 'Classical Source of the "Conception of Mongan"', *Zeitschrift für Celtische Philologie*, 28.1 (1961), 262–71.

Ó Carragáin, É. and A. Thacker, 'Wilfrid in Rome', in N.J. Higham (ed.), *Wilfrid: Abbot, Bishop, Saint* (Donington, 2013), 212–30.

O'Gorman, R., 'Grail', in TNAE, 212–13.

— '*Joseph of Arimathie*': *A Critical Edition of the Verse and Prose Versions* (Toronto, 1995).

— 'The *Gospel of Nicodemus* in the Vernacular Literature of France', in Z. Izydorczyk (ed.), *The Medieval Gospel of Nicodemus: Texts, Intertexts and Contexts in Western Europe* (Tempe, AZ, 1997).

Ó hÓgáin, D., *The Celts: A History* (Cork, 2002).

Okasha, E. and K. Forsyth, *Early Christian Inscriptions of Munster: A Corpus of the Inscribed Stones* (Cork, 2001).

Olivier, A.C.H., 'Postscript: The Nature of the Ribchester Civil Settlement', in B.J.N. Edwards and P.V. Webster (eds), *Ribchester Excavations, Part 2* (Cardiff, 1987), 117–26.

O'Loughlin, T., *Gildas and the Scriptures: Observing the World through a Biblical Lens* (Turnhout, 2012).

Oman, C., *History of England* (London, 1895).

Oppenheimer, C., *Eruptions that Shook the World* (Cambridge, 2011).

O'Sullivan, T.D., *The De Excidio of Gildas: Its Authenticity and Date* (Leiden, 1978).

Over, K.L., 'Transcultural Change: Romance to *Rhamant*', in H. Fulton (ed.), *Medieval Celtic Literature and Society* (Dublin, 2005), 183–204.

Pace, E., 'Geoffrey of Monmouth's Sources for the Cador and Camblan Narratives', *Arthuriana*, 24.3 (2014), 45–78.

— 'Athelstan "Twist-Beard" and Arthur's Tenth-Century Breton Origins for the Historia Regum Britanniae', *Arthuriana*, 26.4 (2016), 60–88.

Padel, O.J., 'Tintagel in the Twelfth and Thirteenth Centuries', *Cornish Studies*, 16 (1988), 61–6.

— 'The Early Welsh Arthurian Poems', in TAOTW, 33–71.

— 'The Nature of Arthur', *Cambrian Medieval Celtic Studies*, 27 (1994), 1–31.

— 'A New Study of the *Gododdin*', *Cambrian Medieval Celtic Studies*, 35 (1998), 45–55.

— *Arthur in Medieval Welsh Literature* (Cardiff, 2000).

— 'Evidence for Oral Tales in Medieval Cornwall', *Studia Celtica*, 40 (2006), 127–53.

— 'Aneirin and Taliesin: Sceptical Speculations', in A. Woolf (ed.), *Beyond the Gododdin: Dark-Age Scotland in Medieval Wales* (St Andrews, 2013), 115–52.

— 'Where was Middle Cornish Spoken?', *Cambrian Medieval Celtic Studies*, 74 (2017), 1–32.

Parry, J.J., 'The Vita Merlini', *University of Illinois Studies in Language and Literature*, 10.3 (1925).

Pearce, S., *The Kingdom of Dumnonia* (Padstow, 1978).

Pflaum, H.-G., *Les Carrières Procuratoriennes Équestres sous le Haute-Empire Romain* (Paris, 1961).

Pflaum, H.-G. (ed.), *Inscriptiones Latines de L'Algérie*, II.3 (Paris, 2003).

Phillips, G., *The Lost Tomb of King Arthur* (Rochester, VT, 2016).

Phillips, G. and Keatman, M., *King Arthur The True Story: The Truth Behind the Romance and Legends of Excalibur, the Holy Grail and the Site of the Real Avalon* (London, 1992).

Phillips, M., *The Table of Less Valued Knights* (London, 2014).

Philpott, R., 'The Romano-British Period Resource Assessment', in M. Brennand (ed.), *The Archaeology of North West England*, I, *Resource Assessment* (Manchester, 2006), 59–90.

Phythian-Adams, C., *Land of the Cumbrians: A Study of British Provincial Origins AD 400–1120* (Aldershot, 1996).

Piquemal, C., '"Culhwch and Olwen": A Structured Portrayal of Arthur?', *Arthuriana*, 10.3 (2000), 7–26.

Pitassi, M., *The Navies of Rome* (Woodbridge, 2009).

— *The Roman Navy* (Barnsley, 2012).

Pohl, W., 'Introduction: The Empire and the Integration of Barbarians', in W. Pohl (ed.), *Kingdoms of the Empire: The Integration of Barbarians in Late Antiquity* (Leiden, 1997), 1–12.

— 'Telling the Difference: Signs of Ethnic Identity', in W. Pohl and H. Reimitz (eds), *Strategies of Distinction: The Construction of Ethnic Communities, 300–800* (Leiden, 1998), 17–69.

Pollard, N. and J. Berry., *The Complete Roman Legions* (London, 2012).

Pope, M.K. (ed.), Thomas, *The Romance of Horn*, 1, *Text, Critical Introduction and Notes* (Oxford, 1955).

Poulson, C., 'Arthurian Legend in Fine and Applied Art of the Nineteenth and Early Twentieth Centuries: A Subject Index', *Arthurian Literature*, 10 (1990), 111–34.

Powell, J.G.F. (ed.), *Cicero On Friendship and The Dream of Scipio* (Oxford, 1990).

Price, J.E. and F.G.H. Price, *A Description of the Remains of Roman Buildings at Morton, near Brading, Isle of Wight* (London, 1881).

Probert, D., 'New Light on Aldhelm's Letter to King Gereint of Dumnonia', in K. Barker and N. Brooks (ed.), *Aldhelm and Sherborne: Essays to Celebrate the Founding of the Bishopric* (Oxford, 2010), 110–28.

Pryce, H. (ed.), *Literacy in Medieval Celtic Societies* (Cambridge, 1998).

Putter, A., 'The Twelfth-Century Arthur', in E. Archibald and A. Putter (eds), *The Cambridge Companion to Arthurian Legend* (Cambridge, 2009), 36–52.

Raffield, B., '"A River of Knives and Swords": Ritually Deposited Weapons in English Watercourses and Wetlands during the Viking Age', *European Journal of Archaeology*, 17.4 (2014), 634–55.

Rahtz, P., *Cadbury-Congresbury 1968–73: A Late Roman/Post-Roman Hilltop Settlement in Somerset* (Oxford, 1992).

Ralegh Radford, C.A., *Arthurian Sites in the West* (Exeter, 1975).

Rance, P., 'Drungus, δρουγγος and δρουγγιστί: A Gallicism and Continuity in Late Roman Cavalry Tactics', *Phoenix*, 58.1 (2004), 96–130.

Rastell, J., *The Passtyme of People, the Chronycles of Dyvers Realmys and Most Specially of the Realme of England*, ed. T.F. Dibdin (London, 1811).

Raynaud de Lage, G., *Alain de Lille Poête du XIIe Siècle* (Montreal, 1951).

Rhŷs, J., *Studies in the Arthurian Legend* (Oxford, 1891).

Rice, T.T., 'The Scytho-Sarmatian Tribes of South-Eastern Europe', in F. Millar, *The Roman Empire and Its Neighbours* (2nd ed., London, 1981), 281–93.

Richmond, I.A., 'The Sarmatae, Bremetennacum veteranorum, and the Regio Bremetennacensis', JRS, 35 (1945), 15–29.

Richmond, V.B., 'King Arthur and his Knights for Edwardian Children', *Arthuriana*, 23.3 (2013), 55–78.

Ridley, R.T., *History of Rome: A Documented Analysis* (Rome, 1987).

Ritson, J., *The Life of King Arthur* (London, 1825).

Rivet, A.L.F. and C. Smith, *The Place-Names of Roman Britain* (London, 1979).

Roach, W., *The Didot Perceval, According to the Manuscripts of Modena and Paris* (Philadelphia, 1941).

Robert, T., 'Safle Cerrig Arthur', *Transactions of the Anglesey Antiquarian Society and Field Club* (1977), 53.

Roberts, B.F., 'Rhai o Gerddi Ymddiddan Llyfr Du Caerfyrddin', in R. Bromwich and R.B. Jones (eds), *Astudiaethau ar yr Hengerdd* (Cardiff, 1978), 281–325.

Roberts, J.M., *The Pelican History of the World* (London, 1976).

Robinson, J.A., *Two Glastonbury Legends: King Arthur and Joseph of Arimathea* (Cambridge, 1926).

Romer, F.E. (trans.), Pomponius Mela, *Description of the World* (Ann Arbor, MI., 1998).

Roques, M., *Les Romans de Chrétien de Troyes*, III, *Le Chevalier de la Charrête* (Paris, 1958).

Ross, A., *Pagan Celtic Britain* (London, 1967).

Rostovtzeff, M.I. et al. *The Excavations at Dura Europos: Preliminary Report of the 6th Season of Work, Oct. 1932–Mar. 1933* (New Haven, CT, 1936).

Roth, J.P., 'The Size and Organization of the Roman Imperial Legion', *Zeitschrift für Alte Geschichte*, 43.3 (1994), 346–62.

— *The Logistics of the Roman Army at War (264 BC–AD 235)* (Leiden, 2012).

Rouse, R., 'Reading Ruins: Arthurian Caerleon and the Untimely Architecture of History', *Arthuriana*, 23.1 (2013), 40–51.

Rowland, J., *Early Welsh Saga Poetry: A Study and Edition of the Englynion* (Cambridge, 1990).

Russell, B., *The Collected Papers of Bertrand Russell*, 2, *Last Philosophical Testament, 1943–68* (London, 1977).

Russell, M., *Arthur and the Kings of Britain: The Historical Truth behind the Myths* (Stroud, 2017).

Ryan, M., 'Los Orígenes de Arturo', *Desperto Ferro*, 36 (2016), 14–21.

Sachs, A., 'Babylonian Observational Astronomy', in F.R. Hodson (ed.), *The Place of Astronomy in the Ancient World* (London, 1974), 43–50.

Salbiev, T., 'Commentary', TOTN, xv–xvii.

Saller, R.P., 'Promotion and Patronage in Equestrian Careers', JRS, 70 (1980), 44–63.

Salway, B., 'What's in a Name? A Survey of Roman Onomastic Practice from *c.* 700 BC to AD 700', JRS, 84 (1994), 124–45.

Salway, P., *Roman Britain* (Oxford, 1981).

Savory, H.N., 'Excavations at Dinas Emrys, Beddgelert, Caernarvonshire', *Archaeologia Cambrensis*, 109 (1960), 13–77.

Sayles, G.O., *The Medieval Foundations of England* (London, 1948).

Schaefer, B.E., 'The Origins of the Greek Constellations: Was the Great Bear Constellation Named before Hunter Nomads first Reached the Americas more than 13,000 years ago?', *Scientific American*, 295 (2006), 96–101.

Scheers, S., 'Celtic Coin Types in Britain and their Mediterranean Origins', in M. Mays (ed.), *Celtic Coinage: Britain and Beyond* (Oxford, 1992), 33–46.

Scherer, A., *Gestirnnamen bei den indogermanischen Völkern* (Heidelberg, 1953).

Schlesinger, A. M., *A Thousand Days: John F. Kennedy in the White House* (Boston, 1965).

Schmolke-Hasselmann, B., 'The Round Table: Ideal, Fiction, Reality', *Arthurian Literature*, 2 (1982), 41–75.

— *The Evolution of Arthurian Romance* (Cambridge, 1998).

Schörner, G., 'Rom jenseits der Grenze: Klientelkönigreiche und der *Impact of Empire*', in O. Hekster and T. Kaizer (eds), *Frontiers in the Roman World* (Leiden, 2011), 113–32.

Schrijver, P., 'What Britons Spoke around 400 AD', in N.J. Higham (ed.), *Britons in Anglo-Saxon England* (Woodbridge, 2007), 165–71.

Scott, J., *The Early History of Glastonbury, an Edition and Study of William of Malmesbury's* De Antiquitate Glastonie Ecclesie (Woodbridge, 1981).

Scott, S., *Art and Society in Fourth-Century Britain* (Oxford, 2000).

Scowcroft, R.M., 'Leabhar Gabhála – Part II: The Growth of the Tradition', *Ériu*, 39 (1988), 1–66.

Sellar, W.C. and R.J. Yeatman, *1066 and All That* (London, 1930).

Sharpe, R., 'Martyrs and Local Saints in Late Antique Britain', in A. Thacker and R. Sharpe (eds), *Local Saints and Local Churches in the Early Medieval West* (Oxford, 2002), 75–154.

Sheehan, S., 'Giants, Boar-Hunts and Barbering: Masculinity in "Culhwch ac Olwen"', *Arthuriana*, 15 (2005), 3–25.

Short, I. (ed.), Geffrei Gaimar, *Estoire des Engleis/History of the English* (Oxford, 2009).

Short, I. and B. Merrilees (eds), *Benedeit: The Anglo-Norman Voyage of St Brendan* (Manchester, 1979).

Shotter, D.C.A., 'The Coinage of Roman Ribchester', in B.J.N. Edwards and P.V. Webster (eds), *Ribchester Excavations, Part 1* (Cardiff, 1985), 86–93.

— *Roman Coins from North-West England* (Lancaster, 1990).

Silverberg, R., *The Realm of Prester John* (Athens, OH, 1996).

Simons, P., 'Pattern and Process of Education in *Le Conte du Graal*', *Nottingham French Studies*, 32 (1993), 1–11.

Simpson, R., *Camelot Regained: The Arthurian Revival and Tennyson 1800–1849* (Cambridge, 1990).

Sims-Williams, P., 'Gildas and the Anglo-Saxons', *Cambridge Medieval Celtic Studies*, 6 (1983), 1–30.

— 'Gildas and Vernacular Poetry', in M. Lapidge and D. Dumville (eds), *Gildas: New Approaches* (Woodbridge, 1984), 169–92.

— 'Cú Chulainn in Wales: Welsh Sources for Irish Onomastics', *Celtica*, 21 (1990), 620–33.

— 'The Early Welsh Arthurian Poems', in TAOTW, 33–71.

— 'Historical Need and Literary Narrative: A Caveat from Ninth-Century Wales', *Welsh Historical Review*, 17 (1994), 1–40.

— 'The Death of Urien', *Cambrian Medieval Celtic Studies*, 32 (1996), 25–56.

— 'The Uses of Writing in Early Medieval Wales', in H. Price (ed.), *Literacy in Medieval Celtic Societies* (Cambridge, 1998), 15–38.

— *The Celtic Inscriptions of Britain: Phonology and Chronology, c. 400–1200* (Oxford, 2003).

— *Irish Influence on Medieval Welsh Literature* (Oxford, 2011).

Sinor, D., 'The Hun Period', in D. Sinor (ed.), *The Cambridge History of Early Inner Asia* (Cambridge, 1990), 177–205.

Siscia, K., *Pannonia Superior: Finds and Metalwork Production* (Oxford, 1995).

Skene, W., *The Four Ancient Books of Wales* (Edinburgh, 1868).

— *Celtic Scotland: A History of Ancient Alban* (Edinburgh, 1876).

Smith, L.T. (ed.), *The Itinerary of John Leland in or about the Years 1535–1543*, 5 vols (London, 1964).

Smith, R.E., 'Dux, Praepositus', *Zeitschrift für Papyrologie und Epigraphik*, 36 (1979), 263–78.

Smyth, A., 'The Earliest Irish Annals: Their First Contemporary Entries and the Earliest Centres of Recording', *Proceedings of the Royal Irish Academy*, 72 C (1972), 1–48.

Snyder, C.A., *An Age of Tyrants: Britain and the Britons AD 400–600* (Pennsylvania, 1998).

— 'The Age of Arthur: Some Historical and Archaeological Background', *The Heroic Age*, 1 (1999).

— *Exploring the World of King Arthur* (London, 2000).

— *The Britons* (Oxford, 2003).

Soulsby, I., *The Towns of Medieval Wales* (Chichester, 1983).

Southern, P., 'The Numeri of the Roman Imperial Army', *Britannia*, 20 (1989), 81–140.

— *The Roman Army: A Social and Institutional History* (Oxford, 2006).

Spaul, J., *Ala 2: The Auxiliary Cavalry Units of the Pre-Diocletian Imperial Roman Army* (Andover, 1994).

— *Cohors 2: The Evidence for and a Short History of the Auxiliary Infantry Units of the Imperial Roman Army* (Oxford, 2000).

Speed, G., *Towns in the Dark: Urban Transformations from Late Roman to Anglo-Saxon England* (Oxford, 2014).

Speidel, M.P., 'The Chattan War, the Brigantian Revolt and the Loss of the Antonine Wall', *Britannia*, 18 (1987), 233–7.

— *Ancient Germanic Warriors* (Abingdon, 2004).

Spence, J. (ed.), *Reimagining History in Anglo-Norman Prose Chronicles* (Woodbridge, 2013).

Spisak, J.W. and Matthews, W. (eds), *Caxton's Malory: A New Edition of Sir Thomas Malory's Le Morte Darthur* (London, 1983).

Staines, D. (trans.), *The Complete Romances of Chrétien de Troyes* (Bloomington and Indianapolis, IN, 1993).

Stancliffe, C., 'The Thirteen Sermons Attributed to Columbanus and the Question of their Authorship', in M. Lapidge (ed.), *Columbanus: Studies on the Latin Writings* (Woodbridge, 1997), 93–202.

Steinbeck, J., *The Acts of King Arthur and his Noble Knights*, ed. C. Horton et al. (New York, 1976).

Stenton, F.M., *Anglo-Saxon England* (3rd ed., Oxford, 1971).

Stephens, G.R., 'A Severan Vexillation at Ribchester', *Britannia*, 18 (1987), 198–209.

Stephenson, D., *Medieval Powys: Kingdom, Principality and Lordships, 1132–1293* (Woodbridge, 2016).

Stevenson, J. (ed.), *Nennii Historia Brittonum* (London, 1838).

Stirling, S.A., *The King Arthur Conspiracy: How a Scottish Prince Became a Mythical Hero* (Stroud, 2012).

Storr, J., *King Arthur's Wars: The Anglo-Saxon Conquest of England* (Solihull, 2016).

Stout, A., 'Savaric, Glastonbury and the Making of Myths: A Reappraisal', *The Antiquaries Journal*, 96 (2016), 101–15.

Strachey, (ed.), *Le Morte Darthur* (London, 1868).

Stuart-Glennie, J.S., *Arthurian Localities: Their Historical Origin, Chief Country, and Fingalian Relations: With a Map of Arthurian Scotland* (Edinburgh, 1869).

Stupperich, R., 'A Reconsideration of Some Fourth-Century British Mosaics', *Britannia*, 11 (1980), 289–301.

Sturzer, N., 'The Purpose of *Culhwch and Olwen*', *Studia Celtica*, 39 (2005), 145–67.

Sulimirski, T., *The Sarmatians* (London, 1970).

Sweetser, E.E., 'Line-Structure and *Rhan*-Structure: The Metrical Units of the *Gododdin* Corpus', in B.F. Roberts (ed.), *Early Welsh Poetry: Studies in the Book of Aneirin* (Aberystwyth, 1988), 139–54.

Swift, C., 'Welsh Ogams from an Irish Perspective', in IWMA, 62–79.

Tatlock, J.S.P., 'The English Journey of the Laon Canons', *Speculum*, 8 (1933), 454–65.

— 'The Dates of the Arthurian Saints' Legends', *Speculum*, 14.3 (1939), 345–65.

— *The Legendary History of Britain: Geoffrey of Monmouth's Historia Regum Britanniae and its Early Vernacular Versions* (Berkeley, 1950).

Taylor, T. (ed.), *The Life of St Samson of Dol* (Llanerch, 1991).

— *The Time Team Guide to the History of Britain* (London, 2010).

Tennyson, Alfred, *Idylls of the King*, ed. J.M. Gray (Harmondsworth, 1983).

Thompson, E.A., 'Gildas and the History of Britain', *Britannia*, 10 (1979), 203–26.

— *Saint Germanus of Auxerre and the End of Roman Britain* (Woodbridge, 1984).

Thornhill, P., 'The Origin of the Legend of King Arthur', *Mankind Quarterly*, 40.3 (2000), 227–85.

Throop, P. (trans.), *Isidore of Seville's Etymologies: The Complete English Translation of Isidori Hispalensis Episcopi*, 2 vols (Charlotte, VT, 2005).

Todd, J.H. (ed.), *The Irish Version of Nennius* (Dublin, 1848).

Tolhurst, F., 'Geoffrey of Monmouth's "Historia regum Britannie" and the Critics', *Arthuriana*, 8.4 (1998), 3–11.

— 'The Britons and Hebrews, Romans and Normans: Geoffrey of Monmouth's British Epic and Reflections of Empress Matilda', *Arthuriana*, 8.4 (1998), 69–87.

Tolkien, J.R.R., 'On Fairy-Stories', in J.R.R. Tolkien, *Tales from the Perilous Realm* (London, 2008), 315–400.

— *The Fall of Arthur*, ed. C. Tolkien (London, 2013).

Tomas, A., *Inter Moesos et Thraces: The Rural Hinterland of Novae in Lower Moesia (1st–6th centuries AD)* (Oxford, 2016).

Tomlin, R.S.O., 'The Curse Tablets', in B. Cunliffe (ed.), *The Temple of Sulis Minerva at Bath, 2, The Finds from the Sacred Spring* (Oxford, 1988), 59–278.

— 'The Inscribed Lead Tablets', in A. Woodward and P. Leach (eds), *The Uley Shrines: Excavation of a Ritual Complex on West Hill, Uley, Gloucestershire, 1977–79* (London, 1993), 113–24.

— 'Writing to the Gods in Britain', in A.E. Cooley (ed.), *Becoming Roman, Writing Latin? Literacy and Epigraphy in the Roman West* (Portsmouth, RI, 2002), 165–79.

Toolis, R. and C. Bowles, *The Lost Dark Age Kingdom of Rheged: The Discovery of a Royal Stronghold at Trusty's Hill, Galloway* (Oxford, 2016).

Toshio, H., 'The Beginning and the Maturity of Nomadic Powers in the Eurasian Steppes: Growing and Downsizing of Elite Tumuli', *Ancient Civilizations from Scythia to Siberia*, 19.1 (2013), 105–41.

Toynbee, J.M.C., *Art in Roman Britain* (2nd ed., London, 1963).

— *Art in Britain under the Romans* (Oxford, 1964).

Treister, M., 'Sarmatian Treasures of South Russia', *Archaeology*, 50.1 (1997), 49–51.

Turner, S., *History of the Anglo-Saxons*, 3 vols (London, 1799–1805).

Twain, M., *A Connecticut Yankee in King Arthur's Court* (New York, 1889).

Ullyot, J., 'Molloy or *Le conte du Graal*', *Modern Philology*, 108.4 (2011), 560–79.

Updike, J., *Roger's Version* (London, 1987).

Vaday, A., 'Limes Sarmatiae', in RAP, 204–12.

— 'Roman Presence in the Barbaricum', in RAP, 213–21.

— 'Barbarian Peoples', in RAP, 222–37.

Van Hamel, A.G., 'Aspects of Celtic Mythology', *Proceedings of the British Academy*, 20 (1934), 207–48.

Verboven, K., 'Demise and Fall of the Augustan Monetary System', in O. Hekster, G. de Kleijn and D. Slootjes (eds), *Crises and the Roman Empire* (Leiden, 2007), 245–57.

Vinogradov, N. B. and A.V. Epimakhov, 'From a Settled Way of Life to Nomadism, Variations in Models of Transition', in KRSS, 240–6.

Virtanen, L., *Finnish Folklore*, trans. T. Dubois (Helsinki, 2000).

Visy, Z., 'Some Notes on the Defence System of Pannonia in the 2nd and 3rd Centuries AD', in G. Hajnóczi (ed.), *La Pannonia e L'Impero Romano* (Rome, 1994), 85–96.

— 'Mapping the SW Limes of Dacia', in W.S. Hanson (ed.), *The Army and Frontiers of Rome* (Portsmouth, RI, 2009), 115–26.

— 'The River Line Frontiers of the Roman Empire', in D.J. Breeze et al. (eds), *Understanding Roman Frontiers: A Celebration for Professor Bill Hanson* (Edinburgh, 2015), 27–36.

Wacher, J., *Roman Britain* (Stroud, 1978).

Wadge, R., 'King Arthur: A British or Sarmatian Tradition?', *Folklore*, 98.2 (1987), 204–15.

Waite, A.E., *The Holy Grail, Its Legends and Symbolism* (London, 1933).

Wallis, F., *Bede: The Reckoning of Time* (Liverpool, 1988).

Walker, G.S.M. (ed. and trans.), *Sancti Columbani Opera* (Dublin, 1957).

Walters, L.J., 'Reconfiguring Wace's Round Table: Walewein and the Rise of the National Vernaculars', *Arthuriana*, 15.2 (2005), 39–58.

— 'Re-examining Wace's Round Table', in K. Busby and C. Kleinhenz (eds), *Courtly Arts and the Art of Courtliness* (Woodbridge, 2006), 721–44.

Warner, M., *Once Upon a Time* (Oxford, 2014).

Watson, R., 'Viking-Age Amounderness: A Reconsideration', in N.J. Higham and M.J. Ryan (eds), *Place-Names, Language and the Anglo-Saxon Landscape* (Woodbridge, 2011), 125–41.

Watts, V., *The Cambridge Dictionary of English Place-Names* (Cambridge, 2004).

West, G.D., *An Index of Proper Names in French Arthurian Verse Romances 1150–1300* (Toronto, 1969).

West, M.L., *Indo-European Poetry and Myth* (Oxford, 2002).

Weston, J.L., *The Quest for the Holy Grail* (London, 1913).

Wheeler, E.L., 'The Laxity of the Syrian Legions', in D.L. Kennedy (ed.), *The Roman Army in the East* (Ann Arbor, MI, 1996), 229–76.

White, R., *Britannia Prima, Britain's Last Roman Province* (Stroud, 2007).

— 'Managing transition: Western Britain from the End of Empire to the Rise of Penda', *History Compass*, 11.8 (2013), 584–96.

White, R.B., 'Introductory Note', in HB, unpaginated.

White, T.H., *The Once and Future King* (London, 1958).

Whitelock, D. (ed.), *Sermo Lupi ad Anglos* (Exeter, 1976).

Wilkes, J.J., *Dalmatia* (London, 1969).

— 'The Danube Provinces', in A.K. Bowman, P. Garnsey and D. Rathbone (eds), *The Cambridge Ancient History*, XI, *The High Empire, AD 70–192* (2nd ed., Cambridge, 2000), 577–603.

— 'Roman Legions and their Fortresses in the Danube Lands', in R.J. Brewer (ed.), *Roman Fortresses and their Legions* (London, 2002), 101–20.

Williams, I. (ed.), *Canu Aneirin* (Cardiff, 1961).

— *Armes Prydein. The Prophecy of Britain*, trans. R. Bromwich (Dublin, 1972).

Williams, J.E.C., 'Brittany and the Arthurian Legend', in TAOTW, 249–72.

Wilmott, T., *Birdoswald: Excavations of a Roman Fort on Hadrian's Wall and Its Successor Settlements, 1987–92* (London, 1997).

Winterbottom, M., 'Columbanus and Gildas', *Vigiliae Christianae*, 30.4 (1976), 310–17.

Wiseman, H., 'The Derivation of the Date of the Badon Entry in the *Annales Cambriae* from Bede and Gildas', *Parergon*, NS, 17.2 (2000), 1–10.

Witts, P., *Mosaics in Roman Britain: Stories in Stone* (Stroud, 2005).

Wolfram, H., 'Neglected Evidence on the Accommodation of Barbarians in Gaul', in W. Pohl (ed.), *Kingdoms of the Empire: The Integration of Barbarians in Late Antiquity* (Leiden, 1997), 181–3.

Wood, D., 'Gildas and the Mystery Cloud of 536–7', *Journal of Theological Studies*, 61.1 (2010), 226–34.

Wood, I., 'The End of Roman Britain: Continental Evidence and Parallels', in M. Lapidge and D. Dumville (eds), *Gildas: New Approaches* (Woodbridge, 1984), 1–25.

— 'The Fall of the Western Empire and the End of Roman Britain', *Britannia*, 18 (1987), 251–62.

— *The Merovingian Kingdoms 450–751* (Harlow, 1994).

Wood, M., *In Search of England* (London, 1999).

Woolf, A., 'An Interpolation in the Text of Gildas's *De Excidio Britanniae*', *Peritia*, 16 (2002), 161–7.

— 'The Expulsion of the Irish from Dyfed', in IWMA, 102–15.

— 'Fire from Heaven: Divine Providence and Iron Age Hillforts in Early Medieval Britain', in P. Rainbird (ed.), *Monuments in the Landscape* (Stroud, 2008), 136–43.

— 'The Early History of the Diocese of Sodor', in S. Duffy and H. Mytum (eds), *A New History of the Isle of Man*, III (Liverpool, 2015), 329–48.

Woolf, G.D., 'How the Latin West was Won', in A.E. Cooley (ed.), *Becoming Roman, Writing Latin? Literacy and Epigraphy in the Roman West* (Portsmouth, RI, 2002), 181–8.

Worthington, H., 'From Children's Story to Adult Fiction: T.H. White's *The Once and Future King*', *Arthuriana*, 12.2 (2002), 97–119.

Wright, N., 'Geoffrey of Monmouth and Gildas', R. Barber (ed.), *Arthurian Literature*, 2 (1982), 1–40.

— 'Gildas's Prose Style and Its Origins', in M. Lapidge and D. Dumville (eds), *Gildas: New Approaches* (Woodbridge, 1984), 107–28.

Wright, T., *The Celt, The Roman and the Saxon* (2nd ed., London, 1861).

Yablonsky, L.T., ' "Scythian-Triad" and "Scythian World" ', in KRSS, 3–8.

— 'New Excavations of the Early Nomadic Burial Ground at Filippouka (Southern Ural Region, Russia)', *American Journal of Archaeology*, 114.1 (2010), 129–43.

Yarrow, S., *Saints and Their Communities: Miracle Stories in Twelfth-Century England* (Oxford, 2010).

Yorke, B., 'Fact or Fiction? The Written Evidence for the Fifth and Sixth Centuries AD', *Anglo-Saxon Studies in Archaeology and History*, 6 (1993), 45–50.

— *Wessex in the Early Middle Ages* (London, 1995).

Zaharade, M. and N. Gudea, *The Fortifications of Lower Moesia (AD 86–275)* (Amsterdam, 1997).

Zimmer, H., 'Review of Gaston Paris' *Histoire Litteraire de la France*', *Göttingische Gelehret Anzeigen* (1890), 735–6.

— *Nennius Vindicatus* (Berlin, 1893).

Zubar, V.M., 'The Crimean Campaign of Tiberius Plautius Silvanus', in D. Braund (ed.), *Scythians and Greeks* (Exeter, 2005), 176–80.

INDEX